Praise for *Alterity and the Evasion of Justice*

This pathfinding volume offers a radical critique of the ways World Christianity has been conceptualized by focusing on what has been excluded or marginalized. Attending to race, gender, sexuality, and culture, contributors present rich methodological insights and astute analyses of local Christian contexts that broaden our historical and theological horizons. I highly recommend it.

Kwok Pui-lan, Dean's Professor of Systematic Theology
at Candler School of Theology, Emory University

Just as women's theology represented the "eruption within the eruption" of liberation theology, so this volume represents the eruption within the eruption of World Christianity. By focusing on alterity, the editors and authors deepen the meaning of World Christianity as a challenge and corrective to Western academic discourse. In giving voice to the "other," they add richness and complexity to understanding Christianity as an intercultural, multiethnic, and gendered world religion. This exciting book continues urgent and creative conversations about World Christianity as public theology, and as a global community in which justice matters. I recommend it very highly.

Dana L. Robert, William Fairfield Warren Distinguished Professor,
and director, Center for Global Christianity
and Mission, Boston University

After an initial burst of interest in World Christianity as a field of study, with a steady flow of publications, it is time for what might be called the second generation of scholars in World Christianity to examine the lacunae in the writings of its pioneers. *Alterity and the Evasion of Justice* is an important and challenging collection of essays that bring to the fore issues left hitherto unexplored, especially those concerning injustice in its multiple forms. Coming from different parts of the globe with their distinctive contexts, the authors of these essays draw our attention to decolonialism, liberation, feminism, queer studies, and race and cultural theories—so many inconvenient truths that vastly expand the horizon of World Christianity. I enthusiastically recommend this volume for courses in the history of Christianity.

Peter C. Phan, Ignacio Ellacuría Chair of Catholic Social Thought,
Georgetown University

Alterity and the Evasion of Justice: Explorations of the "Other" in World Christianity is among the most important books yet to appear in the field of World Christianity. It accurately names and analyzes the silencing of the "other" that has taken place in both the study and practice of World Christianity. It also serves to let the "others" speak and be heard as compelling voices for justice. No one who cares about what is happening in World Christianity can ignore this work.

Dale Irvin, professor of World Christianity,
New School of Biblical Theology

As much as the study of World Christianity has successfully decentered the field by drawing attention to the new expressions of, and dynamics in, Christianity as a global religion, it has also established its own centers of attention and power. Partly this is because Christianity worldwide, as well as in its fresh manifestations, often reinforces social and political norms and hegemonies. The important contribution of this book is that it makes the quest for "the other"—marginalized voices, topics, and perspectives—its central aim. Driven by an ethical passion for social and epistemic justice, the editors and contributors critically engage with questions of gender, sexuality, ecology, and race, to mention just a few areas of investigation, thereby making a significant decolonial intervention in the field. This volume reminds us of what Christianity, at its best, can be: a critical social imagination and a pursuit of new horizons.

Adriaan van Klinken, professor of religion and African studies,
University of Leeds

Womack and Barreto's new volume extends the contextual riches of this thoughtful and very important series, which broadens the scope of global Christian voices and perspectives that have long been neglected or unheard. The focus is on epistemic colonization, which has excluded "certain ways of being and knowing" from their appropriate participation in World Christianity. Here is a refreshing reimagining of what *ecumenical* means: to include religious traditions whose adherents were never before invited to the conversations. Here also is attention to what may be the most challenging issues for Christians in the Global South: naming evasions of justice in their own communities. The reader is drawn in to learn, struggle, and grow through this exciting contribution to the increasingly complex face of World Christianity.

Elsie Anne McKee, Archibald Alexander Professor of Reformation
Studies and the History of Worship, emerita,
Princeton Theological Seminary

World Christianity and Public Religion Series, Vol. 5

Series Editor: Raimundo C. Barreto

Alterity and the Evasion of Justice

World Christianity and Public Religion Series, Volume 5
Series Editor: Raimundo C. Barreto

Alterity and the Evasion of Justice

Explorations of the "Other" in World Christianity

Deanna Ferree Womack
Raimundo C. Barreto

Editors

FORTRESS PRESS

MINNEAPOLIS

CONTENTS

THE WORLD CHRISTIANITY AND
PUBLIC RELIGION SERIES

During the latter half of the twentieth century, scholars began to pay closer attention to the polycentric and culturally diverse nature of Christianity worldwide. In particular, the rapid growth in the number of Christians living in the Global South caught the attention of Western scholars as a trend that would not be reversed in the near future.

A number of books have been written in the attempt to offer clues on how these drastic demographic changes are reshaping Christian identity and relations worldwide. Beyond the fascination with numbers, the rapid growth Global South Christianities and their respective diasporas have experienced in recent decades is giving birth to a new global Christian consciousness with profound cultural, social, and economic implications that demand further scholarly attention. World Christianity scholarship has demonstrated that Christianity can no longer be dismissed as a Western religion. We have stepped into the threshold of a new era. New and creative theological insights have emerged, debunking a Eurocentric hegemonic understanding of Christianity that prevailed in the modern era. Contrary to some assumptions, conversion to Christianity in former Western colonies did not imply the Westernization of converts. On the contrary, Indigenous cultures and spiritualities that were expected to disappear or be absorbed into the colonial civilizational project remain alive and well. In fact, the end of the twentieth century saw a revitalization of indigenous traditions and spirituality. Such resurfacing of indigenous voices significantly contributed to renewed understandings of Christianity that are not at odds with traditional worldviews.

This series engages emerging voices from a variety of Christian expressions around the world, focusing not only on particular histories and practices but also on their theological articulations and impacts on the broader society. If in the modern/colonial world the study of Christianity was predominantly informed by Eurocentric perspectives and priorities, the study of World

Christianity in the beginning of the twenty-first century is more representative of diverse contextual experiences, their interaction through the formation of multidirectional transnational networks, and the relationship between Christianity and other religions. Globalization and mass migration have contributed to deepened exchanges among peoples and cultures worldwide, creating a growing demand for making intercultural communication, intercultural theologies, and interfaith dialogue more central to the study of World Christianity. Likewise, questions about hybridity, liminality, border thinking, and cultural interweaving—particularly in the context of formerly colonized cultures—have also gained more attention.

While new tools have been added to the study of Christianity, particularly in response to the cultural turn in the social sciences, some long-existing problems, nevertheless, still linger and equally require attention. The scientific and technological progress has not mitigated existing injustices and economic asymmetries. Socioeconomic injustice remains as fiercely prevalent as when the first theologies of liberation emerged in the 1960s. As Indian theologian Felix Wilfred reminds us, the demographic shift of World Christianity is not simply a shift "from the West to the South, but a shift of Christianity from the rich and middle classes to the poor." According to him, more than half of all Christians in the world live with less than five hundred dollars of annual income.[1]

In a context marked by disparity and scarcity, standing in solidarity with the poor remains a priority. Yet, a concern with economic justice is not enough. Christians living in contexts marked by widespread poverty and injustice in different parts of the world are asking challenging and complex questions about the reasons for such inequality. The inhuman treatment many migrants, refugees, asylum seekers, and stateless persons receive when crossing borders, for instance, helps increase awareness of the indivisibility of justice, demanding renewed moral commitments, and creative responses to problems that are amounting to a global calamity. Unjust relations based on race, gender, and sexuality, along with land-related disputes and environmental concerns, are part of the public agenda Christians are

---

[1] Felix Wilfred, "Christianity between Decline and Resurgence," in *Christianity in Crisis?*, ed. Jon Sobrino and Felix Wilfred, vol. 3, Concilium 2005 (London: SCM Press, 2005), 31.

called to engage in, both in the Global North and South. The growing awareness of the impact of the colonial hegemonic project upon minoritized groups—especially the eclipsed non-European other—has produced new identity claims of previously silenced voices who are now more vocal about the epistemic injustice they have experienced. On the other hand, their regained visibility is often used to justify the growing fear of difference and a relentless sense of insecurity that are at the heart of multiple forms of nationalist and xenophobic ideologies. Such ideologies are quickly poisoning societies across the world, increasing the risk of violence against those who, perceived as different, are feared and discriminated against.

Considering all these things, public reasoning has become an increasingly important dimension of the study of World Christianity. After all, Christians worldwide are key actors in what scholars commonly refer to as the public sphere. Their public living and thinking are important sources for the interrogation of the impact of religion on public life vis-à-vis themes such as citizenship, public witness, peace, justice, environmental relations, and contemporary migration, among others.

This series, which stems from a partnership between Princeton Theological Seminary and Faculdade Unida de Vitória (Brazil), aims to provide a unique space for sustained dialogue on all these matters. It blends a number of methods and approaches in the burgeoning field of World Christianity, placing them in conversation with other fields of study and disciplines, including public theology, postcolonial/decolonial theory, intercultural studies, migration studies, critical gender theory, critical race theory, queer theory, and globalization studies. The series intentionally gathers religious scholars and theologians representative of diverse Christian traditions and continents into conversation with one another. At its root are two schools related to the Reformed tradition, one located in South America and the other in North America; one that is young (having existed for a little more than two decades) and another with a tradition spanning over two hundred years.

In the first half of the twentieth century, Princeton Seminary appointed John A. Mackay as president after his tenure of almost two decades as a missionary in Latin America. That cross-cultural experience deeply influenced him and impacted his ecumenical thinking. By turning ecumenics into a field of study for the church in the twentieth century,

Mackay, in many ways, anticipated the rise of the field we know today as World Christianity.

> A new reality has come to birth. For the first time in the life of mankind the Community of Christ, the Christian Church, can be found, albeit in nuclear form, in the remotest frontiers of human habitation. This community has thereby become "ecumenical" in the primitive, geographical meaning of that term. History is thus confronted with a new fact.[2]

Faculdade Unida de Vitória, in turn, has a history marked by a commitment to the retrieval of a particular memory. Such memory is linked to theologians such as Richard Shaull and Rubem Alves. Shaull was a pioneer in encouraging young Latin American Christians, such as Rubem Alves himself, Jovelino Ramos, João Dias de Araújo, Joaquim Beato, Beatriz Melano, and others, to take their own social and cultural location as their theological and social locus. In other words, he called them to do theology as Latin Americans. By doing that, he inadvertently contributed to the rise of Latin American liberation theology. Rubem Alves, who studied under Shaull both at the Presbyterian Seminary of Campinas and at Princeton, wrote the first book-length treatise on liberation theology[3] while living in the United States. He was one of the most creative thinkers of his days, having also contributed to other subfields, such as theopoetics.

As an heir of these combined stories, this series is deeply rooted in a long tradition, which continues to be renewed to respond to the challenges and circumstances of a new era. It fosters a dialogue that places priority on voices from the Global South, but which also invites participants from the Global North to engage with their peers from the South.

Furthermore, the series is published in English and Portuguese. Its bilingual nature garners an inclusionary approach. The work of authors

---

2   John Alexander Mackay, *Ecumenics: The Science of the Church Universal* (Englewood Cliffs, NJ: Prentice Hall, 1964), vii.

3   Rubem Alves, "Towards a Theology of Liberation: An Exploration of the Encounter between the Languages of Humanistic Messianism and Messianic Humanism" (PhD diss., Princeton Theological Seminary, 1968).

who originally write in Portuguese (some also in Spanish), and which otherwise would not be available to a broader English readership, are through this series brought to the attention of Anglophone scholars, seminarians, and religious leaders. Similarly, the work of authors who despite being known in the English-speaking world remain largely unknown in Latin America are through this series made available to Latin American scholars who can read Portuguese. Above all, this series shows that it is possible to advance transnational and transcultural scholarly dialogues without placing priority on one particular language as *lingua franca*.

The series has six volumes. The first one, published in Brazil in 2016 and in the United States in 2017, approaches World Christianity as a form of public religion, identifying areas for possible intercultural engagement. Each of the remaining five volumes focuses on specific topics deemed important for a public agenda for World Christianity scholarship in the twenty-first century. Volume two, published in English in 2019, examines migration as an important concern in World Christianity's public discourses. Volume three discusses current approaches to urbanization and identity in World Christianity. Volume four focuses on the public impact of interfaith relations. Volume five presents perspectives on race, ethnicity, gender, and sexuality in World Christianity as part of a broader reflection on the evasion of justice. Finally, volume six brings attention to pressing environmental concerns in World Christianity scholarship, engaging with Global South and Global North eco-theological responses to the imminent planetary crisis.

Finally, in the hope that this series becomes a platform for intercultural and intergenerational dialogue, the editors of all volumes have sought to increase the interaction between seasoned and emerging scholars from all parts of the world, creating a broad table, which may contribute to and enlarge international, intercultural, and interdisciplinary conversations.

Raimundo C. Barreto

ACKNOWLEDGMENTS

This volume began with a panel on alterity and the evasion of justice for the Princeton Theological Seminary World Christianity Conference in 2021, at which the editors presented papers along with Moses Biney and James Taneti. We are grateful to Moses and James for this initial contribution to the volume's theme, and for agreeing to turn their presentations into book chapters. We are grateful as well to the other scholars who contributed chapters, and to Jesudas Athyal at Fortress Press, for his support of this endeavor. We would also like to recognize the contributions of Monika Ottermann, who translated chapters 11 and 12 from Portuguese to English, of Rahimjon Abdugafurov, who prepared the bibliography, and Stephen Ditrolio Cloakley, who prepared the index.

CONTRIBUTORS

Raimundo C. Barreto is associate professor of World Christianity at Princeton Theological Seminary. His research interests include theory and methods in World Christianity, Latin American and Latinx Christianities, intercultural studies, and decoloniality. He is the general editor of the Fortress Press series World Christianity and Public Religion, and the author of *Protesting Poverty: Protestants, Social Ethics and the Poor in Brazil* (Baylor University Press, 2023).

Moses O. Biney is associate professor of religion and society and African diaspora studies at New York Theological Seminary. He holds ThM and PhD degrees in social ethics from Princeton Theological Seminary, and other degrees from universities in Ghana. He is also an ordained Presbyterian minister, and currently serves as pastor of Bethel Presbyterian Reformed Church in Brooklyn, NY; Moderator of the Presbytery of New York City; and Moderator of the Conference of Ghanaian Presbyterian Churches in North America. Dr. Biney is the author of *From Africa to America: Religion and Adaptation among Ghanaian Immigrants in New York* (New York University Press, 2011), coeditor of World *Christianity, Urbanization, and Identity* (Fortress Press, 2021), and general editor of *The Living Pulpit.*

Christina Vital da Cunha is a professor in the Department of Sociology and the Graduate Program in Sociology at Universidade Federal Fluminense. She coordinates LePar—Laboratory for Social Anthropological Studies in Politics, Art and Religion. She is editor of *Religion & Society* journal (https://www.scielo.br/j/rs/), author of *Oração de Traficante*, and coauthor of *Religião e política: uma análise da participação de parlamentares evangélicos sobre o direito de mulheres e de LGBTS no Brasil* (2012), among other books and articles.

Ana Ester Pádua Freire is a Brazilian feminist-lesbian-queer theologian, and holds a PhD and master's in religious studies from the Pontifical Catholic University of Minas Gerais, Brazil. She is ordained in the Metropolitan Community Churches, and is the Latin American representative (2021–2023) for the Global Interfaith Network for People of All Sexes, Sexual Orientations, Gender Identities and Expressions (GIN-SSOGIE). She is also a member of the American Academy of Religion (AAR) and the Brazilian Association of Trans-Homoculture Studies (ABETH).

Jay-Paul Hinds, assistant professor of Pastoral Theology at Princeton Theological Seminary, earned his Master of Divinity and Master of Theology from Princeton Theological Seminary and his PhD from Emory University. While at Emory he also earned a certificate in psychoanalytic studies from the Emory University Psychoanalytic Institute. Hinds's academic interests include the psychology of religion, object relations theory, pastoral theology, Black psychology, critical pedagogy, and the psycho-spiritual development of African American men. His work has been published in the *Journal of Religion and Health* and *Pastoral Psychology*. He is the author of *A Gift Grows in the Ghetto: Reimagining the Spiritual Lives of Black Men*, published by Westminster John Knox Press.

Chammah J. Kaunda (PhD) is a specialist in African Christianity and theology. He is an assistant professor of World Christianity and mission studies at Yonsei University, South Korea. He is also an Extraordinary Professor at the University of the Western Cape in South Africa, and a research fellow for the Southern African Institute for Policy and Research (SAIPAR). He worked as a Senior Research Specialist/Africa Research Fellow for the Human Sciences Research Council in South Africa.

Sun Yong Lee is a PhD candidate in the Department of History and Ecumenics, studying World Christianity and history of religions at Princeton Theological Seminary. She earned an MDiv from Yale Divinity School, and a ThM in church history and BA in journalism from Ewha Womans University. Her research involves the history of Christianity in modern East Asia, Korea in particular. She is interested in Christian women's experiences, with a special focus on women's movements, in their intercultural, interreligious, and transnational encounters. Her research expands on religion in public spheres and in popular culture.

Graham McGeoch is a minister of the Church of Scotland. He teaches theology and religious studies at Faculdade Unida de Vitória, Brazil, and collaborates with UNIperiferias—an international university of the peripheries, based in the favela Maré in Rio de Janeiro, Brazil. His research interests include Orthodoxy, liberation theologies, interreligious dialogue, and the relationship between theology and the social sciences.

Fulata Lusungu Moyo is a feminist ethicist of *ubuntu* and Franklian Logo-therapy student. She holds a PhD in human sciences with a focus on gender, religio-culture, and ethics from the University of KwaZulu-Natal, South Africa. She is a founder of Thimlela-STREAM, a holistic response to survivors of sex trafficking in northern Malawi that focuses on trauma resilience, and healing accompaniment. She is vice president of the Afriaus iLEAC, and a former World Council of Churches staff who pioneered the process of developing the gender justice principles, the globalization of the Thursdays in Black campaign, and Healing Together for community-based trauma healing.

Eve Parker (PhD) is lecturer in modern theology at the University of Manchester, UK. She holds a PhD from the University of St. Andrews, Scotland. Her recent publications include *Trust in Theological Education: Deconstructing 'Trustworthiness' for a Pedagogy of Liberation* (London: SCM, 2022) and *Theologising with the Sacred 'Prostitutes' of South India: Towards an Indecent Dalit Theology* (Leiden: Brill, 2021).

James Elisha Taneti, assistant professor of World Christianity, teaches in the Department of Church History at Union Presbyterian Seminary, and directs the Syngman Rhee Global Mission Center for Christian Education located at the seminary. An ordained minister in the

Presbyterian Church (USA), he has previously ministered in church, classroom, and correctional settings. After completing his theological education at the United Theological College, India, James pursued and received a master's degree at Princeton Theological Seminary and a doctoral degree from Union Presbyterian Seminary. He has authored *History of the Telugu Christians: A Bibliography* (American Theological Library Association, 2011), *Caste, Gender and Christianity in Colonial India: Telugu Women in Mission* (Palgrave, 2013), and *Telugu Christians: A History* (Fortress, 2022).

Kenner R. C. Terra is professor of biblical literature and religious sciences at Faculdade Unida de Vitória, Brazil (FUV). He completed his master's and doctorate in sciences of religion at the Universidade Metodista de São Paulo. He is secretary of the Associação Brasileira de Pesquisas Bíblicas (Brazilian Association of Biblical Studies), coordinator of the Research Group Linguagens da Religião (Languages of Religion) (FUV), and managing member of RELEP (Rede Latino-americana de Estudios Pentecostales). His publications on biblical literature, Pentecostal Hermeneutics, Second Temple Judaism, and Early Christianity include the books *O Apocalipse de João: Caos, Cosmos e Contradiscurso Apocalíptico* (Apocalypse of John: Chaos, Cosmos and Apocalyptic Counter-Discourse) and *Autoridade Bíblica e Experiência no Espírito* (Biblical Authority and the experience of the Spirit).

Deanna Ferree Womack is associate professor of history of religions and interfaith studies at Emory University's Candler School of Theology in Atlanta. Her research focuses on Middle Eastern Christianity, Protestant missions, and Christian–Muslim relations, with particular attention to gender. Womack is the author of *Protestants, Gender and the Arab Renaissance in Late Ottoman Syria* (Edinburgh University Press, 2019) and *Neighbors: Christians and Muslims Building Community* (Westminster John Knox, 2020). She is an ordained minister in the Presbyterian Church (USA), and earned her PhD at Princeton Theological Seminary.

PART 1

ALTERITY AND THE MARGINS OF WORLD CHRISTIANITY

ALTERITY AND THE EVASION OF JUSTICE IN WORLD CHRISTIANITY

Deanna Ferree Womack and Raimundo C. Barreto

What histories, practices, or identities have been left invisible in the field of World Christianity? Which voices and experiences remain marginalized within Christian communities around the globe? How might scholars of World Christianity bring to light situations of injustice and *othering* in these Christian contexts and within the field itself? Does World Christianity need to be decolonized, turned indecent, in order to avoid domestication? As World Christianity has become a robust field of study now represented in multiple academic programs, book series, and scholarly conferences, such questions are pressing for the field's future. They invite us to consider what is missing within the literature, and to make course corrections that will enable World Christianity to stay true to its original purpose—articulated by scholars such as Lamin Sanneh, Andrew Walls, and Dana Robert, among other pioneers—to provide a forum and methodology for studying Christianities in Asia, Africa, and Latin America that Western Christian discourses and Eurocentric scholarship had pushed to the peripheries.

Much has happened since the initial articulation of the field in the late 1980s. The original focus on the previously overlooked Global South Christianities and their diasporas gave way to a more concerted search for connections and relationships worldwide, which, though, continues to prioritize silenced voices and knowledges in the study of World Christianity. Yet, there remain areas and approaches that have not received enough attention in the field. The World Christianity Consultation held at Emory University on October 17–19, 2019, highlighted, for instance, the deficit in the engagement of the field with social ethical concerns.[1] This leads to the question: Are matters of social justice and liberation within the purview of World Christianity scholarship? Pioneers such as Sanneh spoke about the ethical impact of translation on the matter of qualitative power in intercultural relations, and he referred to both an "ethics of commitment to local specificity" and a call to live ethically as neighbors.[2] It would be fair, however, to say that social ethical concerns were not further developed in his work. Likewise, the great interest among World Christianity scholars in the fast-growing Christianities of the Global South has often limited the field's attention to minoritized voices in those contexts. The popularized contrasting picture of a liberal Global North against a morally conservative Global South, for example, has contributed to silencing minoritized progressive Christian voices in Asia, the Pacific, Africa, Latin America, and the Caribbean, including those of women, sexual minorities, and non-Christian religious or nonreligious actors. As most ethnographic studies on Indigenous communities by self-professed World Christianity scholars focus on Christian subjects, they often silence non-Christian voices, subsuming the indigenous into *Indigenous Christian* voices. Finally, while World Christianity has largely succeeded in making scholars at major academic centers in the North Atlantic aware of the stories and experiences of Christians in Africa, Asia, and Latin America, does World Christianity scholarship equally engage with knowledge produced in these regions? Do regions like the Pacific, Latin America and the Caribbean, and the Middle East need more attention in the field? As English has been the dominant language in this burgeoning field, are we paying enough attention to scholarship on Christianity produced in other languages? What methodological and

---

1   See the volume based on the conference proceedings, Jehu J. Hanciles, ed., *World Christianity: History, Methodologies, Horizons* (Maryknoll, NY: Orbis, 2021).

2   Lamin Sanneh, *Translating the Message: The Missionary Impact on Culture*, revised and expanded. American Society of Missiology (Maryknoll, NY: Orbis Books, 2009), 242.

theoretical tools emerging in area studies, for instance, can help World Christianity scholars to do more justice to neglected areas? Which resources are available in the toolkit of World Christianity scholarship to correct some of these oversights?

With these concerns at the forefront, *Alterity and the Evasion of Justice: Explorations of the "Other" in World Christianity* delves into questions of alterity and justice, giving special attention to gender, sexuality, race, and the cultures and regions of the world not widely represented within World Christianity scholarship. This volume contributes to expanding the horizons of the field of World Christianity by emphasizing liberationist concerns in order to consider what the field has overlooked or misrepresented. The authors take explicit cognizance of prominent ways that the field may perpetuate injustice and othering. Engaging literary and literature criticism resources; decolonial, liberationist, feminist, and queer epistemologies; and contributions from critical race and cultural studies, among others; the authors of this volume, coming from a wide variety of contexts in different regions of the world, bring to the fore stories, approaches, and concerns that have often been absent or pushed to the fringes in World Christianity guilds.

As a matter of fact, World Christianity scholarship has challenged Eurocentric modes in the study of religion by elevating marginalized voices of Christians in and from the Global South. This core commitment also should compel scholars to attend to the margins of the field itself. The establishment of the field of World Christianity was, in essence, a way of pushing for justice in response to the Euro-normative and colonizing mentality of studies on Christianity in the twentieth century that either focused on European and North American Christians as representative of Christianity as a whole or identified Christian growth and vitality outside the West as the result of Western missionary efforts. As Dale Irvin explained:

> Without acknowledging as much, the term "Christianity" by itself has too often been reduced to naming one or more of the dominant Western historical forms of the religion, rendering the broader global Christian reality invisible. The study of World Christianity is, in contrast, an emerging field that investigates and seeks to

understand Christian communities, faith, and practice as they are found on six continents . . . It is concerned with both the diversity of local or indigenous expressions of Christian life and faith throughout the world, and the variety of ways these interact with one another critically and constructively across time and space. *It is particularly concerned with under-represented and marginalized communities of faith, resulting in a greater degree of attention being paid to Asian, African, and Latin American experiences; the experience of marginalized communities within the North Atlantic world; and the experiences of women throughout the world.*[3]

The field's alternate narrative is exemplified in Sanneh's argument that Christianity belongs just as much to people "beyond the West" and in his proposal to give "priority to indigenous response and local appropriation over missionary transmission and direction." Sanneh thus inverted the typical Eurocentric argument "by speaking of the indigenous discovery of Christianity rather than the Christian discovery of indigenous societies."[4] This reversal of language, and the field's broader attention to under represented and silenced communities, can be interpreted as a matter of justice that brings Global South Christians to the center of the World Christian movement. This challenges not only the Eurocentric biases in academic studies of Christianity but also calls out the collusion between Euro-American Christianity and colonialism, and the enduring harms inflicted on both Indigenous[5] Christians and Indigenous practitioners of other religions.

Without denying the significance of justice for World Christianity scholars since the inception of the field, the editors and authors of this volume recognize that those concerns have been limited for the most part to restoring balance to asymmetrical narrative power relations in the

---

3   Dale T. Irvin, "World Christianity: An Introduction," *Journal of World Christianity* 1, no. 1 (2008): 1–2.

4   Lamin Sanneh, *Whose Religion is Christianity?: The Gospel beyond the West* (Grand Rapids: Eerdmans, 2003), 10. Italics added for emphasis.

5   This volume capitalizes the term "Indigenous" when used to identify people or in contrast with "Western."

construction of a non-Eurocentric understanding of the Christian story and diverse experience, sometimes also bringing attention to the key agency of women in the field. This latter emphasis can be seen in Irvin's naming of women among the marginalized groups that the field strives to include and in Dana Robert's recognition of global Christianity as a predominantly female movement by the late twentieth century.[6] Also notable is the recent work to uncover the histories of Christian women in the Global South,[7] recognizing their overlooked contributions in the same way that a more developed body of scholarship has already acknowledged the role of Western women in global missions.[8] Yet despite these important gains, the field of World Christianity has rarely acknowledged the *theological*

---

6   Dana L. Robert, "Shifting Southward: Global Christianity since 1945," *International Bulletin of Missionary Research* 24, no. 2 (April 1, 2000): 50; Dana L. Robert, "World Christianity as a Women's Movement," *International Bulletin of Missionary Research* 30, no. 4 (2006): 180–88.

7   Eliza F. Kent, *Converting Women: Gender and Protestant Christianity in Colonial South India* (New York: Oxford University Press, 2004); James Elisha Taneti, *Caste, Gender, and Christianity in Colonial India: Telugu Women in Mission* (New York: Palgrave, 2013); Deanna Ferree Womack, *Protestants, Gender and the Arab Renaissance in Late Ottoman Syria* (Edinburgh: Edinburgh University Press, 2019); Int Dorcas Dah, *Women Do More Work Than Men: Birifor Women as Change Agents in the Mission and Expansion of the Church in West Africa (Burkina Faso, Côte d'Ivoire and Ghana)* (Eugene, OR: Wipf & Stock, 2018); Michelle A. Gonzalez, *Sor Juana: Beauty and Justice in the Americas* (Maryknoll, NY: Orbis, 2003); and Kathleen Ann Myers, *Neither Saints nor Sinners: Writing the Lives of Women in Spanish America* (Oxford: Oxford University Press, 2003). In addition, historical studies on the roles of women missionaries and Christian women of the Global South have appeared in World Christianity conferences, sometimes in prominent ways. For example, the annual conference of the Yale-Edinburgh Group in Edinburgh on June 26–28, 2014, focused on the theme of "Gender and Family in the History of Missions and World Christianity."

8   R. Pierce Beaver, *American Protestant Women in World Mission: History of the First Feminist Movement in North America* (Grand Rapids, MI: Eerdmans, 1980); Dana L. Robert, *American Women in Missions: A Social History of Their Thought and Practice* (Macon, GA: Mercer University Press, 1996); Amanda Porterfield, *Mary Lyon and the Mount Holyoke Missionaries* (New York: Oxford University Press, 1997); Rhonda Anne Semple, *Missionary Women:*

contributions of women in recent decades. In other words, the questions women shaping theological agendas in Asia-Pacific, Africa, the Middle East, and Latin America and the Caribbean have been raising for some time may need further consideration in the literature of World Christianity. Furthermore, as the next section highlights, the field of World Christianity lacks any consistent engagement of feminist, womanist, *mujerista*, and other scholarly contributions from Global South women, including that produced by the Circle of Women Theologians in Sub-Saharan Africa, which brings attention to heteropatriarchal structures that continue to inform our relations and work in academia, church, and society.[9]

Justice, thus, is not upheld methodologically only by filling in gaps or rendering appreciation for heretofore unrecognized contributors. Rather, it is necessary, and especially urgent today, to consider ways that World Christianity scholarship may still perpetuate colonial mentalities and hegemonic norms or fail to recognize the diversity of Christian life expressions around the globe. This book turns its attention to such gaps, which we describe as "the evasion of justice," in connection with the kinds of knowledge and ways of knowing that tend to be validated or neglected in World Christianity scholarship, local voices and experiences that are often left out in studies of local realities, and readings of the Bible that inform understandings of race, gender, and sexuality with damning impact on the lives of women, men, and queer Christians in different contexts around the world.

The editors of this volume seek to bring social, cultural, and epistemic justice to the forefront, including in the select number of authors

---

Gender, Professionalism and the Victorian Idea of Christian Mission (Rochester, NY: Boydell Press, 2003).

9   See, for instance, Mercy A. Oduyoye and Musimbi R. A. Kanyoro, eds., *The Will to Rise: Women, Tradition, and the Church in Africa* (Eugene, OR: Wipf & Stock, 1992); Mercy A. Oduyoye, *African Women's Theologies, Spirituality, and Healing: Theological Perspectives from the Circle of Concerned African Women Theologians* (New York: Paulist Press, 2019); Ivone Gebara, *Out of the Depths: Women's Experiences of Evil and Salvation* (Minneapolis: Fortress Press, 2002); Elsa Tamez, ed., *Through Her Eyes: Women's Theology from Latin America* (Eugene, OR: Wipf & Stock, 2006); and Grace Ji-Sun Kim and Hilda P. Koster, eds., *Planetary Solidarity: Global Women's Voices on Christian Doctrine and Climate Justice* (Minneapolis: Fortress Press, 2017).

whose work the prevailing literature in this field has not yet thoroughly engaged. We highlight alterity in connection with the evasion of justice to remind ourselves and our readers of the persistent othering and continuous erasures of certain ways of being and knowing still reflective of the centuries-old impact of colonial power relations and their lingering influence—the coloniality of power, knowing, and being[10]—on the Western academy and the various disciplines we continue to engage in the study of World Christianity. This is particularly apparent in reference to matters of race, authority, sexuality, knowledge, the economy, and "the general understanding of being" in the world.[11]

Additionally, this volume's attention to the "other" within World Christianity reveals communities that have been excluded and questions of justice that have been neglected in overwhelmingly positive, even triumphalist, studies in our field. As Moses Biney's chapter in this volume argues, although it is necessary to assign positive value to the study of Christianities outside the West in order to challenge Eurocentric expressions of Christianity, glorification of non-Western Christianity can encourage scholars to turn a blind eye to abuses of power and other injustices that occur within Global South churches, just as they do in the Global North.[12] This can be seen, for example, in World Christianity

---

10 This is one of the ways of expressing the multidimensional lingering impact of coloniality. See, for instance, Sylvia Wynter, "Unsettling the Coloniality of Being/Power/Truth/Freedom: Towards the Human, After Man—Its Overrepresentation. An Argument," *New Centennial Review* 3, no. 3 (2003): 257–337; Catherine E. Walsh, "The (De)Coloniality of Knowledge, Life, and Nature: The North American-Andean Free Trade Agreement, Indigenous Movements, and Regional Alternatives," in *Globalization and Beyond: New Examinations of Global Power and Its Alternatives*, ed. Jon Shefner and Patricia Fernández-Kelly (University Park: Pennsylvania State University Press, 2011), 228–48; and Walter D. Mignolo and Catherine E. Walsh, *On Decoloniality: Concepts, Analytics, Praxis* (Durham: Duke University Press, 2013), especially chapter 6.

11 Nelson Maldonado-Torres, "On the Coloniality of Being: Contributions to the Development of a Concept," *Cultural Studies* 21, nos. 2–3 (2007): 240–70 (242).

12 See chapter 4 in this volume, Moses O. Biney, "World Christianity and the Evasion of Social Justice Issues: A Focus on Pentecostalism in West Africa."

scholars' enthusiastic fixation on Christian growth outside the West, a phenomenon that has led the field to neglect communities for which rapid growth is not the defining factor of Christian life.[13] This phenomenon may reflect a lingering colonialist-missionary mentality that focuses on making and counting converts rather than attending to Indigenous people's needs, concerns, and self-identifications. While understandable at the time of the field's infancy, the enduring hesitancy of World Christianity scholarship to critique injustices within Christian communities of the Global South suggests that the field is equipped mainly to change Western presumptions about Christianity but largely unprepared to provide a forum for African, Asian, and Latin American Christian scholars to raise critical questions about their own contexts or to guide scholars and practitioners alike toward justice.

Within this vein, this volume points to gender, sexuality, and race as intersectional themes ripe for exploration within the field, while also identifying regions and areas of study that have fallen outside the dominant World Christianity narrative, including the theological expression of Indigenous and other minoritized communities in the aftermath of European colonization. This collection of chapters from scholars researching diverse contexts around the globe will inform readers about issues that have not garnered enough attention within World Christianity because of the field's limitations, as well as the overwhelming attention scholars have given to its successes.

ATTENDING TO THE "OTHER" IN WORLD CHRISTIANITY

Emmanuel Levinas spoke of alterity in connection with the need to rethink transcendence—a movement of crossing over or going beyond—in contrast with the ontological totality he identified in Western philosophy,

---

13 Devaka Premawardhana, *Faith in Flux: Pentecostalism and Mobility in Rural Mozambique* (Philadelphia: University of Pennsylvania Press, 2018), 8, 10–11; Deanna Ferree Womack, "Middle Eastern Christianity in the Context of World Christianity," in *The Rowman & Littlefield Handbook of Christianity in the Middle East*, ed. Mitri Raheb, Meredith Riedel, and Mark A. Lamport (Lanham, MD: Rowman & Littlefield, 2020), 551–52.

which erased difference by not leaving anything outside.[14] In response to that approach, Levinas identified the face of the other as "the locus of transcendence in that it calls into question the *I* in its existence as a being for itself."[15] Argentinean-Mexican historian and philosopher Enrique Dussel builds on Levinas's insight to point out how, "by controlling, conquering, and violating the Other," Europe became the colonizer of alterity, advancing "the myth of a special kind of sacrificial violence which eventually eclipsed whatever was non-European."[16] Concern over this eclipse of the "other" is at the root of the field of World Christianity, as we have demonstrated in the previous section.

Alterity can be understood not only as limiting and resisting totality and erasure but also as an analogy for the unframeable nature of life, which is always moving beyond totalization toward new possibilities and beginnings.[17] A limited view of alterity, which does not take into consideration its constructive possibilities, may inadvertently reinforce totality, or what Levinas calls "ontological imperialism."[18] Levinas's methodological attention to alterity offers a way beyond ontological imperialism, freeing the other from dependence on the gaze of the *I*. Freed from this imperial gaze, the "other" plays a moral role, summoning the imperial *I* from its exteriority (beyond its totalizing tentacles) and demanding respect and rights. In Latin America, through the insights of Dussel and others on alterity, the face of the other gained more concrete contours as revealing the faces of those who had been eclipsed by the conquering European *I*, the Amerindian, the

---

14   Pierre Hayat, "Preface: Philosophy Between Totality and Transcendence," in Emmanuel Levinas, *Alterity and Transcendence* (London: The Athlone Press, 1999), ix–xxiv.

15   Ibid., xiv.

16   Enrique Dussel, *The Invention of the Americas: Eclipse of "the Other" and the Myth of Modernity*, trans. Michael D. Barber (New York: Continuum, 1995), 12.

17   Oscar Guardiola-Rivera, "On the Apophatic Urgency of Now: A Future for the Philosophy of Liberation," in *Decolonizing Ethics: The Critical Theory of Enrique Dussel*, ed. Amy Allen and Eduardo Mendieta (University Park: Pennsylvania State University Press, 2021), 127–46.

18   Edgar Roberto Moros-Ruano, "The Philosophy of Liberation of Enrique D. Dussel: An Alternative to Marxism in Latin America?" (PhD diss., Vanderbilt University, 1984), 34.

African, the Asian, the poor, etc.[19] Thus, not only in Latin America but in other formerly colonized contexts, Levinas's "other" becomes an embodied being. The victims who were supposed to be eclipsed are concrete beings who not only articulate their existence in the world on their own terms but who also interpellate the *I,* demanding more symmetrical participation in the shared world. The moral interpellation of the face of the "other" disrupts dominant reason, demanding justice in varied forms. For Dussel, "the interpellation of the oppressed (be they poor, women, children, elderly people, the discriminated-against race, the peripheral nation) . . . pragmatically irrupts (in the sense of Austin) within the horizon of the Totality (in the sense of Levinas) dominated by the hegemonic reason . . . ."[20] This occurs while affirming the alternative reasoning and responsible practices emanating from those who are often exploited, ignored, and silenced. Intentionally paying attention to often-unheard voices in World Christianity, this volume makes room for a moral interpellation of those who continue to be impacted by the symbolic and otherwise hegemonizing violence still dominant in the world, including in ecclesiastical and academic contexts that many scholars of World Christianity are forced to navigate.

In this volume, we identify alterity in relation to subjects and communities that have been neglected or intentionally avoided within the field of World Christianity and/or within churches and Christian communities in various parts of the world. Often these two forms of neglect are closely aligned, as individual voices excluded from scholarship are sometimes the same ones who also experience *othering* at the hands of dominant Christian powers. Gender justice is a case in point. Although the field has recognized the significant role of women as leaders and faith practitioners, and although much has been done in recent decades to rectify previous scholarly neglect of women's roles, especially from within Global South communities, bringing women's voices and contributions to the forefront is only

---

19   Enrique Dussel, "Palabras Preliminares, " in *Liberacion Latino Americana y Emmanuel Levinas,* ed. Enrique Dussel and Daniel E. Guillot (Buenos Aires: Editorial Bomum, 1975), 8.

20   Enrique Dussel, *The Underside of Modernity: Apel, Ricoeur, Rorty, Taylor, and the Philosophy of Liberation* (Atlantic Highlands, NJ: Humanities Press, 1996), ix. In the quote above, Dussel is referring to John Austin, *How to Do Things with Words* (Cambridge: Harvard University Press, 1962).

one important step toward grappling with patriarchal oppressions and abuses of power that have occurred not just between Western and Global South Christians in mission fields but also within African, Asian, and Latin American (as well as European and North American) churches.[21]

Such injustices within global Christianity cannot be rectified simply through the acknowledgment of women's contributions or the encouragement of women scholars. Much more attention must be given to the pressing needs of women and girls in Christian communities, particularly in the face of horrific abuses that are often both gender-based and involving sexual exploitation. Important work on this front being done by Asian, African, and Latin American feminist and womanist scholars[22] has

---

21   For one World Christianity approach to this challenge, see Dana L. Robert, "Gender Roles and Recruitment in Southern African Churches, 1996–2001," in *Communities of Faith in Africa and the African Diaspora,* ed. Casely B. Essamuah and David K. Ngaruiya (Eugene, OR: Pickwick Publications, 2013), 116–34.

22   Elza Tamez, *Teólogos da Libertação Falam sobre a Mulher: Entrevistas* (São Paulo: Loyola, 1989); Hyun Kyung Chung, *Struggle to Be the Sun Again: Introducing Asian Women's Theology* (Maryknoll, NY: Orbis Books, 1990); Mercy Amba Oduyoye, *Daughters of Anowa: African Patriarchy* (Maryknoll, NY: Orbis, 1995); Ada María Isasi-Díaz, *Mujerista Theology: A Theology for the Twenty-First Century* (Maryknoll, NY: Orbis, 1995); Kwok Pui-lan, *Introducing Asian Feminist Theology* (Sheffield: Sheffield Academic Press, 2000); Kwok Pui-lan, ed., *Asian and Asian American Women in Theology and Religion: Embodying Knowledge* (Cham: Palgrave Macmillan, 2020); Meehyun Chung, *Another Story of Women's Theology* (Seoul: South Korea: Handŭlch'ulp'ansa, 2007); Judith Casselberry and Elizabeth A. Prichard, eds., *Spirit on the Move: Black Women and Pentecostalism in African and the Diaspora* (Durham: Duke University, 2019); Clarinda Still, *Dalit Women: Honour and Patriarchy in South India* (New York: Routledge, 2017); Evangeline Anderson-Rajkumar, "Turning Bodies Inside Out: Contours of Womanist Theology," in *Dalit Theology in the Twenty-first Century, Discordant voices, Discerning Pathways*, ed. Sathianathan Clarke, Deenabandhu Manchala, and Philip Vinod Peacock (Oxford: Oxford University Press, 2010), 199–214; Min-Ah Cho, "Stirring up Deep Waters: Korean Feminist Theologies Today," *Theology Today* 71, no. 2 (2014): 233–45; Man-Ja Choi, "The Acceptance, Development, and Influence of Feminist Theology in The Korean Church and Society in the 1980s," *Christianity and History in Korea* 18 (2003): 86–87; Ajay Kumar, "Sexual Violence against Dalit

not found a prominent place within World Christianity circles, and such scholarship is almost entirely neglected in World Christianity book series.[23] The chapters in this volume build on some exceptions to this general rule.[24]

Women: An Analytical Study of Intersectionality of Gender, Caste, and Class in India," *Journal of International Women's Studies* 22, no. 2 (2021): 123–34.

23 Although relevant examples of feminist and womanist scholarship can be found in some edited volumes, a survey of major World Christianity series (Fortress, Brill, Routledge, Penn State University Press, Baylor University Press, Oxford University Press) yields no volumes at all to date that even focus on women or gender. Palgrave's Christianities of the World series includes one title: Thien-Huong T. Ninh, *Race, Gender, and Religion in the Vietnamese Diaspora: The New Chosen People* (New York: Palgrave, 2017).

24 Such topics receive somewhat better coverage within journals. Over the past three decades, for example, two major World Christianity journals have published nine articles that engage substantively with feminism/womanism. Marcella Althaus-Reid, "Do Not Stop the Flow of My Blood: A Critical Christology of Hope Amongst Latin American Women," *Studies in World Christianity* 1, no. 2 (1995): 143–59; Musa W. Dube, "Searching for the Lost Needle: Double Colonization & Postcolonial African Feminisms," *Studies in World Christianity* 5, no. 2 (January 1, 1999): 213–28; Aruna Gnanadason, "Jesus and the Asian Woman: A Post-Colonial Look at the Syro-Phoenician Woman/Canaanite Woman from an Indian Perspective," *Studies in World Christianity* 7, no. 2 (2001): 162–77; Kwok Pui-lan, "Christianity and Women in Contemporary China," *Journal of World Christianity* 3, no. 1 (2010): 1–17; Namsoon Kang, "Reclaiming Theological Significance of Women's *Religious Choice-in-Differential*: Korean Women's Choice of Christianity Revisited," *Journal of World Christianity* 3, no. 1 (2010): 18–46; Oyeronke Olademo, "New Dimensions in Nigerian Women's Pentecostal Experience: The Case of DODIM, Nigeria," *Journal of World Christianity* 5, no. 1 (2012): 62–74; Francis Machingura, "'A woman should learn in quietness and full submission' (1 Timothy 2:11): Empowering Women in the Fight Against Masculine Readings of Biblical Texts and a Chauvinistic African Culture in the face of HIV and AIDS," *Studies in World Christianity* 19, no. 3 (2013): 233–51; Yolanda Pierce, "'Leaving Husband, Home, and Baby and All': African American Women and Nineteenth-Century Global Missions," *Journal of World Christianity* 6, no. 2 (2016): 277–90; Sonja Thomas, "'Studying Up' in World Christianity: A Feminist Analysis of Caste and Settler Colonialism," *Journal of World Christianity* 11, no. 2 (2021): 195–209.

The gaps in the field are even more glaring when it comes to the identities and religious expressions of sexual minorities in African, Asian, and Latin American contexts. While gender has often been treated as a synonym for women's experiences, using gender as a lens of study for World Christianity also invites reflection on questions about sexuality and sexual orientation. Such questions are taboo in many churches and have prompted the reinforcement of heteropatriarchal norms. The same appears to be true, for the most part, within studies on World Christianity. Existing scholarship on LGBTQI+ Christian identities, though relevant in geographical focus to World Christianity, is usually rooted in other fields, such as sexuality studies or queer theory, and rarely makes an appearance in World Christianity literature.[25] This is the case, as well, for studies addressing sexual abuse and other forms of sexual marginalization in Global South Christian contexts. Scholars working on these issues

---

25   For example, the following key texts inform this volume but are not widely used in World Christianity literature: Gayle Rubin, "Thinking Sex: Notes for a Radical Theory of the Politics of Sexuality," in *The Gay and Lesbian Studies Reader*, ed. Henry Abelove, Michèle Aina Barale, Daivd M. Halperin (New York: Routledge, 1993): 3–41; Marcella Althaus-Reid, *Indecent Theology: Theological Perversions in Sex, Gender and Politics* (New York: Routledge, 2000); Althaus-Reid, *The Queer God* (New York: Routledge, 2003); Althaus-Reid, *From Feminist Theology to Indecent Theology* (London: SCM, 2004); bell hooks, *Feminist Theory: from Margin to Center* (Boston: South End Press, 1984); Jeremy Carrette, "Radical Heterodoxy and the Indecent Proposal of Erotic Theology: Critical Groundwork for Sexual Theologies," *Literature and Theology: Queering Religion* 15, no. 3 (2001): 286–98; Kimberlé Crenshaw, "Demarginalizing the Intersection of Race and Sex: A Black Feminist Critique of Antidiscrimination Doctrine, Feminist Theory and Antiracist Politics," *University of Chicago Legal Forum* 1, no. 8 (1989): 141–56. A select few scholars have begun connecting such literature specifically to sexually marginalized people in various global Christian contexts: Chammah J. Kaunda, ed., *Genders, Sexualities, and Spiritualities in African Pentecostalism: 'Your Body is a Temple of the Holy Spirit'* (Cham: Palgrave Macmillan, 2020); Adriaan van Klinken, *Kenyan, Christian, Queer: Religion, LGBT Activism, and Arts of Resistance in Africa* (University Park: Pennsylvania State University Press, 2019); Joseph N. Goh, *Living Out Sexuality and Faith: Body Admissions of Malaysian Gay and Bisexual Men* (New York: Routledge, 2019).

must draw their theories and methods from outside the field of World Christianity.[26]

Other forms of exclusion within the field relate to racial, ethnic, cultural, or regional identities. Although racism and ethnocentrism have been salient concepts for exploration within the field of World Christianity since its inception, such discussions have mainly taken place in the context of Western missionary encounters with Indigenous people or in the contemporary context of Global South–Global North relations.[27] These discussions focus mainly on the activities and worldviews of white Western Christians, rarely identifying ways that white supremacist notions can also manifest themselves within Christian communities of color or affect South–South relationships.[28] Similarly, studies emerging from Amerindian peoples and others revisiting World Christian history, theology, praxis, and relations through decolonial epistemological lenses are yet to receive adequate attention in the field.[29]

---

26 See Eve Rebecca Parker, *Theologising with the Sacred 'Prostitutes' of South India: Towards an Indecent Dalit Theology* (Leiden: Brill, 2021). This study on Dalit sacred sex workers who have converted to Christianity in South India draws on Althaus-Ried's *Indecent Theology*.

27 See, for instance, José Carlos Barbosa, *Slavery and Protestant Missions in Imperial Brazil: "The Black Does Not Enter the Church, He Peeks in from Outside"* (Lanham, MA: University Press of America, 2008); Kirstie Close-Barry, *A Mission Divided: Race, Culture and Colonialism in Fiji's Methodist Mission* (Acton, Australia: ANU Press, 2015); and Alan Scott Willis, *All According to God's Plan: Southern Baptist Missions and Race, 1945–1970* (Lexington: University Press of Kentucky, 2005).

28 For a recent contribution in this area, which gives attention to Korean Christian engagements with anti-Black racism, as well as Korean influences on American evangelicalism, see Helen Jin Kim, *Race for Revival: How Cold War South Korea Shaped the American Evangelical Empire* (Oxford: Oxford University Press, 2022). For another recent contribution that pays attention to how white supremacy impacted the self-understanding and missionary practices of Brazilian evangelicals, see João B. Chaves, *The Global Mission of the Jim Crow South: Southern Baptist Missionaries and the Shaping of Latin American Evangelicalism* (Macon, GA: Mercer University Press, 2022).

29 Some of this literature is emerging in the Latin American and Latinx contexts: Michel Andraos, ed., *The Church and the Indigenous Peoples in the*

Regional divisions affect the field as well. World Christianity scholarship has tended to focus on certain areas of the world while neglecting others such as the Indigenous Christianities of the Middle East/North Africa (where Christianity is not growing rapidly and in some countries is actually declining)[30] and Latin America (a predominantly Christian region that nevertheless is underrepresented in the field).[31]

In fact, the Fortress Press series World Christianity as Public Religion, of which this volume is a part, in general seeks to bring attention to some of these issues. Its bilingual or multilingual makeup, for instance, seeks to address the anglophone-centric nature of the field.[32] In addition to being intentionally multilingual, inclusive of a significant number of scholars

---

    Americas: In Between Reconciliation and Decolonization (Eugene, OR: Cascade Books, 2019); Raimundo C. Barreto and Roberto Sirvent, eds., *Decolonial Christianities: Latinx and Latin American Perspectives* (New York: Palgrave Macmillan, 2019); and Elizabeth O'Donnell Gandolfo and Laurel Marshall Potter, *Re-Membering the Reign of God: The Decolonial Witness of El Salvador's Church of the Poor* (New York: Lexington Books, 2022).

30   Middle Eastern Christianity is included in World Christianity anthologies. See, for example, Heather J. Sharkey, "Middle Eastern and North African Christianity: Persisting in the Lands of Islam," in *Introducing World Christianity*, ed. Charles E. Farhadian (Malden: MA: Wiley-Blackwell, 2012), 7–20; Naures Atto, "The Death Throes of Indigenous Christians in the Middle East: Assyrians Living under the Islamic State," in *Relocating World Christianity*, ed. Joel Cabrita, David Maxwell, and Emma Wild-Wood (Leiden: Brill, 2017), 281–301. Few scholars of Middle Eastern Christianity, however, frame their work within the field of World Christianity. For some recent exceptions, see: Womack, *Protestants, Gender and the Arab Renaissance*; Elizabeth Marteijn, "Between Ruins and Remnants: Religious Reinvention and Renewal among Christians in West Bank Palestine" (PhD diss., University of Edinburgh, 2022); Lucy Jane Schouten, "'Everyone Has a Story': Jordanian Churches Reimagine Middle Eastern Christianity in Response to Refugees" (PhD diss., University of Edinburgh, 2022).

31   For more on this topic, see Deanna Ferree Womack's study in chapter 1 of this volume and Raimundo C. Barreto's chapter in Hanciles, *World Christianity: History, Methodologies, Horizons*, 138–57.

32   In all volumes of this series, there are authors who primarily work in a language other than English, including Portuguese, Spanish, and German. All volumes are translated in different directions. Since the series will also

living and working in different countries and continents in the Global South, and promoting intergenerational conversations (always seeking to combine rising and more established contributors), each volume of this series so far has addressed concerns with alterity and justice, although not as thoroughly as this volume. Volume one included chapters addressing theology, ethics, and society; church and gender; and concerns with a migratory epistemology and the politics of "wasting bodies" and unwanted immigration in fortress Europe.[33]

With a focus on migration as public discourse, volume two included chapters on the civic participation of African immigrants in North America, migrant theopolitics, pastoral theology among undocumented immigrants, a theological approach to migration considering xenophobia and xenophilia as antagonistic parameters, responses to the refugee crisis, the interpretation of Ignacio Ellacuria's notion of the "crucified people" to reframe the way of the cross in Central American migration, and the experience of urban migrants in a landless workers' settlement.[34] The third volume turned its attention to matters of urbanization and identity formation, including a chapter on the right to the city, a postcolonial approach to exile in a globalized world, sexual migration and gender diversity, the formation of popular advocacy agents in Brazil, and the rise of cultural popular action in the politically polarized context of mid-twentieth-century Colombia.[35]

Finally, with a focus on interfaith relations, volume four included chapters on counteracting Buddhist nationalism in Burma; cooperation among religious minorities in defense of Indian secularism; the situation

---

appear in Portuguese, authors writing in English are also translated and published in a different language.

33   See Raimundo C. Barreto Jr., Ronaldo Cavalcante, and Wanderley Pereira da Rosa, eds., *World Christianity as Public Religion* (Minneapolis: Fortress Press, 2017).

34   See Afe Adogame, Raimundo C. Barreto, and Wanderley Pereira da Rosa, eds., *Migration and Public Discourse in World Christianity* (Minneapolis: Fortress Press, 2019).

35   See Moses O. Biney, Kenneth N. Ngwa, and Raimundo C. Barreto, eds., *World Christianity, Urbanization, and Identity* (Minneapolis: Fortress, Press, 2021).

of religious intolerance in Brazil from the perspective of a Candomblé Babalawo; race, literature, and religion in contemporary Brazil; necropolitics, religion, and the ecological crisis; interfaith peace activism in Uganda; ecumenical initiatives to combat caste; and the encounter between Western Christianity and African cultures and religions in Southern Africa.[36]

Building on those conversations, this volume makes the issue of justice (or its evasion) and the various forms of alterity the core of its concern. The literature cited in all chapters of this book brings new areas of study/fields into conversation with World Christianity, something that becomes evident in the bibliography at the end of this book.

OVERVIEW OF CHAPTERS

This volume is divided into four parts, each one fleshing out the book's themes in particular ways. The chapters in "Part 1: Alterity and the Margins of World Christianity" advance methodological and theoretical frameworks to address themes of alterity and justice in the field of World Christianity in conversation with Middle Eastern Christian, Latin American ecumenical, African Pentecostal, and South Asian evangelical realities and scholarship.

Focusing on the historical intersections between Arab Christian migrants in the US and American Muslims, in the first chapter, Deanna Ferree Womack uses the concept of religio-racial misrecognition as a lens for exploring two neglected areas within World Christianity scholarship: Middle Eastern Christianity and interreligious engagement. Finding Edward Said's critique of orientalism useful for interpreting white American Protestants' racist discourses about both Islam and Arab Christianity, the chapter complexifies this critique by applying World Christianity principles to highlight the actions, responses, and self-identifications of misrecognized Middle Easterners, South Asians, and African Americans. The second chapter, by Raimundo C. Barreto, approaches the Christian ecumenical movement similarly by applying a decolonial lens. Barreto demonstrates that studies on ecumenism—which have long presupposed

---

36   See Richard Fox Young, ed., *World Christianity and Interfaith Relations* (Minneapolis: Fortress Press, 2022).

the ecumenical movement as operating primarily within a dominant Western Christian framework—must account for shifting realities in which the Global North churches that once imagined themselves as the center of modern Christianity are no longer calling the shots. Offering examples of this rearranged ecumenical table in Latin America, he points to Global South ways of knowing and challenges the field of World Christianity to attend to these voices, including Indigenous Christian voices that engage with traditional religions in ways that the dominant Western Christianity has typically suppressed.

In his study of the confluence between evangelicalism and bhakti tradition among Telugu Christians in India, James Taneti demonstrates yet again how important it is for World Christianity scholars to give due attention to Christian relationships with other religious and spiritual traditions in their own local contexts (chapter 3). This research confronts prevailing norms that reinforce separation between distinct religions rather than recognizing blurred boundaries, hybrid identities, or mutual influences—a salient subject for other studies in this volume contributed by Sun Yong Lee and Eve Parker. Taneti studies Telugu hymns as catechetical tools, including those largely overlooked hymns by Telugu Christian women, through which these bards articulated and passed on a faith that was the product of cross-fertilization between Telugu Christian, Western evangelical, and Hindu worldviews and hierarchical values. The fourth chapter, by Moses O. Biney, then asks how the field of World Christianity ought to understand and approach alterity methodologically. Using examples drawn from Pentecostal ministries and leaders in West Africa, Biney exposes cases of othering and misuse of power, including sexual abuse, that have not been adequately addressed in World Christianity studies, which often focus instead on the successes of church growth in Africa. He therefore proposes a new methodology for identifying and analyzing social justice issues as relevant for African Pentecostalism and for World Christianity generally, advocating a combination of social ethics and everyday religion.

The themes of gender and sexuality raised in Biney's and Taneti's chapters are explored more fully in the middle two sections of this book. "Part 2: Feminism, Masculinity, and Justice" begins with Fulata Lusungu Moyo's study on the response of the church to child marriage practices in

Malawi. Using her mother's testimony and experience as a child bride as a lens through which to examine the Church of Central Africa Presbyterian efforts to end child marriage, Moyo offers a feminist ethics of care and *ubuntu* principles that promote communal relations. Thus, she argues that the church's decision to do justice must include listening to the stories of survivors of child marriage and incorporating their ideas into concrete actions. She warns that if survivors' voices are excluded, the church will end up protecting the perpetrators whom these voices might otherwise expose.

In chapter 6, Sun Yong Lee uses feminist resources as well, in this case engaging with Korean feminist theologians' articulations about Korean Shamanism. Lee focuses on the controversy provoked by feminist theologian Hyung Kyung Chung's performance of a shamanistic ritual aiming to address unresolved sadness and suffering (known as *han*). Rather than taking sides with those who commended Chung's performance or those who critiqued it, Lee proposes an open-question approach to Korean Christian engagement with Korean Shamanism, through which shamanistic concepts present in Korean Christianity can be openly identified, explored, and/or contested as part of a continuing conversation. The last chapter in this section turns to issues of masculinity and race as Jay-Paul Hinds considers the missionary efforts of Black clergymen who styled themselves in the image of the Black messiah, intent on redeeming Africa (chapter 7). Yet, due to the racialized Western patriarchal consciousness and images of Christian masculinity that these clergymen adopted from American culture and then applied to native Africans, Hinds finds that the Black messiah brought a destructive manhood that mimicked the white slave masters' exploitative domination, rather than establishing the kingdom of God in Africa.

Moving on to address questions of sexuality explicitly, "Part 3: Biblical and Theological Approaches to Gender and Sexuality" considers how the Bible and theology have been used to marginalize LGBTQI+ persons and to condone sexual exploitation and violence against women. In response, the four chapters that make up this section advocate biblical and theological interpretations that support the flourishing of all people. In chapter 8, Chamma Kaunda examines Biblicist Pentecostal rhetoric about sexuality in Zambia, focusing on the case of a Pentecostal minister-turned-politician, Godfridah Sumaili, using the Bible to legitimize hierarchical gender and sexual discourses and to deny LGBTQI+ rights. Kaunda argues that the problem is not that Pentecostals reject certain sexual practices, as the rejection of some lifestyles and the choosing of others is a natural human condition. Rather, he explains, their mode of rejection allows for dehumanization of sexual minorities and promotes the status quo of neocolonialism. Kaunda advocates instead a theology of grace, humanization, and solidarity with those whose ideas about life are different from one's own. Ana Ester Pádua Freire's chapter addresses LGBTQI+ experiences within World Christianity as well, focusing on the Brazilian context (chapter 9). Freire frames her study within the category of *desire*, as described in Marcella Althaus-Reid's queer theology—a neglected subject within World Christianity studies that allows for analysis of social actions within the plural possibilities of Christian experiences in Brazil. Presenting two case studies of Brazilian inclusive initiatives—Evangelicals for Diversity and the National Network of Catholic LGBT Groups—Freire uses the marginal epistemology of queer and indecent theology to argue for the belonging of dissident inclusive initiatives within Christianity that challenge the tradition's hegemonic discourses.

The next two chapters then address connections between skewed biblical interpretations, violence, and sexual abuse against women. In chapter 10, Eve Parker weaves ethnographic research on the experiences of Dalit women, and in particular sacred "sex workers" (*devadāsīs*, or temple "prostitutes") of South India, into a critical rereading of the rape and murder of the nameless concubine in Judges 19. Parker gives voice to the sexual narratives of the oppressed as they expose and challenge the religious, political, social, and economic matrix of power. She reinterprets scripture through the lens of Dalit feminist theology in an effort to challenge epistemic and testimonial injustice and call for radical change in theology and praxis today. Kenner R. C. Terra's chapter similarly rereads and deconstructs the negative feminine symbolism in scripture, focusing on the role of the woman throughout the Book of Revelation (chapter 11). Drawing on the tools of contemporary biblical studies, Terra argues that the apocalyptic language of Revelation must be interpreted with critical care and symbolic inversion to avoid upholding gender-based violence and legitimizing misogyny. His proposal finds contemporary urgency in light of the escalating violence against women in Brazilian Christian communities, and the ways that religious language continues to be used to demonize the female body.

"Part 4: Politics of Marginality in Latin American Christianity" concludes with a section focused on Latin America, an area of the world that has not been a major focus within World Christianity circles, despite the large number of studies (in Spanish, Portuguese, and English) on Christianity in this region. The final two chapters focus on Christian groups that are marginalized or overlooked in the region, namely progressive evangelicals and Orthodox Christians. In chapter 12, Christina Vital da Cunha draws on extensive interviews with members of the Brazilian evangelical left to highlight the performances and disputes surrounding progressive evangelical identity and the relationship between the secular and Christian left in Brazil. Focusing on two leftist movements—Popular Evangelical Front and Christians Against Fascism—she observes the political challenges that progressive evangelical candidates face from both conservative evangelical and secular critics while also accounting for the growing political mobilization and electoral successes within Brazil's Christian left. Finally, Graham McGeoch addresses the Orthodox "other" in Latin America, providing a history of this community's growth in a largely Catholic landscape and then focusing on the Russian Orthodox diaspora and recent activities of the Russian Orthodox hierarchy in the region. Discussing the 2016 Joint Declaration of Patriarch Kirill and Pope Francis in Cuba, McGeoch sheds light on Orthodox relations with other churches in Latin America alongside ongoing inter-Orthodox tensions.

Conclusion: Reinscribing Justice

The authors of this volume, although engaging with different subjects of study and bodies of scholarship, all demonstrate that the field of World Christianity can and should offer more concerted attention to questions of justice, and to the plural ways of knowing and of being Christian in global contexts. These studies indicate, as well, that the pursuit of justice and humanization requires learning not just *about* but also *from* those who have experienced othering. Based on such lessons from those who are too often silenced, we hope that readers of this volume will be better prepared to grapple with several conclusions drawn from the research in the following pages.

First, many of the chapters presented here are tied together by the recognition of alternative epistemological (a reference to ways of knowing) and ontological (a reference to multiple ways of being in the world) locations of the various subjects in the study of World Christianity, including the scholars researching in this field. One of the contributions that decolonial, feminist, queer, and other marginal epistemologies offer to World Christianity scholarship is to bring to the fore ways of being/ living and knowing that do not conform to dominant Eurocentric modes of Christianity, nor to neocolonial structures that have developed in the modern/colonial world,[37] including in the Global South. Further, these ways of being, as described by several authors (Womack, Barreto, Lee,

---

37   The concept of modernity/coloniality highlights the incongruence of the rhetoric of modernity, stating that both modernity and (the modern understanding of) Europe itself do not stand independently from the process of conquest and colonization. Modernity/coloniality are two faces of the same coin, a totalizing project that has defined the terms of modern ontologies (the boundaries between being and non-being) and the limits of modern rationality (which knowledges are academically acceptable and validated, and which ones are not). Sustaining this discourse is a rhetoric that interprets history as a progression from traditional societies to modern rationality. Its outcome is the colonial matrix of power, a hierarchized and totalizing ordering of the world that employs the modern concepts of religion, race, and gender to define notions of superiority and inferiority, distinguishing the human from the nonhuman, reason from non-reason, and faith from superstition. The alternative epistemologies this book refers to are constitutive of the decolonial turn, "the movement of theoretical and practical resistance, political and epistemological, to the logic of modernity/coloniality." See Luciana Ballestrin, "America Latina e o Giro Decolonial," *Revista Brasileira de Ciência Política* 11 (2013): 89–117 (105), cited in Raimundo Barreto and Roberto Sirvent, "Introduction," in *Decolonial Christianities: Latin American and Latinx Perspectives*, 2. See also Walter D. Mignolo, *The Darker Side of Western Modernity: Global Futures, Decolonial Options* (Durham/London: Duke University Press, 2011); and Nestor Maldonado-Torres, "Enrique Dussel's Liberation Thought in the Decolonial Turn," *Transmodernity* 1, no. 1 (2011): 1–30.

Parker, and Taneti), do not follow Western notions about distinctions and separations between religious traditions but rather are blurred, fluid, and hybrid.

Second, although these chapters indicate how violence and patriarchy are entangled with colonialism, Western colonialist forms of Christianity are not the only—and not always the most pressing—problem being confronted in the contemporary studies contained in this volume. Rather, the authors acknowledge ways through which Indigenous Global South churches and Christian leaders perpetuate patriarchy and other injustices. These authors apply a critical lens to understand and challenge forms of othering enacted in the name of Christianity, and they model a way of uncovering and addressing abuses of power in World Christianity without reinforcing old Eurocentric stereotypes and generalizations about non-Western cultures. The liberationist concerns of this volume about injustices within African, Asian, or Latin American contexts do not negate the concerns that scholars of World Christianity have always held about power imbalances between the Global North and South. Indeed, there must be a place within World Christianity scholarship for such critiques, particularly those made from within the cultures and traditions being studied, so that the field is not oriented toward informing the Western Christian academy alone but is relevant to scholars in Global South contexts as well.

Third and finally, drawing on the language that Ana Ester Pádua Freire and Eve Parker both employ in this volume, to negate the ways that studies of World Christianity have evaded justice, the field itself may need to be turned indecent. The chapters herein make plain that in pursuit of decency, the field has largely overlooked abuses within Global South Christianities and avoided confronting patriarchy, sexual exploitation, and the dehumanization of queer Christians in these contexts. These authors chart a way forward, challenging the field of World Christianity not to remain tame and safe but to see and give voice to the marginalized "other."

CHAPTER 1

AMERICAN MUSLIMS, ARAB CHRISTIANS, AND RELIGIO-RACIAL MISRECOGNITION

Deanna Ferree Womack

INTRODUCTION

In describing the effects of Islamophobia on young American Muslims today, Interfaith America founder and president Eboo Patel identified widespread experiences of misrecognition. Muslim self-perceptions, he explained, have become scarred by the dehumanizing images of Islam that others in United States society "mirror back" to them.[1] Instances of misrecognition likewise shaped the transition experiences of the earliest Muslims who migrated to the US from the Middle East and South Asia in the late nineteenth and early twentieth centuries. They faced perceptions of civilizational backwardness, accusations of immorality, and the denial of citizenship on the basis of race and geographical origin. At that time, many white American Protestants projected similarly negative views on Arab Christian immigrants. They often misperceived Middle Eastern Christians as Muslims while also identifying South Asian Muslim migrants as Hindus. In a related

---

1   Eboo Patel, "Forward," in Todd H. Green, *Presumed Guilty: Why We Shouldn't Ask Muslims to Condemn Terrorism* (Minneapolis: Fortress Press, 2018), xvii. Originally founded as Interfaith Youth Core, the organization was renamed Interfaith America in 2022. I wish to thank Kyle Lambelet, Susan Reynolds, Joel Kemp, Helen Kim, and Lucila Crena, for generative feedback on this chapter.

27

form of misrecognition, as African American Muslim communities grew between the 1930s and the 1960s, the white American Christian establishment interpreted Black Muslim movements as race-based political movements. Scholars, politicians, and clergy alike discounted or de-emphasized Black Muslim religiosity based on perceptions of race—similar to the way they misidentified Arab and Indian immigrants' religious identities.

That such religio-racial othering continues in the United States today, as Patel noted, is cause for concern for Christian–Muslim relations, for racial equity, and for immigration and refugee protections. Religio-racial misrecognition is also relevant to the study of World Christianity in this era of unprecedented global migration. Since the late nineteenth century, when Christians from outside of Europe began migrating to the US in significant numbers, white Protestant cultural normativity has met them at every turn. It is important, therefore, to understand the history of religio-racial misrecognition that still shapes American Protestant thought patterns and the transition experiences of Christian and Muslim immigrants alike. This chapter explores this history with two aims in mind:

1. To understand how Americans, and especially white Protestants, applied their perceptions of Islam to immigrants and communities of color in the first half of the twentieth century, in religious rhetoric and in public policy; and

2. To explore the responses from such misrecognized populations, and particularly from Arab American Christians, who were notable among the new Christian immigrants to the US coming from outside of Europe in this period.

Because the majority of Arab migrants to the US were Christian, not Muslim, and because Americans nevertheless tended to view Middle Easterners as Muslim, cases of mistaken identity were common in the early twentieth century, as they still are today. Perhaps for similar reasons, the migration histories of Arab Christians have seldom been the focus of World Christianity scholarship. This study helps to rectify this oversight by using historical archives, American newspapers, Arab American periodicals, memoirs, and Muslim missionary publications to explore American Protestant (mis)perceptions of Islam, and responses to such misrecognition from Arab Christians and from Muslims in the US in the first half of the twentieth century.

The first section of this chapter provides historical context, documenting the language about Islam, Muslims, and Islamic cultures that circulated in early twentieth-century America. It attends to the ways in which Protestant missionaries in the Islamic world shaped their constituents' perceptions of the "other" through invented concepts of race and world religions. The second section presents three case studies of religio-racial misrecognition in the US, focusing in turn on Arab Christian migrants, South Asian Muslim migrants, and African American Muslims. The third and final section returns to the experiences of Arab Christian migrants to explore more fully their responses to being religiously misrecognized as Muslims. They variously rejected Muslim identity, reinforced orientalist notions about the Middle East and Islam, appropriated Muslim identity for economic and social gain, and defended Islam and Arab-Islamic culture. The conclusion considers how the lessons learned from these encounters relate to theories and methods for the study of World Christianity today, and to the theme of alterity in global Christian studies.

Before turning to the historical context, I must offer a word on the concept of *misrecognition* as the focal point and interpretive lens for this chapter. Patel drew this term from philosopher Charles Taylor, who dealt with misrecognition briefly in an influential 1994 essay on the "politics of recognition."[2] Taylor explained that when identity is shaped by the misrecognition of others, "a person or group of people can suffer real damage, real distortion, if the people or society around them mirror back to them a confining or demeaning or contemptible picture of themselves. Nonrecognition or misrecognition can inflict harm, can be a form of oppression, imprisoning someone in a false, distorted and reduced

---

2   Nasar Meer, Wendy Martineau, and Simon Thompson, "Misrecognition and Ethno-Religious Diversity," *Ethnicities* 12, no. 2 (April 1, 2012): 131–41.

mode of being."[3] Acknowledging these psychological impacts, this study considers how misrecognition became enshrined in American narratives about Islam. I trace the historical patterns of racialization in rhetoric about Islam and consider the actions, responses, and self-understandings of Middle Easterners, South Asians, and African Americans, whose religious identities were so often misrecognized.[4]

Like studies on orientalism that critique Western colonial abuses and the cultural imperialism of knowledge production about Asia and Africa, this chapter interrogates the actions of white American Protestants who transmitted, internalized, and applied racist discourses about Islam. Assured of their own superiority in the face of alterity, these Protestants orientalized Muslims and Christians from Islamic societies, demonizing them as radically alien based on Euro-American Protestant religious and cultural norms. Yet, as Jacob Berman argued, the basic critique of orientalism "fails to account for the manifold question of agency." Critical scholarly interventions must "do more than detail co-option, misrepresentation, and the discursive practices of hegemony."[5] Therefore, this study is equally interested in the actions, responses, and self-understandings of misrecognized Middle Easterners, South Asians, and African Americans. Moreover, I take seriously the World Christianity principle that *the native Christian can speak.*[6] This study therefore moves beyond the politics of recognition as a mode for promoting multiculturalism and explores the consequences of religio-racial othering on Arab American Christian relationships to Islam.

---

3   Charles Taylor, "The Politics of Recognition," in *Multiculturalism*, ed. Amy Gutmann (Princeton, NJ: Princeton University Press, 1994), 25.

4   As both Patel and Taylor note, identity formation is a fraught, dialogical, and highly complex process. Taylor, "The Politics of Recognition," 37; Patel, "Forward, " xvii.

5   Jacob Rama Berman, *American Arabesque: Arabs and Islam in the Nineteenth Century Imaginary* (New York: New York University Press, 2012), 2.

6   On seeking out and listening to native Christian voices, see Arun W. Jones, ed., *Christian Interculture: Texts and Voices from Colonial and Postcolonial Worlds* (University Park: Pennsylvania State University Press, 2021). On the need to move beyond multiculturalism in understanding misrecognition, see Meer, Martineau, and Thompson, "Misrecognition and Ethno-Religious Diversity," 131–41.

CONTEXT: ALTERITY AND THE NINETEENTH-CENTURY REINVENTION OF ISLAM

In the late nineteenth century, rising transnational travel, the development of global communication networks, and the expansion of US political influence abroad brought American Protestants more information than ever about Muslims and the Islamic world. Long before the United States faced the Ottoman Empire as an adversary in World War I, American politicians, newspaper reporters, and missionaries spoke about the terrible Turks and their oriental despotism. This derisive language represented the Ottoman Empire—the center of Sunni Islam since the sixteenth century—as a political threat. Americans and Europeans alike also marked the inhabitants of this region as religiously and culturally inferior and threatening. Protestant writings applied similar views to Muslims in South Asia while identifying sub-Saharan Africa as a space of competition between Christianity and Islam for converts from African traditional religions. This section focuses on the perceptions of religious, cultural, and racial differences that American Protestants projected onto Islam after the nineteenth century, in conversation with British Protestants and European scholars of religion. Then it explains how such ideas were applied in the missionary reports that brought information about Islam to Protestant readers who had not met Muslims themselves.

American Protestants inherited a long history of European Christian thinking about Islam as an Arab religion that spread by the sword and that was antithetical to Christianity. With the development of the science of religion in the nineteenth century, these preconceptions blended with new ideas about Christianity's superiority in relationship to other world religions. As Tomoko Masuzawa explained, Western Christians had previously understood Islam "as an old menace and invincible foe to European Christendom," but by the early twentieth-century, European and American scholars of religion had categorized Islam within the invented concept of world religions.[7] When standardizing the list of these universal

---

7   Tomoko Masuzawa, *The Invention of World Religions: Or, How European Universalism Was Preserved in the Language of Pluralism* (Chicago: University of Chicago Press, 2005), 179, 204.

religions, philologists and biblical scholars disconnected Christianity from its Judeo-Semitic origins while identifying Islam as "an intrinsically Arab religion, Semitic in its essential nature."[8] They understood this national or ethnic basis to determine Islam's character: as barbaric, dangerous, and aggressive due to the Arab nation's "expansionist ambition." Western Christians also came to understand that Islam was legalistic, ritualistic, and trapped in a state of pre-modern stagnation because of its Semitic origins.[9]

Such notions followed orientalist thought patterns about racial, cultural, and civilizational inferiority of the "East" to the "West." This was apparent, for example, in the way German philologists conceived of an Aryan race consisting of a western branch of "Indo-Germans" and an eastern branch of "Indo-Persians" or "East-Aryans."[10] Yet Islam, when understood as a Semitic religion tied to an Arab nation, fared far worse. As Edward Said contended, the self-reinforcing orientalist attitude "turned Islam into the very epitome of an outsider against which the whole of European civilization from the Middle Ages on was founded."[11] Thus, the reinvention of Islam in the nineteenth century was founded on alterity, or misrecognition, in the sense that categorization and understanding of world religions was premised on Western Christianity as the norm, at the top of a religio-racial hierarchy.

Eurocentric discourses of knowledge about the peoples of Asia and Africa were systematized further in the late nineteenth century with the rise of scientific racism, biological determinism, and a Western obsession with categorizing humanity into racial "types." In the information they disseminated to supporters back home, Protestant missionaries in the Islamic world merged theological claims with orientalist notions and views of Christianity as the pinnacle of world religions. The accounts of both

---

8   Ibid., 191, 205.

9   Ibid., 199, 200. In the late nineteenth century, Judaism was not considered to be a world religion because it was "national," not universal, and for similar reasons, scholars like Abraham Kuenen and Otto Pfleiderer argued that Islam was not a true world religion either. Ibid., 192–204.

10 Ibid., 189, note 10.

11 Edward W. Said, *Orientalism* (New York: Vintage Books, 1979), 70.

American and British missionaries were especially formative for American Protestant culture in the nineteenth and early twentieth centuries. Missionaries sometimes transmitted nuanced explanations of Muslim life, yet nevertheless they usually reinforced perceptions of Christianity's superiority over Islam, of Eastern cultural inferiority to Euro-American civilization, and of white Protestantism as the normative ideal for Christianity and for American identity.[12] This relates to World Christianity because non-Western Christians were judged by the racial categories, but then elevated in status according to Christian and especially Protestant affiliation, as seen in the Arab American Christian citizenship cases described in the second section below.

Although it would be a mistake to cast all Western Christians and missionaries uncritically into the same orientalist mold, the nineteenth- and early twentieth-century missionary enterprise drew from and contributed to Western cultural constructions of Muslims as so-called "Oriental" others. For one example, we can turn to the mission atlas that the Church Missionary Society (CMS), a prominent British Anglican mission agency, published in 1896. This text reflected philological and anthropological views of non-Western societies at the turn of the century as it introduced Protestant readers to the people in global mission fields according to invented religio-racial categories that corresponded to a hierarchy of intellectual capacities and bodily characteristics. The atlas designated three primary human divisions within a racialized hierarchy that posed as scientific fact: "the Negritic or Black, the Mongolic or Yellow, and the Caucausic or White."[13] This third and highest division of the human family included Aryans (European, Iranian, and Indian), Semites (Arab and Abyssinian), and North African Hamites.[14] In British, American, and

---

12 Although what missionaries expressed in private about the cultures they encountered was often more nuanced than what they said in public or wrote for mission supporters, missionaries both followed and reinforced the first two norms of thinking listed above in a period when theories of biological determinism strongly influenced Western Christian thought.

13 *The Church Missionary Society Atlas, Containing an Account of the Various Countries in which the Society Labors and of its Missionary Operations*, 8th Edition (London: Salisbury Square, 1896), 1.

14 Ibid., 2.

other Western missionary practice, such designations determined where nineteenth-century missionaries would devote financial resources and personnel. As we shall see later, such invented racial categories also had devastating consequences in terms of US policy decisions and the physical and emotional violence such policies elicited.

Just as this section of the atlas upheld the intellectual foundations of biological racism, it also signified a specific orientalization of Arabs and others whom the authors deemed to be "Eastern Caucasians." The atlas categorized Europeans as white, along with inhabitants of much of the Islamic world (including North Africans, West Asians, Central Asians, and South Asians). Yet then it distinguished between fair and dark "types," indicating a hierarchy within the peoples considered to be Caucasian. Those with blue or gray eyes and light hair were "serious, steadfast, solid, and stolid." In contrast, black eyes and black or dark brown hair signified a "fiery, impulsive, and fickle" temperament.[15] Vernacular languages also reflected religious and racial identity according to the mission atlas. For example, under the "Semitic" category, the authors described Arabic as "one of the great conquering languages of the world, and representing very emphatically the influence of Mohammedanism."[16] The atlas linked these essentialized features to mental capacities and to spiritual attainment. Quoting William Muir, a Scottish Orientalist who was in close correspondence with British and American missionaries across the Islamic world, it contended that "radical evils flow from the [Islamic] faith."[17]

This CMS atlas was but one example of the widespread Islamic orientalism within Western Protestant missions at the turn of the century.[18] It

---

15 Ibid., 6–7. In a striking parallel to Said's depiction of philology, the document included a lengthy philological explanation of the relationship between global languages and the three "stock races." The highest order of languages matched the highest division of the human race.

16 Ibid., 16.

17 Ibid., 66. These evils, according to Muir, included polygamy, divorce, slavery, prohibition on freedom of thought, intolerance of private judgment, and resistance to the Christian gospel message.

18 The atlas defined the "Mohammedan population of the globe" as that part of the human race corresponding to the phrase "the East." Ibid., 65. In order to explicate the evils of Islam, the atlas turned to Sir William Muir and William

effectively demonstrated the common British and American practice of using geographical origin to map racial, cultural-linguistic, and religious characteristics onto various people groups, along with determining intellectual capacity, character traits, and morality. Each of the case studies I consider next centers around a group that white Americans misrecognized according to these invented religio-racial maps.

CASE STUDIES: ARAB CHRISTIANS, SOUTH ASIAN AHMADIS, AND AFRICAN AMERICAN MUSLIMS

In this section, I highlight three populations that white American Protestants tended to misrecognize in the early- to mid-twentieth century: Arab Christian immigrants, South Asian Muslim immigrants, and African American Muslims. This misrecognition included misidentification of these communities' actual religious traditions and projection of hostile representations onto these communities to exclude them from citizenship or to deny them equal rights in US society. From the colonial period onward, Christians in the Americas who identified themselves as "white" also racialized Islam as "non-white," noting Islam as the religion of a certain number of enslaved West Africans, and wishing to suppress all non-Christian forms of African religiosity.[19]

Middle Eastern Migrants

With advances in transatlantic travel by the late nineteenth century, migrants to the US from the Islamic world came from the Middle East and especially from Ottoman Syria. This Syrian American population was mostly

---

Gifford Palgrave, both of whom Said mentioned in *Orientalism*. See *The Church Missionary Society Atlas*, 66; Said, *Orientalism*, 99, 151, 197, 224.

19 Sylviane A. Diouf, *Servants of Allah: African Muslims Enslaved in the Americas* (New York: New York University Press, 2013); Terry Alford, *Prince among Slaves: The True Story of an African Prince Sold into Slavery in the American South* (Oxford: Oxford University Press, 2007); Omar Ibn Said, *A Muslim American Slave: The Life of Omar Ibn Said*, ed. Ala Alryyes (Madison: University of Wisconsin Press, 2011). The earliest Muslims to reach the Americas in any large number were enslaved West Africans who were forcibly transported to these shores beginning in the colonial period.

Arab and about 90 percent Christian, and it was known for its elite intellectual circle, including famed authors like the Maronite Khalil Gibran. The Syrian American community also included enterprising peddlers (both Christian and Muslim) who established trade networks from the East Coast to the Midwest, often selling souvenirs purportedly from the Holy Land.[20] As Linda Jacobs reported, many Syrian Christians were misrecognized as Muslims, and some of them found that it helped their business enterprises not to correct such mistaken assumptions.[21] Yet persistent questions about Muslim identity did bother some Syrian Christians, like the Protestant Hannah Kurani, who lectured to American church groups, women's circles, and suffragist meetings in several states following her appearance in the women's congress at the 1893 Chicago World's Fair. *The New York Times* reported on one such meeting, saying, "One thing that troubles Mme. Korany is why she should be asked if she is a Christian, when she comes from the land that gave Christianity to the world. Her ancestors, centuries ago, belonged to the old Greek Church."[22]

A more disturbing form of misrecognition taught Syrians by the early twentieth century that it was to their advantage to assert their *Christian* identities when petitioning for US citizenship. In that period when only those deemed legally white could become citizens, judges projected assumptions of inferiority onto Syrian petitioners based on prejudice that geographical origin and skin color made them unfit to be Americans. Some held that true "whiteness" was linked to European ancestry alone,

---

20   Among the Syrian migrants in the US at the turn of the century were also hundreds who came to perform the parts of Islamic world inhabitants or to sell Middle Eastern trinkets and handicrafts at the Chicago World's Fair of 1893. Linda Jacobs, "Playing East: Arabs Perform in Nineteenth-Century America," *Mashriq & Mahjar* 2, no. 2 (2014): 82.

21   Ibid., 80, 90. During such an event sponsored by the Woman's Foreign Missionary Society in Washington, DC in the 1880s, members of a Greek Orthodox Syrian immigrant family dressed up as Muslims and put on a show. Ibid., 91.

22   "A Fair Visitor from Syria," *New York Times* (February 20, 1894): 6. Not Kurani's ancient ancestors but her parents, in fact, converted from Greek Orthodoxy to Protestantism in the nineteenth century. Deanna Ferree Womack, *Protestants, Gender and the Arab Renaissance in Late Ottoman Syria* (Edinburgh: Edinburgh University Press, 2019), 155, 199, note 59.

and that Syrians were "Asiatic," a term used to stigmatize immigrants.[23] This approach was comparable to the ideas of biological determinism and Caucasian hierarchy represented in the CMS atlas. In response, lawyers for Syrian Christians argued "for inclusion in the 'white race' on the basis of membership in the Christian fold."[24] Though religion alone would not become a legal reason for citizenship, the argument moved Syrian Christians closer to the top of this perceived Caucasian hierarchy, and many judges were convinced by this logic. Cases for citizenship were more difficult for Syrian Muslims, however. As Sarah Gualtieri explained:

> Whereas the Christian identity of Syrian applicants in the racial prerequisite cases had been central to their argument for whiteness, Muslim Arabs were at their whitest when stripped of their religious affiliation and rendered part of the Western fantasy of an original "Semitic" race.[25]

The next two case studies further explore how American Christian policymakers applied such religio-racial concepts to Muslims.

South Asian Migrants

A similar approach to citizenship based on ethnology of race affected the status of South Asian Muslims and others from the Indian subcontinent. They were typically all called "Hindu" regardless of religious identity and categorized as Aryan along with actual practitioners of Vedic traditions. Thus, as the CMS atlas indicated, they would have been deemed *Caucasian*, making it possible

---

23   Sarah M. A. Gualtieri, *Between Arab and White: Race and Ethnicity in the Early Syrian American Diaspora* (Berkeley: University of California Press, 2009), 61, 70.

24   Ibid., 57.

25   Ibid., 161. Further attention should be given to the use of the term "Arab" in this period. See Ibid., 159, 161. A Syrian Christian, like Costa Najour, who petitioned for citizenship in Atlanta in 1909, could be proclaimed as a "pure Syrian and a Christian" as distinct from the "Asiatic" Muslim Turks who ruled the Ottoman Empire, and from Arab Muslims who were also deemed "Asiatic" and more regularly denied citizenship. Armenian Christians were also deemed white. Ibid., 70, 158.

to receive US citizenship in the early twentieth century. With the help of caste system analysis, such misrecognition generally worked in the favor of upper-caste South Asian applicants until the notorious 1923 Supreme Court case of Baghat Singh Thind (1892–1967). Thind was an Indian American Sikh and US army veteran who had his citizenship stripped based on an American nativist interpretation that "removed 'white' from the realm of ethnological inquiry and genealogical reckoning, arguing instead that it denoted a race or racial type that . . . had reached its peak in America."[26] The US Supreme Court upheld the judgment that a "Hindu"—as Thind was called—could never be "white."[27] Hindus were lumped together with Arabs as "Asiatic."[28]

Even before Thind's court case, when a prominent Indian Ahmadi missionary named Mufti Muhammad Sadiq arrived in Philadelphia in 1920, religio-racial assumptions nearly prevented him from entering the country. Sadiq would become a spokesperson for South Asian Muslims, and for the Ahmadis' particular understanding of Islam (which emerged with Mirza Gulam Ahmad in 1880s Punjab). Immigration officials confined the Mufti in a detention house for several weeks but eventually permitted him into the US "on the condition that he would not preach polygamy."[29] Of this experience, Sadiq wrote in his English language periodical, *The Moslem Sunrise*, that "if Jesus Christ comes to America and applies for admission to the United States under the immigration laws,

---

26 Jennifer Snow, "The Civilization of White Men: The Race of the Hindu in *United States v. Bhagat Sindh Thind*," in *Race, Nation, and Religion in the Americas*, ed. Henry Goldschmidt and Elizabeth McAlister (Oxford: Oxford University Press, 2004), 261.

27 Ibid., 262; Richard Brent Turner, *Islam in the African-American Experience*, 2nd edition (Bloomington: Indiana University Press, 2003), 117.

28 Snow, "The Civilization of White Men," 260.

29 Turner, *Islam in the African-American Experience*, 116. Polygamy was also a subject Sadiq took up in his first publication of *The Moslem Sunrise*, the newspaper he founded for the Ahmadi mission. This question about polygamy did not necessarily indicate that the immigration agents identified Sadiq as Muslim. Snow explained, "polygamy, child and arranged marriage, abuse of widows, slavery, drunkenness, adultery and sensuality, even feeding one's children to the Ganges crocodiles were all laid at the door of Hinduism." Snow, "The Civilization of White Men," 171.

[he] would not be allowed to enter this country." Sadiq then listed several reasons, including:

> 1. He comes from a land which is out of the permitted zone. 2. He has no money with him. 3. He is not decently dressed. 4. His hands have holes in the palms. 5. He remains bare-footed, which is a disorderly act. 6. He is against fighting for the country. 7. He believes in making wine when he thinks necessary. 8. He has no credential to show that he is an authorized preacher. 9. He believes in practicing the Law of Moses [polygamy].[30]

Sadiq's message about the contradictions of American culture and Western Christianity gained him a multiethnic group of followers in the US, but most converts were African American. What the Ahmadis accomplished in the US, Moustafa Bayoumi argued, was a path toward multiracial and ecumenical unity around Islam so that "African Americans could metaphorically travel beyond the confines of national identities. They could become 'Asiatics' and remain black, and could be proud of their African heritage *and* feel a sense of belonging to and participation with Asia."[31] This brings me to the final case study on African American Muslims.

African American Muslims

By the mid-twentieth century, the close attention that the white press gave the Nation of Islam (NOI) under Elijah Muhammad's leadership after 1934 quickly surpassed the fleeting media attention given to the Ahmadis' multiracial movement. The Ahmadis created a more universalistic movement that "America was not ready to deal with" because

---

30　Moustafa Bayoumi, *This Muslim American Life, Dispatches from the War on Terror* (New York University Press, 2015), 39. Bayoumi quoted Sadiq's statement from "If Jesus Comes to America," *The Moslem Sunrise* 1, no. 1 (April 1922): 55–56.

31　Ibid., 40–41. This added to the positive appropriation of the term "Asiatic" used by the Moorish Science Temple, and later by the Nation of Islam, to signify African American Muslims' connection to the Islamic world.

it violated presumptions about race and religion.[32] For the NOI, on the other hand, identification with Asian and Arab culture and the positive appropriation of the term Asiatic "functioned as a form of ethnographic self-identification for the black Muslims who sought to separate themselves racially, geographically, historically, and spiritually from Western culture."[33] This separatist *race* ideology gave white Americans a great excuse to discount the *religious* appeal of the NOI and the diversity of other African American Muslim movements that they tended to equate with the NOI.[34] Some simply dismissed it as a "cult," while liberal white Christian writers in the 1960s—including Thomas Merton—recognized the NOI as an understandable sociopolitical response to racism. Yet, as Thomas Kidd explained, "Their coverage hardly suggested that the Nation represented a legitimate religious alternative."[35] The term "Black Muslim" emphasized race over religious identity, and it stuck despite the objections of Malcolm X, who explained, "We are black *people* here in America. Our *religion* is Islam. We are properly called 'Muslims'!"[36]

As Jamillah Karim and Dawn-Marie Gibson argued, "The Nation of Islam is not only a Black nationalist movement but also a religious movement . . . unmistakably embedded in the religion of Islam."[37] Misrecognition of this religious reality may be understandable since "mainstream"

---

32   Turner, *Islam in the African-American Experience,* 141. Turner quotes here from Muzaffar Ahmad Zafr.

33   Ibid., 162.

34   Largely overlooked in the American press of the time—and in much of the scholarship on Black Muslims today—were the African American Sunni communities that emerged in the US by the late 1920s. On the diversity within African American Islam, see Robert Dannin, *Black Pilgrimage to Islam* (Oxford: Oxford University Press, 2022); Rasul Hanif Miller, "Black Muslim Cosmopolitanism: The Global Character of New York City's Black Muslim Movements, 1929–1990" (PhD diss., University of Pennsylvania, 2019).

35   Thomas S. Kidd, *American Christians and Islam: Evangelical Culture and Muslims from the Colonial Period to the Age of Terrorism* (Waco: Baylor University Press, 2009), 105, 107.

36   Bayoumi, "East of the Sun (West of the Moon)," 42.

37   Dawn-Marie Gibson and Jamillah Karim, *Women of the Nation: Between Black Protest and Sunni Islam* (New York: New York University Press, 2014), 32.

Muslim immigrant groups dismissed the NOI as sectarian, and since the Nation's "race ideology" and practices did not jibe with American conceptions of religion informed by Protestant culture.[38] Yet other factors came into play too, including the reality that Africans and their descendants were not mapped into Islam as a world religion by the early twentieth century. There were several reasons for this. First, the religion of enslaved African Muslims was historically dismissed or suppressed in North America. Second, most Western scholarship on Islam before the mid-twentieth century centered on the Arab Middle East or on Islamic societies in Asia, reflecting that Islam in Africa was marginal to the growing study of Islam by Orientalists and scholars of religion. Third, Protestant missionaries who sought to convert Muslims in sub-Saharan Africa did not view Islam as indigenous to the region. Rather, they understood Africa as a territory of missionary competition, fearing that the continent would become Islamized if Christian missions there did not gain sufficient support.[39] With such precedents in the background, the religious aspects of African American Muslim work for social change, as a movement led by people of color in the US, has always been downplayed within white Protestant society. What Rahma Abdulaleem says about African American Islam today was true in the mid-twentieth century: "In a nation where race remains a major impediment to a flourishing religious pluralism, racial identity often trumps religious identity."[40] By naming Black Islam as a sociopolitical movement, white American Christians avoided recognizing that Islam had become an indigenous American tradition that offered a religious alternative to Christianity.[41]

---

38   Since the 1980s especially, the NOI has been rightly critiqued for its leaders' anti-Semitic rhetoric.

39   Kidd, *American Christians and Islam*, 99.

40   Rama A. Abdulaleem, "Race, Religious Pluralism and Religious Freedom," in *African Americans and Religious Freedom*, ed. Sabrina E. Dent and Corey D.B. Walker (Washington, DC: Freedom Forum, 2021), 57.

41   *Mr. Muhammad Speaks*, the first publication of the NOI paper that became *Muhammad Speaks*, had this to say about Billy Graham's evangelistic tour of Africa: "Graham came away from his trip visibly shaken because at one point during his tour he was challenged by a Muslim to a healing contest to see whether Christianity is more powerful than Islam. Upon his return to Nairobi from Ruangu-Urundi on his African trip, the evangelist was given a

ARAB AMERICAN CHRISTIAN RESPONSES TO RELIGIOUS MISRECOGNITION

I return in this final section to the experiences of Arab Christian migrants to explore the multiple ways that *native Christians can and do speak*. When immigrating from the Middle East, how did Arab Christians respond to American perceptions about Islam and Islamic culture? How did they react to presumptions that they, themselves, were Muslim? The responses varied, just as Arab Christian migrants came from diverse backgrounds and made choices according to differing socioeconomic, religious, or intellectual goals. I have documented three strikingly different ways that Arab Christian migrants in the US responded to American Protestant views of Muslims and reflected their own approaches to Islam. These responses described below should not be interpreted as a typology that applies to all Arab Christian migrants. Neither were the three responses mutually exclusive, as the examples from the Greek Orthodox Arbeely family will demonstrate.

When Arab Christians arrived in the US, their social status changed from that of a religious minority within an ethnically Arab majority in their homelands to that of an ethnic and cultural minority within a majority Christian and predominantly Protestant society. As described in the earlier case study, white American Protestants often noted Arabs' minority status in racialized terms while also denigrating Islam as the religion of Arabs. One way Arab Christian migrants responded, as seen in many citizenship cases, was to correct such mistaken assumptions about their religious identity and confirm their Christian affiliation. Arab Christians responding in this fashion often exhibited a sense of Christian superiority over Islam or sought to gain sympathy from their

---

note of challenge from the chief of the Ahmadiyya Muslim mission in East Africa, Maulana Sheikh Mubarak Ahmad . . . Africa seeks liberation and freedom which have been denied to men of color in America . . . When Mr. Graham returns to America there is hope that the suffering he has seen will urge him to see the contradiction which comes to the man who is asked to give his heart to God when society disregards him as a person." "Come Home, Billy Graham!" *Mr. Muhammad Speaks: A Militant Monthly Dedicated To Justice For the Black Man* 1, no. 1 (May 1960): 4.

Christian co-religionists by describing the persecution they experienced in the Muslim world. For example, the aforementioned members of the Arbeely family, who promoted themselves as the first family of immigrants from Syria to settle in the US in 1878, played on anti-Muslim sentiments by giving press interviews "that resonated with an American predisposition to see these peoples from the East as fleeing their Muslim overlords."[42]

A similar example came from Layyah Barakat, a Maronite convert to Protestantism who migrated from Lebanon to the US in the 1880s. She became an evangelist for the National Christian Woman's Temperance Union, and a fundraiser for Protestant missions in her homeland. In the memoir she wrote for an American audience, *A Message from Mount Lebanon* (1912), Barakat told of her harrowing escape from the Druze massacres in Mt. Lebanon in 1860, and introduced both Arabic terminology and Arab culture to her readers. She argued that American Christianity was simply the fruit of ancient missionary work initiated by her own Syrian ancestors who first spread the light of the gospel.[43] Although Barakat reaffirmed American prejudices about Muslim (and Druze) violence, she also aimed to expand the worldview of her fellow Protestants in America, opening their eyes to the diversity of global Christianity, and the reality that Western civilization was not the originator of the gospel message. Thus, she and other Arab Christians corrected American Christians' misperceptions about their identities while also defending Arab culture and Middle Eastern Christianity.

In a second common response, Arab Christian (and Arab Muslim) migrants sometimes employed orientalism for economic and social benefit rather than challenging stereotypes about the Middle East. This sort of

---

42   Sarah M. A. Gualtieri, *Arab Routes: Pathways to Syrian California* (Stanford, CA: Stanford University Press, 2020), 142.

43   Layyah A. Barakat, *A Message from Mount Lebanon* (Philadelphia: Sunday School Times, 1912). For another example of Arab American Christian views, see Hani Bawardi's treatment of Naoum Mokarzel, the Maronite intellectual and newspaper editor who wrote vociferously against Muslims, against the Ottoman administration, and against Orthodox Syrians. Hani Bawardi, *The Making of Arab Americans: From Syrian Nationalism to U.S. Citizenship* (Austin: University of Texas Press, 2014), 63, 66, 118, 145, 209.

response can be seen in the Syrian Christians who made a fortune at the 1893 World's Fair as performers or as shop owners, and those who offered exhibitions of "Muslim" cultural displays, such as weddings or sword fights at performance venues or cafes in various parts of the country thereafter. One such event sponsored by the Woman's Foreign Missionary Society in Washington, DC, in the 1880s was billed as "Missionary Reception and Mohammodan [sic] Sword Exercise." There, rather than emphasizing their Christian identities as they did on other occasions, several members of the Arbeely family dressed up and put on a show purporting to be Muslim swordsmen.[44]

Reflecting yet again that individuals and members of the same family might offer different responses to American Protestant presumptions according to the time and circumstance, the Arbeely family exhibited the third common response as well—that of defending Islam and Arab-Islamic culture and challenging categories of Christian–Muslim division. The brothers Nageeb and Ibrahim Arbeely did so as founding editors of the first Arab American newspaper (*The American Star/Kawkab Amirka*), established in 1892 and published in English and Arabic. This paper's English-language articles intended to educate American readers about Islam, according to the stated aim to be "An Oriental Weekly devoted to the development of direct, helpful relations and good understanding between the East and the West." *Kawkab Amirka* included articles to explain Islamic beliefs and practices to English-language readers, and notices about Muslim holidays like Ramadan.[45] In their speaking and published work for English-speaking audiences, elite educated Syrian Christians of all denominations upheld similar notions as those found in *Kawkab Amirka*. The aforementioned Hannah Kurani, for example, explained the Qur'an to the women's circles where she spoke, and she disabused her audiences of the view that all Arab Muslim women were uneducated.[46]

---

44 Jacobs, "Playing East," 91.

45 For more on *The American Star*, see Deanna Ferree Womack, "Syrian Christians and Arab-Islamic Identity: Expressions of belonging in the Ottoman Empire and America," *Studies in World Christianity* 25, no. 1 (2019): 29–49.

46 Kurani also used critiques of Ottoman censorship and persecution to gain sympathy, and exhibited tendencies to use orientalist notions to her advantage. Womack, *Protestants, Gender and the Arab Renaissance*, 155–57.

Similarly, the Maronite author-poets Khalil Gibran and Amin al-Rihani sought to uphold the richness of Arab-Islamic culture in their writings while also dispelling notions of Christian–Muslim hostility. Rihani held strong opinions on the necessity of religious tolerance; he delivered a controversial speech on this topic at the Maronite Society in New York in 1900, and he was eventually excommunicated for his harsh critiques of Maronite sectarianism.[47] He wrote about this experience of excommunication in *The Book of Khalid*, the first novel published in English by an Arab author. The book teaches readers Arabic vocabulary, including religious terms Muslims and Christians used, and ultimately it advocates for the unity of all religions, and for harmony between East and West. Rihani's novel, which his colleague Gibran illustrated, was the forerunner to Gibran's more widely read book, *The Prophet* (1923).[48] The latter used poetic sermons delivered by a wise character named al-Mustapha to reflect Gibran's mystical belief that the key to self-realization and oneness with God lies in love, and not in any religious dogma.[49]

These Arab Christian authors wrote in both English and Arabic, reflecting their aims to bridge and reform both American and Arab culture. While Gibran did so by focusing on "human universals," Berman argued that Rihani's work and his own self-presentation did "not synthesize Arab and American, Islamic and Christian, traditional and modern. He present[ed] them as unreconciled constituent pieces of his [own] contradictory identity."[50] In representing the plurality and flexibility of

---

47   Waïl S. Hassan, "The Rise of Arab-American Literature: Orientalism and Cultural Translation in the Work of Ameen Rihani." *American Literary History* 20, nos. 1–2 (2008): 248.

48   Suheil B. Bushrui, "The Thought and Works of Ameen Rihani: With Special reference to His Writings in English," *al-Hewar* (1999), accessed online September 17, 2022, https://tinyurl.com/mv3kce6h.

49   N. Naimy, "The Mind and Thought of Khalil Gibran," *Journal of Arabic Literature* 5 (1974): 64.

50   Jacob Berman, "Mahjar Legacies: A Reinterpretation," in *Between the Middle East and the Americas: The Cultural Politics of Diaspora*, ed. Evelyn Alsultany and Ella Shohat (Ann Arbor: University of Michigan Press, 2013), 75. Berman goes so far as to say that Gibran offered a "deracinated self-representation as a conglomerate Oriental prophet figure." Ibid., 73.

Arab identity, Rihani's work resisted the "essentialist logic underpinning the criteria for U.S. citizenship" after the 1920s.[51] This also matches with the great diversity of approaches I found in Arab Christian responses to misrecognition.

Those Arab Christian immigrants who took this third, pluralistic approach often reflected their commitments through collaborations with Arab Muslims. Such Christian–Muslim solidarity was a form of resistance to American Protestant presumptions about Islam, but it also arose naturally out of shared Arab-Islamic heritage and Arab Christians' experiences living alongside Muslims in their home contexts. Such Arab Christian–Muslim collaboration in US immigrant communities occurred, for example, in the earliest Arab American cultural organizations, and in Arab American activism on behalf of Palestinian statehood following the Second World War.[52]

CONCLUSION

The need to resist essentialist logic runs through each of the case studies presented here while connecting with three key principles in the field of World Christianity: (1) that Christianity has authentically taken root in multiple cultural contexts and cannot be defined by Eurocentric norms, (2) that to understand the global diversity and local particularities of Christianity, we must look at the ways that individuals and communities represent themselves, and (3) that the study of World Christianity requires consideration of movement across cultural, denominational, and religious boundaries.[53] Taking these principles seriously would change the

---

51 Ibid., 66, 67.

52 Bawardi, *The Making of Arab Americans*, 190–295. Like *Kawkab Amirka* and the *Syrian World,* Arab American organizations like the Arab National League and the Institute for Arab American Affairs sought to educate Americans about the Arab world, and particularly about Palestinians' history and present realities.

53 On this third principle, see Dale Irvin's definition of World Christianity as a threefold conversation in Dale Irvin, "World Christianity: An Introduction," *Journal of World Christianity* 1, no. 1 (2008): 2.

way we think about Christianity, but they might also help us interrogate the ways that Christian rhetoric and Christian scholarship have misrepresented other global religions, and perpetuated what Eboo Patel described as "the odor of prejudice in the atmosphere [that] does internal damage to identity."[54]

The odor of anti-Muslim prejudice in the twenty-first century American public sphere subjects American Muslims to the internal damage of misrecognition, and to threats of actual violence against Muslim bodies and places of worship. This prejudice has historical roots in white American Protestant judgments about Muslims as dangerous "others." As my study revealed, this pattern of misrecognition has affected American Muslims and Arab American Christians alike. Because Arab Christians in the US have so often been misidentified as Muslims, I compared their experiences to those of actual American Muslims and examined a variety of ways Arab American Christians responded to American misperceptions in the early twentieth century. Arab Christian migrants and Muslim migrants from the Middle East and South Asia faced the same nativist laws in the early twentieth century. Yet in many cases, claims to Christian identity challenged the religio-racial prejudice of US policy, and offered Arab Christians an easier path to US citizenship due to the equation between Christianity, whiteness, and Western civilization. The field of World Christianity has rejected this dangerous equation, yet the field's focus on Global South Christians in their homelands or in immigrant contexts may upset assumptions about Christian ethnicity without challenging the ways white Christians racialize Muslims and contribute to anti-Islamic discourses in the West.

If the field of World Christianity includes conversations "across borders with other religious faiths," as Dale Irvin maintained,[55] then along with the many existing studies of missions to and conversions from other faiths, we need studies of comparative religions and interfaith collaborations. In the US context, this includes attending to Arab American Christian understandings of Islam and challenging the racial injustices that Christians and Muslims from immigrant backgrounds and African American Muslims still experience today. As this volume proposes, the

---

54   Patel, "Forward," xvii.

55   Irvin, "World Christianity: An Introduction," 2.

overwhelmingly positive, even triumphalist, focus on Christian growth in the Global South can blind the field to contexts like the Middle East where interreligious encounter is a daily reality for Christian minorities. The recovery of such neglected Christian voices in response to religio-racial misrecognition, then, is a matter of justice, and an essential task for scholars of World Christianity.

CHAPTER 2

RECONFIGURING THE *OIKOUMENE*: WORLD CHRISTIANITY, ECUMENISM, AND EPISTEMIC JUSTICE

Raimundo C. Barreto

WORLD CHRISTIANITY AND THE EXPANSION OF THE CHRISTIAN *OIKOUMENE*

The origins of World Christianity as a field of study are deeply interconnected with the rise of the ecumenical movement.[1] As Dale Irvin has deftly argued, "world Christianity has its historical roots in the disciplines of missions, ecumenics, and world religions."[2] Irvin also noticed that the phrase "World Christianity" can be understood as a rebranding of the body of scholarship that emerged from the twentieth-century ecumenical movement "called 'ecumenics' and 'ecumenical studies.'"[3] Whereas the relationship World Christianity has with mission studies is commonly

---

1   An earlier version of this essay was published in *The Ecumenical Review*. See Raimundo C. Barreto, "World Christianity and Global Justice: Ecumenical Demands and Possibilities," *The Ecumenical Review* 74, no. 1 (2022): 16–31. See also Raimundo C. Barreto, "The Challenge for Christian Unity and Reconciliation Today from a Decolonial Perspective," *International Review of Mission* 111, no. 1 (2022): 70–87.

2   Dale Irvin, "World Christianity: An Introduction," *Journal of World Christianity* 1, no. 1 (2008): 1–26 (2).

3   Dale Irvin, "World Christianity: A Genealogy," *Journal of World Christianity* 9, no. 1 (2019): 5–22 (7).

accepted, the connection between ecumenics and World Christianity has not received the same amount of attention. While not intending to rehearse Irvin's argument, it is important to draw attention to another connection he restates, namely the more established affinity between missions and Christian unity at the origins of the twentieth-century ecumenical movement. Citing renowned ecumenist Henry P. Van Dusen, who already in 1947 affirmed the inescapable connection between Christian missions and Christian unity, Irvin reminds his readers that those "two branches of ecumenical Christianity" are united "into one single *world Christian movement.*"[4]

In 1964 John A. Mackay, one of the great ecumenists of the twentieth century, also pointed to that connection by drawing attention to the rise of *the new global reality* of the Christian faith.

> A new reality has come to birth. For the first time in the life of mankind *[sic]* the Community of Christ, the Christian Church, can be found, albeit in nuclear form, in the remotest frontiers of human habitation. This community has hereby become "ecumenical" in the primitive, geographical meaning of that term. History is thus confronted with a new fact.[5]

Mackay's use of the word ecumenical here draws attention to the geographical presence of the church in all parts of the world. Without using the kind of vocabulary that would become more common after his lifetime, Mackay underscores the global geographical presence of the Christian churches in his days to argue for the importance of studying "the Church" on a global scale.

Despite the clear flow connecting the discipline of ecumenics in the second half of the twentieth century and the later rise of World Christianity as a field of study, the relationship between the ecumenical movement of

---

4   Henry P. Van Dusen, *World Christianity: Yesterday, Today, Tomorrow* (New York: Abingdon-Cokesbury Press, 1947), as per Irvin, "World Chiristianity: A Genealogy," 8. *Italics* are mine.

5   John Mackay, *Ecumenics: The Science of the Church Universal* (Englewood Cliffs, NJ: Prentice-Hall,1964), vii.

the twentieth century and the rise of World Christianity cannot be defined as one of simple continuity—or historical transmission.[6] This chapter's closer examination of the developments in that area in the second half of the twentieth century, with attention to Indigenous agency, helps bring a more complex picture to light.

Some ecumenists, in fact, have interpreted the drastic demographic and cultural changes at the root of the rise of World Christianity not as something that undergirds ecumenism but instead as a movement that furthers the fragmentation of Christianity. In his study about the ecumenical implications of the Southward demographic shift at the epicenter of World Christianity, Wesley Granberg-Michaelson draws attention to the following data: (1) the number of member churches belonging to the World Council of Churches (WCC) at the time of his writing was 349 churches; and (2) the number of Christian denominations in the world was estimated as about 43,800.[7] Granberg-Michaelson understands these numbers as both a predicament and an opportunity. His study also notes that "the fast-growing Pentecostal churches, energetic evangelical churches throughout the global south, congregations of the African Instituted Churches, and other highly contextualized forms of emerging Christianity function in ecclesiological worlds almost completely separate from traditional ecumenical structures."[8] The implication is that since the fastest-growing forms of World Christianity today are highly contextualized or local, and tend to operate outside existing ecumenical structures, they make the ecumenical task more challenging.

Such a sense of fragmentation is intensified by the distinct nature of the walls dividing Christians at the beginning of the twenty-first century. Cultural difference is one of the important issues that exacerbate Western

---

6   Andrew F. Walls, *The Cross-Cultural Process in Christian History: Studies in the Transmission and Appropriation of Faith* (Maryknoll, NY: Orbis Books, 2001), 22.

7   Wesley Granberg-Michaelson, *From Times Square to Timbuktu: The Post-Christian West Meets the Non-Western Church* (Grand Rapids: Eerdmans, 2013), 53, Kindle edition.

8   Ibid.

scholars and ecumenists' sense of unfamiliarity with the cultural realities shaping the Christianities of the Global South. In ecumenical dialogues focused on doctrinal differences born, for example, from the schisms in the sixteenth-century Protestant Reformation, there is a sense of familiarity, as Walls noted, that partly derives from a theological background commonly "shaped by the interaction of Christian faith with Greek philosophy and Roman Law."[9] By contrast, Walls continues, "the most striking feature of Christianity at the beginning of the third millennium is that it is predominantly a non-Western religion."[10]

Therefore, differently from modern Christian divisions addressed in earlier ecumenical dialogues, the distinctions considered in connection with "non-Western Christians," more evident in the current century, tend to be of a cultural nature, and have yet to receive full attention in contemporary ecumenical relations. In this historical juncture, one can no longer assume that the understanding of the Christian faith and practice in a given context might be mediated through theological reasoning informed by Greek philosophy or Roman law. Other knowledge traditions ought to be brought to the ecumenical table and demand the same kind of consideration. Drawing on decolonial approaches, methods, and praxis,[11] this chapter advances a World Christianity approach to ecumenics that includes voices and knowledge traditions that the dominant Western Christianity has usually suppressed as a matter of epistemic justice.

The field of World Christianity emerged in response to visible and unspoken Eurocentric hegemonic assumptions often present in the modern study of Christianity. As Irvin points out, "Without acknowledging as much, the term 'Christianity' by itself has too often been reduced to naming one or more of the dominant Western historical forms of this

---

9 Andrew F. Walls, "Eusebius Tries Again: The Task of Reconceiving and Re-visioning the Study of Christian History," in *Enlarging the Story: Perspectives on Writing Christian World History*, ed. Wilbert R. Shenk (Maryknoll, NY: Orbis Books, 2002), 1. Cited in Granberg-Michaelson, op. cit., 138.

10 Ibid.

11 See, for instance, Walter D. Mignolo and Catherine E. Walsh, *Decoloniality: Concepts, Analytics, Praxis* (Durham, NC: Duke University Press, 2018).

religion, rendering the broader global Christian reality invisible."[12] Relocating their attention to other historical Christian experiences around the world, many first-generation World Christianity scholars focused primarily on the indigeneity of Global South Christian experiences, thus offering a corrective to the prevailing Eurocentric understanding of the Christian faith that perceived Global South Christianities as peripheric to and derivative of European Christendom.[13] By emphasizing Christianity's indigeneity in African societies, for instance, Lamin Sanneh and other African scholars rejected Western Christian claims of prominence and control of Christian self-understanding while also validating and reaffirming Indigenous cultures—previously dismissed as inferior and superstitious—as competent to interpret the gospel and shape their Christian faith on their own terms.

Whereas such a historiographical shift has helped correct cultural injustice by bringing to the fore historically marginalized Christian voices, it also amplified the existing diversity among Christians worldwide. This chapter argues that such a renewed focus on difference does not need to create a dismissive attitude in regard to ecumenical concerns. On the contrary, it can expand the notion of the Christian *oikoumene* in new ways, giving voice to previously excluded peoples and cultures. In other words, the demographic and cultural expansion of the *oikoumene* contributes a wider methodological and theoretical toolkit for the study of World Christianity. In what follows, I highlight the potential that the increasing emphasis on the reconfiguration of World Christianity has to transform and expand the notion of the *oikoumene,* especially through concerted attention to emerging demands of epistemic justice. Drawing on concrete ecumenical networks initiated in the Global South, more prominently in Latin America, this chapter advances the proposal of a liberative intercultural dialogue in response to lingering colonial disparities that continue to challenge Christians and non-Christians today, concluding that, if engaged through decolonial lenses, World Christianity might point

---

12   Irvin, "World Christianity: An Introduction," 1.

13   Lamin Sanneh and Michael J. McClymond, "Introduction," in *The Wiley Blackwell Companion to World Christianity,* ed. Lamin Sanneh and Michael McClymond (Hoboken, NJ: Wiley-Blackwell, 2016), 1–17.

the way to ecumenical renewal and to a more expansive understanding of ecumenical relations.

The Continuing Relevance of the Ecumenical Ideal

William Temple's affirmation during his inauguration as the Archbishop of Canterbury in 1942 that the ecumenical movement was the great new fact of his era was an exultation that marked the heyday of a vivacious twentieth-century ecumenism.[14] At that time, ecumenism was expanding as one of the most vibrant movements generated by a Christendom that had finally expanded its reach globally. The worldwide reach and public significance of the ecumenical movement in the mid-twentieth century inspired Uruguayan theologian Julio de Santa Ana to speak of that century as *the time of ecumenism* in the history of Christianity."[15] From being an ideal, an aspiration, a dream nourished especially by young European and North American Christian leaders at the end of the nineteenth century, the ecumenical movement rose to prominence in the decades following the World Missionary Conference in Edinburgh (1910) through specific initiatives and organizations that would culminate in the formation of the World Council of Churches in 1948.

Toward the end of the twentieth century, though, the ecumenical progress seen in previous decades began to show signs of exhaustion, leading some to wonder whether an ecumenical crisis or winter was underway.[16] The question many started to ask was: Would the ecumenical movement still be a vital force in the dawn of a new century?[17] With the

---

14   William Temple, *The Church Looks Forward* (New York: Macmillan, 1944), 2. Cited in William R. Burrows, Mark R. Gornic, and Janice A. McLean, *Understanding World Christianity: The Vision and Works of Andrew F. Walls* (Maryknoll, NY: Orbis Books, 2011, Kindle Edition), Kindle Location 2888.

15   Julio de Santa Ana, "The Ecumenical Movement at the Crossroads," *Student World* 1 (2003): 11–23 (11). *Italics* are mine.

16   See, for instance, Ola Tjorhom, "An 'Ecumenical Winter'? Challenges in Contemporary Catholic Ecumenism," *The Heythrop Journal* 48 (2008): 841–59.

17   See Michael Kinnamon, *Can a Renewal Movement be Renewed? Questions for the Future of Ecumenism* (Grand Rapids, MI: Eerdmans, 2014). Especially chapter 14.

boom of independent churches, particularly in the Global South, it became clear that the *oikoumene* envisioned by twentieth-century ecumenists had changed significantly, and the earlier ecumenical structures built in the previous century seemed insufficient to address new emerging ecumenical challenges.

Some aspects of the twentieth-century ecumenical ambitions have turned into sources of frustration, often because of the slow pace in the reception of ecumenical dialogues and the practical impossibilities hindering the realization of the ecumenical ideal of structural unity. However, other areas of ecumenical activity continue to be perceived as extremely significant and necessary. That is the case, for example, with ecumenical work for peace, justice, and reconciliation in a drastically divided world, as exemplified in the ecumenical support to the anti-apartheid struggle,[18] and the ecumenical accompaniment and action for human rights in Latin America.[19] Drawing on the work of German educator Ernst Lange, Kinnamon describes the ecumenical movement as a movement for peace.[20]

Shaped amidst the political and military conflicts of the Cold War era, the ecumenical movement developed "a profound sense of relatedness" that went beyond the churches.[21] As we move into the third decade of the twenty-first century, though, the world remains highly divided. Considering the deadly nature of current world tensions and conflicts, the Christian ecumenical witness for peace and justice remains as important as it has ever been. There are nearly thirty active armed conflicts and situations of political tension and instability around the world today, and a total of 70.3 million people worldwide displaced by

---

18 Ian Macqueen, "Ecumenism and the Global Anti-Apartheid Struggle: The World Council of Churches' Special Fund in South Africa and Botswana, 1970–75," *Historia* 62, no. 2 (2017): 87–111.

19 Charles R. Harper, *O Acompanhamento: Ecumenical Action for Human Rights in Latin America, 1970-1990* (Geneva: WCC Publications, 2006).

20 Ernst Lange, *And Yet It Moves* (Geneva: WCC Publications, 1979), 147, in Michael Kinnamon, *Can a Renewal Movement Be Renewed?* Kindle location 473.

21 Ibid.

those conflicts.[22] As in the case of the recent Russian invasion of Ukraine, some of these conflicts remind us that the nuclear annihilation threat is as alive as ever. Other conflicts are related to the scarcity of vital resources tied to a greedy system of global capitalism and the related rapidly increasing environmental crisis. Furthermore, the past few years have shown an intensification of attacks on democratic institutions, and an accelerated growth of authoritarianism and nationalism in various countries.[23] Bigotry, racism, xenophobia, anti-Semitism, Islamophobia, misogyny, homophobia, transphobia, and other forms of discrimination and intolerance remain widespread. Likewise, socioeconomic inequalities continue to be a major cause of death and exclusion of hundreds of millions across the globe. The prolonged impact of a pandemic that has killed more than 6.4 million people in the past two and a half years has magnified the obscenity of those inequalities.[24]

Finally, whereas the world where Christians are called to live out their faith today is as fractured as it was when the ecumenical movement first emerged, the circumstances and nature of the prevailing conflicts have drastically changed. We are now living in a digital era, where social media has become a megaphone for hatred, extremist discourses, and misinformation, as algorithms are increasingly used to create artificial bubbles that reinforce distortions of reality and bump up conspiracy theories.

If the broader *oikoumene*, the whole inhabited world, remains so drastically wounded and divided, the over two billion Christians living in such a world are no less fragmented. The difference, as noted earlier, is the nature of Christian divisions today. Christians around the world are increasingly divided by culture, race/ethnicity, views on sexuality, and

---

22   Council of Foreign Relations, *Global Conflict Tracker*, last updated January 28, 2022, accessed February 1, 2022, https://tinyurl.com/3twuhr7x.

23   See Raimundo Barreto and João Chaves, "Christian Nationalism is Thriving in Brazil: Bolsonaro's Faith-Based Enablers," *The Christian Century* 138, no. 24 (2021): 22–25.

24   Nabil Ahmed, *Inequality Kills: The Unparalleled Action Needed to Combat Inequality in the Wake of COVID-19* (Oxford, UK: Oxfam International, 2022), accessed February 1, 2022, https://tinyurl.com/ysvsmbr2.

socioeconomic conditions. While these sorts of divisions are not necessarily new, they are impacting a large number of Christians worldwide in new ways, in a world where hegemonic views on race, gender, sex, and class are constantly challenged. The new configurations of the differences that separate most Christians around the world today, as Walls highlights, challenge us to move beyond ecumenical criteria based on "confessional comprehensiveness" toward those based on "ethnic, cultural, and geographical comprehensiveness."[25]

Likewise, the nature of the ecumenical movement itself must be reconsidered. As Dale Irvin notices, the modern ecumenical movement that emerged in the beginning of the twentieth century was deeply influenced by powerful "lingering memories of Christendom East and West." In Irvin's words,

> The churches or communions that formed the Ecumenical Movement in the 20th century . . . were mostly the descendants of Protestant communions that had formed along state lines in Europe and, although disestablished, continued to align themselves with the dominant culture and its political and social life, in North America.[26]

The relocation of previously suppressed theological voices of the Global South to the centerstage in recent ecumenical debates provides a unique platform for those who used to exist in the peripheries of Eurocentric modern Christianity to help shape the ecumenical agendas of today, promoting new ways of being Christian—and human—in the contemporary world.[27] In such a context, new epistemologies stemming from the

---

25   Walls, *The Cross-Cultural Process in Christian History*, 57.

26   Dale Irvin, "Specters of a New Ecumenism: In Search of a Church 'Out of Joint,'" in *Religion, Authority, and the State: From Constantine to the Contemporary World*, ed. Leo D. Lefebure (New York: Palgrave Macmillan, 2016), 3–32 (17, 20).

27   Mario I. Aguilar, "Public Theology from the Periphery: Victims and Theologians," *International Journal of Public Theology* 1 (2007): 21–337 (324).

study of World Christianity can prompt new approaches and methodological tools to engage the study of ecumenism, not as a static movement shaped in the mid-twentieth century but as a dynamic movement, which continues to change as both Christianity and the world are also rapidly changing. Among other things, a World Christian approach to ecumenism can create renewed opportunities for the sharing of previously unheard, overlooked, and unexplored Christian stories and narratives that enrich and expand the Christian community (the ecumenical *oikoumene*), making room for creative reconfigurations and reinventions of Christian identity and relations. This renewed approach to ecumenical relations would not only dislodge the hegemonic status of Western rationality but also legitimize *otros saberes*, other forms of knowing and knowledge deeply connected to the experiences and histories of the subaltern, which privilege respect, solidarity, conviviality, and intercultural dialogue, without overlooking cultural and epistemic asymmetries and injustice.[28] The rise of new subjects in the ecumenical movement, as I will show below, is generating new ecumenical networks, which can both challenge existing ecumenical institutions and contribute to their renewal and transformation.

As the sections below demonstrate, the ongoing changes in the ecumenical movement are not to be confused with a sign of decline. They can alternatively indicate renewal and reimagination. As previously marginalized voices and experiences take a seat at the ecumenical table, they bring with them their own ecumenical aspirations. Such aspirations tend to be articulated from the bottom-up, dialogically and interculturally. In such a context, the movements from the Global South are increasingly claiming, as Enrique Dussel points out, more protagonist roles in designing new methods and setting the agenda for an intercultural dialogue "that is critical of and goes beyond the European 'I.'"[29]

---

28   Roberto E. Zwetsch, "Apresentação," in *Conviver. Ensaios para uma Teologia Intercultural Latino-Americana*, ed. Roberto E. Zwetsch (São Leopoldo, Brazil: Editora Sinodal/EST, 2015), 17–23 (18).

29   Enrique Dussel, "Agenda for a South-South Philosophical Dialogue," *Human Architecture* 11, no. 1 (2013): 3-18 (3).

Reimagining Ecumenism

While the ecumenical structures built in the first half of the twentieth century resulted from the initiatives of Western missionary agencies, the latter part of the century began to see the rise of new ecumenical initiatives that primarily stemmed from the agency of Global South subjects. One of the most significant of those initiatives was the Ecumenical Association of Third World Theologians (EATWOT), formed in 1977.[30] EATWOT has contributed significantly to expand theological exchange and cross-fertilization among Asian, African, and Latin American Christians—along with minoritized groups in Western countries. In 2005 a similar network, the World Forum on Theology and Liberation (WFTL), was created in connection with the World Social Forum (WSF). In its first meeting, in Porto Alegre, Brazil, the WFTL articulated in theological terms the hope for a better world manifest in the WSF slogan "Another World is Possible."[31] These networks formed by individuals deeply rooted in grassroots movements, churches, and faith-based organizations replicate a multitude of similar ecumenical and interfaith networks formed on the local and national levels. They exemplify some of the new shapes and forms ecumenicity is taking nowadays.

Similar ecumenical and interreligious forums and networks have followed suit in recent decades. Churches Witnessing with Migrants (CWWM), for instance, is an ecumenical and interfaith network formed in 2008, in Manila, at the initiative of the National Council of Churches of the Philippines, which has grown into an international, interfaith, and tripartite group of migrants/refugees, migrant-serving institutions, and religious bodies focused on the plight of migrants, refugees, asylum seekers, and trafficked persons—with special attention to forced mobility or forced migration. CWWM brings religious leaders, scholars, activists, and migrants together, putting their collective resources and efforts in the service of forcibly dislocated peoples. Although initiated in the Global

---

30   M. P. Joseph, *Theologies of the Non-person: The Formative Years of EATWOT* (London: Palgrave Macmillan, 2015), ix.

31   Luiza E. Tomita, "Brief Historical Introduction to the World Forum on Theology and Liberation," in *Religion, Human Dignity and Liberation*, ed. Gerald Boodoo (São Leopoldo, Brazil: Oikos Editora, 2016), 9.

South, CWWM has invited North Atlantic churches such as the United Methodist Church and the American Baptist Churches to join their efforts. This is an example of an ecumenical initiative in which the churches that used to see themselves as the center of modern Christianity are no longer calling the shots. In ecumenical settings like those that CWWM provides, Western churches join by invitation as participants in a rearranged ecumenical table.[32] Likewise, this is not merely an ecumenical initiative to help migrants. It is a network which includes migrants among its leaders.

By the same token, a new Latin American ecumenical initiative called *Red Continental Cristiana por la Paz* (RECONPAZ) emerged in 2014 as a result of efforts led mainly by the Christian Ecumenical Council of Guatemala, the Baptist Peace Fellowship of North America, and other ecumenical organizations in Mexico, Guatemala, El Salvador, Nicaragua, Puerto Rico, Colombia, Chile, and Brazil. Global Ministries (the common missional witness of the Christian Church and the United Church of Christ in the US), and the International Ministries of the American Baptist Churches are co-sponsors. As in the case of CWWM, RECONPAZ is a fluidly structured ecumenical network that brings voices from churches, social movements, activists, and scholars together, decentering Western hegemony without excluding Western churches and individuals. Its leadership is wholly Latin American, although some of those leaders are supported by US-based mission organizations. Those organizations participate as co-sponsors and partners, but are not part of the governance of RECONPAZ. This peace network was initially conceived by a group of twenty-eight Latin American Baptist leaders from ten different countries gathered during the Fourth Global Baptist Peace Conference, on February 9–14, 2009, in Rome. That group of Christian leaders and peace activists wrote a Latin American and Caribbean Peace Declaration, which, among other things, condemned

> the attack on life as a system and structure at the national and global level performed by savage capitalism; the arms industry that feeds the arms race and militarism in the world, provoking war and violence; the unfair distribution of natural resources and the

---

32   For more on the CWWM, see https://tinyurl.com/4tykc6vk. Accessed on August 22, 2022.

wealth of peoples; the unfair privatization of science and technology . . .; the use of political power to favor economic interests of specific groups and individuals . . . in international relations; racism, sexism, the 'objectification' of women, and the degrading treatment of economic immigrants; drug trafficking and the ideological tyranny exercised by power groups that control the big media such as the written press and television; [and] the abuse of natural resources and the destruction of the environment, risking the future of new generations.[33]

This Peace Declaration also called for the cessation of the economic blockade against Cuba, and for respect for the life, culture, and worldview of Indigenous peoples and Afro descendants. While in Rome, the group came to the conclusion that the spirit of that declaration needed to be organically fleshed out. The Declaration demanded action, which could be articulated through what was initially imagined as a Latin American and Caribbean Baptist Peace Network.

The result of those conversations, however, was more ecumenical. On January 20–26, 2014, in San Cristóbal de las Casas, Chiapas, a group of fifty Christians from several Christian confessions, including some individuals who had contributed to the Rome Declaration, formed what was initially called *Red Afro-Indígena-Latino América y Caribe de Iglesias por la Paz* (RAILAC). Participants in that inaugural conference came from various parts of the continent, showcasing Abya Yala's cultural and ethnic diversity, with significant Tzeltal and Tzotzil Mayans, Zoques, and Afro-descendant representation. They committed to start "a pilgrimage to learn to walk together in the construction of peace within the painful realities of violence and injustice" their people experienced on a daily basis.[34]

---

33 RECONPAZ, "Declaracion Latinoamericana y del Caribe," Cuarta Conferencia Global Bautista por la Paz, Feruary 9–14, 2009, Rome, Italy, accessed on August 23, 2022, https://tinyurl.com/mstaysjm.

34 RECONPAZ, "Conferencia Inaugural de la Red Afro-Indígena-Latino América y Caribe de Iglesias por la Paz (RAILAC por la paz)," accessed on August 23, 2022, https://tinyurl.com/5n7nuada.

While ecumenically Christian, the organization renamed RECONPAZ that same year expanded its horizons, joining hands with other religious traditions and nonreligious grassroots organizations. This ecumenical network has created "a space for listening and dialogue" and "for the analysis of the situation of war and violence" in the region, taking the participants' "testimonial experiences of peacebuilding" as the basis for its activities. It advances "pastoral intervention at different levels of personal and community life as signs of hope" and witness "of the fellowship of churches for peace."[35] Discerning meaningful ways to address the various forms of systemic violence that kills, in particular, large numbers of Latin Americans of African and Indigenous descent, RECONPAZ promotes an ecumenism aimed at "rapprochement and collaboration for the work of building peace and solidarity among peoples." Finally, it fosters respect and appreciation of distinct religious and cultural traditions, "[re]claiming the dignity of all peoples."[36]

CWWM and RECONPAZ are international ecumenical networks deeply rooted in local and regional initiatives. Similar ecumenical efforts are flourishing on the local and national levels. They often fly under the radar of those who confuse the ecumenical movement with the privileged ecumenical structures that emerged through the coordinated agency of predominantly European and North American Christian agencies throughout the twentieth century.

In Brazil, the national reality I have examined more closely, these new movements are often called "popular ecumenical initiatives."[37] As in the cases aforementioned, they stem from complex networks involving individual leaders, churches, national ecclesiastical agencies, and social movements. These are some examples of popular ecumenical action in Brazil:

1. *Centro de Estudos Bíblicos* (CEBI)—An ecumenical association created by two Catholic biblists and two Protestant ecumenical leaders who, reading the Bible with the poor in

---

35   Ibid.

36   Ibid.

37   See Raimundo C. Barreto, "Vatican II, Medellin, and Ecumenism: A Brazilian Protestant Perspective," *Journal of World Christianity* 9, no. 2 (2019): 187–202 (194).

Northeast Brazil, developed a dialogical method[38] to study the biblical texts from the "reality" of the poor "and in defense of life." This communal method of biblical study has spread to many other countries, and is known as "Popular Reading of the Bible."[39]

2. *Centro Ecumênico de Evangelização, Capacitação e Assessoria* (CECA)—An ecumenical civil society organization focused on the education of advocacy agents in the state of Rio Grande do Sul, with an emphasis on gender and human rights. CECA's main goal is to educate grassroots community for citizenship based on a faith articulated through ecumenical and inter-religious conversations. Among other things, CECA trains Brazilian women in impoverished communities to serve as advocacy agents capable of organizing their communities in the fight, especially against gender-based violence.[40]

3. *Comissão Ecumênica dos Direitos da Terra* (CEDITER)—A Land Rights Commission created in 1982 in response to a five-year famine that impacted Northeast Brazil and to "serious land conflicts, with the truculent presence of squatters who disturbed small farmers . . . in the Middle São Francisco."[41] In partnership with CESE, the PCUSA, and *Igreja Presbiteriana Unida* (IPU), CEDITER has developed a number of advocacy programs and initiatives to protect

---

38 See Ira Shor and Paulo Freire, "What is the 'Dialogical Method' of Teaching?" *The Journal of Education* 169, no. 3 (1987): 11–31.

39 CEBI, "O Nascimento," accessed on August 23, 2022, https://tinyurl .com/3wr897fw. See also Carlos Mesters, *Defenseless Flower: A New Reading of the Bible* (Maryknoll, NY: Orbis Books, 1989).

40 Claudete B. Ulrich and Nivia Ivette Núñez de la Paz, "Christianity and Urbanism: The Ecumenical Training and Advisory Center (CECA) and the Formation of the Popular Legal Agents," in *World Christianity, Urbanization and Identity,* ed. Moses O. Biney, Kenneth Ngwa, and Raimundo C. Barreto Jr. (Minneapolis: Fortress Press, 2021. Kindle Edition), 223–40.

41 CEDITER, "Histórico," accessed on August 23, 2022, https://tinyurl.com/ y8u6c7d6.

small farms and Indigenous and Quilombola communities. It has assisted thousands of starving families, organized rural workers' associations, coordinated the struggle against squatters threatening the poor in the region, advocated for people displaced due to the construction of a major dam, and created a number of rural development projects in the past four decades.

4. *Centro Ecumênico de Serviço à Educação Popular* (CESEEP)—"A Latin American ecumenical center for popular education founded in 1982," CESEEP provides "educational services to social movements and communities of the different Christian Churches in their pastoral and of human promotion,"[42] informed by Paulo Freire's Popular Education. CESEEP also accompanies the human rights and citizenship formative work "of popular movements, social pastorals, communities and churches."[43] While its headquarters is in São Paulo, its action spans throughout Latin America and the Caribbean.

5. *Coordenação Ecumênica de Serviço* (CESE)—Founded in 1973, it is a vanguard ecumenical organization in the defense of human rights and the promotion of peace and justice in Brazil.[44] CESE facilitates the relationship "between churches, aid agencies, and social movements" based on "the principles of solidarity and the ecumenical sharing of resources."[45] The capillarity of its social projects has enabled CESE to interact with a large number of communities and popular organizations, including churches not affiliated with the ecumenical movement.

---

42 CESEEP, "História," accessed on August 23, 2022, https://tinyurl.com/muwevrxw.

43 Ibid.

44 Derval Dasilio, *Jaime Wright: O Pastor dos Torturados* (Rio de Janeiro: Metanoia Editora, 2012), 40.

45 Anonymous, "CESE: An Ecumenical Service, a Commitment to Human Rights," *International Review of Mission* 85, no. 338 (1996): 409–16 (409).

6. *Koinonia Presença Ecumênica e Serviço*—Founded in 1994, in Rio de Janeiro, *Koinonia* affirms "the diaconal vocation of the ecumenical community."[46] It is today one of the most important Brazilian ecumenical organizations, providing "services to historically and culturally vulnerable groups in the process of social and political emancipation."[47] *Koinonia* coordinates with other ecumenical organizations to "develop communication and information actions, dialogue with state and multilateral organizations and the defense of economic, social and cultural rights as a strategy for the structural fight against poverty."[48] Its areas of action include rural workers' rights, an educational program called "Ecumenism, Dialogue and Formation," educative work on health and rights, the protection of traditional lands, which include those of Quilombola communites and Candomblé worship houses, the formation of ecumenical and civil society networks, and documentation of human rights violations, the core focus of its predecessor, the Ecumenical Center of Documentation and Information, created during the years of the dictatorship.[49]

All these ecumenical organizations have joined ecclesiastical councils such as the Latin American Council of Churches (CLAI) and the Brazilian National Council of Churches (CONIC) to form the Ecumenical Forum Act Brazil (FEACT), a space for solidarity and sharing "in which each participant sees itself represented in the actions and initiatives of the other members."[50] FEACT is currently formed by twenty-three organizations and

---

46 Koinonia, "Histórico," accessed on August 23, 2022, https://tinyurl.com/2p8p9hsb.

47 Andréa Carvalho Oliveira, "Direito à memória das comunidades tradicionais: organização de acervo nos terreiros de candomblé de Salvador, Bahia," *Ciência da Informação* 39, no. 2 (2010): 84–91 (84).

48 Ibid.

49 Ibid., 85. See also Barreto, "Vatican II, Medellin, and Ecumenism," 194.

50 See Rafael Soares de Oliveira et al., eds., *Ecumenismo, Direitos Humanos e Paz: A Experiência do Fórum Ecumênico Brasil* (Rio de Janeiro, Brazil: Fe Brasil, 2006).

seven churches. Guiding its actions is the conviction that "our planet and our cause cannot leave anyone out; we are all part of the same future and a Common House." As a national ecumenical body, FEACT is affiliated with "the ACT Alliance, a global coalition of 151 faith-based organizations and churches, working together in more than 125 countries."[51] Here, the circle is closed. The connection between the local and the global is fully established. The difference, however, is that it begins with networking on the local and national levels. The expansion of such ecumenical coalitions leads all the way to an international ecumenical organization related to the WCC. These Brazilian examples of popular ecumenical action, along with international networks such as EATWOT, WFTL, CWWM, and RECONPAZ, exemplify the kind of new ecumenical initiatives working closely with communities and popular movements whose stories and knowledges can enrich, transform, and expand the ecumenical movement today.

The Demands of Epistemic Justice

Although associated with ecumenical structures and institutions stemming from the World Missionary Conference in 1910, the ecumenical networks and initiatives abovementioned show that the ecumenical movement in the twenty-first century increasingly depends on a complex web of initiatives that can move from the local to the global through multiple layers of intercultural networks of solidarity. Such initiatives not only highlight the rise of new ecumenical agendas and agents, but they also allow for often-ignored knowledge traditions to challenge hegemonic ways of thinking and knowing still dominant in ecumenical mechanisms and structures.

Another recent example of that kind of process took place in an international online seminar—"The Brazilian Tragedy: A Risk for Our Common Home?"—organized by a coalition of Brazilian ecumenical organizations, including CONIC, the National Conference of Bishops of Brazil's

---

51   Coletivo de Comunicação Feact-Brasil, "Organizações do Feact-Brasil atuam no fortalecimento da Justiça de Gênero em meio à pandemia da covid 19," *Medium*, accessed on August 23, 2022, https://tinyurl.com/8r4pk32x.

(CNBB) Justice and Peace Commission, FEACT, and other human rights and sociobiodiversity organizations. The seminar aimed "to carry out dialogue between national and international ecumenical churches, faith-based organizations and other organizations for the defense of human and socio-environmental rights, to articulate international support strategies to face the Brazilian contemporary tragedy that presents itself as an imminent global risk."[52]

The aforementioned "tragedy" refers to the dismantling of democratic, educational, and human rights organizations by the Brazilian right-wing authoritarian government at that time, and its consequences—which include the loss of more than six hundred thousand lives to COVID-19, the constant burning of the Amazon rainforest to exploit its land, the killing of Indigenous leaders, the dismantling of public universities, and the thirty-three million Brazilians struck by hunger. The forum sought to convey the message that these tragic problems are not only the concern of Brazilians. They are tragedies with consequences for all life inhabiting the Common House (the planet).

International representatives participated in the seminar at the invitation of the Brazilian organizers. People from other religious traditions and nonreligious organizations, along with representatives from international organizations such as the United Nations and the Vatican, came together to learn from one another and coordinate action in response to these problems.

Considering that the Black and Indigenous Brazilian populations are more directly impacted by these problems, Indigenous and Afro-Brazilian thinkers and activists were invited to speak in different sessions

---

52   The program and lineup of the seminar can be found here: https://tinyurl .com/53hb8krf. The title of the seminar was inspired by a document submitted to the Federal Senate's Committee of Inquiry (CCI) for COVID-19 on April 28, 2021 by a group of sociologists, lawyers, public health professionals, journalists, and economists to denounce the mishandling of the pandemic by the Bolsonaro administration, and its lethal consequences to the Brazilian population and to the world. See "The Tragedy of Brazilian Coronavirus/ Covid-19: An Analysis of the Federal Government's misgovernment, 2020-2021," accessed on December 7, 2022, https://tinyurl.com/5xfy356b.

of the event. One of those sessions was titled "Social and Human Rights: Aggravated Inequalities," and featured two distinguished speakers: (1) Benilda Brito, a consultant at the United Nations for the Nzinga-Collective of Black Women of Belo Horizonte, and an activist for education of the Malala Network, and (2) Indigenous leader, environmentalist, philosopher, poet, and author Ailton Krenak.[53] These two speakers pointed to the fact that the crisis—the Brazilian tragedy—that alarmed the seminar's participants was nothing new for them. For the African descendants and the Brazilian Indigenous population, that crisis started long ago. Because those communities have resisted for so long, their ways of living and their knowledge of the world may have something to teach us about the best ways to respond to such crises. The relevance of those contributions mainly resides in the way these speakers associated the historical injustices Indigenous and Black Brazilians experience on a daily basis with the epistemic injustice that has insisted on erasing their ways of being and knowing for five centuries.[54]

---

53   I served as moderator of this session, which also had Monsignor Bruno-Marie Duffé and Christine Jeangey from the Vatican's Dicastery for Promoting Integral Human Development as speakers. Other important speakers at this event were João Pedro Stedile, the historical leader of the Brazilian Landless Workers Movement; former WCC general secretary Olav Fykse Tveit; Brazilian sociologist Jessé José Freire de Souza; Nara Baré, the first woman to serve as chairperson of the Coordination of Indigenous Organizations in the Brazilian Amazon (COIAB); and Peter Prove, Director of the Commission of the Churches on International Affairs at World Council of Churches.

54   The framework of epistemic injustice highlights a cultural construction "based on an earlier philosophical lexicography that developed the trope of 'civilization' as a mode to justify rights to land, resources, and human labor within the colonial empires claimed by the European monarchs." It is based on the understanding that "the cultural constructions of the past continue to inform Western law and policy and are profoundly linked to both testimonial and hermeneutical forms of epistemic injustice." Rebecca Tsosie, "Anthropology, and the Legacy of Epistemic Injustice," in *The Routledge Handbook of Epistemic Injustice*, ed. Ian James Kidd, Jose Medina, and Gaile Pohlhaus, Jr. (New York: Routledge, 2019), 356–68 (356).

For both Brito and Krenak, the criminal[55] neglect with which President Jair Bolsonaro treated a pandemic that has disproportionately killed Black and Indigenous Brazilians stands in continuity with the historical genocide of Brazilians of African and Indigenous descent. Brito began her remarks by stating her social and epistemic locus:

> I am a survivor of racism. . . . Death has a color of preference in this country. . . . The Brazilian tragedy began when the first African was brought here by force . . . . As a Black woman, the only time I feel I am in our common home is when I am in the traditional homes, the *terreiro de Candomblé*, among Indigenous communities, among those who respect our ancestry.[56]

By doing that, she underscored the connection between the common disregard for Afro-Brazilian ancestral knowledge and the racism ingrained in the Brazilian society. The attempt to erase African religions is just one of the many faces of the violence which constantly seeks to dehumanize Black Brazilians.

> When we suffer racism, we have our identity denied. Racism dehumanizes us. . . . Without our ancestors we don't have an identity. . . . Our people have a different logic, a circular one. In a circle, one cannot see the beginning or the end. Everyone belongs equally. Everyone is important. This is what our communities believe as equal rights. How to believe in democracy in a country that denies the racial injustices committed against us, affirming the myth of racial democracy? If they deny that racism is real, then there is no need to fight for antiracist policies; all remain the same.[57]

---

55 See Pedro Fonseca and Maria Carolina Marcello, "Brazil pandemic probe to recommend Bolsonaro face 11 criminal charges," *Reuters*, accessed on October 24, 2021, https://tinyurl.com/2nsj7nmp.

56 The recording of this session of the seminar "A Brazilian Tragedy" can be found in the following link, https://tinyurl.com/y4b5pz5f. All quotes from this session were transcribed and translated by the author.

57 Ibid.

Brito speaks as a member of a community that has for centuries experienced racism through acts of religious intolerance against African-derived religions. While these atrocious acts are vile in themselves, Brito draws attention to the fact that their origin resides in a worldview that continues to dehumanize Afro-Brazilians by treating their deities dismissively if not worse.

The alternative path she offers is the radicalization of the concept of democracy, which, she insists, "can be learnt from the practices of the *Quilombola* and Indigenous communities." In those communities, democracy begins with "a radical affirmation that all of us are human beings." Therefore,

> To know if there is democracy in a society or a community, one must see how the black community lives there. Do they have enough food, do they have houses, do they have access to education and health care? No? Then, there is no democracy. . . . Black women in Brazil cannot relax while their children are not back home, because of racism and police violence. They are busy trying to survive. . . . 83% of all people detained unjustly are black.[58]

In her remarkable talk, Brito made a drastic call for Christians concerned with the tragedy impacting Brazil and the Common House to listen to those who have been on the receiving end of oppression for five hundred years. Truly democratic societies must place the reality, experiences, and knowledge of those who have become (not by their own will) the most vulnerable at the center stage. Such a move requires a concerted effort to understand the counterhegemonic rationality of both Indigenous and Black Brazilian communities.

This is why Brito speaks of the "circular" logic of her ancestral communities. Afro-Brazilian communities offer important epistemological and ontological contributions to the building of real democracy by bringing to the table a deeper communal understanding of inclusion, equality, and participation, which is manifested in *rodas* (circles) *de Oyé* (a circle where those with a function in the *terreiro de Candomblé* dance in

---

58   Ibid.

circles at the sound of drums), the *rodas de samba, rodas de capoeira, rodas de cantiga, rodas de conversa*, and other circular symbols and rituals of inclusion that are so prominent in Afro-Brazilian traditions.[59]

Brito challenges assumptions of Christian superiority. While Christians are welcome to engage the struggle against racism and other forms of social, economic, and cultural oppression that Black Brazilians face on a daily basis, they cannot come to the table pretending to be saviors. The long history of racial and religious prejudice in Brazil has not only excluded ways of knowing and experiencing the world that can be vital for our future but has also treated them as lesser—nonvalid—knowledges. Brito's prophetic challenge to the organizers and participants of that seminar shows the way that our understanding of ecumenism in today's world can be interrogated and reconfigured.

Ailton Krenak offered similar contributions. Like Brito, he began by acknowledging his ancestors. Then, he criticized the binary perspective on truth the Christian colonizer brought to the land we now call Brazil, highlighting the problems it continues to cause, in particular to his family, the Indigenous people, and reinforcing that the "Brazilian tragedy" began long ago. In order to affirm the Christian God, the only true God, all the Indigenous deities had to be denied. Therefore, the ongoing denial and objectification of the Indigenous "other," and of the lands they live in, stems from

---

59   *Rodas de Oyé* and *Samba de Roda* are examples of ritual dancing in Afro-Brazilian culture and religion. In 2005 UNESCO declared that *Samba de Roda*, from the Recôncavo Basin in Bahia, is an oral and intangible heritage of humanity. Capoeira, which also forms circles, is a symbol of resistance, combining elements of music, ritual dance, and martial art. *Rodas de cantiga* gather people in circles to sing popular songs. *Roda de conversa* is a structured space of dialogue where all participants, sitting in a circle, are invited to contribute to a conversation or discussion on a given theme. In all these cases, the circle is intended to represent the inclusivity and participation of the whole community. Even when being a ritual space, the *roda*, or circle, is also a space of interaction and knowledge production. See Eloisa Domenici, "Samba de Roda and the Threat of Epistemicide on the North Coast of Bahia," *MUSICultures* 48 (2021): 142–67; and Mika Lillit Lior, "Circling With/ In the Saint: Bahian Candomblé's Feminist Poiesis and Dark Horse Kinetics" (PhD diss., University of California, 2021).

the exclusivist logic at the root of the colonial enterprise. "Enough with 'the truth'!", Krenak emphatically stated. "We need to debunk hegemonic truth in order to make room for other truths. We must move from universalism to the pluriverse where our narratives can coexist as part of the broader social biodiversity."[60]

Both Brito and Krenak underscored key epistemic and ontological injustices that Christians are confronted with in their encounters with Indigenous and African-derived cultures, which have often led to the suppression of non-Western knowledges—an *epistemicide*.[61]

While the study of World Christianity has so far focused preferentially on the transcultural nature of Christianity, paying special attention to cultures that were not previously taken seriously in the study of Christianity, it still needs to become more epistemically inclusive. By bringing non-Western cultures to the center stage, World Christianity has paved the way for an epistemic turn in the study of Christianity.[62] Such a turn, however, must be more intentionally constructed to include non-Christian Indigenous voices.

The act of thinking inevitably takes place through sentient bodies, which are geographically, socially, and culturally situated. People like Benilda Brito and Ailton Krenak are keenly aware of that. Their thinking/feeling the world emanates from communally situated bodies. They think/feel in relationship with a community that is inclusive of the living and the dead—many of which were brutally silenced. Since colonial domination implied the silencing of colonized bodies and a systemic effort to cut Indigenous peoples off from the cultural/religious traditions of their ancestors, Brito and Krenak's proclamation of a logic that promotes ways of knowing otherwise is exemplary of the kind of decolonial move that needs to be

---

60   Seminar "A Brazilian Tragedy," second day, accessed on October 23, 2021, https://tinyurl.com/y4b5pz5f. All quotes were transcribed and translated by the author.

61   Boaventura de Souza Santos, *If God Were a Human Rights Activist* (Stanford, CA: Stanford University Press, 2015), 56.

62   Raimundo C. Barreto, "The Epistemological Turn in World Christianity: Engaging Decoloniality in Latin American and Caribbean Christian Discourses," *Journal of World Christianity* 9, no. 1 (2019): 48–60.

taken seriously in the study of World Christianity today. As Catherine Walsh explains,

> Decoloniality . . . implies the recognition and undoing of the hierarchical structures of race, gender, heteropatriarchy, and class that continue to control life, knowledge, spirituality, and thought, structures that are clearly intertwined with and constitutive of global capitalism and Western modernity . . . Decoloniality, in this sense, is not a static condition, an individual attribute, or a lineal point of arrival or enlightenment. Instead, decoloniality seeks to make visible, open up, and advance radically distinct perspectives and positionalities that displace Western rationality as the only framework and possibility of existence, analysis, and thought.[63]

Citing Nelson Maldonado-Torres, Walsh speaks of a decolonial attitude that denotes the "responsibility and the willingness to take many perspectives, particularly the perspectives and points of view of those whose very existence is questioned and produced as dispensable and insignificant."[64] Thus, the turn to the constructive aspect of decoloniality through the proposition of "relational ways of seeing the world, including the relation between privilege and oppression" is key.[65] Without attention to epistemic justice, both World Christianity scholars and ecumenists risk overlooking their own biases. It is not hard to see that most field studies in World Christianity privilege Christian voices as representative of broader Indigenous communities, often silencing non-Christian Indigenous communities. Such a selective hearing of Indigenous voices perpetuates epistemic injustice and the continued silencing of non-aligned, inconvenient voices.

---

63   Catherine Walsh, "Decoloniality as/in Practice," in *On Decoloniality: Concept, Analytics, Praxis*, 15–102 (17).

64   Nelson Maldonado-Torres, *Against War: Views from the Underside of Modernity* (Durham, NC: Duke University Press, 2008) 8, cited in Walsh, op. cit., 17.

65   Walsh, op. cit.

Toward a Liberative Intercultural Ecumenism

There is another possible way ahead for the study of World Christianity that can potentially encourage new ecumenical practices and perspectives. Such an approach takes into consideration a broader diversity of voices in any given context. Orlando Espin talks about "inter-trans-culturation" as an alternative path to older emphases on inculturation in Christian interactions with non-Western cultures. His proposal demands openness for another to "witness to me, in an open inter-discursive dialogue, what he or she understands and lives as truth."[66] The expected outcome of such a dialogue is to move "into an ever-deepening and continuing dialogue where truth is discovered and affirmed, over and over, through mutual witnessing, contrasting dialogue, and non-colonizing reflection."[67]

The guiding assumption of such dialogue is that truth is not a static, ready-made commodity that can be possessed by particular individuals and communities. On the contrary, "'truth' results from intercultural dialogue and contrast, and not from arguments and concepts born within a cultural horizon foreign to me and designed to convince me by pulling me away from my own cultural horizon."[68] Resembling Krenak's pluriversal perspective, Espin states: "Truth will only unveil itself to us if we are willing (in intercultural dialogue) to risk contrasting our own truth with the truth claims and truth expressions originating in other cultures."[69]

Considering both reality and truth "plurichrome and plurivalent," Espin is weary of claims of "universal validity" because such claims have "usually accompanied the history of power and colonization and [have] been all too frequently legitimized by these."[70] Alternatively, he suggests that religions can claim "universal relevance," offering a truth claim from within particular cultural or religious systems "to others who may find the claim to be useful, suggestive, or even true, thereby opening for and

---

66   Orlando O. Espin, *Idol and Grace: Traditioning and Subversive Hope* (Maryknoll, NY: Orbis Books, 2014, Kindle Edition), Loc. 1491.

67   Ibid.

68   Ibid.

69   Ibid., Loc. 1515.

70   Ibid.

within the recipients new perspectives—questions and themes, answers and solutions, practices and approaches—that had hitherto remained closed, unclear, or ignored."[71] This dialectical process of intercultural dialogue and contestation potentially leads to a processual unveiling of truth that, nevertheless, avoids "the trappings of empire, imposition, or idolatry."[72]

Espin's "inter-trans-culturation" offers a path to overcome the binary understanding of truth that Krenak identified as destructive to his people and culture because it does not make room for the *convivência* among multiple truth claims.[73] This dialogical praxis has a liberative potential to inform contemporary ecumenical engagement and expand our understanding of the "ecumenical" through the inclusion of geographies, cultures, and knowledges hitherto invisible under the cloak of modernity/coloniality.

Dale Irvin has hinted that the ecumenical movement is still haunted by the specter of Constantine. As mentioned earlier, the ecumenical movement that arose in the twentieth century mirrored the spirit of the times—the modern nation-state. As social, economic, and political structures today tend to organize themselves as "fluid assemblages of cross-border networks often coalescing around specific local issues but with trans-local or transnational (global) consequences," a new ecumenism that is also shaped up through similar "fluid assemblages and cross-border flows of globalization and exile" may be emerging.[74]

This chapter not only has shown some concrete examples of how this reconfiguration of the *oikoumene* is shaping up but has also unveiled its epistemic implications—especially showing how this new ecumenism

---

71   Ibid., Loc. 1528.

72   Ibid.

73   Espin defines *convivir* (Spanish) as meaning "to live-with," and implying, "among other things, that those who conviven are actually present with and to one another for a sufficiently prolonged period of time and, further, that their presence with and to one another engages them with and in one another's daily lives in ways that each considers sufficiently meaningful and sufficiently mutually respectful." Ibid., Loc. 1503.

74   Irvin, "Specters of a New Ecumenism,'" 24–25.

offers Christian and societal structures still tainted by lingering colonial disparities the means to resist and overcome historical epistemic injustices. Consequently, the ecumenical structures emerging in the twenty-first century can benefit from engaging the body politics of knowledge brought to the ecumenical table by formerly colonized bodies, which point to alternative ways for reconnecting and coexisting.

CHAPTER 3

EVANGELICALISM AND BHAKTI TRADITION AMONG TELUGU CHRISTIANS

James Elisha Taneti

INTRODUCTION

Telugu[1] Christians, located in the southern region of India, are drawn primarily from the Dalit communities, formerly considered untouchable and ritually defiling. They are placed outside the four-tiered caste system and thus are left without access to land, natural resources, or power-sharing. The dominant castes constitute less than 25 percent of all Christians. Yet they strongly influenced the evolution of Telugu Christianity—its theologies and practices—and they continue to do so. The imprints of the bhakti (piety) tradition embraced by caste Christians and the evangelicalism transported by Protestant missionaries reside harmoniously in the Telugu Christian piety and beliefs. Bhakti is a tradition within Hinduism that stresses the individual's faith in and devotion to a personal God (*swayam bhagawan* or *ishta daivam*). The word "bhakti" literally means "sharing." A *bhakta* is believed to share a relationship or bond with a personal deity. Bhakti *marga* (path) is one of the four paths or disciplines with which an individual is believed to attain liberation or *moksa*. The tradition at its inception was a protest movement against caste and gender inequalities, and was later domesticated by the dominating caste. Within Telugu Christianity, bhakti and evangelical traditions converged, resulting in a distinct spirituality. Caste and gender shaped this confluence.

The reasons for this blending of traditions are many. In the eighteenth century, Telugu Catholics composed *Prabhandas* (hymns)

---

1   A linguistic group in southern India.

in praise of their newly found deity, while their missionary counterparts translated catechisms using Brahminical dialect and idioms.[2] In the nineteenth century, it was Brahmins who translated the Bible into Telugu. In the traditional caste system, Brahmins are considered to be at the top of the caste hierarchy. With their ritual and literary powers, they legitimize and perpetuate the caste system and the economy that it established. And throughout the history of Telugu Christians, Brahmins composed songs through which Telugu Christians continue to affirm their faith today. With their songs, writings, and translations, Brahmin Christians brought remnants of bhakti traditions into the transmission and appropriation of the Christian message among the Telugu Christians. They initially introduced the bhakti tradition into Telugu Christian theology. Christians of both Dalit and Sudhra backgrounds retained and appropriated the tradition in their Christianity. In the four-tiered Indian society, Sudhras are placed at the bottom and the Dalits outside the caste system altogether. In Telugu society, Sudhras own lands and therefore dominate the social processes. While appropriating their version of Christianity, Telugu Protestants, in particular, collaborated with European and North American missionaries with evangelical leanings.

In his illuminating analysis of how communities hear and appropriate the Christian faith, Lamin Sanneh identified multiple partners in the process of translation.[3] The vernacular of the recipient community is one. The message transmitted by the missionary is another. In the case of Telugu Christians, there is a third partner, that is, the Hindu, especially bhakti, worldview. The faith and practices of the Dalit converts differed from those of Hindu traditions. Dalits brought their beliefs with them at the time of their group conversations to Christianity in the late

---

2   Pulidindi Solomon Raj, "Christian Prabhandha Literature," in *Striving for Excellence: Educational Ministry in the Church*, ed. Siga Arles and Brian Wintle (Bangalore: Center for Contemporary Christianity, 2007), 394. Solomon Raj defined *Prabandhas* as poetry with an opening prayer (*praveshika*) and occasional references to the ancestors.

3   Lamin Sanneh, *Translating the Message: The Missionary Impact on Culture* (Maryknoll, NY: Orbis, 1989), 51.

nineteenth century and the early twentieth century. Dalit worldviews, the bhakti tradition of their Hindu neighbors, and the evangelicalism of the Protestant missionaries together contributed to the evolution of Telugu Christianity. Telugu Christianity, therefore, is Christo-centric, marked with missionary enthusiasm and the posture of personal submission to Christ.[4] The personal is blended with the familial due to women's leadership. This chapter seeks to examine the traces of evangelicalism, bhakti tradition, and women's leadership on Telugu Christianity. In order to do so, I study select hymns (*kirtans*) written by female and male writers, to accentuate the theme of bhakti, and also to identify the layers within Christian bhakti.

Why do I study hymns to understand the beliefs of the Telugu Christian community? Beliefs, for Telugus, are often preserved, expressed, and celebrated in the spoken word. Telugu Christians articulate their faith in their sermons and hymns. Hymns function as catechetical tools. Some of the Telugu Christian hymns were written by Dalits themselves, but most were by Brahmin or Sudhra Christians, indicating the cross-fertilization of worldviews in Telugu Christian theology. Brahmins and Sudhras had access to literacy to compose songs, and Dalit Christians embraced these songs and the worldview that came with them. Purushottham Choudary (1803–1890), Pulipaka Jaganatham (1826–1896), Bhanumurti Chetti (1882–1973), and Abel Boanerges Masilamani (A. B. Masilamani, 1914–1990) are among such influential high-caste bards. For our purposes, I will limit my study to the hymns composed by A. B. Masilamani, a male bard, and three female writers—Philipp Gnanaratnamma (1890–1960), Vesapogu Gulbanamma (1905–1971), and Kommu Krupa (early twentieth century). All of the songs, except that of Krupa Kommu, belong to the second half of the twentieth century. While Masilamani was a Sudhra, the women were Dalits. Telugu Christians—Dalit and non-Dalit, men and women—graciously welcomed these writers and continue to sing their songs, allowing them to shape their spirituality. In this chapter, I will

---

4   Arun Jones studies the confluence of bhakti tradition and American evangelicalism in another region of India in greater detail. See his book *Missionary Christianity and Local Religion: American Evangelicalism in North India, 1836–1870* (Waco, TX: Baylor University Press, 2017).

first briefly introduce the beginnings of Telugu Protestantism, and then examine influences of bhakti tradition in the hymns written by a male bard and three female writers.

BEGINNINGS OF TELUGU PROTESTANTISM

The beginnings of Roman Catholicism among the Telugus date back to the early sixteenth century, and those of Protestantism to the early eighteenth century. German Pietistic missionaries located in Tharangabadi were the earliest of Protestants to have shown missionary interest in Telugus. Benjamin Schultze, who arrived in Tranquabar in 1712, learned Telugu and completed the translation of the Bible into the language by 1734, a project his illustrious predecessor Bartholomaus Ziegenbalg had wished to undertake. Schultze eventually moved to Vepery and ministered among the Telugus in Chennai. At the dawn of the nineteenth century, both the General Baptist missionaries located in Serampore and those of the London Missionary Society located in Visakhapatnam connected with Telugus and undertook translation projects. Their evangelistic efforts among the Telugus yielded limited results.

Christianity among Telugus grew in number in the second half of the nineteenth century. Three events played crucial roles in the transmission and translation of the Christian message in the nineteenth century—one in the North Atlantic region, and another in South India, while the third swept through both continents. First, the wave of evangelical revivals in the 1830s heightened missionary interest among Protestants in the United States. Of the fifteen Protestant missionary societies that arrived among the Telugus in the nineteenth century, thirteen arrived after 1833.[5] The change of British colonial policy toward missionaries,

---

5   These included the London Missionary Society (1805), Society for the Propagation of the Gospel (1826), Plymouth Brethren (1833), American Baptist (1835), Free Church of Scotland (1837), Church Missionary Society (1841), American Lutherans (1842), American Reformed (1853), American Episcopal Methodists (1857), German Lutherans (1865), Canadian Baptists (1868), British Wesleyans (1878), Russian Mennonites (1889), Salvation Army (1895), and American Mennonites (1899). In addition, there were a few unaffiliated missionaries who either worked alone or collaborated with others.

especially its openness to missionaries of non-British origins, was a factor in this surge.

Second, in the Indian subcontinent, marginalized groups organized themselves to seek better social status in the second half of the nineteenth century. Shanar women in South Travancore, an adjacent region, fought for legislation that would allow them to wear clothing above their waists, just as their counterparts in "higher" castes did.[6] Among the Telugus, Dalits in Kristna, Kurnool, and Prakasam districts converted to Christianity as groups in the second half of the nineteenth century. Among other reasons, quests for social respect and spiritual fulfillment may have been the primary motives behind these conversions.

Third, the cultural climate engineered by the marginalized on both continents shaped the motives of both missionaries and Telugu converts. Struggles for the emancipation of the slaves in North America resulted in the American Civil War, and subsequent declaration of the abolition of slavery. This influenced the American Baptist missionaries John Clough, Harriett Clough, and Emma-Rauschenbusch Clough, for example, who witnessed the baptism of blood during the Civil War, and the subsequent abolition in the United States in the 1860s, and were inclined to join similar struggles in the Indian subcontinent. Their British counterparts had earlier witnessed their own version of social reforms, including the abolition of slavery in the 1830s.

As a result of group conversions of Dalits in the second half of the nineteenth century, Christianity had become a religion of the Dalits, and is still identified as such. In an attempt to gauge the percentage of Dalits in the Telugu church today, I have randomly consulted with Telugu colleagues who specialize in the history of Telugu Christianity, and roughly estimate that at least three fourths or more of Telugu Christians are of Dalit background.[7] The lack of data did not deter Pulidindi Solomon Raj, a Lutheran

---

6   Joy Gnanadason, *A Forgotten History: A Story of the Missionary Movement and the Liberation of People in South Travancore* (Columbia, MO: South Asia Books, 1996). The Shanar, traditionally toddy-tappers, were at the bottom of the Tamil society in the middle of the nineteenth century.

7   The church historians consulted include Injumuri Asheervadam, Pavuluri Srikanth Chittibabu, Kanithi Ranjit Kumar, Michael Kumar Chatterjee, and

scholar, from identifying the Telugu Christian community with Dalits.[8] The group conversions mentioned in the preceding paragraph, and those that followed in other regions, radically changed the social fabric of the Telugu church.

The demographic change in the church significantly altered the theological outlook of the Telugu church. With the marginalized in its pulpits and pews, Christianity recovered its subversive character. In their effort to improve their social status, Dalit Christians reclaimed Christ and salvation as having implications of holistic life and social status. They integrated into their Christianity the enlightenment values of equality, freedom, and the right to organize. Salvation was not confined to a person's interior experience but rather it was an experience that pertained to one's social relationships.

Despite being a numerical minority, preachers and bards of "caste" origins dominated the translation of the Christian message in Telugu. Before going further, let me add a brief note on the caste system among the Telugus. Telugu society is stratified into castes. Some groups were considered outcastes. A person's birth determines their caste, and subsequently occupation and geographical location. In this agrarian society, the landowning Sudhra communities control natural resources, social life, and human labor. Brahmins, Vaishyas, and Kshatriyas (the three "higher" castes) buttress the religious, economic, and administrative systems to support the hegemony of the landowning Sudhras. The latter narrate history, interpret the present, and cast the vision for the future through their writings, speeches, and films. Deprived of a share in the land, Dalits are forced to provide cheap labor to the landowning Sudhras. Needless to say, the Hindu community evolved a religious worldview that would support this economic system.

As mentioned earlier, the dominant Hindu worldviews infiltrated the process of transmission of evangelical Christianity as Protestant missionaries employed Brahmin Bible translators and language teachers, starting in the nineteenth century. We do not know who assisted Benjamin Schultz, a

---

Chandra Sekhar. The suggested numbers were between a vague "majority" to 90 percent. But all of them hinted at a number between at least 70 and 80 percent.

8   Raj, "Christian Prabhandha Literature," 393.

German missionary in Chennai, in translating the Bible into Telugu in the 1730s. Anandarayaru, a Marathi Brahmin from Kadapa, helped the Baptist missionaries in Serampore and the London Missionary Society missionaries in Visakhapatnam in translating portions of the New Testament a century later.[9]

Considering Brahmins as pundits in the Telugu language, Protestant missionaries also employed them to teach the Telugu language. The terms and concepts used in Americus Timpany's theological *Compendium* and John McLaurin's Bible *Commentaries* indicate the degree of Sanskritic influences in the transmission of evangelical Christianity among the Telugus.[10] The practice of employing Brahmins to teach continued even until the 1960s. It was the world of these Brahmin scholars that the missionaries were introduced to. It was the same world that dominated the translation of the Christian message into Telugu.

Christian bards of "high" caste descent influenced the faith formation of Telugu Christian communities. Purushotham Chowdhari (1803–1890), a Gouda Brahmin, was a prominent voice in the formative years of Telugu Protestant Christianity. Ordained a catechist in 1836 by the London Mission Society, Chowdhari served the mission for twenty-seven years, and the Odisha Baptists twenty-five years.[11] With more than 130 hymns, Chowdhari inculcated the bhakti ethos of a devotee's submission to a personal god. In lieu of Krishna or Rama, Christ became the object of personal devotion. Praise for the redeemer God, admission of guilt, and gratitude for the grace received are common threads in his hymns.[12] At

---

9   S. M. Hooper and W. J. Culshaw, *Bible Translations in India, Pakistan and Ceylon* (Bombay: Oxford University Press, 1963), 81.

10   A. V. Timpany, *Compendium of Theology* (Cocanada: n.p., 1879); John McLaurin, *Telugu Commentary on the New Testament: Acts of Apostles*, vol. 4 (Madras: SPCK, 1902); John McLaurin, *Telugu Commentary on the New Testament: Gospel according to St. John*, vol. 3 (Madras: SPCK, 1906); John McLaurin, *Telugu Commentary on the New Testament: The First Corinthians to Philippians*, vol. 4 (Madras: SPCK, 1906).

11   John Chowdhari, *Biography of the Rev. Purushottam Chowdhari* (Madras: The Christian Literature Society, 1906), 27.

12   Rayi R. Sundara Rao, *Telugulo Chraistava Sahityam* (Chennai: Rayi Foundation, 2016), 17–35. Citing Sudha Ratnajali, Kanithi Ranjit Kumar classifies

least seventy of his hymns are listed among the nine hundred songs in the current *Andhra Chraistava Kirtanalu* (Andhra Christian Hymnal).[13] Chowdhari also assisted in the revision of the Telugu Bible. Chowdhari is just one prominent example of many such song writers.

In addition to these hymns, the influence of Western evangelicals on the beliefs and hymnody of the Telugu Christians continued. Translations of at least 132 English hymns from Europe and North America are listed among the nine hundred hymns in the Telugu hymnal. Except for those written by Martin Luther, the sixteenth-century German Protestant reformer, all other hymns were composed by Pietists or evangelicals in the late eighteenth and nineteenth centuries. Most of them were written for liturgical and sacred occasions, and therefore are sung more often than some Telugu hymns. Thus, both evangelical and bhakti traditions continued to shape the Telugu church in the postcolonial era, that is, after 1947.

Masilamani and His Hymns

To understand the coming together of bhakti and evangelical influences, let us now study the songs by A. B. Masilamani (1914–1990), an influential writer in the Protestant communities in the second half of the twentieth century. Born in a mission hospital compound, Masilamani grew up a Baptist. His mother Saramma was a schoolteacher. As a Biblewoman (a woman preacher), she also preached and modeled Christian faith. Masilamani's father, Gershon Paul, was a nurse at Christian Medical Center in Pithapuram. After completing high school in Samarlakota, Masilamani pursued basic training at Baptist Theological Seminary in Kakinada where he studied under Chetti Bhanumurti, another prolific hymn writer. It is not surprising that in a seminary consisting predominantly of Dalits, Masilamani, a Visva Brahmin (goldsmith), and Bhanumurti, a Vaishya

---

Chowdahri's songs into thirteen types. See also Sudha Ratnanjali Samuel, *Purshothama Chowdari Jeevitha Charitra* (Chennai: Christian Literature Services, 1997), 73.

13   *Andhra Chraistava Kirtanalu* (Privately published by K. Matthew Henry in Tenali, 2014).

(merchant community), bonded well. They shared a love for classical music. Bhanumurti, who also ministered at the adjacent Baptist church located in Kakinada, composed several heart-touching hymns, seventeen of which are sung in Telugu churches even today. Masilamani's interest in theater and music matured at the seminary, making him a prolific hymn-writer and eloquent preacher. Masilamani eventually pursued graduate and doctoral studies in Canada and India. His education at McMaster Divinity School and Acadia Divinity School further rooted him in evangelical faith.

The beginnings of Masilamani's ministry coincide with the birth of the Indian Union, and the formation of greater Andhra Pradesh.[14] He first ministered in the Convention of Baptist Churches in the Northern Circars in the 1950s and 60s, and later founded New Life Associates in 1970, a federation of congregations and charitable agencies, which he led until his death in 1990. In addition to his hymns and sermons, he wrote short books and published a popular magazine *Kapari* (Shepherd), a preaching resource for Telugu clergy. With his versatile gifts, Masilamani actively shaped the faith of Telugu Christians for more than four decades in independent India.

Masilamani's flair with words continued late into life, resulting in forty-four hymns, ten of which are listed in the Telugu Christian Hymnal.[15] Masilamani also translated English hymns, such as "Blest Be the Tie That Binds" by John Fawcett, a British evangelical. This hymn resonates with the common themes in his songs, such as adoration, repentance, and hope. Most of Masilamani's hymns were written for huge gatherings of Telugu Christians who assembled annually in Vijayawada under the auspices of the Andhra Christian Council. He was a regular preacher at these annual gatherings. After preaching a sermon, Masilamani taught a hymn that would summarize his sermon. His hymns thus functioned as catechetical tools. These annual gatherings were ecumenical with an attendance drawn from diverse Protestant communities: the Church of South India, Andhra Evangelical Lutheran Church, and Baptist churches. This collaboration necessitated a broader and conciliatory tone. Not all Masilamani's songs

---

14   The greater Andhra Pradesh was bifurcated into the states of Andhra Pradesh and Telangana in 2014.

15   Kumar, "The Elements of Bhakti in the Lyrics of Acharya A. B. Masilamani," 45.

were composed for these ecumenical gatherings, but he might well have had huge audiences in mind, as he was a much sought-after preacher.

The accent in these hymns on one personal and visible God emerged out of the bhakti tradition, as did the genre used to articulate this Christology. Telugus have been singing praises of their *ista dhaivam* (beloved God) since the sixteenth century. Rayi R. Sundara Rao in his illuminating book *Telugulo Chraistava Sahityam* (Christian Literature in Telugu) analyzed the prominence of music in bhakti tradition, and how pervasive that tradition was in the Telugu Christian hymns.[16] Kanithi Ranjit Kumar, the Principal of Baptist Theological Seminary in Kakinada, concurs with Sundara Rao and highlights the influences of bhakti in Telugu hymnody.[17]

Given the bhakti influences in Telugu Christian piety, Christ became the object of worship, an *avatar* (visible personification) of God. In a song that narrates the conversation between Jesus and two convicts on the cross (Luke 29:39–43), Masilamani interpreted Jesus as the face of God. In the emaciated countenance of the crucified Jesus, humanity can see God revealed, Masilamani believed. Given their daily experiences of servitude and forced labor, this portrait of God in the crucified Christ would have appealed to Telugu Baptists, most of whom were Dalits. Goddesses in the Dalit pantheon often were victims of rape or murder before being deified by the Dalit community. The song *"Prabhu yesuni vadhanamalo"* ("In the Countenance of Jesus") connects incarnation to the daily struggles of Dalit Christians:

> *In the face (countenance) of Jesus, I see my God (My God revealed*
> > *Godself)*
> *Grace was poured out at Calvary to redeem the sinner*
> *My soul yearned for heaven and eternal life*
> *In the face of Jesus, I see my God*
> *Trapped in wickedness and brutality,*
> *I wandered in all directions with the weight of my sin*

---

16 Rao, *Telugulo Chraistava Sahityam*, xxi.

17 Ranjit Kumar Kanithi, "The Elements of Bhakti in the Lyrics of Acharya A. B. Masilamani: Its Implications for Mission and Its Relevance to the Convention of Baptist Churches in the Northern Circars" (MTh thesis, Serampore University, 2005), 45.

Greedy after money and with animal instincts,
I deteriorated towards the ebbs of death
In the face of Jesus, I see my God

Kindly remember me, Jesus,
when you arrive with your kingdom on earth
I plead and weep, hear my plea
In the face of Jesus, I see my God

You will partake in the other world today with joy
I journey towards the Lord with heaven as my last breath
In the face of Jesus, I see my God![18]

Masilamani further explicated his Christology in a hymn enti-tled "*Yesu Kristu Dhevudu,*" which literally means "Jesus Christ is Lord." This lyrical confession of faith, especially its recurring prelude, reveals Masilamani's Christology. The song offers worshippers a way to sing their Christology.

Jesus Christ is the Son of God
Jesus Christ is the Son of Man
Jesus Christ is God; Jesus is Lord
He is worthy to praised

The power of God's righteousness is manifest in Jesus' cross
The image of God of gods is in the name of Jesus
Priceless is the Word of Yahweh; a delight to God's people

(Jesus is) the glory without end
An incarnation of God who carries our burdens
The Lord of heavens and celestial beings
The source of universal creativity

---

18   My translation of the hymn "*Prabhu Yesuni Vadanamulo.*" This and the other hymns translated in this chapter come from *Andhra Chraistava Kirtanalu* (Privately published by K. Matthew Henry in Tenali, 2014).

The giver and head of the entire world
The generous giver of grace every day

(Jesus is) the name the sin fears
An offering of grace to the sinner
The voice of love to the seeking humanity
An offer of heavenly bliss
A song of forgiveness of sin
A gift of strength and the true sacrifice

(Jesus is) the Lord of people's life
The light that rules the world
The final judge of all the living
The victor who conquered life and death
The flame that transforms the evil world[19]

Drawing from the titles used for Jesus in the gospels, Masilamani presented Jesus as both Son of God and Son of Man.[20] In this song, Masilamani drew heavily from Paul's letter to Colossians 1:15–20 and highlighted the universal lordship of Jesus Christ. In the bhakti tradition, devotees worshipped their most favored god and on occasions swapped their gods depending on the seasons in life. But they seldom placed gods in competition nor claimed one to be the only avatar of the Ultimate Reality. Finding themselves in a context of social conflict and perpetual marginalization, Telugu Christians may have embraced the missionary claims of the finality of Christ.

The belief in the universal lordship and uniqueness of Christ often motivates the missionary consciousness of Telugu Christians. The highest number of hymns in the Telugu hymnal praise and adore Christ, while the second largest center on the church's missionary obligation. Telugu Christians construe mission as preaching about Christ and inviting the hearer to faith in him. Masilamani's song *"Dhevuni Varasalamu"* ("We Are God's Heirs") reveals Telugu Christians' self-perception as those on

---

19   My translation of the hymn *"Yesu Kristhu Dhevudu."*

20   Mark 8:29, 31, 38. Cf. Matthew 11:27 and Luke 22:29. The title "Son of God" is used numerous times in the Gospel according to St. John.

the mission of preaching Christ. Using a military tone and vocabulary, the singer lifts up Jesus's cross as the rallying banner. Masilamani's hymn "*Randi Suvartha Sunadhamo*" ("Come with the Gospel Melody") is another example of the missionary enthusiasm of the Telugu Christians.

Come to the presence of gracious Jesus
With the melodies of the gospel
With amazing songs of the cross
With the music of cymbals and sitar

Only Jesus is the destiny of humanity
Only Jesus is the location for human righteousness
Only Jesus is the sanctifying name
Jesus shines as the holy name for Christians

Only Jesus is the image of divine love
Only Jesus is the reflection of omnipresent God
Only Jesus is the Lord of the people
Only Jesus is the safe haven for the poor

Only Jesus carried the cross
Only Jesus gives eternal life
Only Jesus has the authority to forgive
Jesus helps those who pray

Only Jesus is the illuminator in the church
Jesus is the only peace within a soul
Only Jesus is the living light within a family
Jesus blesses the innocent children

Only Jesus is the way to heaven
Only Jesus is the heaven on earth for worshippers
Only Jesus is the strategy for world peace
Jesus is the sure hope for humanity[21]

---

21   My translation of the hymn "*Randi Suvartha Sunadhamutho.*"

The song invites the singer to worship and preach the gospel because Jesus, according to the writer, is the only way to God. Within the religiously pluralist context of India, worship is a site and moment of witness. It is more so because Dalits worship in streets and in sanctuaries with loudspeakers. Every song and sermon is an invitation.

Reminiscent of the Hindu bhakti songs, the posture of submission runs through Masilamani's hymns. Devotees find themselves helpless even to follow God. Recognizing the need for grace, the devotee completely submits to the deity. Masilamani accentuated this attitude of submission. According to his most popular song *"Margam Chupumu Intiki"* ("Show Me the Way Home"), which relates the parable of the prodigal son (Luke 15: 11–32), the worshipper is a penitent wanderer who needs God's help to turn to God.

Show me the way home to my father's house
Show me the sweet world of love to my eyes
Show me the way home to my father's house
Show me the sweet world of love to my eyes

To me who wandered with love for sin, a famine struck
Grant me wholeness as I repent and seek father's blessing
To me who does not deserve your countenance
Lord, your cross instilled confidence
Show me the way home . . .

Considering wealth as everything and worldly pleasure as heavenly
I have left father for the worldly delights to ruin my life
God, I return to you begging with folded hands
Show me the way
Show me the way home . . .

Hoping that life would be better in far off lands, I lost the way
All friends I trusted deserted me, impoverished I am
Pour out your grace on me, Gracious God
Deem me blessed
Show me the way home . . .

With the sting of hunger, I have sold my sense of shame
Gutted I have been ostracized even by pigs
Habituated to grief, I reached the ebbs of wickedness
Grant me shelter, as the humanity within awakens
Show me the way home . . .

Complaining that I am not your son and the house is a prison, I left
Be merciful as I beg to work as one of your slaves
Do not turn me away as I have none else to go to
Receive me with forgiveness
Show me the way home . . .

My father saw me, came running, embraced me and wept
He gave me new life, took me home, and blessed me
My life story will be a witness to Jesus' love in this world
Show me the way home.[22]

In this song, written both to retell a biblical story and to invite the listener to faith in God, Masilamani highlighted human rebellion and the need for God's grace. The wayward son repents and returns to God with folded hands, a gesture symbolizing total submission to the Deity. God shows the way, grants new life, and welcomes the lost individual back. In addition to bringing Dalits closer to their Hindu neighbors' bhakti tradition, the posture of submission also reinforces Hinduism's hierarchal values.

As mentioned earlier, almost all the hymns composed by Masilamani were hewn from biblical passages. They retell events in the life of Jesus, and highlight the redemptive power of Jesus's death and resurrection. For example, Masilamani's song *"Andhala Thara Arudhinche Nake"* ("The Blessed Star That Descended for Me") relates the journeys of magi and shepherds to find solace to their spiritual yearnings at the feet of baby Jesus. Another song, *"Basillenu Siluvalo,"* narrates the passion story. Masilamani's leadership of the Bible Society of India as Auxiliary Secretary for the state of Andhra Pradesh attests to his faith that the Scripture,

---

22   My translation of the hymn *"Margam chupumu intiki."*

when retold, is capable of transforming individuals. It also reflects Telugu Christians' approach to the Bible. Accustomed to transmitting the truth in oral stories, Dalit Christians, in imitation of and/or competition with Hindus, embraced Christian scripture and found its retelling transforming and empowering.

WOMEN BARDS AND THEIR THEOLOGIES

Women have been instrumental in the spread of Christianity among the Telugus. In public, they led the community as Biblewomen, schoolteachers, and health workers. And at home, they interpreted the Christian message to their children and husbands. Despite their active leadership, their ability to influence the Telugu Christian faith via hymns has been limited. Only three Telugu women writers find place in the hymnody. Pilli Vijaya Charles, Vesapogu Gulbanamma, and Kommu Krupa together contributed four songs to the collection of nine hundred hymns mentioned earlier. However, Gogu Syamala in her *Nalla Proddhu: Dalitha Streela Sahithyam (1921–2002)* adds two more women writers to the list, Katta Chandramma and Phillip B. Gnanarathnam, whose hymns have not been listed in the hymn book.[23] All five of these hymn writers were Dalits. Their songs, except the one by Kommu Krupa, were written in the second half of the twentieth century, contemporaneously with Masilamani. This absence of women's voices attests to the gender biases in the Telugu Christian community.

There are some resemblances between the theologies of these five women and that of Masilamani. First, Christ is the *ista dhaivam,* the focus of their worship. In fact, Christ is the only way to the transcendent God. Second, they share missionary enthusiasm. Third, they draw extensively from the Bible, sometimes verbatim. Fourth, the posture of submission runs through each of their hymns, not that of resistance reminiscent of pre-Christian Dalit spiritualities. The women, however, went beyond the element of personal piety to include faith formation at home.

The hymn *"Sree Yahweh Nee Kosungedha"* ("I Offer You") by Vesapogu Gulbanamma (1905–1971) attests to the motive of submission or bhakti.

---

23   Gogu Syamala, *Nalla Proddhu: Dalita Streela Sahityam* [Black Dawn: Dalit Women's Literature] (Hyderabad: Hyderabad Book Trust, 2003).

Gulbanamma, another Baptist and an older contemporary of Masilamani, was a Dalit. After her high school education at Preston Institute in Jangaon, Gulbanamma successfully pursued her associates and undergraduate degrees, and a licentiate of teaching at Madras Christian College.[24] She later earned a Master of Arts degree from a school in the United States, and served as the headmistress at her alma mater in Jangaon.[25] Given her education and social ranking afforded by her profession, she embraced and promoted the bhakti tradition in Christianity. In choice of terms and theological inclinations in her hymn, Gulbanamma sounds as Sanskritic as her male counterparts did.

O Yahweh, I offer you the best of my treasures.

I will be without fear and with devotion in your presence.
I fall at your feet, with humility; I will give every bit of myself to thee.
I will worship without delay. Accept me, O Father!

You are always my king; I am your child.
Mine is a sinful life in your holy sight;
Grant me new life.

I offer myself, O God; fill me with your devotion!
Fill me with your blessed/auspicious powers, O Lord![26]

Like their male counterparts did, women writers like Gulbanamma drew from the biblical texts. This resonates with the practices of Telugu Biblewomen, who masterfully read, memorized, recited, and interpreted the biblical passages. In the following hymn *"Yehova yandhu bhakti bahuga kaligi undi"* ("With an Immense Devotion to God"), Gulbanamma attests to that biblical mastery by skillfully paraphrasing Psalm 128.

---

24 Syamala, *Nalla Proddhu*, 40.

25 William Arthur Stanton, *Out of the East: India's Search for God* (New York: Flemming H. Revell, 1938), 72. Cf. Syamala, *Nalla Proddhu*, 40; Rao, *Telugulo Chraistava Sahityam*, 343.

26 My translation of the hymn *"Sree Yehovah Nee Kosungedha."*

> *Blessed are those with those who run families*
> *with abundant devotion (bhakti), and*
> *walk in the paths of the Glorious One*
>
> *The fear of the Lord blesses the poor.*
> *You will verily enjoy the fruit of your labor.*
>
> *Your wife will produce like a vineyard, and*
> *your children will delightfully grow to be like olive trees.*
>
> *Your devotion (bhakti) to God will ensure you longevity;*
> *you therefore with the Lord's mercy will see your children's children.*

The above hymn resonates with the unique foci of the Telugu Biblewomen, both in drawing from the Bible and also in its accent on the Christian home. The hymn invites parents to raise children in devotion. It moves past the personal relationship of individual devotees or *bhaktas* with God to that of families with God. The songs of Katta Chandhramma and Pilli Vijaya Charles also highlight the themes of Christian home life and character. They share an implicit mission of raising children with a lifestyle they perceive to be Christian.

There is also a claim in the women's hymns about a two-pronged mission, one of learning and another of doing. Philip Gnanaratnamma (1890–1960) was a schoolteacher and a Lutheran. She studied and later taught at Stall Girls' School in Guntur. Gnanaratnamma composed seven hymns.[27] Of the seven hymns she composed, two of them were meant to be sung at the beginning of the worship service. Her hymn *"Chakkani Yesuswami Na Chakki Kegudhinche"* ("Beloved Jesus Has Drawn Close to Me") is noteworthy for our purposes. While emphasizing the divine immanence, Gnanaratnamma extolled God's care for every individual. "The one who sends sun and rain on the trees also endows me with joys and sorrows," she sang. Later in the hymn, Gnanaratnamma prayed that the Lord grant her the hands of Martha and the mind of Mary, recognizing the

---

27   Rao, *Telugulo Chraistava Sahityam*, 338–39. Cf. Syamala, *Nalla Proddhu*, 38–39.

importance of both in Christian life.[28] Gnanaratnamma's songs of invocation do not present themselves as departing from the songs composed by her male counterparts but the accent on the divine imminence and affirmation of Martha and Mary as models of Christian piety does. She seems to understand mission to be nurturing responsible Christian families and pursuing a life characteristic of Martha's hands and Mary's mind.

CONCLUSION

In almost all cases, the songs analyzed herein were primarily written to be sung in the context of community worship. They were meant to proclaim the good news of God revealed in Christ, making worship an evangelistic moment. In hymns, Telugu Christians confess Christ not only as their Lord but as the Lord of all, often putting the community at odds with other communities and making worship a site of conflict. And through hymns, Telugu Christian bards teach faith to the community, making worship an educational event.

At the outset, there is theological consensus among the twentieth-century Telugu hymn writers. Christ is the one and only Lord. Christians are called to live a life of devotion or submission (bhakti), a departure from the Dalit spirituality of resistance. They accept the Bible as the source of authority in matters of belief and practice, which is a departure from the notion of locating authority in divine oracles and spoken wisdom. Located at the margins, Telugu Christians share missionary enthusiasm, as evident in the hymns studied here. Given their gender and the perceptions of their roles, women bards emphasized the mission of creating Christian homes. These writers and the Telugu Christians draw from evangelicalism and bhakti traditions, making space for their pasts and their neighbors.

---

28   Rao, *Telugulo Chraistava Sahityam*, 340. Cf. Syamala, *Nalla Proddhu*, 39.

CHAPTER 4

WORLD CHRISTIANITY AND THE EVASION OF SOCIAL JUSTICE ISSUES: A FOCUS ON PENTECOSTALISM IN WEST AFRICA

Moses O. Biney

World Christianity as a discipline has far too often evaded the discussion of social justice issues. As a discipline that "seeks to investigate and understand Christian communities, faith, and practice as they are found on six continents,"[1] it must notice and point out injustices in these contexts, even if it seeks to be nonjudgmental. To do this, World Christianity scholarship must, among other things, employ methodologies of study that allow for deep inquiry, as well as critique of harmful beliefs and practices of the Christian communities being studied. Using examples from West African Pentecostalism, this chapter explores the complexities of alterity in religious practice and the lack of adequate methodologies for capturing and addressing injustices in World Christianity. It calls on scholars, particularly those who study African Pentecostalism, to pay closer attention to problems of alterity, and seek creative methodologies to unearth and address social justice issues in their research and writing.

Starting with a general overview of alterity and its role in religion, this chapter will outline the nature and importance of Pentecostalism in

---

1   Dale T. Irvin, "What is World Christianity?" in *World Christianity: Perspectives and Insights*, ed. Jonathan Y. Tan and Anh Q. Tran S. J. (Maryknoll, NY: Orbis Books, 2016), 4.

World Christianity, and African Christianity in particular. Then it will detail some of the activities of Pentecostal ministries and leaders in West Africa to reveal some of their dubious teachings and dangerous practices, and will follow up with an examination of issues of power and othering in Pentecostalism. Additionally, it will accentuate the existing tensions between Euro-American epistemologies and theologies of African Indigenous culture and religion regarding community, prosperity, evil, and salvation, and their combined influence on West African Pentecostalism. The chapter will then discuss issues of justice and othering in World Christianity, and provide suggestions for a new methodology for studying the discipline.

Religion and Alterity

Alterity is a term used in philosophy, anthropology, and other social sciences to refer to the concept of "otherness." Its meaning and use are as varied as the scholars who employ the term. The key question most seek to answer revolves around the relationship between the self and the "other."[2] The answers to this conundrum, as found in the writings of Edmund Husserl, Maurice Merleau-Ponty, Claude Lévi-Strauss, Emmanuel Levinas, and other philosophers,[3] range from the notion of radical alterity, which places the "other" in the realm of subjectivity, to the understanding of the "other" as engaged in an intersubjective and indeterminate relationship with the self.

Levinas (1906–1995), who popularized alterity as an ethical concept, for instance, argued that radical alterity is a necessary condition for human existence.[4] He believed that the relationship between the self and the

---

2   Although Levinas's concept of *Altrui* is often translated as Other, this chapter follows the terminology used throughout this volume in rendering it as "other."

3   Latin American scholars such as Enrique Dussel and Juan Scanonne also have made alterity an important category in their work.

4   Bernhard Leistle, ed., *Anthropology and Alterity: Responding to the Other* (New York: Routledge, 2017), 32.

"other" is an intersubjective engagement within which the "face" represents the self of the "other." Writing in his *Totality and Infinity*, he stated:

> What we call the face is precisely the exceptional presentation of self, incommensurable with the presentation of realities simply given, always suspect of some swindle, always possibly dreamt up. To seek truth, I have already established a relationship with a face which can guarantee itself, whose epiphany itself is somehow a word of honor. Every language as an exchange of verbal signs refers already to this primordial word of honor. The verbal sign is placed where someone signifies something to someone else. It therefore signifies an authentication of the signifier.[5]

Unlike René Descartes, Hegel, Husserl, and others who emphasized the self's need to conquer, consume, or take control of the "other" to survive or thrive as an ontological necessity, Levinas argued that the encounter between the self and "other" imposes on the self a responsibility for the "other."[6] Levinas's views, though largely philosophical, provide an entry point into the anthropological study of the "other." Worth mentioning here is the work of Bernhard Waldenfels who, building on the ideas of Levinas, attempts to bridge the gap between the radical and empirical "other" in his notion of the "other" as alien [*Fremd*].

Another way of understanding alterity is to shift the discursive focus from the "other" whose relevance lies simply in the fact that they can or must be known (epistemic "other") to the "other" who is situated in a political, cultural, linguistic, or religious context (moral "other"). It is this moral "other" who constitutes the focus of my discussion. In the context of this chapter, I use "alterity" interchangeably with "otherness" in an anthropological sense to mean the cultural/religious "other." Embedded in this use is also the notion of *othering*, which is the social and psychological means of exclusion and marginalization of the "other." My intention here is not to provide an exhaustive definition of the concept of alterity but to lay

---

5   Emmanuel Levinas, *Totality and Infinity: An Essay of Exteriority* (Pittsburgh: Duquesne University Press 1969), 202.

6   Ibid., 202–3.

enough groundwork for discussion of religious othering by West African Pentecostals.

All religions create otherness. They do so largely through their structures and perceived sacredness. By structures, I mean the entire apparatus of religious organizations—economic, political, social, and religious—through which they affirm and promote certain persons, projects, principles, and practices and not others. Through their doctrines, strategies for evangelism and mission, and cultural beliefs and practices, religious communities often otherize people. West African Pentecostals are no exception. It will become evident in the next section of this chapter how they create otherness.

PENTECOSTALISM IN WEST AFRICA

Scholars of World Christianity have documented well the astronomical growth of Pentecostalism in the Global South.[7] As Cephas Omenyo points out, there are numerous types of Pentecostals in West Africa. Among these are the (1) African Independent Churches (AICs) and their current mutations, (2) Classical Pentecostal movements (beginning in West Africa in 1906 and organized into churches in the 1920s), (3) Neo-Pentecostal and Charismatic Renewal groups (FGBMF, Aglow International and others), (4) Charismatic Renewal Groups within mainline denominations (e.g.,

---

7   The following are some helpful readings on African Pentecostalism: Ogbu U. Kalu, *African Pentecostalism: An Introduction* (Oxford University Press, 2008); Ogbu U. Kalu, *The Collected Essays of Ogbu Uke Kalu*, vol. 1: African Pentecostalism: Global Discourses, Migrations, Exchanges, and Connections, ed. Wilhelmina J. Kalu, Nimi Wariboko, and Toyin Falola (Trenton: Africa World Press, 2010); Paul Gifford, *Ghana's New Christianity: Pentecostalism in a Globalizing African Economy* (Indiana University Press, 2004); Nimi Wariboko, *Nigerian Pentecostalism*, Rochester Studies in African History and the Diaspora, 62 (Rochester, NY: University of Rochester Press, 2014); Nimi Wariboko, *The Pentecostal Hypothesis: Christ Talks, They Decide* (Eugene, OR: Cascade Books, 2020); J. Kwabena Asamoah-Gyadu, *Contemporary Pentecostal Christianity: Interpretations from an African Context* (Oxford: Regnum Books, 2013); J. Kwabena Asamoah-Gyadu, *Pentecostalism in Africa: Experiences from Ghana's Charismatic Ministries* (Minneapolis: Fortress Press, 2021).

The Bible Study and Prayer Group), and (5) Independent Pentecostal/ Charismatic churches and ministries.[8]

Since the 1980s, Pentecostalism has gained a dominant presence on the religious landscape of West Africa. The ubiquitous presence of Pentecostalism is observable through the many Pentecostal and Charismatic churches and ministries that spring up in many cities, towns, and villages in all seventeen West African countries. Thus, among other things, Pentecostalism is a major driving force behind the growth of Christianity in West Africa, and Africa as a whole.

Writing about Pentecostalism and renewal in Africa, J. Kwabena Asamoah-Gyadu notes:

> The Christian communities in Africa that I describe as Pentecostal include older Pentecostal denominations of both foreign and local provenance, and the various contemporary Pentecostal renewal movements, churches, and transnational fellowships such as the Full Gospel Businessmen's Fellowship International. Within the last century these streams of pneumatic Christianity have together transformed the face of Christianity in Africa.[9]

Additionally, he opines that the future of Christianity in Africa will be determined by how seriously churches are open to the work of the Holy Spirit. Similarly, appreciation of Pentecostals and their importance to the growth and expansion of African Christianity, and World Christianity in general, is shown in the works of many other authors.

In a recently published book, *African Pentecostalism and World Christianity*, edited by Nimi Wariboko and Adeshina Afolayan, the authors present an interdisciplinary discussion of the interplays that exist between World Christianity and African Pentecostalism. This book, which,

---

8   Cephas Omenyo, *Pentecost Outside Pentecostalism: A Study of the Development of Charismatic Renewal in Mainline Churches in Ghana* (Zoetermeer, The Netherlands: Boekencentrum Publishing House, 2006), 94.

9   J. Kwabena Asamoah-Gyadu, *Sighs and Signs of the Spirit: Ghanaian Perspectives on Pentecostalism and Renewal in Africa* (Eugene, OR: Wipf & Stock Publishers, 2015), 177.

according to its authors, investigates and interrogates the critical junctures at which World Christianity invigorates and is invigorated by African Pentecostalism, is important for our current discussion. Among other things, it provides a very current and periscopic view of African Pentecostalism through its seventeen scholarly essays. The overall tone and tenor of the book is positive. It casts African Pentecostalism in a glowing light. However, a few of its chapters raise certain critical issues regarding social justice and otherness worth exploring here.

In chapter 10 of the said book, entitled "Proclaiming Good News to the Poor (Isa 61: 1–2; Luke 4:1–19): Pentecostalism and Social Justice in Ghana,"[10] Patrick Kofi Amissah calls for a more balanced approach to dealing with spiritual and social justice issues among Ghanaian Pentecostals. Focusing his discussion on the teaching and programs of the Church of Pentecost (CoP) in Ghana, he argues that though the denomination's Pentecost Social Services (PENSOS) addresses issues of poverty through its disaster prevention, relief services, economic empowerment, health services, and educational support programs, it needs to do more. He suggests that the denomination, for instance, must take seriously the support of persons with disabilities as a ministry and provide both their spiritual and material needs.

Another social justice issue he recommends that the CoP must address in Ghana is violence against women and girls. Though much of this discrimination and violence is embedded in cultural attitudes and practices such as widowhood rites, female genital mutilation, and shrine slavery, Amissah points out that the actions and statements of some influential Pentecostal leaders unfortunately promote negative attitudes against women and girls.[11] He quotes several such utterances that he considers demeaning. Bishop Agyinasare of the World Miracle Church International, for instance, is said to have advised women abused in marriage to "rise up

---

10   Patrick Kofi Amissah, "Proclaiming Good News to the Poor (Isa 61: 1–2; Luke 4:1–19): Pentecostalism and Social Justice in Ghana," in *African Pentecostalism and World Christianity: Essays in Honor of J. Kwabena Asamoah-Gyadu*, ed. Nimi Wariboko and Adeshina Afolayan (Eugene, OR: Pickwick Publications, 2020) 153–68.

11   Ibid., 167.

and use their spiritual weapons" instead of complaining,[12] saying, "You are not the first woman to be beaten by your husband and will not be the last." Archbishop Duncan Williams, head of the Action Chapel International, is also quoted as saying that marriage is a privilege for which women must be thankful. He claimed they should stop misbehaving, and that, however intelligent or beautiful a woman is, she will "rot in her beauty and intelligence unless a man proposes and marries her."[13] The high positions these "men of God"[14] occupy, and the honor accorded to them, make their statements and their attitudes slighting girls and women very dangerous, as they influence the beliefs and behaviors of their large membership and fan base.

In another chapter of *African Pentecostalism and World Christianity*, "The Need for Theologizing from the Experience of the 'other' in Contemporary Christianity in Africa," the author, Faith Lugazia, reiterates the fact that women continue to be subjected to demeaning characterizations in African Christian theology and cultures. She points particularly to the religious and cultural worldview of women as witches or persons prone to the effects of witchcraft. Her words are worth quoting here:

> Women in Africa have been defined by their experience of oppression. This includes oppression in such mystical forms like being bewitched, being possessed by demons or ancestral spirits whose consequence is to hinder the life progress of women. In Tanzania, there is a belief that the ancestral spirit that possesses a woman becomes the husband that prevents any physical marriage.[15]

---

12   Ibid.

13   Ibid.

14   The term "man of God" derived from the Bible, Micah 6:8 for instance, is used by many Pentecostals to refer to their pastors who are incidentally largely men.

15   Faith K. Lugazia, "The Need for Theologizing from the Experience of the 'Other' in Contemporary Christianity in Africa," in *African Pentecostalism and World Christianity: Essays in Honor of J. Kwabena Asamoah-Gyadu*, ed. Nimi Wariboko and Adeshina Afolayan (Eugene, OR: Pickwick Publications, 2020), 237.

She continues by naming other gender-based injustices women suffer in churches. For example, she says:

> Where both a boy and a girl are caught in adultery, and the girl becomes pregnant, she is punished by the church by being put under church discipline as if committing adultery is only a woman's misconduct.[16]

Among other things, Lugazia suggests that African Christian theology must allow space for the stories of these women and girls, whom she considers the "other." Theologizing from the perspective of the "other," she says, will assist the church to bring into focus the negative experiences that women encounter. Women in this way can name and own their experiences, and find ways to challenge and get rid of the causes of their oppression.

I have referenced the above chapters for two main reasons. First, to show like every human institution, African Pentecostalism and Christianity in general is not without social injustices, and lacks adequate social programs to ameliorate them. And, second, this study points out that there are scholarly African voices that draw attention to social justice issues, such as poverty and injustices against women, girls, and the disabled.[17]

The most complex portrait of West African Pentecostalism—the good, the bad, and the ugly—can be found in newspapers and on social media platforms such as Facebook, YouTube, and WhatsApp. Here, the full gamut of the beliefs, practices, and programs of several Pentecostals are on display. These social media pages are replete with audio and video recordings and stories of the activities—preaching, "prophetic" declarations, worship, healing, and deliverance services, etc.—of Pentecostal churches and ministries. Such

---

16 Ibid.

17 Many African scholars, such as Mercy Oduyoye and theologians in the Circle of Concerned African Women Theologians, have addressed and continue to discuss and write about these matters. However, within World Christianity and in published studies of African Pentecostalism, the concern is less evident. Another exception is Fulata Moyo's chapter in this volume, "Child Marriage, the Untold Story of My Mother, and the Church in Africa."

activities and stories often capture both positive practices and services as well as excesses such as bullying, manipulation, and extortion by some of the leaders of these Pentecostal-Prophetic-Charismatic churches. They particularly reveal the excesses associated with "deliverance" (exorcism) and prophetism that have become part of the modus operandi of many Pentecostal and Charismatic churches in West Africa, and the complex social and economic conditions that make these possible. A couple of short videos I reviewed on Facebook and YouTube for this chapter revealed some of the most unspeakable abuses I have ever seen meted out to church members. One such video shows Daniel Obinim, variously called Bishop, Angel, Prophet Obinim, Founder, and leader of International God's Way (Obinim Ministries), in Ghana stepping on the belly of a pregnant woman in 2014.[18] Another clip shows the same Bishop Obinim in 2016 flogging two teenagers, a boy and a girl, in front of a large congregation. They were alleged to have engaged in sex, resulting in the girl's pregnancy.[19] Despite the call for his prosecution from Amnesty International (GH), and a temporary arrest by the Ghana Police in 2016 in connection with the flogging incident, he continues to operate as a pastor and is as controversial as ever.

Some other videos showed complete lack of common decency, invasion of privacy, and sexual harassment in the ministries involved. One such clip shows a male pastor and his male associate bathing female members of his congregation in public view. This, he claims, was to make them clean and holy.[20] This same pastor who goes by the name Pastor Blinks and leads the End Time Church of Grace in Ghana is seen in another video clip shaving off the pubic hair of his female church members.[21] Speaking

---

18   Scoop TV, "Ghanaian Pastor Steps & Kicks A Pregnant Woman," May 26, 2015, YouTube video, 1:10, accessed June 14, 2022, https://tinyurl.com/mt35464n.

19   Francis Kennedy Ocloo, "Moralist High Priest Bishop Obinim Publicly Flogging a Pregnant Woman for Sinning," August 17, 2016, YouTube video 2:59, accessed June 14, 2022, https://tinyurl.com/2w9sk7ua.

20   Blinks TV, "Ghanian Pastor Blinks Bath his Female Congregants During 31st December Watch Night," December 31, 2021, YouTube video 4:28, accessed June 16, 2022, https://tinyurl.com/39x3rt88.

21   Emmanuel Akyeam, "Pastor Blinks Caught On Camera Shaving Private Parts of His Church Members," October 12, 2020, YouTube video 4:46, accessed June 16, 2022, https://tinyurl.com/y5u6ta7r.

in Twi, a Ghanaian language, he claimed that he had been instructed by God to do this for those who need economic breakthroughs. A sixty-five-year-old woman whose underparts he shaved is heard saying, "If you can make me prosperous by shaving my pubic hair, shave all of it." Such sexual exploitation and abuse are not peculiar to West African Pentecostals. A BBC documentary on Pentecostal churches in Africa, particularly in South Africa, shows cases of rape and other abuses by some of these pastors.[22] Another YouTube clip reveals pastors beating demons out of people and instructing congregation members to eat grass, drink petrol, and eat rats to receive healing or have favor with God.

While these and other such abuses are horrific in themselves, what is even more dangerous are the hermeneutical distortions, concoctions, and prophetic chicanery that are used as the basis for these acts. In many cases, their church members and adherents, particularly the poor and needy, who hope to better their lives, are swindled out of their financial and other material resources. The key motive for establishing many of these Pentecostal churches and ministries is financial. This is evident from the many dubious fundraising methods used by these pastors, prophets, and evangelists, which include asking members and adherents to pay membership fees,[23] "sow seeds," or purchase all kinds of supposed spiritual aids to receive blessings.[24]

The brand of African Pentecostals who have gained the most fame and notoriety on social media are the Independent Pentecostal/Charismatic churches and ministries founded and led by individuals, many of whom go by titles such as Apostle, Prophet, Bishop, Archbishop, Angel, and others.

---

22   BBC African News, "Fake Pastors and False Prophets Rock Churches in South Africa," March 13, 2019, YouTube video, accessed June 16, 2022, https://tinyurl.com/rurf2cnf.

23   Ghanaweb, "Agradaa goes berserk over membership fee," May 20, 2022, accessed June 14, 2022, https://tinyurl.com/2p8ecaa5.

24   These supposed spiritual aids include anointing oil, special candles, salt, and onions. One pastor in Nigeria even sells "the blood of Jesus," a red grape-looking drink for N4,000 or N7,000, depending on the size of the bottle. It is supposed to be a cure for every disease. Adom Online, "'Blood of Jesus' for sale in churches; sparks controversy," October 16, 2017, accessed June 14, 2022, https://tinyurl.com/bddvhnnw.

These congregations and ministries are often unaffiliated with larger denominations or religious associations. Thus, they operate mostly under the instructions of their founders or leaders, who are unrestrained by any ecclesiastical or governing bodies. Many of these often "prophesy" about national issues, and especially the demise or downfall of political leaders and public figures. In an article on the Ghanaweb entitled "Mahama and Chief Imam are alive; Owusu Bempah is a liar,"[25] the author, Charles Addai, recounts the story of Rev. Isaac Owusu Bempah, founder and leader of Glorious Word and Power Ministry in Ghana, who prophesied the deaths of the National Chief Imam of Ghana, Sheik Nuhu Sharabutu,[26] and His Excellency John Dramani Mahama, the leader of the National Democratic Party (the main opposition party) and former President of Ghana, in December 2019.[27] These two persons, who were supposed to die in 2020 according to Bempah, were still alive at the time of writing in June 2022. In the said article, the author cautions Ghanaians to beware of these "false prophets" who he claims seek power and money.

West African Pentecostals and Power

Central to Pentecostal belief and theology is the power and action of the Holy Spirit. This power is transformational and regenerative. Whoever has the Holy Spirit, therefore, according to Pentecostal belief, has

---

25 Ghanaweb, "Mahama and Chief Imam are alive; Owusu Bempah is a liar," January 1, 2020, accessed June 16, 2022, https://tinyurl.com/yshf6ucd.

26 The National Chief Imam or Grand Mufti of Ghana is the title for the highest Muslim authority in Ghana. He is the leader of all Muslim communities in Ghana, and represents them in national affairs and interreligious gatherings. The current Chief Imam, Sheik Osman Nuhu Sharabutu, was 103 years old at the time of writing.

27 There was a huge uproar in Ghana immediately after this prophesy on December 31, 2019. Many news outlets, including the BBC, reported that groups of Muslim youth armed with machetes stormed a congregation of Rev. Bempah and destroyed some property. They stopped after the Imam condemned the attack and asked them to cease their actions. BBC News Online, "Ghanaian Isaac Owusu-Bempah's church stormed over prophecy," January 3, 2019, accessed June 14, 2022, https://tinyurl.com/2ukcs5j6.

power to defeat demonic forces, evil persons, and circumstances. Such a belief is reflected in the language of "success," "victory," "taking territories," "prosperity," and other motifs common among Pentecostals and Charismatics. Related to this belief in the power of the Holy Spirit is the strong belief in "deliverance," that is, the practice of exorcising a person or place, or of providing protection from the influence of demons or evil spirits. The Western binary notion of "Holy Spirit" vs. "Demonic Spirits," for instance, has heavily influenced the definition and exclusion of the "other" among West African Christians and Pentecostals, in particular. Analyzing these and other social conditions is necessary in providing a more balanced picture of the successes and challenges of Christianity in Africa.

I have mentioned elsewhere that the purpose and practice of deliverance, as well as the underlying worldview, is akin to exorcism in Indigenous African healing. As I point out:

> In both cases, healing is premised on the belief that there are malignant forces that seek to destroy or impede human progress. To overcome these forces, one needs to tap into the power of a superior force or being. The priest, diviner, or deliverance official as the case may be, can reverse the actions of the forces in people's lives.[28]

One essential difference, however, is that in the case of traditional healing, the priest aims at restoring health and wellness not only to the individual(s) undergoing exorcism but also to the entire community. Unlike the traditional priests who seek communal harmony as part of their healing, many Pentecostal pastors use the practice of deliverance for self-promotion and financial gain. Commenting on the prominence of "deliverance thinking" among Charismatics (Neo-Pentecostals) in Ghana, which she says attributes poverty, sickness, and the inability to make progress in life to the influence of demons and evil spirits, Jane Soothill points out the belief that "demonic influence may persist even after Christian

---

28   Moses Biney, *From Africa to America: Religion and Adaptation among Ghanaian Immigrants in New York* (New York: New York University Press, 2011), 97.

rebirth and must be expelled by prayer, Bible study and prophetic powers of the man or woman of God."[29] The supposed ability of these prophets and priests to perform miracles such as healing of the sick, praying for people to find well-paying jobs, and warding off evil and mischievous spirits has created an aura of power and authority around them. In many cases, these "men and women of God" are not shy to tout their "powers" at every opportunity.[30]

Regarding the importance of the spiritual powers of individual preachers and prophets, Soothill remarks:

> A moment of connection with Ghana's chosen prophets can turn someone's life from a path of failure or disappointment to one of significance and success (and often this can take place with little or no reference to God at all).[31]

Besides claiming spiritual power, Pentecostal leaders and churches in West Africa have become important players in the politics of their respective countries. Many of them have gained prominence in the courts of government and influenced political decisions. Ebenezer Obadare, Professor of Sociology at the University of Kansas, in his *Pentecostal Republic*, for instance, asserts that "the Nigerian democratic process since 1999 is ultimately inexplicable without recourse to the emergent power

---

29　Jane Soothill, "A Critical Approach to the Concepts of 'Power' and 'Agency' in Ghana's Charismatic (Neo-Pentecostal) Churches," in *Sprit on the Move: Black Women and Pentecostalism in African and the Diaspora*, ed. Judith Casselberry and Elizabeth A. Prichard (Durham: Duke University Press, 2019), 151.

30　Most independent Pentecostal church leaders are male. For this reason, many of the injustices recorded were perpetrated by male leaders against women who often constitute the majority membership of their churches. There are, however, some women leaders who are referred to variously as "woman of God," "prophetess," or "Evangelist," and who also engage in dubious practices. For example, Nana Agradaa, a traditional fetish priest who formed a church and calls herself Evangelist Patricia, was critiqued for requiring her congregation to pay a "membership fee" of three hundred Ghanaian cedis. See footnote 23.

31　Soothill, "A Critical Approach," 152.

of Pentecostalism, whether as manifested in the rising political influence of Pentecostal pastors or in a commensurate popular tendency to view socio-political problems in spiritual terms."[32]

The sacred personas associated with Pentecostal and Charismatic leaders and the political influence they possess contribute in no small way to the othering that takes place in and outside these churches.

Pentecostals and Alterity

Alterity, as indicated earlier, centers on the relationship between the self and the "other." The study of this relationship must extend beyond mere observation of physical interaction(s) between the self and the "other" to include the larger sociocultural context, and dynamics such as the motives at play in the relationship and the undergirding racial-ethnic, class, and gender issues.

Anthropologists who have written about alterity have raised critical questions, such as: What is the essential nature of the "other"? How does one respond to the "other"? The second question, which raises the issue of representation, is more relevant for our current discussion. In trying to represent the "other," scholars use terms such as "radical other," "empirical other," and "alien." Representation means more than merely seeing the "other." It means how one fabricates the "other" in one's imagination. Construction of the "other" also involves the construction of self. In other words, our perception of the identity and worth of the other person(s) is based not only on the intrinsic value of the "other" but also on our own assessment of the status of the "other" in relation to our own status. Othering thus begins with a psychological position of "not one of us." Practically, this position excludes or relegates to the margins of society persons who do not fit the norm of a particular social group.

Early in the last century, West African Pentecostals were the "other" in relation to the mainline denominations at that time—such

---

32   Ebenezer Obadare, *Pentecostal Republic: Religion and Struggle for State Power in Nigeria* (London: Zed Books 2018), 1. For another example of Pentecostal politics, in chapter 8 of this volume, see Chamma Kaunda's "The Public Bible, Politics, Gender, and Sexuality in Zambia."

as Anglicans, Catholics, Methodists, and Presbyterians—due to their biblical literalism and the low level of education of most leaders and members. Things have changed immensely in the last fifty years. The preponderance of Pentecostal and Charismatic churches and ministries, as well as the general popularity of Pentecostal styles of worship, has caused a shift in the religious landscape of West Africa. Now Pentecostals, the once Christian underdogs, are prominent and powerful. Paradoxically, however, they are also engaged in *othering*, as was once done against them. This occurs in two main ways, first, through the construction of a sacred and spiritually powerful persona. Many Pentecostal leaders construct themselves as powerful, prosperous, and holy men and women. Second, they objectify others through demonizing, prophetic manipulation, and peddling political influence. The poor, sick, and disabled are considered as "others" who are afflicted by the evil power of the devil or are themselves complicit in their own and others' woes due to their possession of evil powers. Such persons are often stigmatized and sought out to be "delivered" from the "powers of darkness." Many times, the spiritually weak or wicked persons are subjected to indignities, some of which were mentioned earlier. This othering is often conditioned by the binary understanding of persons and occurrences as either good or evil, controlled by God or Satan.

Considering this, it is important to revisit Levinas's notion of the true relationship between the self and the "other" in ethical and spiritual terms. The relationship is transcendent, that is, beyond and above the entities involved. The face of the "other," though powerless, defenseless, and destitute, compels the self to be compassionate and merciful. As Levinas put it, "The Other who dominates me in his transcendence is thus the stranger, the widow and the orphan, to whom I am obligated."[33] This spiritual and moral ethic reflects both the teachings of Christ and an essential principle for community living and building in West Africa. Unfortunately, however, the attitudes and practices of othering by some Pentecostal leaders are counter to these values.

---

33   Levinas, *Totality and Infinity*, 215.

WEST AFRICAN CHRISTIANITY, JUSTICE, AND THE "OTHER"

Scholarship on West African Christianity has largely been defensive and cautious. This may be the unintended consequence of reacting to colonial and racist descriptions of African religions and culture. In the last two centuries, African scholars have had to counter the numerous mischaracterizations of African peoples' religious beliefs and practices promoted by Western missionaries, anthropologists, and armchair historians, many of whom believed that African religious and cultural practices were barbaric, superstitious, and incompatible with Christianity.[34] Unfortunately, in their attempt to repudiate these claims, many African scholars have failed to critique injustices that occur within African Christianity.

One would have hoped that the works of prominent scholars of African Christianity, such as Sanneh, Asamoah-Gyadu, and Ogbu Kalu would have been far more forceful in their critique of abuses in West African Pentecostalism. Understandably, positive portrayals are needed to counter previously negative perceptions of African religious beliefs and practices. For generations, Euro-American scholars wrote in ways that diminished the importance of African Christianity and theology in global Christianity, and this still occurs even now.[35] Yet with the shift of the center of Christianity from the Western world in the last fifty years, and the expansion of Pentecostal/Charismatic Christianity, many non-African scholars of African Christianity feel uncomfortable critiquing the religious beliefs and practices of Pentecostals, perhaps out of fear of being called racist, ethnocentric, or unpatriotic. Description and analysis of African Pentecostalism

---

34   Robert Moffat, the Scottish pioneer missionary to South Africa for over fifty years, for instance, is quoted as saying, "Satan has employed his agency with fatal success, in erasing every vestige of religious impression from the minds of the Bechuanas, Hottentots and Bushmen; leaving them without a single ray to guide them from the dark and dread futurity, or a single link to unite them with the skies." Edwin W. Smith, *African Ideas of God: A Symposium* (London: Edinburgh Press, 1961), 83.

35   This surely calls for a forceful response. Nonetheless, in doing so, discussions and analyses of social justice issues in African Christianity should not be pushed to the backburner.

by African and non-African scholars alike is therefore generally positive, even sometimes adulatory and triumphalist.

It is therefore fair to ask whether scholars of West African Christianity are intentionally evading issues of justice in their research or simply lack the appropriate methodologies for studying social justice. I believe both problems are occurring. Related to the second problem, it must be noted that there is no one single methodology in World Christianity but rather numerous historical, missiological, phenomenological, anthropological, intercultural, and comparative approaches. Many of the first-generation scholars of African Christianity such as Sanneh, Kalu, John Mbiti, Kwame Bediako, and Andrew Walls favored historical and missiological approaches. While these approaches and their specific methodologies may be helpful in addressing injustices, that has not been the foci so far. What is needed now, considering the abuses in African Pentecostalism, are specific methods for identifying and analyzing social justice issues. The next section will speak to this need in World Christianity and suggest new ways of overcoming some of the field's present challenges.

Methodological Considerations in World Christianity

The late Lamin Sanneh in his very eye-opening book *Whose Religion is Christianity?* defines World Christianity as:

> the movement of Christianity as it takes form and shape in cultures that previously were not Christian, societies that had no bureaucratic tradition with which to domesticate the gospel. In these societies Christianity was received and expressed through the cultures, customs, and traditions of the people affected. World Christianity is not one thing, but a variety of indigenous responses through more or less effective local idioms, but in any case, without the European Enlightenment frame.[36]

---

36   Lamin Sanneh, *Whose Religion Christianity? The Gospel Beyond the West* (Grand Rapids, MI: Wm. B. Eerdmans, 2003), 22.

Sanneh's definition is less about the academic field than about the nature and process of World Christianity as a movement. Nonetheless, it helps us to understand what scholars of World Christianity must study. By this measure, World Christianity as a field focuses on the study of the beliefs and practices of Christianity in two-thirds of the world. Dale Irvin is even clearer on this point. He states:

> As a field of study, World Christianity has its historical roots in the study missions, ecumenics and world religions. It continues to pursue a three-fold conversation across borders of culture (historically the domain of mission studies), borders of confession and communion (historically the domain of ecumenics) and the borders of religious faiths (historically the domain of world religions). Beyond these, it seeks to engage in other areas of the theological curriculum of the social sciences. . . . World Christianity seeks to foster the study and practice of both local and translocal ways of knowing and doing. It is connected to both the local and global. It is an attempt to broaden the universe of Christian understanding to reflect the open-ended nature of the divine.[37]

This definition captures not just the present but also the past and future of World Christianity. Irvin's hope for a broader sphere of study for the field is obvious here. For much of the field's existence, and even today, scholars of World Christianity have researched based on the unwritten principle of the "West and the rest"—where the West refers to Europe and North America. How can World Christianity accomplish its goal of studying the beliefs and practices of Christian communities worldwide and critique their practices of injustice without othering these communities or appearing to do so? As Irvin points out:

> The study of World Christianity is a prelude to engaged activity. New rationalities and new knowledge are manifest not only on theories and methods but also in practices. Diverse experiences

---

37   Irvin, "What is World Christianity?", 5.

of pastoral care, cultural life, gender identity, healing and sexual orientation are sources of new theological insight and reflection.[38]

The complexity of such an enterprise requires multiple and diverse forms of hermeneutics, theological analyses, and methodological innovation. As of now, World Christianity is yet to fully accomplish this goal. I suggest that as the field seeks to provide, in the words of Irvin, "a three-fold conversation across borders of cultures," scholars must pay attention to two important issues. First is the issue of classification, and second is methodology. By classification, I mean how scholarship is classified as "World Christianity." It is unclear at this point what constitutes the boundaries of the field and who sets those boundaries. In other words, which studies and publications can be considered as World Christianity? Much of the literature which passes as "World Christianity" often focuses heavily on missiology, ecumenism, church history, and new Christian movements to the neglect of works on feminism, theology, social ethics, and other areas of inquiry.[39] This reflects alterity in scholarship.

Since World Christianity seeks to be interdisciplinary, it will need to incorporate more diverse genres and methodological foci into its body of literature and research. This cannot be the sole task of scholars of World Christianity since most academic disciplines continue to adhere to archaic and inflexible methodologies and disciplinary boundaries. However, scholars of World Christianity can explore the use of new methodologies, and teach their students to use them also.

---

38   Ibid., 26.

39   Take, for instance, the works of Mercy Oduyoye and the Circle of Concerned African Women Theologians. While they offer deep theological analyses of African Christianity and its engagement with traditional African cultures and other religions, and with social structures such as patriarchy and poverty, these theologians are infrequently mentioned in syllabi and bibliographies for World Christianity. Similarly, works that deal with ethics and social justice in Africa comparatively gain less attention in World Christianity discussions, such as Jean Marc-Ela, *African Cry* (Eugene, OR: Wipf & Stock, 2005); Marc-Ela, *Faith as an African* (Eugene, OR: Wipf & Stock, 2009); Peter Paris, ed. *Religion and Poverty: Pan-African Perspectives* (Durham: Duke University Press, 2009).

Martha Frederiks and Dorottya Nagy in their edited volume, *World Christianity: Methodological Considerations,* advocate for an approach that has "multiple perspectivity, both in terms of multidisciplinary and in terms of representing a diversity of contexts and viewpoints."[40] Using the variety of chapters of their book as a basis, they propose and discuss five elements that are essential to an approach to World Christianity: context, analytical concepts, methods, sources, and units of analysis. I am particularly concerned with their third element—diverse methodologies. The authors indicate:

> By underscoring the fruitfulness of the multidisciplinarity and interdisciplinarity of a World Christianity approach, the editors urge scholars to step out of their comfort zones and explore new methods, intersecting methods and fields or even create new ones.[41]

I agree with this recommendation. African Christianity needs, among its various methods of study, one that combines principles of Social Ethics with the study of Everyday Religion. This will be extremely helpful in addressing social justice issues in West African Pentecostalism. Social Ethics, as an academic discipline, is an American invention.[42] Inspired by the protestations of social gospelers of the 1880s, including Washington Gladden, Richard Ely, Josiah Strong, George Herron, and Walter Rauschenbusch, it was formed and shaped in the classrooms of institutions such as Harvard University, Andover Seminary, and Chicago Theological Seminary. It concerns itself with issues of the human condition like wealth, poverty, war, peace, and justice and their implications for society.

Everyday Religion is a new area within Religious Studies that seeks to understand the lived religions of persons and groups, particularly

---

40 Martha Frederiks and Dorothya Nagy, "Methodological Considerations: Convergences," in Martha Frederiks and Dorothya Nagy, eds., *World Christianity: Methodological Considerations* (Boston: Brill, 2021), 293.

41 Ibid., 301.

42 On this subject, see Garry Dorrien, *Social Ethics in the Making: Interpreting An American Tradition* (West Sussex: U.K. John Wiley & Sons: 2011), 1.

outside institutional settings and structures. In other words, it privileges individual spiritual experiences and social contexts over fixed categories and statistical equations. According to Nancy Ammerman, one of its foremost proponents, scholars who use this approach for the study of religion are:

> interested in the ways in which nonexperts experience religion. Everyday religion may happen in both private and public life, among the privileged and nonprivileged people. It may have to do with mundane routines, but it may also have to do with the crises and special events that punctuate those routines. We are simply looking for the many ways religion may be interwoven with the lives we have been observing.[43]

A combination of the two approaches will involve the study of ethical issues in the everyday religious practice of persons and institutions, and their implications for the larger society. Practically, this would require methods such as the recording and reporting of personal stories of persons at both the centers and peripheries of various World Christianity contexts, as well as the review and assessment of the social media postings and current activities of religious congregations, ministries, and leaders. This proposed hybrid approach, which is both sociological and anthropological, can use familiar ethnographic tools of research such as interviews, observation, and mapping.

This approach offers scholars three key tools. First, it involves the ability to examine closely and carefully the social and religious lives of persons, especially the marginalized, through their daily experiences and relationships. Second, it offers tools with which to critique the lapses and abuses in/of religious practices and institutions. Third, through this approach, scholars can influence their own disciplines methodologically to discover and critique injustices that often hide in the crannies of lexical and philosophical argumentation.

---

43   Nancy Ammerman, ed., *Everyday Religion: Observing Modern Religious Lives* (New York: Oxford University Press, 2007), 5.

Conclusion

The main goal of this chapter was to highlight the comparably minimal attention paid to social justice issues in World Christianity through the lenses of West African Pentecostalism. Broadly, it sought to address issues of alterity and methodology in World Christianity. Alterity exists in World Christianity in both its practice and its scholarship, as revealed through the beliefs and practices of West African Pentecostalism, and the inadequate scholarly attention given to those who endure abuses and exclusions in such contexts.

World Christianity as a field of study is still under construction. Though currently growing with a vibrant scholarship, the scholarly discourse indicates that the field remains in need of "conceptual clarity and consistency"[44] as well as methodological innovation. I agree with Frederiks's assertion that the Christian communities, beliefs, and practices that constitute the subject matter for World Christianity are part of an "entangled world."[45] Christians are intertwined with and even shaped by the social, economic, cultural, political, historical, and religious realities of their local and global contexts. Approaching Christianity with this understanding involves the study of the numerous and diverse causes and effects, both past and present. Also, the peculiarities of the context and implications for individual and communal lives will need to be considered. This calls for appropriate methodology. I have suggested a methodological approach that combines the principles and practices of Social Ethics and Everyday Religion as a way of probing religious persons and practices within specific contexts. Additionally, this approach will create opportunities for listening to the stories of the "other," and understanding the ecology and cultural geography of the persons, places, and practices under study. With these insights, scholars of World Christianity will be well equipped to shine light on commendable practices and critique excesses such as those identified in West African Pentecostalism.

---

44   Peter Phan, "World Christianity: Its implications for History, Religious Studies and Theology," *Horizons* 39, no. 2 (Fall 2012): 171–88.

45   Frederiks and Nagy, *World Christianity*, 29.

PART 2

FEMINISM, MASCULINITY, AND JUSTICE

CHAPTER 5

CHILD MARRIAGE, THE UNTOLD STORY OF MY MOTHER, AND THE CHURCH IN AFRICA: A FEMINIST ETHICS OF *UBUNTU*

Fulata Lusungu Moyo

NAVIGATING THE WIDE TERRAIN

The Church of Central Africa Presbyterian (CCAP)[1] defines child marriage using the Malawi government's definition as "a marriage in which either one of the parties, or both, is or was a child under the age of 18 at the time of the union."[2] In this chapter, I retell the story of my late mother, Ellina Nchawaka Nyaphakati, as a child marriage survivor, in order to wrestle with

---

1   The roots of the Church of Central Africa Presbyterian can be traced to the Livingstonia Mission of the first Scottish Presbyterian missionaries of the Free Church of Scotland in 1875. From the onset, there was a vision to unite the Nkhoma Mission established by the Dutch Reformed Mission via South Africa and the Church of Scotland's Blantyre Mission. Following the second Anglo-Boer War (1899-1902) in South Africa, it was only in 1924 that Livingstonia and Blantyre Synods joined to form the CCAP. Two years later, in 1926, Nkhoma Synod also joined the CCAP. Due to the presence of Malawian migrants, the CCAP later established the Harare Synod in Zimbabwe and the Zambia Synod that has its congregations in Lusaka, Copperbelt, and Lundazi. Each synod is autonomous in polity, mission, and ministries. Christoff Martin Pauw, *Mission and Church in Malawi: The History of the Nkhoma Synod of the Church of Central Africa, Presbyterian 1889-1962* (Wellington, South Africa: Christian Literature Fund Publishers, 2016).

2   The Malawi Government, "The Marriage, Divorce and Family Act" (Lilongwe: Malawi Government, 2015), 14.

121

questions about the role of the church in Malawi to resist and help end child marriage. Though my mother was not married in the church, she was baptized in and faithfully attended church services at the CCAP[3] in the Synod of Livingstonia, northern Malawi. She held hope that the church's mission to spread the good news of salvation was inclusive of social justice. Yet the CCAP did not address the gender injustices that she experienced or her exploited childhood. I contend that the hope that kept her in the church was the possibility of hearing about the God of Hagar, who sees oppressed women like her and promises justice. As Genesis 16:11, 13 affirms: "the LORD has given heed to your affliction. . . . she named the LORD who spoke to her, 'You are El-roi.'"

Like the biblical woman who was ostracized because of purity laws and had to come behind Jesus and touch the hem of his garment, for my mother, the church was this face of Jesus. Jesus rewarded the unnamed woman's courageous transgression by providing a platform for her voice to be heard, thus restoring her dignity and transitioning her from invisibility to visibility.[4] Likewise, my mother courageously and consistently attended church "from behind doors," although denied full communion because of polygamy. Ellina's story is still the story of many girls and women today.

According to the World Vision 2021 report,[5] Malawi remains heavily burdened with child marriage. Approximately 42 percent of girls marry before the age of eighteen years, and 9 percent marry under fifteen. This means that when my mother Ellina was a child bride, the number of girls marrying under the age of fifteen was much higher. Since it is a challenge within Malawi to find written records for such information, the existing records in other parts of the world can help.

Statistics confirm that child marriage remains today's living reality in every part of the world—cutting across countries, regions, religions, cultures, races, and ethnicities. Rachel B. Vogelstein reiterates that child

---

3   I focus on the response of the CCAP to child marriage because it is my home church as well as that of Ellina whose story shapes this chapter.

4   Isabelle Hamley, *Embracing Justice* (London: SPCK, 2021), 132.

5   Kate Shaw, Tendai Chigavazira, and Tamara Tutnjevic, *COVID-19 and Child Marriage: How COVID-19's Impact on Hunger and Education is Forcing Children into Marriage* (World Vision International October 2021), accessed August 19, 2022, https://tinyurl.com/5a5p5afy.

marriage occurs across boundaries of existing religions. For example, she estimates that 40 percent of Hindu and Muslim marriages in India in 2014 were child marriages, while in Bukina Faso and Ethiopia, this practice was prevalent among Muslims and Christians alike.[6] It is apparent that our world is still built on kyriarchal[7] systems and mindsets that tend to value girls less than boys. As such, within contexts of poverty, insecurity, and limited access to quality education and work opportunities, child marriage is often seen as the best option for vulnerable girls.

Yet the CCAP's claim to holding a holistic approach to the propagation of the gospel should translate into addressing the evils of child marriage. The CCAP historically holds the belief that the gospel and the training of church ministers go hand in hand with the running of hospitals, health care facilities, schools, and colleges, as well as ensuring that people have access to safe water and electricity. In affirmation of this approach, Anne-Lise Quinn argues that:

The Livingstonia Missionaries came to Malawi with a message, both religious and social, that many people found significant and relevant in a rapidly changing world. Over the years the religious communities of the CCAP have, however, imbued the church

6 Rachel Vogelstein, *Ending Child Marriage: How Elevating the Status of Girls Advances U.S. Foreign Policy* (New York/Washington: The Council on Foreign Relations, 2013), 3, 5.

7 By coining "womanist" as "a Black feminist or feminist of color," Alice Walker started the conversation about the intersectionality of oppressive systems that Kimberlé Crenshaw built on, and Elisabeth Schüssler Fiorenza further developed by coining "kyriarchy" from the ancient Greek word for lord/master, *kyrios*. Kyriarchy as a term extends patriarchy to encompass and connect to other structures of oppression and privilege, such as racism, ableism, homophobia, capitalism, and other social markers, in recognition of the intersectionality of oppression into overlapping, traversing, and complicated power dynamics. Alice Walker, *In Search of Our Mothers' Gardens: Womanist Prose* (New York: Harcourt Brace Jovanovic, 1983), xi; Kimberlé Crenshaw, "Demarginalizing the Intersection of Race and Sex: A Black Feminist Critique of Antidiscrimination Doctrine, Feminist Theory and Antiracist Politics," *University of Chicago Legal Forum* 1, no. 8 (1989): 141, 156; Elisabeth Schüssler Fiorenza, *Changing Horizons: Explorations in Feminist Interpretation* (Minneapolis: Fortress Press, 2013), 7.

with many of their own values and practices, thereby making it more meaningful to them as a social and religious institution.[8]

It is with the above conception of *missio ecclesiae* that Girls Not Brides[9] affirms the important role played by religious actors. Their "Theory of Change on Child Marriage" outlines four interlinked strategic pillars. These are:

- Empowering girls with information and skills to be able to exercise their rights;

- Working with families and communities to understand the risks of child marriage and find alternatives for girls;

- Ensuring education, health, child protection, and other services are available for them;

- And creating a supportive legal and policy environment.[10]

To further navigate the church's response to child marriage, in this chapter, I use my mother's marriage to Ncumayo, and later to my father as a case study. The Indigenous wisdom of the Sankofa, the Akan tribes' mythical bird, symbolizes the journey of remembering the past injustices suffered by my mother so as to guide the pursuit of a more just future. Since all of the information about her experience was orally transmitted to me as a story,[11] I have, therefore, created a letter imagined to have been written by Ellina to me less than three months before she died on July 3, 2006.

---

8   Anne-Lise Quinn, "Holding on to Mission Christianity: Case Studies from A Presbyterian Church in Malawi," *Journal of Religion in Africa* XXV (Leiden: E.J. Brill, 1995): 4.

9   Girls Not Brides describes itself as a global partnership with its secretariat based in London, United Kingdom, and working with colleagues based in Mexico City, Mexico; Nairobi, Kenya; and New Delhi, India. See the Girls Not Brides website, accessed August 19, 2022, https://tinyurl.com/y7h7dfa8

10 Girls Not Brides, "Theory of Change," last modified July 9, 2014, https://tinyurl.com/3kuwh8uv.

11 My mother's letter imaginatively written by me uses the information shared by Ellina Nchawaka NyaPhakati during some of the mother–daughter conversations over the years often triggered by my frequent inquisition. An

The following letter contains five parts. First, there are salutations and introductory remarks that explain her reasons for the letter. The second part gives Ellina's background of poverty that forced her to vulnerably succumb to child marriage. The third narrates her experiences of violations in the polygamous relationship. The fourth part focuses on her restoration into the church's full communion and her rise to leadership. Fifth and finally, it talks about turning her woundedness into resources for activism against child marriage.

The Case Study of Ellina Nyaphakati: A Mother's Letter to Her Scholar-Activist Daughter

To my daughter, Fulata Lusungu
*   -You who defied that which our ancestors held as normalcy.*
*   -Yet to be born feet-first at twenty-five weeks and survive is the act*
of God.

I am writing this letter to you today on your forty-fifth birthday, April 27, 2006, not knowing how much time I will have to live after the first stroke left me partially paralyzed. This letter has to be written so that I can help shed more light about my life as your mother, who seemed to hold so many mysteries. Being born in the early 1920s and being molded by the cultural expectations of that time makes even writing this letter difficult. Yet, knowing you, my last-born daughter, and your daring to evoke conversation on "taboo" issues, it is better that I write rather than suffer the embarrassment of trying to have a face-to-face conversation with you.

I remember that in 2005, you asked me some culturally difficult questions as part of your research concerning girls' socialization into gender and sexuality roles through the rites of passage. I am still trying to wrap these concepts around my head. After getting over my shock at some of your questions, I realized that if I did not share my experiences with

---

earlier version appeared in Fulata Lusungu Moyo, "Called to Lament Injustice and Prophesy Equality, Justice, Peace and Healing for All – Honoring Rev Dr. Nyambura Njproge," in *That All May Live: Essays in Honour of Nyambura J. Njoroge*, ed. Ezra Chitando, Esther Mombo, and Masiiwa Ragies Gunda (Bamberg: University of Bamberg Press, 2021), 47–57.

you, then those missing parts of my story would obliterate some crucial pieces of what has shaped me as your mother. So, this letter is my attempt to answer those questions that I avoided at that time.

Why did I marry at such a young age, and to a much older man? As a Presbyterian Christian who knew the stance of the church against polygamy, why did I still choose to marry your already-polygamous father? I was "raised" by my old grandmother because my mother had to raise younger children in another village away from my brother Godfrey and me. Like many men of his age, my father erroneously believed that going to work in the South African mines was the only way to alleviate our poverty. When he stopped communicating with my mother, and his intermittent financial support also stopped, his family believed that he was dead. So, after observing a period of mourning, the family arranged a widowhood inheritance for my mother as their traditional way of caring for young widows.

My mother moved to the Mhangos, inherited by one of my father's cousins. My older brother and I remained in the village with my father's mother. I lost my childhood as I instantly became a responsible "unpaid maid" for my brother and my very old grandmother, who needed a great deal of care. It was a very difficult life with no playtime. So, when at around thirteen years of age,[12] I met a seventeen-year-old boy, Ncumayo, who told me that he loved me, I did not hesitate to elope with him and went to live with him.

After some months of bliss, like my father, Ncumayo also decided to go to South Africa to improve our livelihood. My attempt to convince him otherwise fell on deaf ears. I saw the same stubbornness in my father. Meanwhile, soon after Ncumayo left for the city of gold, Johannesburg, his uncle started abusing me by yelling insults at me. I tried to endure in anticipation of my husband's return, but as months went on and his letters stopped coming, I lost any anchor of hope and I left Ncumayo's home.

My brother felt scandalized by my deserting my marriage and punished me by battering and hurling insults at me for causing family dishonor.

---

12   My mother's ages are mainly based on estimates, an attempt to reconstruct such ages from her narrative to me. It is more likely that she was eleven or twelve when she eloped with Ncumayo, although in my previous written account, I described her as being thirteen years old. Moyo, "Called to Lament Injustice," 53.

I strongly considered going back to my marriage because, in retrospect, I could endure verbal violence much easier than the combination of physical and mental abuse. But I received the sad news that Ncumayo had killed himself. I was heartbroken. I still do not know what caused his death. Was it my leaving?

Then your father, who was a postmaster general for Mzimba District Post Office Services, started courting me. I tried to resist him, but the daily abuse by my brother and the bleakness of my future made me revalue my options. Marrying your father was more dignity-enhancing than remaining at the mercy of my abusive brother. So, I eventually accepted your father's hand in marriage. I was about fifteen, and he was about thirty-nine or so years old when we married under the customary law in 1936 or 1937.[13] He had told me about his two wives, even though his first wife was no longer living with him because of a severe case of postpartum depression. She died soon after our marriage.

One reason your father used to justify his polygamy was his need for male children. Until then, his first and second wives had only daughters. So, when I conceived, I hoped it was a boy. Your father was a very caring and peace-loving man. I heard of husbands that were violent to their families, but my husband was different, even to my co-wife and his two daughters.

Meanwhile, as a pregnant teenager, I did not know the biology of my body or what to expect. So, in my ninth month, when my co-wife, Nyajele, sent a woman to "help," in desperation to know, I believed her and obeyed every instruction. She asked me to nakedly sit on my husband's shirt that she rolled into a coil. Then she started pressing fiercely hard around my belly while shushing me not to scream from the pain she caused. I was drenched in pain and unavoidable screams escaped as tears uncontrollably flowed because of the racking pain.

Soon after the woman left, the continued spasms of pain that I later learned were part of labor pains led to a still birth of my first-born son. My co-wife had the audacity to accuse me of childishly killing my son. Out of anger, your father threatened to kill me for irresponsibly killing his only son. He was so angry that he left me alone at his village away from his duty station.

I lived alone in my husband's village until 1940, when he came and took me back. From a total of eleven pregnancies, five girls and only one boy survived. I was already in my early forties, and your father

---

13   Ibid.

was a sixty-five-year-old retiree when you were born. Your birth defied all odds. Considering our ages, your father and I did not expect to have another baby. Yet, surprisingly, I conceived. When I was about twenty-five weeks pregnant, your father angrily battered me, accusing me of producing only one boy and probably carrying another girl. In retrospect, I understand that his peers were laughing at him for wastefully investing in the education of girls—knowing well that in the isiNgoni patrilineal system, his daughters' education would benefit those they would marry.

Soon after this pummeling, I prematurely delivered a tiny bundle that came out feet-first, weighing less than a kilo. You, Fulata, smoothly came out without endangering my life, contrary to the usual dangers of breech birth. The traditional midwife who helped me deliver at home cautioned me not to get attached to this preemie, who would not survive beyond two weeks after birth. After two weeks, however, I went into a rhythm of motherhood of such an extraordinarily tiny baby. Your brother, Zondiwe, and your sister, Fanny, were still around to experience your zest for life. The rest of your sisters were away: Linley was already married, Patricia was going to university, and Irene was at secondary school.

Meanwhile, I also received the news that my father was actually alive and had returned from South Africa. I was so angry with him that I didn't want to even see or talk to him. What a stubborn man who had sacrificed the welfare of our whole family for nothing! Evidently, he was deported in dire poverty by the South African government. We do not know what happened to his resources after working for such a long time. Did he have a South African family? Or was he a victim of the TEBA[14] agreement's unfulfilled promises? I am clueless.

It is true that both my elopement at thirteen years of age and my marriage to your father are unacceptable to the CCAP canon. I have explained the desperation that led to such choices. As you also know, your father went ahead and married two more wives after me: your stepmother, Nyachavula, soon after your sister Linley was born. Nyachavula gave birth to two daughters. As you recall, your father married your last stepmother, Nyakhowoya, in his seventies, and she was already menopausal.

---

14   TEBA, "TEBA'S Perspective on Lesotho's Labour Migration," last updated June 18, 2015, https://tinyurl.com/cntkcz3y.

Unlike me, your father resolved his church membership by founding a branch of the African Abraham Church, which accepted polygamy. I often hoped that the CCAP leadership would accept me back on the basis of my faithfully participating in the life of the church. Yet this happened only after Anyajele died, and I was "elevated" as my husband's first wife. After the ritual of **Chiwera** (Restoration), I was accepted back into the church's full communion. Thus, I joined the **Umanyano** (women's guild), became a deacon, and soon became an elder and could influence church decisions.

I became preoccupied with the exercise of scrutinizing the ages of girls who were getting married, insisting for a minimum of eighteen years of age for marriage. While **Umanyano** space remained closed to conversations around gender-based violence, it was not easy to convince parents and communities against child marriage, especially if it was connected to livelihood and survival.

So, my dear daughter, with this letter, I am passing the baton onto you—to dare the church to be in the forefront of resisting, challenging, and ending child marriage. I know you are already doing something about this, but even more can be done, especially with all the resources you have in education, networks, and experience. Mobilize others to help build a movement that resists the sacralizing of gender-based violence! I am counting on you, Fulata, and I am full of love, faith, and hope. God bless you, my daughter.

Your Amama.

THE FEMINIST ETHICS OF UBUNTU: THE CASE STUDY AND THE CHURCH'S RESPONSE

I use feminist ethics of *ubuntu* (FEU)[15] to analyze my mother's experience in exploration of the church's response, or lack thereof. FEU, as a theoretical

---

15   Unlike D. Hall, Dirk Louw, and Louise Du Toit, who argue for a feminist ethics of care and *ubuntu*, I insist on feminist ethics of *ubuntu* because to say "care and *ubuntu*" or "feminist ethics and care" is unnecessarily redundant and therefore tautological. To have *ubuntu* is to care, just as ethics of care is actually a feminist approach to ethics. Laura D'Olimpio, "Ethics Explainer: Ethics of Care," last updated May 16, 2019, https://tinyurl.com/22bjcmxx; D. Hall, Dirk Louw, and Louise Du Toit, "Feminist Ethics of Care and Ubuntu," *Obstetrics & Gynecology Forum* (February 2013): 29–33; Ramathate Dolamo, "Botho/Ubuntu: The Heart of

framework that helps analyze my mother's story, is my contextualization of feminist ethics of care in the Malawian communitarian ethos in which my mother's story is situated. This framing is theologically and epistemologically necessary so as to establish the relevance and meaning of my mother's story as an example that exposed the church's indifference to child marriage back then. As an African theologian, I agree with Ramathate Dolamo's argument that the notion of *ubuntu* promotes communal relations and interaction between individuals and their respective communities as an expression of their spirituality of being interconnected and interdependent.[16] Like Sinentlanhla Sithulisiwe Chisale,[17] I reiterate that *ubuntu* in its very essence promotes equality and justice, as people are not defined according to social markers of gender, race, class, age, different abilities, or any other category. They have a personhood as moral agents, as well as dignity as *imago Dei*. Therefore, it can be argued that at the onset, FEU offers a critique of kyriarchal biases that privilege male and Western approaches that emphasize individualism and abstract theorizing. Instead, by accenting the African's preference of relationship, experience, and community, FEU situates the church as a fellowship of activists and doers of justice, merciful accompaniers of survivors of injustice, and God's vessels for the transformation of the world. Therefore, examining Ellina's letter using FEU brings out three areas of analysis to the conversation on the church's response to child marriage:

- The critical study of why poverty in the community remains a bedfellow of child marriage.

- The exploration of the church as a safe space for engaging with the voices of the survivors of child marriage for their resilience and healing.

- The clarion call to the church to enable and support the movement of desacralizing child marriage as gender-based violence.

African Ethics," *Scriptura* 112 (2013): 1; Sinenhlanhla Sithulisiwe Chisale, "Politics of the Body, Fear and Ubuntu: Proposing an African Women's Theology of Disability," *HTS Teologiese Studies/Theological Studies* 76, no. 3 (August 2020): 1-10 (2).

16   Ramathate Dolamo, "Botho/Ubuntu: The Heart of African Ethics," *Scriptura* 112 (2013): 1.

17   Chisale, "Politics of the Body," 2.

CCAP, Poverty, Orality, and Child Marriage

The 2018 marriage audit by the CCAP's Nkhoma Synod confirms that there are still no formal procedures for age verification. Unfortunately, the rural communities' birth records are still often transmitted only orally. Even for those birth records from formal health care facilities, only a few are kept safely by families. Furthermore, this mapping exercise indicated that age cheating by the couples is very high and contributes to child marriages being officiated in the church. If anything, this suggests that child marriages may be far more prevalent within the church than currently recognized. As one minister in the Malembo Presbytery explained:

> We mostly rely on the information provided by the bride and the groom and their relations, which is documented by the church elder of the area from where the couple is coming from. We do not have any sophisticated age verification strategy, except checking their faces if their appearance is in line with the recorded age. For example, last year, I blessed the marriage which indicated that the bride's age was 19, but after one week, we realized that her actual age was 16.[18]

The Very Reverend Dr. Timothy P. K. Nyasulu[19] affirms the above. Regrettably, for both synods, the crucial burden of determining the age of the couple still rests on the shoulders of the marriage-officiating clergy who must orally scrutinize the couple before admitting them to take their marital vows. So even the CCAP's vouched-for holistic approach to mission as inclusive of addressing child marriage can remain fragile if this crucial

---

18   Malawi Interfaith Aids Association (MIAA), *Mapping of Marriages Officiated in Nkhoma Synod Congregations* (Lilongwe: MIAA/CCAP Nkhoma Synod, 2018), 30.

19   Associate Professor Rev. Dr. Timothy P. K. Nyasulu is a former Moderator of the CCAP General Assembly (Livingstonia, Blantyre, Nkhoma, Zambia, and Harare Synods), so his input into this essay is very critical since he carries the voice that has overall authority when it comes to CCAP polity and policies. Interviewed virtually by the author, February 2, 2022.

age validation stays at the mercy and integrity of the marriage-officiating clergy. This problem will continue unless the CCAP contextualizes the *National Strategy on Ending Child Marriage (2018–2023)* and translates its following objectives into implementable activities. Such projects would not only become the concern of the developmental arms of the synods but would also become mainstreamed into all ministries of teaching, preaching, and leadership development of clergy and laity. The following are the NSECM objectives:

- To facilitate a positive change in the cultural norms, attitudes, behavior, beliefs, and practices that support and promote child marriage

- To increase access to quality, equitable and relevant education

- To improve access to comprehensive sexuality education and SRH information and services for adolescent girls and boys

- To strengthen the incomes of girls, families, and communities with the provision of economic and other livelihood opportunities for the benefit of girls and their families

- To foster an enabling legal and policy framework which is fully enforced to end child marriage

- To strengthen multisectoral implementation and coordination mechanisms and monitoring and evaluation structures for ending child marriage[20]

The above objectives contextualize resonantly with the four inter-linked strategies in the Girls Not Brides's theory of change, and can also be traced in the two synods' Child Protection Policies. Ironically, child marriage is not mentioned in either policy as an example of gender-based violence. Meanwhile, it is the Nkhoma Synod's *Mapping of Marriages Officiated in Nkhoma Synod Congregation Report* that becomes the key

---

20   MIAA, *Mapping of Marriages*, 18.

document addressing child marriage in the CCAP. The Child Protection Policies' commitments, however, remain essential to this conversation. Below are the seven commitments from the CCAP Synod of Livingstonia's Child Protection Policy:

- Valuing, respecting, and listening to children.

- Prohibiting all staff from engaging in child abuse, exploitation, or neglect.

- Ensuring child-safe screening procedures when hiring staff, particularly those whose work brings them into direct contact with children.

- Maintaining strong child protection systems and procedures for staff.

- Training its staff and providing a common understanding of child protection issues to inform planning and practice.

- Investigating, responding, and reporting suspected allegations of child abuse, exploitation, or neglect perpetrated by personnel.

- Providing adequate and appropriate resources to implement this policy and ensure that it is communicated and understood.[21]

Rev. Nyasulu clarified that the Livingstonia Synod AIDS Programme had to finalize the Child Protection Policy in 2021 because many organizations were demanding a written child protection policy. He reiterated that:

In the church the process was rigorous in the sense that for the pastor to allow the marriage to take place in church, the two (the

---

21   CCAP Synod of Livingstonia, *Child Protection Policy* (Mzuzu: Synod of Livingstonia, 2020), 6.

boy[22] and the girl) had to meet the pastor and announce their intentions. Then the pastor would discuss with them, their parents and sometimes even the teachers if they are a school going age, so as to determine if they have completed school. The pastor has to also determine that lobola [so-called 'bride price' decided by the family of the bride-to-be and settled by the family of the groom-to-be] and other formal traditional processes have been respected. Then the pastor can commence the marital counselling either at a church or at the pastor's home, before the publication of bans are announced at the congregation, so as to give the community a chance to respond in case there are impediments to the process. If there are objections based on age or other factors, then the marriage will not take place in the church. This ensures that the church does not work alone. It is likely that during the time when your mother was married, 15 years was regarded a good age for girls to get married. But since then, times have changed and 15 years of age is no longer allowed as an acceptable age for marriage.[23]

Both synods attest to the above marriage preparations aimed at equipping couples holistically so that they are well informed about their roles and responsibilities in marriage. While this process seems to put the onus of ensuring marriage preparation in the sole hands of one officiating clergy, it is assuring to find the following established procedures in the synod aimed at providing a more systemic verification of the couple's ages:

1. They must have attended and reached the Confirmation Class (*Kalasi ya Usonyezo*) which confirms that they are full members of the church;

---

22   According to Rev. Nyasulu, in the popular traditions in northern Malawi, a boy becomes a man after marriage, and while a girl is admitted to adulthood after the puberty rites, she also ceases to be a girl after marriage. Unlike central Malawi, where the aChewa communities have elaborate puberty rites of passage, in northern Malawi, such elaboration is not commonly known. Rev. Nyasulu, interviewed virtually by the author, March 15, 2022.

23   Rev. Dr Nyasulu, interviewed virtually by the author, March 15, 2022.

2.   They must have attended Counseling Sessions (*Chilangizo*);

3.   They must have attended sessions for those in courtship (*Maphunziro a opalidwa ubwenzi*).[24]

While such ecclesial efforts are important, without addressing certain existing contextual realities, these efforts fail to drive lasting change. Apart from other harmful cultural practices, like the prioritizing of boys in education, poverty and lack of economic opportunities are identified as key drivers of child marriages. According to Maria Harti, in rural areas where poverty, traditions, and lack of infrastructure and services prevail, girls live in situations of deep vulnerability and are exposed to situations of systematic discrimination based on age, social status, education, and health.[25] The Malawi government affirms the connectedness of child marriage and economic factors thus: "poor families and even girls themselves from such poor households may consider child marriage as a strategy for reducing their economic stress and poverty."[26]

In my mother's experience, poverty was the push factor that made her opt for child marriage, apart from the added gender-based violence at the hands of her brother. Although her letter makes it clear that her act of "deserting" her first marriage was viewed by her brother (and probably the rest of the "extended" family) as an act of family dishonor, one is left wondering whether that childhood elopement was also considered an act of family dishonor but silently accepted as the best rescue strategy from poverty.

In her desperation to escape poverty and other hardships, Ellina dared to elope with a fellow teenager, and afterward, she went into a more church-communion-breaching union with my polygamous father. What

---

24   MIAA, *Mapping of Marriages*, vii.

25   Maria Harti, "Reducing Vulnerability of the Girl Child in Poor Rural Areas: Activities of the International Fund for Agricultural Development" (report for the UNICEF Innocenti Research Center, Florence, Italy, September 25–28, 2006), 3.

26   Malawi Government, *National Strategy on Ending Child Marriage, 2018-2023* (Lilongwe: Ministry of Gender, Children, Disability and Social Welfare; UNFPA & Plan Malawi, 2018), 15.

the church did not provide after restoring her into full communion was the process of accompaniment toward healing from her traumatic memories borne of these hardships. The church shallowly understood her salvation as restoration to full communion, without the consideration to address the impact of her suffering.

Rev. Nyasulu[27] reminded me that the fact that my fifteen-year-old mother married my polygamous father outside the church meant that the CCAP Livingstonia Synod could not have influenced such a decision, even if the church had already established rhetoric against child marriage. It is also important to reiterate that in contexts of utter desperation, the affected families can manipulate information to trap even those churches with clear anti-child marriage policies into sacralizing child marriage.

In addition to my mother's own activism against child marriage, and the story of Livingstonia Synod's commitment as shared by Rev. Nyasulu, elements of gender justice, especially regarding women's leadership in the church, can be dated to the period of the CCAP's foundations. T. Jack Thompson's research affirms that Livingstonia Synod was a pioneer in ordaining women elders as early as 1922, even before the Church of Scotland (its mother church) dared such a step.[28] Yet inexplicably, its sister synod, Nkhoma, does not yet ordain women elders.

THE CHURCH AS SAFE SPACE OF ACCOMPANIMENT FOR RESILIENCE AND HEALING

In line with the feminist ethics of *ubuntu*, the process of accompaniment of survivors of child marriage would involve the availability of safe spaces where survivors' voices are prioritized as critical to the process of building resilience and healing. However, the clear exclusion of survivors' voices in the mapping of marriages officiated by Nkhoma Synod's congregations could easily be an expression of the ongoing stigmatization of women's

---

27 Rev. Timothy Nyasulu, interviewed virtually by author, March 17, 2022.

28 T. Jack Thompson, *Christianity in Northern Malawi: Donald Fraser's Missionary Methods and Ngoni Culture* (Leiden: E. J. Brill, Studies in Christian Mission, 1995), xvi.

experiences of gender-based violence, which is also connected with the church's general conspiracy of silence around sexuality. Moreover, when it comes to sexual violations and abuse of women and girls in Malawi, the tendency still is to blame the victim. Questions like the following are still echoed among community members: Where was she? What was she wearing?[29] So this acknowledgment of the problem in the mapping of marriages report could be just an excuse, rather than admitting that the church has not yet provided safe spaces for such voices to be heard. Instead, it is acknowledged that there was:

> Inability to interview individuals who are/were in child marriage . . . Due to the sensitivity of the issue, the research team was asked to make prior arrangements with the congregations if it was to interview this group of people. However, due to time and resource constraints, these arrangements were not made. Therefore, the views of the people who are involved in child marriage themselves have not been incorporated in this report.[30]

The neglect described above is a serious aberration for the church that is to be a community of doers of justice for all. The decision to do justice has within it the courageous intentionality of acknowledging the injustice, as well as building knowledge by listening to the stories of survivors of such injustice so as to incorporate their ideas in shaping justice. Otherwise, by excluding such voices, the church is in turn protecting the perpetrators of child marriage that such voices might expose. This might mean that, in essence, the CCAP is, in this twenty-first century, still covering up for the perpetrators of child marriage. This is the same old story, reflected even in the biblical narrative found in John 8:1–11, where the woman is blamed and exposed, while the male perpetrator is protected and made invisible. I often wonder what the scribes and Pharisees who brought this woman for Jesus to judge meant when

---

29   Fulata Lusungu Moyo, "A Quest for Women's Sexual Empowerment through Education in an HIV and AIDS Context: The Case of Kukhonzekera Chinkhoswe caChikhristu (KCC) among Amang'anja and Ayao Christians of T/A Mwambo in Rural Zomba, Malawi" (PhD diss., University of KwaZulu-Natal, South Africa, 2009), 13–14.

30   MIAA, *Mapping of Marriages*, 13.

they argued: "Teacher, this woman was caught in *the very act of committing adultery*." But they brought *only* the woman and not the lover!

The use of FEU that ascertains the equality and justice of every member—as with personhood and dignity—makes the above mapping exercise lose its essence and relevance. By silencing or trivializing the survivors' voices, the mapping became unjustly incomplete. Not only has it protected the perpetrators but it has also sustained the obsolete slogan by presenting the privileged monopolizing decision-makers as the "voice of the voiceless." No one is voiceless, but we know that tables of decision-making can be so monopolized by those in power that certain voices are un/intentionally silenced by exclusion. This oversight is a clear indicator that the church is not ready to shift its theology to holistically resist the evil caused by child marriage. For until there is readiness to be confronted by the voices of survivors in order to shape the processes of justice and healing, the church cannot effectively oppose and end these cycles of child marriage.

In her study of similar suffering in a Latin American context, Nancy Pineda-Madrid underscores the importance of the presence of the survivors' stories of injustice and violence for effective action for justice. She argues for a Christian understanding of salvation that encompasses resistance of evil. She quotes the Belgian Catholic theologian Edward Schillebeeckx, who argued that the task of theology should safeguard a belief in the hope of a liberating and caring power that, according to Pineda-Madrid, loves women and men, and thus empowers them to work toward overcoming social evils.[31] She asserts that the incapacitating effect of the overwhelmingly strong presence of evil can give the understanding that such evil is unchangeable, and consequently evoke a temptation for communities "to continue to gaze voyeuristically in disbelief upon the evil."[32] In my mother's story, her choice of staying married to my father, even after the two incidents of gender-based violence, could speak to this paralyzing fear of irreversibility of evil. Therefore, the silence of the church signifies that its theology and understanding of *missio ecclesiae* was not as daring and

---

31 Nancy Pineda-Madrid, *Salvation and Suffering in Ciudad Juárez* (Philadelphia: Fortress Press, 2011), 97.

32 Ibid.

holistic as the CCAP claims. For our faith as the church should open us to the sensibilities of the "victimized"/survivors, whether still alive or dead, so that their experiences and the remembrance of their stories command our attention to act. The four elements of the practice of resistance that Pineda-Madrid identifies articulate what the CCAP commitment to resisting child marriage should also involve. These include:

1. Claiming a space so as to enable the suffering to be present;

2. Ensuring that the presence of suffering is not allowed to be all consuming in the community;

3. Protecting the claimed space so that the victimized are enabled to be released from their experience of evil;

4. Providing the accompaniment so that the survivors can know the healing experience of God's saving presence—the social dimension of salvation.[33]

In my mother's letter above, it is clear that the CCAP did not create a space where girls' stories of their suffering could be shared or memorialized. Neither were religious symbols like the cross intentionally used to make visible to their community the existence of such suffering. In 2005 when I was finalizing my ethnographic PhD research, I carried out a contextual Bible study with twenty-six women in church leadership positions using 2 Samuel 13:1–22 about the rape of Tamar by her stepbrother Amnon. I asked, "How many of you have heard a passage like this preached or used in a church context?" None raised a hand. Everyone who spoke was surprised that such a story was in the Bible.[34]

Moreover, even the women-claimed spaces in the church, like that of *Umanyano* (the women's guild), have not been inviting spaces for such stories. Even after my mother's *Umanyano* days, it has remained a coopted space for kyriarchal essentialization of a Christian woman as a submissive wife who suffers silently with dignity.

---

33   Ibid., 98.

34   Moyo, "A Quest for Women's Sexual Empowerment," 24–25.

The Church's Influence and The Movement of Resistance

Since my mother's lifetime, the absence of spaces for sharing narratives of suffering has meant that no movements for resisting such injustices are built with the participation and support of the church—especially since religion[35] remains the greatest influence of Malawian community life. This means that working with religious leaders to combat child marriage is an imperative strategy that can ensure an effective and sustainable impact. The religious leaders as spiritual guides are among the most respected figureheads in Malawian communities. They can play critical roles in changing existing norms, and be key allies in the building of movements of resistance and ending child marriage. They can:

- Refuse to perform child marriages;

- Seek training to build their own capacity and boost their ability to reflect on solutions;

- Raise awareness of the harmful consequences of child marriage through preaching and teaching against it;

- Make public statements and commitments in advocacy against child marriage;

- Collaborate with development actors in boosting girls' education and girls' empowerment.

This awareness raising and capacity building should start within the church, especially in the youth, women's, and men's ministries. Otherwise, young girls and women will still be socialized by older women to sacrifice their good for the good of everyone else, especially that of men. These women use biblical texts like Ephesians 5:22–33 and Proverbs

---

35   The 2018 Housing Census estimates 77.3 percent of the 17.6 million Malawians as Christian, and 13.8 percent as Muslim. National Statistics Office, *2018 Malawi Population and Housing Census: Main Report* (Zomba: National Statistics Office, May 2019), 19, accessed August 24, 2022, https://tinyurl.com/54s8hhkj.

31:10–31 to emphasize the understanding in support of stereotypical gender roles.

ALUTA CONTINUA

It is important to acknowledge the present efforts of the church to limit vulnerability to child marriage, especially as documented by the developed Child Protection Policies. Yet, the reality that child marriage still happens in the church has become an emergency, making it urgent for the church to review the epistemological conception of its holistic mission. My mother's story and the church's acknowledgment of the existing loopholes around determining the real ages at which the couples are married by the church show that the church must, with intentionality, devise a more holistic response that embraces education, health care, and community advocacy and involvement so that the existing loopholes that jeopardize the current responses are effectively remedied. Clearly, written policies are important, but they need to be translated into more accessible communication that includes ongoing sermons, skits, songs, poetry, artistic images, and advocacy messaging using radio programs and other electronic media communication. Otherwise, such policies remain only for the benefit of researchers, and for accountability to funding partners.

As child marriage is an important part of the social evil that the church is actively resisting, procedures for age verification must be formalized. As the church carries out its ministry of healing and wholeness, there is a pressing need for the creation of safe spaces of grace, also in the women's guild, that welcome survivors to share their stories in nonjudgmental contexts. And with appropriate accompaniment, survivors can then create their theologies of hope, recapture the meaning of their lives, and freely participate in sacramental life that enables them to embrace body, soul, and spirit in the mystery of wholeness. As such, this chapter is a clarion call to the church to intensify its desacralizing response to child marriage.

CHAPTER 6

RETHINKING THE SHAMANISTIC CONCEPT OF *HAN-PU-RI* IN KOREAN FEMINIST THEOLOGY

Sun Yong Lee

INTRODUCTION

Korean Shamanism, or *Musok* (*Mukyo*) in Korean,[1] is an Indigenous belief and a religious phenomenon practiced and transmitted by shamans (*mudang*).[2] The shaman functions as a mediator between humans and

---

1   The author would like to express her sincere gratitude and appreciation to the following persons: Deanna Ferree Womack and Raimundo César Barreto Jr., the editors of this volume, for their valuable guidance and suggestions for this chapter; Richard Fox Young and Chloë Starr, for their criticisms and insights, which have encouraged her to pursue the study. Korean words in the texts are rendered in the McCune-Reischauer system. Korean names follow the standard order of surname followed by the given name in the text, unless a name is used in the Western order elsewhere. All translations of Korean texts are mine.

 While shamanism is a general term describing religious practices centering on shamans, Korean Shamanism is capitalized to indicate specific reference to the kind of shamanism practiced in the Korean peninsula. Its Korean titles, "*musok*" or "*mukyo*," are used interchangeably. Tae-gon Kim and Tongshik Ryu, "Musok," *Encyclopedia of Korean Folk Culture*, accessed October 29, 2021, https://tinyurl.com/yc474dmm.

2   Here, I use the word shaman without capitalization as an inclusive term, primarily referring to female shamans. Although *mudang* means female shaman in the Korean language, it is often used as an inclusive term for both male and female shamans. Female or male descriptions of a shaman are used only when

143

gods through rites called *kut*.[3] When it comes to conversations about the relationship between Christianity and Korean Shamanism, the Seventh Assembly of the World Council of Churches (WCC) in Canberra in 1991 colors the discourse. That year's theme was "Come, Holy Spirit - Renew the Whole Creation." Hyun Kyung Chung, a Korean feminist theologian, gave a keynote address in the form of a ritual. With the sound of drums, Chung appeared on the stage, dressed in a white Korean traditional dress, holding a scroll of paper. Reading from the scroll, she "invoked the spirits of women and men oppressed through the ages," and concluded by calling the "spirit of the Liberator, our brother Jesus." Finally, she burned the paper into ashes.[4] The ritual resembled a *kut* in Korean Shamanism. Chung called her performance a *"ch'ohonje,"* a soul summoning ritual known as a rite to appease the souls who have died with unresolved sadness and suffering, known as *han*.[5]

---

gender needs to be specified. For the ancient origin of Korean Shamanism, see chapter 7 in Sarah Milledge Nelson, *Shamanism and the Origin of States: Spirit, Power, and Gender in East Asia* (Walnut Creek, CA: Left Coast Press, 2008).

3   *Kuts* are various in terms of their kinds, objects, functions, and structures. According to Ryu Tongshik, three main patterns of *kut* include "Prayers for blessings," "Rites for Remedy of Diseases," and "Rites for the Soul of the Dead." This chapter focuses on the *kut* for the Soul of the Dead. Tongshik, Ryu, *The History and Structure of Korean Shamanism*, translated by Jeong-il Moon (Seoul: Yonsei University Press, 2012), 317–22.

4   Steinfels vividly described her performance: "Amid the sound of gongs, drums, and clapsticks, the 34-year-old churchwoman was joined onstage by young Korean dancers wearing white like herself and two Australian aborigines in loincloths and body paint. . . . Reading from a rice-paper scroll, Dr. Chung invoked the spirits of women and men oppressed through the ages. 'Come,' she began, 'spirit of Hagar, Egyptian, black slave woman exploited and abandoned by Abraham and Sarah, the ancestors of our faith.' 'Come,' she eventually concluded, 'spirit of the Liberator, our brother Jesus.' . . . Then, deftly rolling the scroll into a cone, she set it aflame and let the ashes drift into the air." Peter Steinfels, "Clash at Canberra: A Feminist Radical's Keynote Renews an Ancient Debate on Christian Diversity," *New York Times*, March 16, 1991, sec. 1.

5   *Han* is a collective emotion of anger and sadness that is distinctive in Korean culture and in Korean people's minds. See footnote 28 and Hellena Moon,

Chung's *ch'ohonje* caused a firestorm. Her keynote ended with a standing ovation from the participants. Theologians highlighted Chung's presentation as a powerful way to evoke interreligious and intercultural conversations, and shed light on Korean women's presence in the Korean religious landscape.[6] However, Korean Protestant churches, mainly evangelical churches such as the Presbyterian Church in Korea (Koshin),[7] strongly criticized Chung's performance as "uncritical syncretism."[8] Some participants left the ceremony during the ritual, and some criticized her for performing a "shaman (*mudang*) practice" at a Christian gathering.[9] Some even threatened to withdraw membership from the Council.[10] A Korean minister recounted the scene in a media interview as "too much to tolerate," and a Korean scholar described Chung's address as "crossing the line,"[11]

"Genealogy of the Modern Theological Understanding of Han," *Pastoral psychology* 63, no. 4 (August 2014): 420.

6 Volker Küster, *A Protestant Theology of Passion: Korean Minjung Theology Revisited*, Studies in Systematic Theology, vol. 4 (Boston: Brill, 2010), 103–5.

7 The term "evangelical" is a contested category. Here, the term is used in a minimal way, referring to Christians who share the conviction about salvation through Jesus Christ and reject the idea of salvation outside the church. Along with Korean evangelical Protestant churches, the Eastern Orthodox Church also strongly reacted against Chung's presentation in Canberra. For a sketch of the responses to Chung's keynote speech, see Volker Küster, *Theology of Passion*, 103–5.

8 In this discussion, the word "syncretism" was used in a judgmental way to criticize the amalgamation of different religious traditions as being tainted. On the concept of syncretism, see Hans G. Kippenberg, "In Praise of Syncretism: The Beginning of Christianity Conceived in the Light of a Diagnosis of Modern Culture," in *Syncretism in Religion: A Reader*, ed. A. M. Leopold and J. S. Jensen (London: Equinox, 2004), 29–38.

9 Hyŏnju Yi, "Ch'ohonje ihu WCC ohiryŏ t'rpokŭmjuŭit'ro hoegwi (WCC Returns to Evangelicalism after the Ch'ohonje," *igoodnews.net*, May 28, 2013, https://tinyurl.com/24df8jsh.

10 Pui-lan Kwok, "Interfaith Dialogue from the Perspective of Feminist Theology in the Multireligious and Multicultural Context of Asia," in *Women and Christianity*, ed. Pui-lan Kwok, vol. 3 (London: Routledge, 2010), 234.

11 Here, theologian Park Sungwon draws upon the WCC's Guidelines on Dialogues with People of Living Faiths and Ideologies. Park states, "The WCC guidelines on interreligious dialogues warn us to be careful 'in attempting to

widening the gap between those who welcomed Chung's ritual and those who were against it.

The controversy is ongoing in Korean churches today, but without much progress in terms of narrowing the gap between these divergent views. In 2021 the Ecumenical Committee of the Presbyterian Church of Korea (PCK, Tonghap) published a booklet titled "Gospel and Ecumenical Faith: The Root and Identity of PCK," explaining PCK's approach to the ecumenical movement, especially the church's involvement in the WCC. This publication includes a Q&A section on misunderstandings related to the WCC and a question that reads, "Is it true that a *ch'ohonje* was offered in the WCC meeting?" In the answer, the author acknowledges the controversy caused by Chung's performance and briefly explains the theological themes surrounding the controversy, such as syncretism. But he concludes by drawing the line, saying that "the *ch'ohonje* performance was her own and her act does not represent the WCC's official position."[12] This answer was a carbon copy of the WCC's position on Chung's presentation, at least since 2013,[13] implying that the same question has been asked and answered in the same way for over a decade.

This chapter acknowledges the long-lasting impact of the controversy over Chung's keynote address in Canberra. Rather than focusing on the

---

"translate" the Christian message for a cultural setting or in approaches to faiths and ideologies with which Christians are in dialogue partnership, as they may go too far and compromise the authenticity of Christian faith and life.' And Chung's shamanistic *ch'ohonje* crossed the line." Hyungki Yi and Sung-won Park, "Chŏnghyŏn'gyŏng kyosuŭi k'aenbŏra ch'onghoejuje kangyŏne taehayŏ (Regarding Hyun Kyung Chung's Keynote at the Canberra Assembly)," *Han'gukkidokkongbo*, August 30, 2013, https://tinyurl.com/2p93uh5e.

12   Byung-joon Chung, "Segyegyohoehyŏpŭihoee taehan ohaewa chinsil (Q&A) WCC (Misunderstandings and truths about the WCC)," in *Pokŭmgwa Ek'yumenik'al Shinang: Taehanyesugyojangnohoe (PCK) Ŭi Ppuriwa Chŏngch'esŏng* (Seoul: Han'gukchangnogyoch'ulp'ansa, 2021), 66.

13   Preparing for the 10th WCC Assembly in Pusan, Korea in 2013, the WCC Korean Committee for the Preparation of the 10th Assembly made official comments on Chung's *ch'ohonje* performance. The WCC Korean Committee for the Preparation of the 10th Assembly, "GETI/ KETI Sajŏn'gyoyuk (Workshop)" (document, Seoul, 2013), 18–19.

controversy itself, I interrogate its impact on Christian conversations about Korean Christian engagement with Korean Shamanism and think about ways for Korean churches to move the conversation forward in the future. This chapter primarily deals with Christian approaches to and discussions on Korean Shamanism, rather than a mutual, formal process to obtain understanding between different religious traditions. This research begins by revealing that the controversy over Chung's Canberra performance revolves around the question of whether Korean Christianity engages with Shamanism as a religion or traditional culture. Beyond the divided approaches to Korean Shamanism, this chapter suggests an open-question approach to Korean Christian engagement with Korean Shamanism, where shamanistic rituals, symbols, and concepts adopted into or present in Korean Christianity are identified, explored, challenged, and even contested for continuing conversations. In this approach, I identify the shamanistic practice of *han-pu-ri,* meaning "to resolve or untangle *han*" in the Korean language, as a key concept behind Hyun Kyung Chung's engagement with Korean Shamanism in her theology. Drawing upon diverse scholarly works on Korean Shamanism within studies of Korean Christianity and studies of Korean religions, I offer a sociocultural and theological analysis of the concept. I argue that the concept of *han-pu-ri* offers resources to construct Korean theology embodying Korean women's collective aspiration for liberation from social oppression. However, its weaknesses must also be acknowledged. I further argue that women's experiences in the *han-pu-ri* ritual were not always liberating, and the concept contains women-oppressive structures.

Korean Shamanism: Korean Indigenous Culture or Religion?

The critiques against Chung's keynote speech at the WWC 1991 Assembly revolved around several themes such as uncritical syncretism and misconceptions of the Holy Spirit.[14] Theologian Yŏnghan Kim argues that

---

14 There have been strands of scholarship debating the question of whether Korean Shamanism is a custom/culture as *Musok* (shaman customs) or a religion as *Mukyo* (shaman religion). However, this chapter does not refer

interreligious conversation is an engagement between religions from the perspective of "a common humanity," not a fusion of different spiritualities but that Chung's soul-summoning *"kut"* was a fusion between the Holy Spirit in Christianity and the spirits in Korean Shamanism, a practice that Kim rejects.[15] Sŭngho Kim, a scholar of Christian ethics, describes Chung's performance not as a Christian engagement with Korean culture but as an amalgamation of the different religious traditions such as Korean Shamanism, the Confucian Kwan In, and the nirvana of Buddhism.[16] Missiologist Youn-Jung So explores Chung's pneumatology in-depth, and problematizes her understanding of the Holy Spirit as "life energy (ki/chi)" and

to the discussion on the term "religion" in defining Korean Shamanism. Rather, culture and religion are used to indicate the different ways in which Korean theologians engage with Korean Shamanism. On the term "religion" and Korean Shamanism, see chapter 2 in David Kwang-sun Suh, *Theology, Ideology and Culture* (Hong Kong: World Student Christian Federation, Asis/Pacific Region, 1983); Shalon Park, "The Politics of Impeaching Shamanism: Regulating Religions in the Korean Public Sphere," *Journal of Church and State* 60, no. 4 (2018): 636–60.

15   Here, Kim intentionally used *"kut"* instead of saying *ch'ohon je* (祭). While *je* is a general term for ritual, *kut* is a specific term for shamanistic ritual. Kim points out Chung used the *cho'hon kut* to call the Holy Spirit in various forms of spirits, including the spirits of dead souls such as Hagar, Uriah, Jephthah's daughter, Joan of Arc, people killed in Hiroshima and Nagasaki by atomic bombs, and then the spirits of earth, air, and water. Yŏnghan Kim, "WCC haeksim nonjŏme taehan sinhajŏk sŏngch'al-ll (Theological Reflection of the Key Issues Related to WCC)," *K'ŭrisŭch'ŏn t'udei*, November 3, 2013, https://tinyurl.com/ycyb223d.

16   Sŭngho Kim, "Chŏnghyŏn'gyŏng kyosuŭi kijoyŏnsŏl, WCC chonggyo tawŏnjuŭiŭi kŭkch'l (Hyun Kyung Chung's Keynote Speech, the Pinnacle of WCC's Religious Pluralism)," *K'ŭrisŭch'ŏn t'udei*, May 23, 2013, https://tinyurl.com/4h9zt3yp. Kwan In (Guanyin/Kuan Yin) is not necessarily a Confucian figure. In her speech, Chung introduced Kwan In as "the goddess of compassion and wisdom by East Asian women's popular religiosity. She is a bodhisattva, enlightened being . . . Perhaps this might also be a feminine image of the Christ." Hyun Kyung Chung, "Come, Holy Spirit – Renew the Whole Creation" in *Signs of the Spirit: Official Report of the Seventh Assembly of the World Council of Churches*, ed. Michael Kinnamon (Geneva; Grand Rapids: WCC Publications/World Council of Church Internet Archives, 1991), 46.

"*bodhisattva* (Kwan In)," the latter meaning a goddess in Buddhism and East Asian women's popular religiosity, as diverging from Christian doctrine.[17]

While these scholars approach Chung's presentation from different angles, they ground their arguments on the shared premise that Chung's *ch'ohonje* is a *kut*, a ritual of Korean Shamanism engaging with shaman spirituality, cosmology, and goddesses. In his essay, it is noteworthy that Yŏnghan Kim describes Chung's ritual as "*ch'ohon kut*," not "*ch'ohonje*." He replaces the word "*je* (祭)," meaning a ritual in a general sense, with "*kut*," a term specifically referring to a shaman rite.[18] Sŭngho Kim also argues that Chung colored her keynote speech with Korean Shamanism at the expense of Christian identity.[19] So Youn-Jung points out that Chung played the role of a shaman in the ritual.[20] The Ecumenical Committee of the Presbyterian Church of Korea echoes this view and describes Chung's performance as "an act of Korean Shamanism (*Musok haengwi*)."[21] These critiques shaped the shared memory that Hyun Kyung Chung appeared as a shaman and offered a *kut* at the WCC 10th Assembly in Canberra.

Meanwhile, the counterarguments in support of Chung's actions center on the use of Indigenous culture as a source of theology. Hyun Kyung Chung explained her performance as a cultural interpretation of Korean Shamanism, implying that the shamanistic elements in her *ch'ohonje* were representations of Korean culture. In a media interview in 1991, she commented on the critiques against her *ch'ohonje*, defining the ritual as "an expression of 'Christianity grafted into our [Korean] culture.'"[22]

---

17   Youn-Jung So, "Chŏnghyŏn'gyŏngŭi honhapchuŭijŏk sillone kwanhan pip'anjŏk yŏn'gu- sŏngnyŏngnonŭl chungsimŭro (A Critical Study on Pluralistic Theism by Jung, Hyun Kyung: A Perspective in Holy Spirit)," *Pogŭmgwa sŏn'gyo* 9, no.1, (2008): 222.

18   Kim, "WCC haeksim nonjŏme taehan sinhajŏk sŏngch'al-Il (Theological Reflection of the Key Issues Related to WCC)."

19   Kim, "WCC chonggyo tawŏnjuŭiŭi kŭkch'i."

20   So, "Honhapchuŭijŏk sillone," 215.

21   Chung, "Segyegyohoehyŏpŭihoe(WCC)e taehan ohaewa chinsil(Q&A) WCC (Misunderstandings and truths about the WCC)," 66.

22   Yonhap News. "Kaesin'gyogye, 'Honhapchuŭi Sinhak' Nonjaeng (Protestant Debate over Syncretism)" *Yonhap News*, April 24. 1991, https://tinyurl.com/y9saabvf.

Asian American feminist theologian Kwok Pui Lan welcomed Chung's presentation as it represented "the rights of younger churches to use their own cultural resources to articulate theology."[23] Theologian Volker Küster also focused on the cultural aspects of Chung's presentation, describing it as "a performance . . . successfully weaving music, dance, symbolic acts, and slide projections together with her speech in a synthesis of the arts."[24] From this perspective, Chung's presentation was a Christian interpretation of Korean traditional cultures drawn from Korean Shamanism.

While the responses to Chung's *ch'ohonje* diverge on whether the shamanistic elements of the presentation should be understood as an amalgamation of different religious expressions or a cultural engagement, the boundary between religion and culture is not clear-cut. The Korean Protestant churches, mainly evangelical churches, refuse to engage with Korean Shamanism due to the fear of syncretism and religious pluralism. However, despite this rejection, Korean Christianity has been in close conversation with traditions drawn from Korean Shamanism since their first encounters. A good example is the *Sungmi* (holy rice) offering widely practiced throughout the twentieth century. Women would collect a handful of rice every time they prepared a meal and offer it to the church. Church historian Deok-Joo Rhie argues that the *Sungmi* offering originated from the Korean women's practice of offering rice to the shamanistic home god called *Sungju* (house lord).[25] On the other hand, theologians such as Hyun Kyung Chung actively engage with Korean Shamanism as an indispensable cultural source of their theology. But culture and religion are entangled in Korean Shamanism. Theologians have engaged regularly with shamanistic spirituality and theology reflected in and expressed through Korean Shamanism. For example, although Chung defended her *ch'ohonje* in Canberra by describing her performance

---

23   Kwok, "Interfaith Dialogue," 234.

24   Küster, *Theology of Passion*, 103.

25   In Korean shamanistic belief, *sungju* is the collective name for the god appointed to each house. *Sungju* governs the blessings and calamities of the household. Geunhye Yim, "Sungju," *Encyclopedia of Korean Folk Culture*, accessed May 20, 2012, https://tinyurl.com/4ppv69vr; Rhie, Deok-Joo. *A Study on the Formation of the Indigenous Church in Korea, 1903–1907* (Seoul: The Institute of the History of Christianity in Korea, 2000), 157–58.

as a cultural representation of Korean Shamanism, she acknowledged elsewhere that *Musok* represents "women's popular religiosity."[26] Therefore, the conversations on the Christian relationship with Korean Shamanism call for a new approach beyond the binary framework of religious syncretism and cultural engagement.

REFRAMING THE NARRATIVE: FROM OPPOSING SIDES TO OPEN QUESTIONS

In contrast to the opposing-sides approach to Korean Shamanism, I suggest a holistic approach to the conversation by shifting the focus to open questions that foster Christian conversations about interreligious engagement. The traditional questions asked about the relationship between Korean Christianity and Shamanism often force interlocutors to choose one of two opposing sides. However, open questions expand the scope of the conversation in diverse directions by considering "why," "what," and "how." Such questions include: Why have Korean theologians engaged with Korean Shamanism? What are the shamanistic elements, symbols, or concepts being used? How effective are those elements, symbols, or concepts in fulfilling a theological task?

Exploring these open questions through an analysis of Korean Christian engagement with Shamanism, this section limits its scope to Korean feminist theologians' interests in Korean Shamanism, with a focus on Chung's theology of *han-pu-ri*. Here, it is noteworthy that Korean feminist theologians' interests did not grow in a vacuum. Korean theologians such as Tongshik Ryu and David Kwang-sun Suh have explored the relationship between Christianity and Shamanism in constructing Korean theology.[27] Feminist theologians have drawn upon this rich tradition of

---

26 Along with Korean Shamanism, she lists Kwan In of folk Chinese Buddhism and Filipino worship of Ina as reflecting women's popular religiosity in Asia. Hyun Kyung Chung, *Struggle to Be the Sun Again: Introducing Asian Women's Theology* (Maryknoll, NY: Orbis Books, 1990), 112.

27 These theologians include but are not limited to the first-generation theologian Ryu Tong-shik, who engages extensively with Korean Shamanism in constructing Korean contextual theology, and Minjung theologian David

Christian engagement with Korean Shamanism in theology. Chung is also heavily influenced by Minjung theologians' interests in Korean Shamanism. Her *han-pu-ri* theology contains her earlier theological vision for Korean feminist theology, foregrounding her *ch'ohonje* performance in Canberra. Considering the long-lasting impact of her presentation on the conversation about Korean Christianity and Korean Shamanism, analyzing the theology behind Chung's performance is a necessary step to further the conversation.

Women's *Han*, Liberation, and Korean Shamanism in Korean Feminist Theology

Korean feminist theologians' interests in Korean Shamanism originate from their primary theological task of naming and resolving Korean women's suffering, expressed in the concept of *han,* a collective and underlying sentiment of agony distinctive in Korean people's minds.[28] Dealing with *han* is a primary task of Korean theology.[29] The experiences of *han* are not bound to Korean women only, but women's *han* is increased

---

Kwang-sun Suh. See Tongshik Ryu, *Han'gukchonggyowa kidokkyo (Korean Religions and Christianity)*, 2nd ed. (South Korea: Taehan'gidokkyosŏhoe, 1993); Suh, *Theology, Ideology, and Culture*, 31–51.

28   There is no equivalent English word for *han*. The National Institute of Korean Language defines *han* as "a sentiment of sadness, agony, and regret (or resentment) accumulated in one's heart." Suh Nam Dong, a Minjung theologian, defines *han* as "the suppressed, amassed, and condensed experience of oppression caused by mischief or misfortune so that it forms a kind of 'lum' in one's spirit." Moon's description of *han* is also helpful: "*han* is considered to be a national characteristic of the Korean people and to be the root of Korean culture and spirituality." "Han," *Standard Korean Language Dictionary*, s.v., accessed May 18, 2022, https://stdict.korean.go.kr; Nam Dong Suh, "Towards a Theology of Han," in *Minjung Theology: People as the Subjects of History*, ed. Yong Bock Kim and Christian Conference of Asia (Singapore: Commission on Theological Concerns, 1981), 65, quoted in Chung, "'Han-pu-ri': Doing Theology from Korean Women's Perspective," 30; Hellena Moon, "Genealogy of the Modern Theological Understanding of Han," *Pastoral Psychology*, no. 63 (August 1, 2014): 420.

29   Korean Minjung theology also locates Korean people's *han* at the center of its theological inquiry. See Suh, "Towards a Theology of Han," 55–69. For more

through gendered oppressions. Chung points out the "gender specificity" of women's experiences of *han* by saying, "Korean women have been suffering with Korean men . . . however . . . Women suffer just because they are women. The people with domination have exploited women in particular ways using the female gender ideology."[30] Her examples include the deprivation of Korean women's freedom under the strict Confucian social order in the Chosŏn Dynasty (1392–1910), the Japanese colonial state's exploitation of women's sexuality during World War II, and the violent suppression by the government and male coworkers of women factory workers' rights for unionizing and protest in the 1970s.[31] Chung argues that these gender-specific oppressions are accumulated in Korean women's *han*, unresolved and compounded by ongoing injustice. Based on this awareness, the necessity of a women-liberating theology has become more apparent.

In this chapter's analysis, liberation means a framework to explore one's experience of freedom and the theology built upon those experiences. The core question is: Who liberates whom from what? Korean feminist theologian Meehyun Chung offers a helpful framework to analyze the concept of women's liberation in feminist theology.[32] She argues that the primary concern of liberation is women's struggles with gender inequality, and the urgent task is to change the social, cultural, political, and religious structures sustaining the inequality. She also highlights that women are not only objects but also subjects of their liberation. Lastly, Meehyun Chung adds an important dimension to the notion of liberation, the ability to imagine liberation. She concludes, "Even though a theology is written by and practiced by women, if the theology lacks in the vision of women's liberation, it cannot be a feminist theology."[33]

---

on the relationship between Korean Shamanism and Minjung theology, see chapter 2 in Suh, *Theology, Ideology, and Culture.*

30   Chung "'Han-pu-ri': Doing Theology," 31.

31   Ibid., 32.

32   Meehyun Chung, *Tto Hanaŭi Yŏsŏng Shinhak Iyagi (Another Story of Women's Theology)* (Seoul: South Korea: Handŭlch'ulp'ansa, 2007), 271–72.

33   Ibid.

In search of sources to construct women-liberating theology, Korean feminist theologians turned to Korean Shamanism. In the 1980s, the first generation of feminist theologians actively sought a new theology to address the issues of oppression and discrimination against women in Korean religious, social, and cultural contexts.[34] They identified theological sources within the nexus of multiple Korean traditional religions.[35] Theologians like Yi Sŏnae, Yi Ujŏng, Pak Sun'gyŏng, Choi Man-ja, and Ch'a Oksung have inquired about the potential of Korean faith traditions in providing resources for women's liberation.[36] While Confucianism was often the target of criticism as the pillar of patriarchy, Korean Shamanism and Taoism were located on the opposite end of the spectrum as faith traditions that provided spaces for women's subjectivity and authority.[37] As I will discuss further below, Hyun Kyung Chung's theology falls within this strand with her interests in Korean Shamanism as a source of the liberating impetus in Korean women's experiences.

CHUNG'S LIBERATION THEOLOGY AND THE SHAMANISTIC CONCEPT OF *HAN-PU-RI*

Since her performance in Canberra in 1991, Hyun Kyung Chung has been at the forefront of the conversations about the relationship between Korean Christianity and Korean Shamanism.[38] For Chung, Korean Shamanism is an indispensable source for Korean women's theology. Chung envisions Asian women's theology as both women-liberating and distinctively Asian: women-liberating by using women's experiences as the primary texts of

---

34   Min-Ah Cho highlights their social justice orientation as the distinctive characteristic of Korean feminist theologians in this period. Min-Ah Cho, "Stirring up Deep Waters: Korean Feminist Theologies Today," *Theology Today* 71, no. 2 (2014): 234.

35   Ibid., 238–39.

36   Chung Meehyun offers the genealogy of these theologians. Chung, *Yŏsŏng Shinhak*, 305–8.

37   Man Ja Choi, "The Acceptance, Development, and Influence of Feminist Theology in The Korean Church and Society in the 1980s," *Christianity and History in Korea* 18 (2003): 86–87.

38   Chung, "Han-Pu-Ri': Doing Theology," 27–36.

theology, and Asian by drawing upon women-centered Asian popular religiosity. According to Chung, popular religion including Korean Shamanism embodies women's spirituality of such resistance and liberation.[39] This "women's popular religiosity" reflects their "subversive power to transform the abstract, misogynist, institutional religions into women-affirming, body-loving, and nature-honoring spirituality."[40]

Chung's focus on *han* and Korean Shamanism was nothing new considering the ways earlier generations of Korean theologians drew on Korean Shamanism.[41] However, the novel element she introduced was her theological integration of the shamanistic way of dealing with *han*, using the concept of *han-pu-ri*. The term "*han-pu-ri*" has been widely used in many different contexts.[42] However, in Chung's conceptualization, the word refers to a shaman's process of resolving the *han* of dead souls in *kut*. In Korean shamanistic cosmology, a person who dies with unresolved *han* is considered a threat to the world of the living. Their soul becomes a "*han-ridden*" angry ghost and remains in this world, causing illness, misfortune, and even death to the living. Korean shamans intervene in the situation by offering a *han-pu-ri kut*. As a mediator between this world and the world of gods, the shaman communicates with *han-ridden* souls to resolve their *han*. She also offers food, music, and dance until the dead souls finally rest in peace.

---

39 Chung, *Struggle to Be the Sun*, 112.

40 Ibid., 111–12.

41 Chung considers herself as a second-generation liberation theologian and draws extensively upon the discourse on Korean Shamanism in Minjung theology, where Korean Shamanism is defined as the theology of *han* and shamans as the priests of *han*. Hyun Kyung Chung, "Opium or the Seed for Revolution?: Women-Centered Religiosity in Korea," in *The Power of Naming: A Concilium Reader in Feminist Liberation Theology*, ed. Elisabeth Schüssler Fiorenza (Maryknoll, NY: Orbis Books; SCM Press, 1996), 275–83.

42 *Han-pu-ri* (a noun) or *han-eul-pul-da* (a verb) are general words often used in the everyday language across culture and religion. However, the terms have gained currency in Christian theological circles. Minjung theologians have explored *han-pu-ri* with a focus on the ways in which Korean Shamanism reflects the nature and characteristics of *han*. David Kwang-sun Suh, *Theology, Ideology, and Culture*.

In her analysis of *han-pu-ri kuts*, Chung identifies three steps of *han-pu-ri*. The first step is *speaking and hearing*. The shaman gives the *han*-ridden persons or ghosts the chance to break their silence. The shaman enables the persons or ghosts to release their *han* publicly. The shaman makes the community hear the *han*-ridden stories. The second step is *naming*. The shaman enables the *han*-ridden persons or ghosts (or their communities) to name the source of their oppression. The third step is *changing* the unjust situation by action so that *han*-ridden persons or ghosts can have peace.[43]

Chung finds a parallel between the *han-pu-ri* ritual and Korean women's theological methodology. In 1984 the Korean Association of Women Theologians (KAWT) held the "Second Consultation for the Establishment of Feminist Theology in Asia" and published the conference proceedings.[44] In Chung's reading of the report, she identified the three-step methodology at work in Korean women's theological approach to *han*.

Women theologians took the following steps. They started their theologizing from listening to the Han-ridden women's stories. They invited women from the bottom stratum of Korean society such as farmers, factory workers, and slum-dwellers, and listened to their life stories. After this step, the women theologians did social analysis with the help of social scientists and other women who knew the structural aspects of the problem. They then moved to the theological reflections with the questions raised by the former two steps. The next step was to check with the original storytellers and communities whether the articulated theology made sense to them and empowered them. The final step was action. KAWT participated in various demonstrations and organized protests in order to solve Korean women's Han.[45]

---

43 Chung, "Han-Pu-Ri': Doing Theology," 29.

44 Korean Association of Women Theologians, *Second Consultation for the Establishment of Feminist Theology in Asia* (Seoul, KAWT, 1983), quoted in Chung, "Han-Pu-Ri': Doing Theology," 35–36.

45 Ibid., 35.

Chung points out the parallel between the three steps of speaking and hearing, naming, and changing in the KAWT meeting and those as performed in the shamanistic *han-pu-ri* ritual. Unfortunately, Chung's interesting comparison has not been contextualized further into a theological concept. In her monograph, *Struggle to Be the Sun Again*, published in 1990, Chung describes the methodology for the creation of Asian women's theology in three steps, echoing her earlier theological methods of *han-pu-ri*. She contends that the method begins with women's *storytelling* and continues with *critical social analysis* of the stories by theologians, leading to *theological reflections*. However, here, Chung's three-step method does not engage with Korean Shamanism. Instead, she draws on the Women's Committee of the Ecumenical Association of Third World Theologians's (EATWOT) method of "listening to individual's situation, social analysis, and theological analysis."[46]

Still, Hyun Kyung Chung's approach to *han-pu-ri* as a feminist theological method powerfully addresses the problems and limits of androcentric and Western-centric theology, and sheds light on the source of Korean women's empowerment within Korean tradition.[47] In her three-step *han-pu-ri* method, the emphasis on speaking and hearing women's voices exposes the exclusion of women from theological inquiries, and highlights the importance of including women's experiences as they are spoken by women themselves. Chung argues that women's telling of their life experiences has been the center of Korean women's experience of resistance and liberation in Korean Shamanism. She points out, "*Han-pu-ri* became one of the few spaces where poor Korean women played their spiritual role without being dominated by male-centered religious authorities. *Han*-ridden women got together and tried to release their accumulated *han* through *han-pu-ri kut*."[48] From this perspective, the primary task of Korean feminist theology is to reinstate the space of *han-pu-ri*. In this way, Korean women's theology can be a Korean theology truly constructed by and for women.

---

46   Chung, *Struggle to Be the Sun*, 103–9.

47   Küster, *Theology of Passion*, 104–5.

48   Chung "'Han-Pu-Ri': Doing Theology," 35.

UNANSWERED QUESTIONS: RETHINKING THE SHAMANISTIC CONCEPT OF *HAN-PU-RI*

While it is undeniable that Chung's use of the concept of *han-pu-ri* contributes to highlighting women's presence and Indigenous agency in constructing Korean women's theology, her use of the concept of *han-pu-ri* in relation to its liberating effect needs further clarification. Some further questions include how the concept of *han-pu-ri* facilitates women's experiences of freedom in shamanistic rituals. This section examines Korean women's experiences in *han-pu-ri kuts* and approaches the task with open questions drawing upon the multiple dimensions of liberation as a framework defined earlier in this chapter. The question is: Who liberates *whom* from *what* in the *han-pu-ri* ritual? I affirm that the *han-pu-ri* process in Korean shamanistic rituals has the potential for facilitating Korean women's collective experiences of resolving *han*; however, the concept of *han-pu-ri* also reflects women-oppressive power dynamics of the *han-pu-ri* process in the ritual.

The Subjects of *Han-pu-ri*: Mudangs' Experiences of Liberation and Oppression

In *han-pu-ri kut*, women are the subjects of the *han-pu-ri* process. Korean Shamanism has traditionally been a women's sphere. The majority of shamans are women. Women are the primary clients, initiators, and participants of its rituals, and there are also female gods.[49] During the Chosŏn Dynasty, Confucianism limited women to the roles of housewives and mothers, and it was exceptional for a woman to have a public role leading rituals with spiritual authority.[50] In his analysis of women's experiences in Korean Shamanism, Jonghyun Lee, a scholar of social work, highlights the role of shamans as powerful mediators in overcoming women's subordinate position under patriarchy, invoking deities and spirits by moving "beyond and above the profane world," and addressing

---

49   Man Ja Choi, "Feminine Images of God in Korean Traditional Religion," in *Frontiers in Asian Christian theology: Emerging Trends*, ed. R. S. Sugirtharajah (Maryknoll, NY: Orbis Books, 1994), 80–89.

50   Ibid., 35.

women's sufferings through "speaking, laughing, crying, dancing, and singing with the spirits and spectators."[51] A *kut* performed by a woman shaman was a visual embodiment of women's freedom from Confucian gender norms.

On the other hand, the focus on the dominant presence of women within Shamanism has a danger of simplifying the complicated women's experiences of agency, and of overshadowing women's struggles behind the scenes. When examining a similar misunderstanding of women's experiences in South Asia, Indian feminist historian Janaki Nair brings attention to the problems of using gender as a unified subject. She points to the dilemma of uncritical gendered labeling, through which women's history closes its eyes to women's voices of struggle in order to present the past as an account of heroic women.[52] In her study of the historical reconstructions of the Telangana People's Struggle, an Indian movement against feudal oppression, also known as a women's movement, Nair argues that the dominant presence of women in the movement did not mean gender was at the center of their political mobilization. In her words, "rather, the post hoc feminist interrogation produced a feminist recollection of that magic time, a reconstruction of the movement understood through the lens of gender."[53] To challenge such rosy narratives of women's experiences, Nair suggests a critical rereading of feminist historiography by disturbing the unified category of gender and searching for the unheard voices in the shadows.

In a similar vein, a close reading of women's stories in Korean Shamanism reveals their unheard struggles. Korean anthropologist Kim Ŭnhŭi's analysis of Korean *mudangs*' life stories provides helpful insight into the diverse experiences of shamans. Kim interviewed seven *mudangs* in the northern Jeolla province in South Korea in the early 2000s. As Kim sheds light on the multifaceted aspects of their lives as a *mudangs*, daughters, wives, mothers, and women through their storytelling, some of their stories reveal their bitterness over their lives as shamans. In their

---

51   Jonghyun Lee, "Shamanism and Its Emancipatory Power for Korean Women," *Journal of Women and Social Work* 24, no. 2 (May 2009): 192–93.

52   Janaki Nair, "The Troubled Relationship of Feminism and History," *Economic and Political Weekly* 43, no. 43 (October 25–31, 2008): 62.

53   Ibid.

narratives, they describe making a choice of sacrifice and enduring their fate as shamans. The most important motivation for their choice was their identity as a mother. A mother of two children became a *mudang* in the fear that if she rejected the role, her children might be pursued by the spirits in her place.[54] She states, "It is my duty to make sure there will be no more shaman in my family."[55] A fifty-six-year-old *mudang* also echoes this narrative. She became a *mudang* in her fifties after hearing another shaman telling her that if she refused her fate as a shaman, the god would chase her son, and if not him, then her granddaughter. The *mudang* recounts, "I thought I would rather sacrifice myself . . . So, I received [the spirit] . . . I could not bear the idea of sacrificing my little ones."[56] One may describe these *mudangs* as liberators of *han*, but they are under the possession of their gods, hoping that their own *han* would be resolved one day.

The Objects of *Han-pu-ri*: Dead Souls, Women, and their *Han*

The purpose of *han-pu-ri* in Korean Shamanism is twofold: to release *han* of dead souls and that of the living. In this pursuit, a shaman deals with the dead souls' problem of *han* as a means of ensuring her clients' welfare. In shamanistic cosmology, shamans are given authority and power to mediate between the two, creating a triangular relationship among shaman, *han*-ridden souls, and clients. And this relationship is formed and performed through a *kut*. While a *kut* treats *han* as a spiritual matter to be dealt with

---

54 There are two kinds of shamans: *sesŭmmu* (hereditary) and *kangsinmu* (god-possessed). While the hereditary shaman inherits the role through marriage or family lineage and becomes a shaman after training, the god-possessed shaman becomes one through the experiences of being possessed by shaman gods, such as ancestor spirits and general spirits. All seven *mudangs* in Kim's book are god-possessed *mudangs*. Ŭnhŭi Kim, *Yŏsŏng Musoginŭi Saengaesa* (*Life Stories of Women Shamans*), Chŏlla Munhwa Ch'ongsŏ (Seoul: Muneyŏn'gusa, 2004), 25–35.

55 The *mudang* explains that if the chosen one refuses the god's possession, the god pursues another member of her family, often her child or grandchild. Kim, *Musoginŭi Saengaesa*, 85.

56 Ibid.

by a ritual, Christian theologians engaging with Korean Shamanism have highlighted the social space offered by a *kut* as an essential part of the *han-pu-ri* process. Choi Man-ja problematizes the critiques against *kut* as a mythical and primitive religious ritual. She contends that *kut* needs to be understood as an archetype of a social movement and a channel of collective resistance.[57] Kim Jin, a Korean philosopher, highlights *kut* as a social and public event, through which a community affirms their collective commitment to address and liberate from the social oppressions.[58]

However, the focus on the communal aspects of *kut* still leaves the question of what happens within the triangular relationship among shaman, *han*-ridden souls, and clients in the *han-pu-ri* process. Korean woman theologian Chung Jae-Yeon asks whether women have always experienced liberation in the *han-pu-ri* ritual.[59] In exploring the relational dynamics in *kut*s, I am mindful of the diversity in *han-pu-ri kut* in its structures and practices depending on the shamans who perform the ritual or on the locations and regions where it is performed. The various ritual forms include *ssitkim, ogu, chinogwi, haewon, dojang,* and *suwang kut.*[60] This diversity raises challenges in analyzing *han-pu-ri kut* as a single entity or a unified practice. Therefore, this section will focus on the primary functions of the *kut*, as Tongshik Ryu, a theologian and scholar of Korean religions,

---

57   Choi, "Yŏsŏngsinhakchŏk Haesŏk," 243–45.

58   Jin Kim, "Musoksinanggwa hanŭi sinhak (Shamanistic Faith and the Theology of Han)," *Theological Thought* (Sinhaksasang) 67 (1989): 992–94.

59   Jae-Yeon Chung, "Chonggyowa han'gugyŏsŏng: Musoge taehan yŏsŏngsinhakchŏk koch'al (Religion and Korean Women: Rethinking Korean Shamanism from the women's theological perspectives)," *Han'gugyŏsŏngsinhak* 6 (1991): 38–41.

60   Each *kut* varies in its primary focus, orders, or ritual practices. For example, *ssitkim kut,* meaning "to cleanse," focuses on the "cleansing" ritual, using water treated with herbs. On the other hand, *ogu kut* is shaped by Buddhist practices, and, in some cases, the shaman would dress like a Buddhist monk and recite chants or invocations. For details on each kind of *kut*, see Hongyun Cho, *Han'gugŭi Mu (Mu of Korea)* (Seoul: Chŏngŭmsa, 1983); Yŏnggŭm Yi, *Chŏnbuk Ssitkimgut: Chŏn'gŭmsunŭi Muga (Nothern Jeolla Ssitkim Kut)* (Seoul: Minsogwŏn, 2007); Taedo Son, "Chosŏn Hugiŭi Musok (Musok in the Latter Period of Joseon Dynasty)," *Han'gungmusok'ak* 17 (2008): 189–270.

summarizes: "praying for blessings, expelling the devil of the plague, and sending off the dead souls to the other world."[61]

What happens in the arena of *kut* is a power game between shamans and *han*-ridden souls. The analysis of the *han-pu-ri* ritual reveals the power dynamics of oppression within *han-pu-ri kut,* where shamans impose force upon dead souls, and both shamans and dead souls are perceived as passive beings: shamans possessed by gods, and dead souls possessed by *han*. The concept of *han-pu-ri* in Korean Shamanism rests on the premise that the dead souls are passive beings. They are unable to resolve their own *han* by themselves. In the shamanistic practice of *han-pu-ri,* the dead souls cannot initiate the ritual nor actively participate in the process, except by speaking through the shaman in a given situation. In many cases, the angry souls are conceived as mentally disoriented. No matter what their original beings were like, once they die with accumulated un-resolved *han*, it is believed that they become irrational and malevolent entities: *han*-ridden souls.[62] Therefore, the release of their *han* should be done by a third person; the dead souls are helpless and passive beings that desperately need shamans to function as their liberators. The client's relationship to the shaman is also one of submission. Laurel Kendall's observation of two *kuts* affirms this objectification of the participants in *kuts*. Kendall describes, "Neither Mrs. Yi nor Mrs. Min [the client of each *kut*] was a full participant in the *kut* held on her behalf, Mrs. Min because she was drugged and temporarily insane, and Mrs. Yi because she did not know the procedures and had to be coached by the shamans."[63] In this context, it is safe to say that *han-pu-ri kut* is a one-way power game in which a passive being imposes force upon

---

61   In his categorization of shaman rituals, Ryu uses the term "exorcism" as an overarching category, equivalent to "*han-pu-ri kut,*" indicating that the primary purpose of *kuts* is to prevent malevolent souls from intervening in the life of the living. Tongshik Ryu, *The History and Structure of Korean Shamanism*, trans. Jeong-il Moon (Seoul: Yonsei University Press, 2012), 521.

62   Buyŏng Yi, *Han'guğŭi syamŏnijŭmgwa punsŏk simnihak: kot'onggwa ch'iyuŭi sangjingŭl ch'ajasŏ* (*The Korean Shamanism and Analytical Psychology with Special Reference to the Symbols of Suffering and Healing*) (Seoul: Han'gilsa, 2013), 437.

63   Laurel Kendall, *Shamans, Nostalgias, and the IMF: South Korean Popular Religion in Motion* (Honolulu: University of Hawaii Press, 2009), 63.

another passive being. And the shamanistic concept of *han-pu-ri* projects this passivity of the participants into the *han-pu-ri* ritual.

In *han-pu-ri* rituals, shamans, often perceived as liberators, are also in a passive role under submission to the gods. In Korean Shamanism, a shaman has an exclusive relationship with a certain god, and in this relationship, the god is called *momju* (a body owner).[64] In this power dynamic, the god dominates the shaman, and the shaman entirely submits to the god. The choice of interrelating is solely made by the god and has less to do with the shaman's own will. This one-sided oppressive relationship is well-demonstrated in the process of becoming a shaman through *sinbyŏng* (possession sickness). In his article, "What is Korean Shamanism?" Kim Tae-gon describes this process in detail:

> A woman suddenly experiences an altered state of consciousness. She shows symptoms of what people around her interpret as a mental disorder; . . . She is unable to take food, and, as her body grows weak. . . . In extreme cases, and still in a trance, she follows the spirits around, roaming wildly through streets and fields. . . . This is the point at which the community accepts what they now believe inevitable; that the spirit will force her to become a mudang.[65]

This description is open to various interpretations. While speaking about the passivity of shamans and the oppression imposed on them in the process of becoming a shaman, Kim Tae-gon describes the *sinbyŏng* functions as a rite of passage that confers divine authority on the woman as a *mudang*. However, the woman's agency to make her life choices is still denied and violated in the process. A *mudang*'s voice testifies to her struggles in this relationship, stating, "You have no choice once you are chosen by the ancestor (meaning a spirit who possesses a shaman). You could even

---

64   The exclusive relationship between the god and the *mudang* is one of the distinctive characteristics of Korean Shamanism. Tae-gon Kim, "What Is Korean Shamanism?," in *Korean Shamanism: Revivals, Survivals, and Change,* ed. Keith Howard (Seoul: The Royal Asiatic Society, Korea Branch, 1998), 20.

65   Kim, "What Is Korean Shamanism?," 21.

get killed. It would be better if I get killed, but they won't even let you die. So, that is why I am doing what I do."[66] For her, being a shaman is an unwanted fate that she endures under constant pressure and regret. A *mudang* may offer a space of *han-pu-ri* for others, but is bound by "another form of subordination to the spirits."[67]

CONCLUSION

The controversy over Chung's *ch'ohonje* has limited the scope of the conversations about the Christian engagement with Korean Shamanism to the issue of identifying Korean Shamanism as a religion or as culture. The opposing sides widened the gap between those who voiced concerns against uncritical religious syncretism and those who welcomed Chung's interpretation of Korean Shamanism as the cultural representation of Korean religiosity. However, this chapter points out that culture and religion have been entangled since the first encounters between Christianity and Korean Shamanism. Rather than affirming or rejecting the opposing sides, this chapter invites reflection on the complexity of Korean Christianity's relationship with Korean Shamanism, asking the open question: Who liberates *whom* from *what* in the Korean shamanistic ritual of *han-pu-ri*? This chapter does not claim to offer a complete answer. Rather, it uses the question as a framework to raise caution against oversimplified understandings of Korean women's experiences of liberation in Korean Shamanism and to explore the multiple dimensions of liberation that arise when using the concept of *han-pu-ri* in Korean feminist theology. The shaman, as a performer of the *kut*, embodied Korean women's resistance against Confucian gender norms, and Korean women expressed their aspiration for liberation by participating in the *han-pu-ri* ritual. Meanwhile, women's experiences in the *han-pu-ri* process were not always liberating for the shamans performing the ritual or for the clients participating. In some

---

66   Ŭnhŭi Kim, *Yŏsŏng Musoginŭi Saengaesa* (*Life Stories of Women Shamans*), Chŏlla Munhwa Ch'ongsŏ (Seoul: Muneyŏn'gusa, 2004), 59.

67   Man-Ja Choi. "Han'gungmusoge Taehan Yŏsŏngsinhakchŏk Haesŏk (Feminist Theological Interpretation of Korean Shamanism)," *Korean Journal of Christian Studies* 7, no. 1 (1990): 244–45.

cases, their agency was compromised within the dominant and submissive dynamics of shamans, *han*-ridden souls, and clients. With this open approach beyond the binary between culture and religion, this analysis affirms that the concept of *han-pu-ri* provides useful resources for theologians to construct theologies that reflect Korean women's aspirations for resolving their *han,* and for Korean Christian women to reaffirm their potential to pursue liberation. But at the same time, this study sheds light on possible women-oppressive dynamics that may be inherited in the concept.

For further conversations on Korean Christianity's relationship with Korean Shamanism, the task of asking open questions does not end here. To convey that many more questions remain, here, I conclude with an insight from the Korean decorative knot, Maedeup. Making a Maedeup begins with carefully choosing threads to form base strands, then the next step is to weave and tie the strands, creating a beautiful pattern.[68] As we create a Maedeup—or in this case, a conversation about Korean Christian engagement with Korean Shamanism—the first step is to pull out a thread, but a single thread does not make a Maedeup. To envision a theology that is truly women-liberating, truly Korean, and truly Christian, more threads need to be collected to create a cord, and then tied into a beautiful knot.

---

68   "Maedeupjang, Decorative Knot Craft," *National Intangible Heritage Center, Research & Archiving Division*, accessed May 19, 2022, https://tinyurl.com/eck5dbfk.

CHAPTER 7

THE BLACK MESSIAH GOES HOME: THE BLACK CHURCH, BLACK MANHOOD, AND THE MISSION TO REDEEM AFRICA

Jay-Paul Hinds

INTRODUCTION: GOING HOME

Home is the place where one belongs. Home is where one feels secure. Home is the place to which one returns when the world, and its many dangers, become too overwhelming. Home is important. Without question, it is devastating—physically, psychologically, and spiritually—when one's home is lost. In *Homesickness: An American History*, historian Susan J. Matt shares the story of Rev. Father J. M. McHale, who, in 1887, left Ireland to lead a congregation in Brooklyn, New York. Soon after his arrival, according to Matt, Rev. McHale began to waste away, as he lamented, "I cannot eat; my heart is breaking . . . My dear country [Ireland], I will never set foot on your green shores again."[1] Homesickness was prevalent throughout antebellum America as many migrants grew ill as they pondered the reality that vast swaths of land and abundant bodies of water separated them from their homes.

While many migrants adjusted to the idea that modern life necessitated their separation from home, some remained entranced by fantasies of returning to their native homeland. And there were some who endeavored

---

1. Susan J. Matt, *Homesickness: An American History* (New York: Oxford University Press: 2011), 3.

167

to make the fantasy a reality, risking all, even death, to go back home. For Black slaves in America, Africa was home. Matt notes that for many slaves, the trauma of homesickness began to have deleterious effects during the Middle Passage, far before they set foot on American soil. "En route to America, slaves were stripped naked and faced dreadful and life-threatening conditions on the overpacked ships that transported them across the Atlantic," writes Matt.[2] Some were so overwhelmed by despair that they "threw themselves overboard."[3] Suicides became common practice for the enslaved Africans who wanted to return home, by any means necessary. There was a common belief among slaves from West Africa "that after death, individuals were reincarnated in Africa and would be free."[4] For many slaves who survived the Middle Passage, the desire to return home—to be free—did not wane but intensified, now suffused with West African religious beliefs and practices.

In *Black Folktales*, African American writer Julius Lester recounts the story "People Who Could Fly," which tells of a group of slaves who had recently arrived from Africa to a South Carolina plantation. The narrative states that on a sweltering day the slaves had become overwhelmed by the inhumane working conditions. One of the slaves was a pregnant woman—"her body curved with child"[5]—who fainted. Lester offers a vivid depiction of the white overseer's vicious response to the pregnant woman's condition, as he writes,

> Before the body struck the ground, the white man with the whip was riding toward her on his horse. He threw water in her face. "Get back to work, you lazy [n-word]! There ain't going to be no sitting down on the job as long as I'm here." He cracked the whip against her back and, screaming, she staggered to her feet.[6]

---

2   Matt, *Homesickness*, 21.
3   Ibid.
4   Ibid., 13.
5   Julius Lester, *Black Folktales* (New York: Grove Press, 1991), 100.
6   Lester, *Black Folktales*, 100.

Upon seeing this, the other slaves fell silent, their voices and bodies rendered mute by this violent act. The white man's primary concern was not the well-being of the pregnant woman but instead that the day's work be completed before nightfall. Nothing else mattered. Not the terrible working conditions. Not the pregnant woman's pain. Nothing. Therefore, he issued a warning, "If you [n-word] don't want a taste of the same, you'd better get to work!"[7] So the slaves returned to their labor. This time, however, according to the folktale, an uncanny slave, a young witch doctor, made his way through the field, whispering something, "a strange word,"[8] to several slaves. While this was happening, other slaves began to succumb to the overbearing heat. Lester shares,

> A few moments later, someone else in the field fainted, and, as the white man with the whip rode toward him, the young witch doctor shouted, "Now!" He uttered a strange word, and the person who had fainted rose from the ground, and moving his arms like wings, he flew into the sky and out of sight.[9]

Now! Now! Now! The shout continued to echo throughout the plantation, until, finally, the witch doctor yelled, "Now! Now! Everyone!"[10] It was time for all of them to go home. The slaves had suffered enough; they were tired of "a taste of the same."[11] And so "all of the Africans dropped their hoes, stretched out their arms, and flew away, back to their home, back to Africa."[12]

Such stories of return to Africa continued among Black communities in the years after emancipation. This chapter seeks to explore how some African American clergymen during the late eighteenth century, the formative years of the Black church, shared a vision of redeeming their true home, Africa. Several prominent African American clergymen,

---

7   Ibid.
8   Ibid., 102.
9   Ibid.
10   Ibid.
11   Ibid., 100.
12   Ibid., 102.

however, were not content with just returning home per se but rather were also convinced that Africa needed to be redeemed, made anew, by men who were God's chosen representatives—the Black messiah. Much more will be shared throughout this chapter on the concept of messianism, and how it influenced African American clergymen in the early Black church. For now, though, it is worth considering a helpful insight offered by historian Wilson Jeremiah Moses, who states that "the Afro-American messianic myth has thrived because its rhetoric is familiar to the people of the United States, who envision themselves as a 'redeemer people.'"[13] He goes on to add that "black messianism has always been reinforced by the messianic strains in American culture."[14] Although not the exclusive preserve of American culture, messianism, as utilized by African American clergymen, was suffused with American notions of a nation and a people having a manifest destiny to redeem the world. But why did these clergymen believe that Africa needed redemption? After all, wasn't Africa their home?

There are scholars in the fields of World Christianity and missions, such as Andrew Barnes, who have discussed how some Africans desired that the "civilized black people"[15] of the United States return to Africa in order to redeem Africa, particularly through industrial education. However, this study suggests that what African American clergymen (that is, as God's civilized Black men) were on a mission to redeem in Africa was not only their homeland but more specifically their own manhood. For centuries, Africa had been depicted and categorized as the land of and for primitive people—put another way, it represented the antithesis of the Christianized American man. Many African American clergymen subscribed wholeheartedly to a negative view of Africa as a primitive nation in need of enlightenment. Unfortunately, the mission to redeem Africa could not be separated from the mission to spread what Moses describes as "the experience of

---

13 Wilson Jeremiah Moses, *Black Messiahs and Uncle Toms: Social and Literary Manipulations of a Religious Myth* (University Park: Pennsylvania State University Press, 1993), 1.

14 Ibid., 1.

15 Andrew E. Barnes, *Global Christianity and the Black Atlantic: Tuskegee, Colonialism, and the Shaping of African Industrial Education* (Waco: Baylor University Press, 2017), 64.

white domination in the modern world."[16] African American clergymen, therefore, desired to remake their home, Africa, in the image of what they had experienced in America, particularly in the South, because they had accepted the Euro-American way of life as exemplifying God's plan for humankind. Furthermore, their conviction was that Africa would become the place where a kingdom of Black manhood, one mimicking all the deleterious values of Christianized American manhood, was destined to reign.

To begin, I will examine the emergence of the idea of Africa as a primitive land in need of redemption, and how this idea flourished in the West during the nineteenth century. Second, I provide an analysis of the ways in which the Sambo figure served as a defaming symbol of Black manhood, a symbol which Black clergymen sought to overcome not only through their leadership roles in the Black church but by their missionary efforts in Africa as well. Third, I consider how the missionary efforts of Black clergymen in Africa, especially in Liberia, evince that some Black clergymen qua Black messiah did not redeem Africa. Instead, due to their adopting a racialized Western patriarchal consciousness, these Black clergymen often recreated in Africa an oppressive way of life that they themselves experienced in America.

Veiled Visions of Africa

Is Africa the Black man's home? Before addressing this question, I believe it wise to better understand the meaning of the word "home." According to Merriam Webster's dictionary, "home" is defined as (1) one's place of residence, (2) a familiar or unusual setting: congenial environment, and (3) a place of origin. Along with these definitions, however, home is also described as a place "providing residence and care for people with special needs."[17] This definition, far more so than the first ones discussed, suggests that home is a place where one can find nourishment, protection, and, if needed, healing from trauma. But what about those persons who have so-called special needs? What kind of home is needed for such persons? When thinking about persons with such needs, one often conjures images

---

16   Moses, *Black Messiahs*, 8.

17   *Merriam-Webster*, s.v., "home," https://tinyurl.com/uxv5ywk5.

of, say, a nursing or orphan home, or a home for the mentally or physically challenged (or disabled). These are designated places (or homes) of care that serve persons with specific needs.

In an insightful essay titled "Home," novelist, essayist, and social critic Toni Morrison shares that home is not simply a place but an idea, and, even more so, a memory of an idea. Morrison asks, "What do we mean when we say [or think of] home?"[18] Of course, this is not an easy question to answer, particularly given that home can mean so many different things. For one, home means different things in different contexts. Morrison problematizes the idea of home by suggesting that in the twenty-first century, due to globalization, mass migration, and several sociopolitical issues that are causing an epidemic of homelessness, home as an idea and a reality has been destabilized. Morrison avers that the loss of place, which exacerbates a sense of homelessness, was often the experience of Black slaves and dislocated native populations in the United States. Morrison states,

> The relocation of peoples has ignited and disrupted the idea of home and expanded the focus of identity beyond definitions of citizenship to clarifications of foreignness. "Who is the foreigner?" is a question that leads us to the perception of an implicit and heightened threat within "difference." We see it in the defense of the local against the outsider; personal discomfort with one's own sense of belonging.[19]

Throughout Morrison's oeuvre, one is confronted with the poignant question, "Am I the foreigner in my own home?" A noteworthy example of feeling out of place in one's own home is found in her novel *The Bluest Eye*, a story that depicts how a young African American girl named Pecola is traumatized by her community, even the persons in her home, because of her dark skin. There are other places where Morrison courageously interrogates how home is not a given for minoritized communities. In another essay titled "The Foreigner's Home," Morrison observes,

---

18   Toni Morrison, *The Source of Self-Regard: Selected Essays, Speeches, and Meditations* (New York: Alfred A. Knopf, 2019), 17.

19   Ibid., 19.

> African and African American writers are not alone in coming to
> terms with these problems [alienation and homelessness], but they
> do have a long and singular history of confronting them. Of not being
> at home in one's homeland; of being exiled in the place one belongs.[20]

Throughout their history in the United States, African Americans have been made to feel like foreigners, the "other," for whom the promises of citizenship, the right to call this land their home, have remained elusive. Morrison offers an imaginative analysis of this "being exiled in the place one belongs" in her novel *Song of Solomon*, as she focuses on how the aforementioned folktale of the flying Africans helped African Americans confront this alienation or sense of homelessness. The focus of our discussion here is not on *Song of Solomon* but instead on the problematic manhood that it seeks to address. At its core, the novel is about Milkman Dead's need to find home because he has been alienated by his environment. His environment has designated Milkman Dead as a problem. And, unfortunately, there is no home in America for a Black man with this special need.

Morrison's ruminations on foreignness bring to mind a poignant question: "How does it feel to be a problem?"[21] Sociologist, historian, and civil rights activist W. E. B. Du Bois (1868–1963) asks this in his influential essay "Of Our Spiritual Strivings." Du Bois goes on to ask, "Why did God make me an outcast and a stranger in mine own house?"[22] Du Bois then describes the terror that is experienced by those who are entrapped within the veil of race. These are segments of the American populace who have been made to suffer the "strange experience" of being a problem.[23] Most observers focus on the "peculiar sensation, this double-consciousness"[24] that Du Bois explicates in the essay. What is of significance for us here is Du Bois's diagnosis regarding the Black man's inability to attain "self-conscious manhood."[25] Because of his race, Du Bois avers, the Black man is not able to

---

20 Ibid., 8.

21 W. E. B. Du Bois, *The Souls of Black Folk* (1903; repr., New York: Barnes & Noble Classics, 2003), 7.

22 Ibid., 8.

23 Ibid.

24 Ibid., 9.

25 Ibid.

achieve a unified sense of selfhood, a "true self-consciousness."[26] According to Du Bois, "[The Black man] simply wishes to make it possible for a man to be both a Negro and an American, without being cursed and spat upon by his fellows, without having the doors of opportunity closed roughly in his face."[27] The lack of opportunity for the Black man, the problem, is not simply due to the machinations of race and racism. Much of this racial hostility has to do with the centuries-old disregard many in the West have for the Black man's home: Africa. Not only is the Black man a problem but his home, Africa, is a problem as well. Morrison explains that, throughout most of Western literary, philosophical, and theological traditions, Africa has been deemed a "dark continent in desperate need of light."[28] According to those who hold this view, Africa has nothing to offer the world but is instead "a huge needy homeland to which we were said to belong but that none of us had seen or cared to see, inhabited by people with whom we maintained a delicate relationship of mutual ignorance and disdain, and with whom we shared a myth of passive, traumatized otherness."[29] It is not surprising, then, that so many African Americans view not only themselves as a problem but perceive their home, Africa, which should be a place of refuge, as a problem as well. Though it is daunting to pin down one specific source of this view of Africa, the work of philosopher G. W. F. Hegel was influential in inculcating a negative image of Africa in the Western intellectual tradition.

Hegel sought to explore the development of Spirit (or Mind) in history in his notable work *The Philosophy of History*. Hegel contends that the essence of Spirit is "activity; it realizes its potentiality—makes itself its own deed, its own work—and thus becomes an object to itself."[30] For Hegel, the primary means by which one is able to perceive the activity of Spirit in history is through the "Spirit of a People," which indicates the continual development (or growth), via a dialectical process, of a "new National Spirit."[31] Spirit is what keeps a nation and its people alive. That is to say, Spirit is what keeps a nation

---

26   Ibid.

27   Ibid.

28   Morrison, *The Source of Self-Regard*, 9.

29   Ibid.

30   G. W. F. Hegel, *The Philosophy of History* (Mineola: Dover Press, 1956), 73.

31   Hegel, *The Philosophy of History*, 75.

from being restricted to its glorious past or naively enamored by a hoped-for future. Instead, Spirit keeps a nation in a state of constant renewal, confident in what is occurring in the "essential now."[32] The great nations reflect the work of the Spirit by leaving an indelible mark on history, particularly in the development of culture. For example, Hegel points out that Western nations have had the greatest effect on history, and to a lesser extent, the nations of Asia have been influential as well. However, he has little regard for Africa's role in history. It is worth mentioning that Hegel does not view Africa as a monolith but as a nation divided into three unequal parts. First, he identifies the northern coastland, that is, places such as Tunisia, Morocco, and Algeria, as European Africa; next there is the area that surrounds the Nile, mainly Egypt, which is designated as being connected to Asia; and last is what he terms the "real" Africa (or African proper), the region that lies south of the Sahara, referred to as the darkest place on the dark continent.

> Africa proper, as far as History goes back, has remained—for all purposes of connection with the rest of the World—shut up; it is the Gold-land compressed within itself—the land of childhood, which lying beyond the day of self-conscious history, is enveloped in the dark mantle of Night.[33]

As for the people who occupy this dark continent, Hegel says,

> In Negro life the characteristic point is the fact that consciousness has not yet attained to the realization of any substantial objective existence—as for example, God, or Law—in which the interests of man's volitions are involved and in which he realizes his own being. This distinction between himself as an individual and the universality of his essential being, the African in the uniform, undeveloped oneness of his existence has not yet attained; so that Knowledge of an absolute Being, an Other and a Higher than his individual self, is entirely wanting.[34]

---

32   Ibid., 79.
33   Ibid., 91.
34   Ibid., 93.

This damning and misleading view of Africa is contested by Du Bois, who in *The World and Africa* remarks, "there can be little doubt but that in the fourteenth century the level of culture in black Africa south of the Sudan was equal to that of Europe and was so recognized."[35] Unfortunately, a positive view of Africa and its culture was replaced in post-Enlightenment European thought with the supposedly enlightened idea that Africa and its people had nothing to offer the world.

The emergence of this negative idea of Africa is explored in philosopher V. Y. Mudimbe's *The Invention of Africa: Gnosis, Philosophy, and the Order of Knowledge*. Mudimbe argues that various schools of thought, such as anthropology, emerged in the nineteenth century during the same time that modern missionaries were being sent to Africa. In fact, when divulging where he attained information about the benighted state of Africa, Hegel states, "the copious and circumstantial accounts of Missionaries completely confirm this."[36] Certainly, the "facts" provided by the sciences and missionaries supported the idea of the "inherent superiority of the white race" and "the necessity for European economies and structures to expand to virgin areas of the world."[37] But this was not enough. Something more, something transcendent, was needed to justify not only the negative idea of Africa but also the exploitation of the land and its people. Therefore, as Hegel suggested, the civilized West viewed Africa as a godless land, void of religious beliefs and practices that reflected a developed civilization. Mudimbe posits that as Africa was depicted as a land void of religious beliefs, Christian missionaries developed three approaches to the redemption of this forsaken land: (1) a total negation of Africa's purported "primitive" religions and gods, (2) an effort to demonstrate to the Africans the superiority of Christianity, and (3) the imposition of rules that forced converts to conform to the social mores of the colonizing nation.[38] The stated goal of these efforts was not simply to create

---

35   W. E. B. Du Bois, *The World and Africa: An Inquiry into the Part which Africa Played in World History* (New York: International Publishers, 1965), 44.

36   Hegel, *The Philosophy of History*, 93.

37   V. Y. Mudimbe, *The Invention of Africa: Gnosis, Philosophy, and the Order of Knowledge* (Bloomington: Indiana University Press, 1988), 17.

38   Ibid., 53.

religious converts but, even more significantly, docile subjects that could be exploited by colonizing powers.

In *The Idea of Africa*, Mudimbe argues that Western expansion, via colonization, had a deleterious effect on the spiritual lives of Indigenous populations. Mudimbe says, "disagreement [between the enlightened and the civilized] then appears as a powerful criterion . . . it arranges the gap which distance and difference have created in light of these colonizing practices . . . the scenarios of reducing other landscapes, other peoples, other values to a normative paradigm."[39] Mudimbe is pointing to a paradigm of encounter that is most evident in how the West has interacted with Africa. The idea that Africa is a land that must be forced to fit, by various forms of violence, within a "normative paradigm" (i.e., a civilized way of life) guided how many leaders of the early Black church viewed their home. In fact, the model of normativity was so prevalent that during the formative years of the Black church, some leaders, most of whom were men and were slaves or first-generation descendants of slaves, had a vision of remaking Africa, their home, into a place that resembled the American South. Black nationalist Martin R. Delaney was confident, for example, that it was the Black man's calling to Christianize and, by extension, enlighten his African brethren. Delaney, whom we will return to later, was but one of many Black leaders who were trying to overcome the slanderous images of Black men as perpetual children, most evident in the popularized Sambo figure. To understand how this ideal developed, it is worth examining, first, the emergence of Sambo and the various ways Black men sought to fight against this damning image.

The Sons of Sambo Rebel

The Sambo figure started as a myth, but later became a reality. Sociologist William H. Turner, in his essay "Myths and Stereotypes: The African Man in America," remarks that 'reality itself is often defined within the context

---

39   V. Y. Mudimbe, *The Idea of Africa* (Bloomington: Indiana University Press, 1994), 6.

of the myths and stereotypes developed to account for it."[40] But what are these myths, especially those that create oppressive realities for minoritized groups, supposed to accomplish? "They serve," Turner says, "to lessen the cognitive-load of modern man inasmuch as we must codify and categorize the infinite amount of information on which reality itself is based."[41] Therefore, if we return to the discussion in the previous section regarding Africa, a myth was created about Africa's fallen state—that is, its uncivilized status—because colonizing powers never intended to know the rich cultural and religious histories of Africa. Instead, they created a myth that could easily be codified and categorized by those who sought to exploit the continent. Likewise, given Turner's argument, it has also been much easier for white America to categorize Black men, for instance, as lazy, childlike, angry, and libidinous than to seriously consider the daily realities of Black life that invalidate such labels. According to Turner, many whites believed the myth purporting that the Sambo was the original "proper personification" of the Black man in America. But what was it, exactly, about Sambo, in mythology and reality, that made him so beloved by white America and, at the same time, so harmful to the image—and, more important, self-image—of Black men?

In *Sambo: The Rise and Demise of an American Jester*, historian Joseph Boskin provides an insightful overview of how the Sambo figure emerged, and was popularized, in American culture. Boskin has it that the Sambo figure was the first "truly indigenous American humor character throughout the culture, transcending region and ethnicity."[42] Sambo's appeal was not humor alone, however. Another interesting trait that made the Sambo figure appealing was his inability to feel sorrow. This myth regarding Sambo's personality originated on the plantation, where slave-masters often marveled at how slaves could suffer while still experiencing

---

40   William Turner, "Myths and Stereotypes: The African Man in America," in *The Black Male in America: Perspectives on His Status in Contemporary Society*, ed. Doris Y. Wilkinson and Ronald L. Taylor (Chicago: Nelson-Hall, 1977), 122.

41   Turner, "Myths and Stereotypes," 122.

42   Joseph Boskin, *Sambo: The Rise and Demise of an American Jester* (New York: Oxford University Press, 1986), 8.

joy, that is, "that people so oppressed could sing and dance."[43] It was not long before the myth regarding the slave's ineluctable joy was turned into a performative reality through various forms of entertainment. "On the plantations, it was expected that one of the slaves' primary tasks was to entertain the whites," writes Boskin.[44] Unfortunately, this readily available entertainment affixed an image in the American mind of the Black man as a perpetual child. In fact, historians agree that slavery was founded and maintained through the paternalistic master–slave relationship. The master wanted to be recognized as a divine-like figure, akin to a heavenly father, the one to whom slaves remained absolutely obedient. To achieve this, however, slave masters had to make the plantation the slave's home. For example, slaveowner Bennet Barrow kept a diary detailing how he controlled the estimated two hundred slaves on his cotton plantation in Louisiana. In an entry on May 1, 1838, Barrow writes:

> The very security of the plantation requires that a general and uniform control over the people of it should be exercised. What are to protect the planation from the intrusions of ill-designed persons when every body is a broad? Who can tell the moment when a plantation might be threatened with destruction from fire—could the flames be arrested if the negroes are scattered throughout the neighborhood, seeking their amusement. Are these not duties of great importance, and in which every negro himself is deeply interested to render this part of the rule justly applicable, however, it would be necessary that such a settled arrangement should exist on the plantation as to make it necessary for a negro to leave it . . . You must, therefore, make him as comfortable at Home as possible, affording him, What is essentially necessary for his happiness—you must provide for him Yourself and by that means create in him a habit of perfect dependence on you.[45]

---

43 Ibid., 45.

44 Ibid., 46.

45 Edwin Adams Davis, ed., *Plantation Life in the Florida Parishes of Louisiana, 1836–1846, as reflected in the Diary of Bennet H. Barrow* (New York: AMS Press, 1943), 406–7.

After offering his advice to fellow slavemasters, Barrett goes on to suggest that the upshot of all of this is that "the Negro who is accustomed to remain constantly at Home, is just as satisfied with the society of the plantation as that which he would find elsewhere."[46] The plantation, then, was the slave's home, but it was a home that created and maintained an inequitable power structure that ensured the slavemaster could produce dependent, Sambo-like behavior in slaves.

As Sambo, the slave's dependency on the slavemaster was limitless. So much so that, in his influential text *Slavery: A Problem in American Institutional and Intellectual Life*, historian Stanley Elkins contends that chattel slavery significantly altered the personality of slaves. Elkins points out that the unique personality types found amongst slaves were produced by what he terms the "closed system of the plantation," a system that was so complete because everything about the slave's life was under the slavemaster's control. Living under these conditions created the Sambo personality type, which Elkins describes as follows:

> The characteristics that have been claimed for the type come principally from Southern lore. Sambo, the typical plantation slave, was docile but irresponsible, loyal but lazy, humble but chronically given to lying and stealing; his behavior was full of infantile silliness and his talk inflated with childish exaggeration. His relationship with his master was one of utter dependence and childlike attachment: it was indeed this childlike quality that was the very key to his being. Although the merest hint of Sambo's "manhood" might fill the Southern breast with scorn, the child, "in his place," could be both exasperating and loveable.[47]

Throughout *Slavery*, Elkins focuses on how the closed system of the plantation sustained "infantilism as a normal feature of behavior."[48] An essential part of Sambo's childish behavior was that he was required to be in

---

46   Ibid., 407.

47   Stanley Elkins, *Slavery: A Problem in Institutional and Intellectual Life*, 2nd ed. (Chicago: University of Chicago Press, 1968), 82.

48   Ibid., 86.

awe of and identify with the absolute power of the slavemaster. Elkins observes that the system is likened to that of the patriarchal household, stating, "the plantation offered no really satisfactory father-image other than the master."[49] He goes on to add that "absolute power for him meant absolute dependency for the slave—the dependency not of the developing child but of the perpetual child. For the master, the role most aptly fitting such a relationship would naturally be that of the father."[50] Needless to say, slavemasters who were committed to maintaining this exploitive father–son relationship expected their male slaves to display all the characteristics of a dutiful son, the Sambo. Elkins's thesis regarding Sambo's filial piety is confirmed by historian John W. Blassingame, who notes that "the master and slave lived and worked together on such intimate terms that they developed an affection for each other, and the slave identified completely with his master."[51] But is this true? What of the documented slave rebellions telling of ways enslaved people fought against slavemasters and, by extension, the Sambo image?

An overlooked, and often misunderstood, example of this rebellion is found in Harriet Beecher Stower's well-known novel *Uncle Tom's Cabin*, published in 1852. The dominant interpretation of the novel is that Uncle Tom, the main character, was the embodiment of the dutiful slave, a Sambo. Even today, to be called an Uncle Tom denotes that a Black person, particularly a Black man, is overly supportive of social policies and causes that are championed by the white community. Wilson Jeremiah Moses argues that such a view limits the complexity of Uncle Tom. Moses states that "the character of Uncle Tom was not originally intended to be pejorative."[52] Uncle Tom was no Sambo, for unlike Sambo, Uncle Tom did not exhibit absolute obedience to his slavemaster, Simon Legree. For instance, during an episode in the novel in which his owner demands that Tom commit acts of violence against fellow slaves, he refuses to obey. Also, due to his deep spirituality, Tom did not display *absolute* dependence upon

---

49 Ibid., 113.

50 Ibid.

51 John W. Blassingame, *Slave Community: Plantation Life in the Antebellum South*. Rev. ed. (1972; repr., New York: Oxford University Press, 1979), 304.

52 Moses, *Black Messiahs*, 49.

his slavemaster—that is, Legree was not Tom's god. This is evident when Tom says to Legree, "My soul an't yours, mas'r. . . . It's been bought and paid for by the One that's able to keep it."[53] The slavemaster's desire for absolute control—of the soul and the body—of the slave is vividly described by Stowe, who, in *A Key to Uncle Tom's Cabin*, shares that "only this office of master . . . contains the power to bind and loose, and to open and shut the kingdom of heaven, and involves responsibility for the soul as well as the body."[54] Tom, however, rebels against the notion that Legree, or any other earthly potentate, owned his soul.

Slaves also undertook more direct forms of rebellion that sought to militate against the Sambo-making system of the plantation. One finds this in the stories of uncontrollable slaves—slaves who would never bow to slavemasters, no matter how much they were punished. Frederick Douglass was such a slave. Douglass shares the story of his physical encounter with Edward Covey, referred to as the Negro-breaker, in his autobiographical narrative, *My Bondage, My Freedom.* Covey had a reputation as a slavemaster who possessed the skill of bending even the most obdurate slave to his will. Covey could turn a rebellious slave into a Sambo. The man himself was terrifying, and, according to Douglass, the conditions on his plantation were just as bad. In a letter written from Scotland in 1846 to abolitionist William Lloyd Garrison, Douglass states that Covey's plantation was so terrible that "[his] soul was crushed and [his] spirits broken."[55] But Douglass's low emotional and spiritual state did not last. Something happened, eventually, that changed him, and it was a change that lasted the rest of his life. Douglass discusses his monumental transformation from the enslaved "ordinary Negro," Frederick Bailey, to the freeman Frederick Douglass, who was a new, empowered man.[56] It was a complete

---

53 Harriet Beecher Stowe, *Uncle Tom's Cabin: Or Negro Life in the United States* (1852; repr., London: Wordsworth, 1995), 331.

54 Harriet Beecher Stowe, *A Key to Uncle Tom's Cabin: Facts and Documents upon Which the Story Is Founded* (1852; repr., Bedford, MA: Applewood Books, 1970), 39.

55 Frederick Douglass, 1846, quoted in *Frederick Douglass: Selected Speeches and Writings*, ed. Philip S. Foner (Chicago: Lawrence Hill Books, 1999), 22.

56 Ibid., 22–23.

conversion. What brought about this radical transformation in Douglass? He confesses that his physical altercation with Covey, a flagrant act of rebellion—an act a Sambo would never commit—was the turning point in his life because, through this violent confrontation, he attained "a sense of his own manhood."[57] Manhood was what he gained from this conversion, and nothing mattered more to Douglass than achieving this status. "I was a changed being after that fight. I was nothing before; I WAS A MAN NOW," writes Douglass.[58] Douglass likens his acquisition of power-filled manhood to a redemptive religious conversion:

> A man, without force, is without the essential dignity of humanity. Human nature is so constituted, that it cannot honor a helpless man, although it can pity him; end even this it cannot do long, if the signs of power do not arise. . . . After resisting him [Covey], I felt as I had never felt before. It was a resurrection from the dark and pestiferous tomb of slavery to the heaven of comparative freedom. I was no longer a servile coward, trembling under the frown of a brother worm of the dust, but my long-cowed spirit was roused to an attitude of manly independence.[59]

According to historian John David Smith, the confrontation "released Douglass from the chains suppressing his will and identity and gave him self-confidence to act on his own regardless of the circumstances."[60] Douglass's victory over Covey was not his triumph alone but became a template of how Black men could overcome the shame of the Sambo figure. Ultimately, his message of redeemed manhood would become the clarion call for Black leaders, the Black messiahs, who wanted to lead the oppressed to a new age of liberation. The message was clear: acquiring a powerful manhood would denote authentic liberation. Only a true man was free. But this, too, proved problematic for Black manhood, as it was

---

57 Frederick Douglass, *My Bondage and My Freedom*, ed. John David Smith (1855; repr., New York: Penguin Books, 2003), 181.

58 Douglass, *My Bondage*, 181.

59 Ibid., 180.

60 John David Smith, "Introduction," in Douglass, *My Bondage*, xxxiii.

informed by a model that overvalued patriarchal, violence-laden, and overly Christianized forms of Western manhood.

THE BLACK MESSIAH'S MISSION TO REDEEM AFRICA (AND HIMSELF)

The Sambo figure was not the only slave character to emerge during slavery, particularly in the antebellum South. John Blassingame shares that "Nat" was depicted as the other side of Sambo. While Sambo was dependent, childish, and jovial, Nat was "revengeful, bloodthirsty, cunning, treacherous and savage."[61] The myth of Nat is based on the life of Nat Turner, a preacher and revolutionary who led the most violent slave revolt in US history. Unlike earlier slave revolts, such as the Haitian San Domingo revolt (1791–1804), led by general Toussaint Louverture, Nat Turner's had a supernatural element that terrified the South's slave-owning class. Scholar of African American literature William L. Andrews reports that before the start of the revolt on August 21, 1831, Turner received a series of "heavenly" visions between the years of 1825 and 1831. In one especially prophetic vision, Turner "learned of his messianic task: to 'fight against the Serpent' in the approaching eschaton."[62] From these kinds of messianic visions, Turner got the fierce courage to start the revolt that, in Andrew's words, "traumatized the white South."[63] Nat Turner's status as not simply a revolutionary but even more so a messianic figure is evident in Wilson Jeremiah Moses's statement that Tuner was "superficially reminiscent of the wrathful, retributive messiah."[64] American history has been filled with figures, mostly men, who have been viewed as messiahs—that is, modern-day deliverers who were sent to redeem the oppressed.

Moses suggests four different patterns of messianism: (1) "The expectation or identification of a personal savior—a messiah, a prophet or a

---

61   Blassingame, *Slave Community*, 225.

62   William L. Andrews, "Nat Turner," in *The Oxford Companion to African American Literature*, ed. William L. Andrews, Frances Smith Foster, and Trudier Harris (New York: Oxford University Press, 1997), 739.

63   Andrews, *Oxford Companion*, 739.

64   Moses, *Black Messiahs*, 65.

Mahdi [messianic figure in Islam]"; (2) "The far more important theme of racist messianism—a concept of the redemptive mission of the black race"; (3) "Messianic symbolism—journalistic and artistic representations of certain black individuals as symbolic messiahs"; and (4) "anyone with a special mission from God."[65] Moses also adds that messianism is "the perception of a person or a group, by itself or by others, as having a manifest destiny or a God-given role to assert the providential goals of history and to bring about the kingdom of God on earth."[66] In his essay "The Black Church: Manhood and Mission," historian William H. Becker states that some leaders in the formational years of the African Methodist Episcopal (AME) Church, the first independent Black denomination, believed themselves called by God to redeem their fallen brethren in Africa. Bishop Henry M. Turner, who traveled to West Africa in 1891, declared that "there is no reason under heaven why this continent [Africa] should not or cannot be brought to God in twenty-five years—say thirty at most."[67] The Reverend S. F. Flegler, a pastor who led a group of AME settlers to Liberia, claimed that "Africa is the home of the Negro, the land where he is free, and where he has the best opportunity for the best development."[68]

Becker suggests that what these leaders wanted to develop, and even more important, to have recognized in Africa, was their manhood. "The assertion of black manhood was in turn a conscious motive and dominant theme in the black appropriation of the common nineteenth century dogma that it was the black American's special providential calling to win his African brother to Christianity. Black manhood and black mission in Africa come to be tied together in the black Christian mind," writes Becker.[69] The independent Black congregations that emerged during the late nineteenth century provided a unique space for Black men to become independent, thereby negating much of the stigma associated with the Sambo figure. Becker identifies three integral elements that, for some leaders in the Black church, guided the Black man's mission to Africa:

---

65 Ibid., 1.

66 Ibid., 4.

67 Becker, "The Black Church," 329.

68 Ibid., 330.

69 Ibid., 323.

(a) the American black man has been prepared for mission work by divine providence, through Christianization and education in the U.S.; (b) being thus blessed by God, Afro-Americans are obligated to bring these blessings to their African brothers; (c) Afro-Americans possess a "superior fitness" for African mission because of their racial kinship with Africans and because they can adapt to the African climate more successfully than white missionaries.[70]

Unfortunately, some of the Black leaders who engaged in the missionary efforts to redeem their African brethren maintained a negative view of Africa, the nation, and its people. For instance, L. J. Coppin, AME Bishop of South Africa, said in 1902 that "In their isolated condition, the people [of Africa] have for long centuries become the victims of customs and habits not in keeping with the better life which is the result only of Christian civilization."[71] Just as Hegel had claimed decades prior in *The Philosophy of History*, Coppin, too, viewed Africa as an uncivilized continent in need of what the civilized West, or the Christianized United States, had to offer. Some observers believed that Africa could not be redeemed. For instance, nineteenth-century historian W. Winwood Reade expresses a similar perspective in "Efforts of Missionaries Among Savages," wherein, after seeing the work of American Protestant missionaries, he laments that missionary efforts cannot change the "wretched creatures" in Africa.[72] Black missionaries from America remained hopeful that they could make a change. Nevertheless, there seems to have been little thought as to how the natives in Africa, especially in colonies like Liberia, often designated as a "black man's place,"[73] would receive the Black messiahs who, they were being told, had come to redeem them. Historian James Ciment reports that some natives referred to the new settlers as "black white men," mainly because both the Black and white settlers viewed the natives as "heathens

---

70 Ibid., 329.

71 Ibid., 331.

72 W. Winwood Reade, "Efforts of Missionaries among Slaves," *Journal of the Anthropological Study of London* (1865): 163–83.

73 James Ciment, *Another America: The Story of Liberia and the Former Slaves Who Ruled It* (New York: Hill & Wang, 2013), xviii.

to be redeemed, or savages to be conquered."[74] In some instances, Black settlers reproduced the same oppressive systems they were attempting to escape in America. For instance, Peyton Skipwith, an emancipated African American, was sent with his wife and children to Liberia in 1833. In his first letter from Liberia, Skipwith describes the settlers' treatment of the natives as follows: "poor souls [the natives] they beat unmercifully, and more than half starve them, and all the labor that is done at all, is done by these poor wretches."[75] This treatment was often handed out by former slaves and freedman who were sent as missionaries to Africa; most of whom believed that you can "do all you can for them [the natives] and they will still be your enemy."[76] Ciment argues that Skipwith's attitude toward the natives in Liberia "sounds all too familiar to us if not to the former slaves and freedmen who embodied it."[77] Other settlers did not view the Africans as enemies but still had the attitude that it was their duty to make certain their primitive brethren wholeheartedly adopted a civilized—and, more to the point, Christianized—way of life.

Few leaders preached the gospel of this civilized way of life more than abolitionist and Black nationalist Martin R. Delany. Delany strongly supported the idea that African Americans should return to Africa, particularly in a missionary capacity. In *Search for a Place*, Delany expounds on his belief that it is the Americanized Black man's calling to redeem Africa. He was confident that these chosen missionaries should be Black men whose vision for a new kingdom in Africa included "commerce, transportation, crops—including cotton—and he sees in this and other tropical and other semitropical lands the hope of competing successfully with the economy of the American South."[78] If this vision were realized, then Africa, in essence, would be a replica in toto of the exploitive capitalist regimes of the American South. But Delaney's vision was not restricted to commerce. He also believed it was the Black man's calling to bring about more

---

74   Ciment, *Another America*, xix.

75   Ibid., 70.

76   Ibid., 71.

77   Ibid.

78   M. R. Delany and Robert Campbell, *Search for a Place: Black Separatism and Africa, 1960* (Ann Arbor: University of Michigan Press, 1969), 16.

fundamental changes to the natives—that is, their whole way of being in the world needed to be radically changed. Delaney states,

> The improved arts of civilized life must now be brought to bear, and go hand in hand in aid of missionary efforts which are purely religious in character and teaching. . . . Christianity certainly is the most advanced civilization that man ever attained to, and where propagated in its purity, to be effective, law and government must be brought in harmony with it.[79]

And he offers the following as the signs that the natives are in fact becoming more civilized:

> I would suggest for the benefit of missionaries in general, and those to whom it applies in particular, that there are other measures and ways by which civilization may be imparted than preaching and praying—temporal as well as spiritual means. If all persons who settle among the natives would, as far as it is in their power and comes within their province, induce, by making it a rule of their house or family, every native servant to sit on a stool or chair; eat at a table instead of on the ground; eat with a knife and fork (or *begin* with a spoon) instead of with their fingers. . . . [And] have them to wear some sort of a garment to cover the entire person above the knees, should it be but a single shirt or chemise, instead of a loose native cloth thrown around them. . . . I am certain that it would go far toward impressing with some of the habits of civilized life.[80]

In order to understand Delaney's stance, it is worth returning to Moses's definition of messianism, as he states that it is "the perception of a person or a group, by itself or others, as having a manifest destiny or a God given role to assert the providential goals of history and to bring about the kingdom

---

79   Delaney, *Search for a Place*, 109.
80   Ibid., 105–6.

of God on earth."[81] Is there anything about the Black messiah's return to Africa—especially in Liberia—that exhibited the kingdom of God on earth? What changes occurred to signify that the Black messiahs were able to "lead [Africa] in the direction of righteousness"?[82] One could certainly argue that the righteousness of a civilized way of life, rooted in Western patriarchy, was the *sin qua non* of this kingdom. In the end, however, this vision and the reality it created were no kingdom of God. For some natives, the only thing the Black messiah returned with was the glory of a destructive form of manhood, one that mimicked the exploitive domination of the white slavemasters whose reign in the American South established hell on earth, not the kingdom of God, for enslaved Black people.

Conclusion: A Taste of the Same

In the introduction to this essay, I shared the story of the flying Africans, as told in "People Who Could Fly." An important aspect of this narrative is when the slave driver threatened the slaves with the warning, "If you [n-word] don't want a taste of the same, you'd better get to work."[83] "A taste of the same" refers to the slave driver whipping those slaves who, due to severe conditions, could not complete the day's work. This warning has reverberated through the African American experience. Countless stories tell how "a taste of the same" has caused great sorrow, led some to do harm to others, and forced many within the African American community to abandon all hope. Unfortunately, due to the constant oppression of "a taste of the same," some no longer value their blackness. A germane example of this is provided in writer and activist James Weldon Johnson's *The Auto-biography of an Ex-Colored Man*, wherein, upon witnessing a lynching, the protagonist laments that he "belonged to a race that could be dealt with so [brutally]," adding that "my heart turned bitter within me."[84] The

---

81   Moses, *Black Messiahs*, 4.

82   Ibid., 5.

83   Lester, *Black Folktales*, 100.

84   James Weldon Johnson, *The Autobiography of an Ex-Colored Man*, in *James Weldon Johnson: Writings*, ed. William L. Andrews (New York: Literary Classics of the United States, 2004), 113.

ex-colored man confesses that this bitterness had become so intense that he no longer wanted to self-identify nor be identified as a Negro.

> All the while, I understood that it was not discouragement or fear, or search for a larger field of action and opportunity that was driving me out of the Negro race. I knew that it was shame, unbearable shame. Shame at being identified with a people that could with impunity be treated worse than animals.[85]

Due to this shame, the ex-colored man in Johnson's novel cuts himself off from his Black cultural heritage by investing his sense of selfhood totally in the "white side of the color line."[86] He is tired of living with the daily pain of "a taste of the same."

The Black messiah was supposed to offer a remedy to "a taste of the same," but did this occur? Wilson Jeremiah Moses sees a problem with the messianic myth in that because it is formed out of a Christian ethos, it is "driven by the same zealous, narrow-minded, self-righteous Protestantism that has so often worked against [Black people]."[87] Of course, as discussed above, this is evident in how some Black clergymen, in their missionary roles, sought to assert their manhood by redeeming Africa—or, more to the point, remaking Africa into the image of the civilized West. Nevertheless, in so doing, the Black missionaries who held this view were giving their African brethren, the very ones they were sent to redeem, "a taste of the same." It is worth recalling that Peyton Skipwith, the former slave who was sent to Liberia in 1833, tells of the terrible treatment—physical beatings, starvation, etc.—the natives received at the hands of the recently arrived Black settlers. Physical violence, when it occurred, was only part of the problem, however. The larger issue was the Christian West's arrogant assertions of racial and cultural superiority that certain African American clergymen had adopted wholeheartedly when going home to Africa. Ciment suggests that all of this

---

85 Johnson, *The Autobiography*, 115.

86 Herman Beavers, "The Autobiography of an Ex-Colored Man," in *The Oxford Companion to African American Literature*, ed. William L. Andrews, Frances Smith Foster, and Trudier Harris (New York: Oxford University Press, 1997), 40.

87 Moses, *Black Messiahs*, 238.

was a primary cause of the larger "social ills" (or various forms of social oppression) that Skipwith believed the Black settlers brought with them from America to Liberia.[88]

This chapter has argued that the central social ill that afflicted Black men in America was their inability to achieve manhood. The Black messiah hoped that his return to Africa could remedy this illness. According to Becker, Edward W. Blyden, a clergyman, scholar, and Liberian government official, made the "most uncompromising . . . argument that the manhood and mission of the black man was not [in America] but in Africa."[89] In sum, Blyden averred that God had allowed African slaves to be brought to America to be Christianized (and civilized), and then it was their calling to "return home to Christianize Africa."[90] Blyden says, "God sent us here [to America] to be trained so that we might return to the land of our fathers and take charge of it, develop it and defend it."[91] In order to accomplish this, however, the Black messiah often looked upon himself as a savior whose manhood demanded that he have absolute control over Africa, the land and its people. It should come as no surprise, then, when Bishop Henry M. Turner, a noted A. M. E. leader, boasts, "One thing the black man has here [in Africa] . . . and that is manhood, freedom and the fullest liberty. He feels like a lord and walks the same way."[92] It was the same pattern of male domination, only now in a different shade. A taste of the same!

---

88   Ciment, *Another America*, 56.

89   Becker, *The Black Church*, 322.

90   Ibid.

91   Ibid.

92   Ibid.

PART 3

BIBLICAL AND THEOLOGICAL APPROACHES TO GENDER AND SEXUALITY

CHAPTER 8

THE PUBLIC BIBLE, POLITICS, GENDER, AND SEXUALITY IN ZAMBIA

Chammah J. Kaunda

INTRODUCTION

Zambia is a context without a sharp distinction between the natural order and symbolic order. The symbolic world of religion forms the background against which the normal or everyday life experiences take place. Symbolic power is the most pervasive, invisible, readily accessible form of power in the world. It is embedded in social structures, relationships, politics, religions, and so on. Religion is a lived metaphor and substratum of triumphs and defeats of everyday ways of interacting, looking at, and doing things. Scholars have argued that the reason religion and public life remain inseparable in Africa is because it is fundamentally through spiritual framework that Africans think about the world today.[1] It is a pervasive cultural system of meaning, which often functions as the overarching and overriding principle of everyday life.

In Zambia, to be precise, Christianity has been deeply entrenched in this public cultural symbolic system, which often is utilized to create, construct, replicate, and perpetuate a particular social order or reality.[2] For Christians, the Bible as a symbolic system of the invisible realm plays

---

1   Stephen Ellis and Gerrie ter Haar, *Worlds of Power: Religious Thought and Political Practice in Africa* (London: C. Hurst & Co., 2004), 2.

2   For a detailed explanation of symbolic structures and symbolic power, see Pierre Bourdieu, *Language and Symbolic Power*, ed. J. Thompson, trans. G. Raymond and M. Adamson (Cambridge, MA: Harvard University Press, 1991).

a decisive, pivotal, and determining function in the daily lives of many Zambian Christians, who make up more than 95 percent of the national population.[3] Yet Zambia is not just a majority Christian nation but a Pentecostal[4] nation—deeply entrenched in Pentecostal culture, religious expression, and public imagination. Zambia's Pentecostal population is about 23.6 percent of the Christian national population.[5] These statistics are confirmed by Operation World, which cites the number of Charismatics in mainstream Christianity as 25.8 percent, and Evangelical-Pentecostals as 25.7 percent.[6] According to these figures, if Charismatics in mainstream Christianity were included, over half of Zambia's population would subscribe to pentecostalized and charismatized forms of African spirituality. These statistics do not just indicate unparalleled growth of Pentecostalism, but rather, they demonstrate a radical shift in the character, nature, and spiritual orientation of Zambian Christianity and African spirituality generally.[7]

After I give a concise history of Zambian Christianity, I will explain the role of the Bible in African Pentecostalism. Then attention is turned to consider how Rev. Godfridah Sumaili, during her tenure (from 2016 to 2021) as Minister of the now-defunct Ministry of National Guidance and Religious Affairs (hereafter, MNGRA), deployed the Bible in the Zambian

---

3   Zamstats, "Zambia 2010 Census of Population and Housing National: Analytical Report" (December 2012), https://tinyurl.com/mxucu9j7; See also Index-Mundi, "Zambia Religions" (December 7, 2019), https://tinyurl.com/4r4hdx7x.

4   Throughout this chapter, the terms "Pentecostal," "Pentecostals," and "Pentecostalism" are used in reference to the broader, multiple, and diverse communities that identify with the movements (classical, neo-Pentecostalism, and Charismatics [both Protestant and Catholic]) who stress the ongoing missional activity of the Holy Spirit in the world.

5   Todd M. Johnson and Gina A. Zurlo, eds., *World Christian Database* (Boston: Brill, 2016).

6   Jason Mandryk, ed., *Operation World Country Profiles*, 7th edition (Colorado Springs, CO: Biblica, 2010), 895.

7   Allan H. Anderson, "Stretching Out Hands to God: Origins and Development of Pentecostalism in Africa," in *Pentecostalism in Africa: Presence and Impact of Pneumatic Christianity in Postcolonial Societies*, ed. Martin Lindhardt (Leiden: Brill Academic, 2015), 54–74.

public as symbolic power to legitimize the religious nationality of power in the context of gender and sexuality. The religious nationality of power refers to political utilization of spirituality and religious symbols as intangible technologies of control, subjugation, reproduction, and perpetuation of power dynamics to shape all relationships in the nation between husbands and wives, parents and children, religious leaders and congregants, citizens and politicians, and so on. I argue that the public Bible in Zambia has been deployed as a total system of symbolic death, and that citizens experienced this monotheistic ideological system as a totalizing, monopolizing, ultimate, imposing, and pervasive frame of understanding and articulating Zambia as a nation embedded in a unified meaning. Sumaili's pentecostally constructed politics exhibited what Achille Mbembe describes as necropolitics or the "politics of death,"[8] meaning death as literal and as a metaphor of injustice and violence.

The Story of Zambian Christian Heritage at a Glance

The story of Zambian Christian heritage dates to 1851 with Dr. David Livingstone's search for the source of the Nile River. This British Congregationalist, pioneer medical missionary with the London Missionary Society (LMS), and explorer in Africa is perceived as the spiritual father of Zambia as a Christian nation. It has been argued that Livingstone's exploration work "inspired more European missionaries to undertake the difficult journey to central Africa to establish Christian mission centers."[9] By 1878, only five years after his death, LMS began mission work in Northern Rhodesia (contemporary Zambia). A few years later, missionaries from various other churches and mission societies—including the Roman

---

8   Achille Mbembe, "Necropolitics," *Public Culture* 15, no. 1 (2003): 11–40 (27).

9   Isaac Phiri, "Why African Churches Preach Politics: The Case of Zambia," *Journal of Church and State* 41, no. 2 (1999): 323–47, (324–25); see also Isaac Phiri, *Proclaiming Political Pluralism: Churches and Political Transitions in Africa* (Westport, CT: Praeger, 2001), 16. For a concise study missionary work in Zambia from late 1800 up to 1924, see Robert I. Rotberg, *Christian Missionaries and the Creation of Northern Rhodesia 1880–1924* (Princeton, NJ: Princeton University Press, 1965).

Catholic Church, the English Primitive Methodist Mission, the Paris Evangelical Missionary Society, the Dutch Reformed Church, Seventh-day Adventists, Baptists, Brethren in Christ, and Anglicans—also entered the country.[10] It is important to mention, however, that Zambia did not exist as a nation when Livingstone first arrived in 1851.[11] In addition, although Livingstone never indicated that he had such a vision of colonization of Africa,[12] he remains a problematic figure for discussing the emergence of imperialism and colonialism in Africa.[13] Nevertheless, the Livingstone myth continues to be adapted to a variety of political and religious contexts in Zambia.[14] John Mackenzie stresses:

> It is perhaps inevitable that the life of the great mythic figure of African exploration, David Livingstone, should itself have become the subject of a number of historical myths. His legendary status turned him into an icon that was constantly invoked throughout the imperial period. He was lionised to a greater extent than almost any other figure of the nineteenth century such that he was

10   Bwalya S. Chuba's book provides a concise and detailed account of the history of Christian missions, cultural conflicts, and development of ecumenical relations in Zambia. See his *A History of Early Christian Missions and Church Unity in Zambia* (Ndola: Mission Press, 2013); see also Ted Olsen, "One African Nation under God," *Christianity Today* 46, no. 2, (2002): 36–43.

11   Phiri, "Why African Churches Preach Politics"; Phiri, *Proclaiming Political Pluralism.*

12   John M. Mackenzie has spelled out many misconceptions labeled against Livingstone as prophet of imperialism and colonialism. See his "David Livingstone – Prophet or Patron Saint of Imperialism in Africa: Myths and Misconceptions," *Scottish Geographical Journal* 129, no. 3-04 (2013): 277–91.

13   David Spurr, *The Rhetoric of Empire: Colonial Discourse in Journalism, Travel Writing, and Imperial Administration* (Durham: Duke University Press, 1993); Dane Kennedy, *The Last Blank Spaces: Exploring Africa and Australia* (Cambridge, MA: Harvard University Press, 2013); Megan Ward with Adrian Wisnicki, "Livingstone's Global Sources: Livingstone's 1870 Field Diary," (April 25, 2017), https://tinyurl.com/yc3yu24p.

14   John M. MacKenzie, "David Livingstone, the Construction of the Myth," in *Sermons and Battle Hymns,* ed. Graham Walker and Tom Gallagher (Edinburgh: Edinburgh University Press, 1990), 24–42.

elevated to the status of a Protestant saint endowed with virtues that, for a period, placed him almost beyond criticism.[15]

For example, Livingston's deathbed prayer at Ulala village in Chief Chitambo's chiefdom in Serenje, northern Zambia, in 1873 is regarded to have "laid the spiritual foundation for Zambia."[16] He prayed, "Lord, on this land where I rest my bended knees, may arise a mighty Christian nation that will become a beacon of light and hope to the continent of African [sic] and the rest of the world." Nearly a century and a half later, on October 25, 2015, during the ceremony for the construction of the National House of Prayer, former president Edgar Lungu described Christianity as a "national faith" of Zambia. He challenged the audience to "consider this prayer by David Livingstone." He asked them, "Are we not living in the days of the fulfillment of that Great Prayer?" He concluded that "obligation is now upon us to play our part to share the love of Christ."[17] Many Zambian Pentecostals believe that Livingstone's:

> prayer opened up Zambia to faith in Christ. And his exploration brought schools, hospitals and churches. Kenneth Kaunda, and his freedom fighters were first fruits of the missionary passion. But Livingstone's prayer did more. It pointed to a political dispensation rare in modern times . . . When President FTJ Chiluba declared Zambia a Christian nation on December 29, 1991, to our knowledge he had no idea of Livingstone's death bed prayer. But Chiluba reset the tone for our republic.[18]

Livingstone was the first Christian to have walked over Zambia and died in the nation where his heart was buried. He is regarded by most Pentecostals as the founding father of Zambian Christian spirituality.[19]

---

15   MacKenzie, "David Livingstone."

16   Derek Mutungu, "Reflection: Zambia National Day of Prayer and Fasting" (October 18, 2015).

17   Edgar C. Lungu, "Greetings!" 25 October, 2015, https://tinyurl.com/r7zetu8x

18   Mutungu, "Reflection."

19   Charles Mwewa argues that the influence of missionaries such as Livingstone and the Roman Catholic Bishop Joseph Dupont on Zambia had already

Historians of Zambian Christianity, such as Marja Hinfelaar and Isaac Phiri, have argued that the idea of a Christian nation did not arise with Chiluba's declaration in 1991 but rather its foundation was already present at national independence and in Kaunda's philosophy of humanism.[20] As Hinfelaar observes, "Christianity was firmly embedded in Zambian society at the time of Independence, and its mission-educated leaders fully understood the importance of the consent and blessings of the churches."[21] Hinfelaar's argument is important because the mission-educated politicians were aware that European missionaries were at the forefront of British colonization of Zambia. They were not merely the carriers of the Christian message but were also the first to enter and live among Indigenous societies that would eventually become colonized.[22]

In 1888 Cecil Rhodes, a British businessman in South Africa and Prime Minister of the Cape Colony, began the great imperial adventure into Central Africa. In the same year, Northern and Southern Rhodesia (now Zambia and Zimbabwe, respectively) were proclaimed a British political domain. With Southern Rhodesia annexed by the British Empire and granted a self-governing colony status in 1923,[23] the political administration of Northern Rhodesia was completely taken over by the British government in 1924. In 1953 both Northern and Southern Rhodesia were joined with

---

    implied the declaration. See his *Zambia, Struggles of My People & Western Contribution to Corruption and Underdevelopment in Africa* (Lusaka: Maiden Publishing House, 2011).

20   Phiri, *Proclaiming Political Pluralism*; Marja Hinfelaar gives a concise history of Catholic political engagement in Zambia since 1994 in "Legitimizing Powers: The Political Role of the Roman Catholic Church, 1972–1991," in *One Zambia, Many Histories: Towards a History of Post-colonial Zambia*, ed. Jan-Bart Gewald, Marja Hinfelaar, and Giacomo Macola (Lusaka: Lembani Trust, 2009): 129–43; David M. Gordon, *Invisible Agents: Spirits in a Central African History* (Athens: Ohio University Press, 2012).

21   Hinfelaar, "Legitimizing Powers," 130. See also Phiri, *Proclaiming Political Pluralism*, 16.

22   Owen White and J. P. Daughton, eds., *In God's Empire: French Missionaries and the Modern World* (Oxford: Oxford University Press, 2012), 6.

23   The colony was self-governing in all domestic affairs. The British government retained control of external affairs and a final veto in relation to legislation directly affecting Black Africans.

Nyasaland (now Malawi) to form the Federation of Rhodesia and Nyasaland. It has been observed that "Northern Rhodesia was the center of much of the turmoil and crisis that characterized the federation in its last years."[24] On December 31, 1963, the Federation was dissolved. And in less than a year, on October 24, 1964, Northern Rhodesia became independent as the Republic of Zambia. Mission education played a critical role in the process of political consciousness, which culminated in the struggle for decolonization. Christianity, nationalism, statecraft, and political consciousness have been intrinsically interwoven since the arrival of Livingstone. However, this relationship has always been complex, contentious, fluid, hybrid, and volatile. Here we can also appreciate the power of the unintended consequences of the translation of Christianity in Zambian Indigenous societies. According to Lamin Sanneh, Bible translation gave rise to the "indigenous discovery of Christianity" in which local people encountered Christianity through Indigenous spiritual frameworks, based on their concrete spiritual, social, political, economic, and relational needs and experiences. The Indigenous discovery left "the way open for indigenous agency and leadership."[25] It "stimulated indigenous religious and cultural renewal," it "strengthened vernacular languages in their diverse particularity and enormous multiplicity," and it "encouraged the role of recipient cultures as decisive for the final appropriation of the message."[26] In this view, Christianity became less of a new religious product or construction than a reconstruction, reascension, and revitalization of a preexisting symbolic capacity of Indigenous spiritual systems. In a way, the resulting psycho-culturally translated Christianity is a continuation of the African quest for abundant life through a spiritual idiom.[27] Insistently, the spiritual consciousness of

---

24 US Dept. of State, Bureau of Public Affairs, "Zambia, Republic of," in *Department of State Publication: Background Notes Series* (New York: Department of State Publication, 1989), 1–8, (3).

25 Lamin Sanneh, *Whose Religion is Christianity? The Gospel Beyond the West* (Grand Rapids, MI: William B. Eerdmans, 2003), 25.

26 Lamin Sanneh, *Translating the Message: The Missionary Impact on Culture* (Maryknoll, NY: Orbis, 1989), 208.

27 Kwame Bediako, "African Theology," in *The Modern Theologians: An Introduction to Christian Theology in the Twentieth Century*, ed. J. Ford (Cambridge: Blackwell, 1997), 428–43.

Zambian Christians is "not so much a chronological past as an 'ontological' past."[28] As Kwame Bediako argues, "The theological importance of the religious past, therefore, consists in the fact that together with the profession of the Christian faith, it gives an account of the same entity—namely, the history of the religious consciousness of the African Christian."[29] Therefore, in the story of Zambian Christian heritage, we are not merely dealing with another phase of spiritual consciousness but also with an incarnation and exemplification of Africa's continuous quest for abundant life, life-giving politics, dignity, authenticity, freedom, and reconstruction of cultural identity.[30] This is a reconceptualization and reformulation of Christianity according to Indigenous apprehensions of reality.[31]

Hence, some major political and societal transformations in Zambia from anticolonial politics resulted in independence from British colonial imperialism; the defeat of Zambia's longest-serving mainline Protestant-informed authoritarian president, Kenneth David Kaunda; and the ushering in of democratization embedded in Pentecostal ideology in 1991.[32] Christianity has played a vital role in all these political developments and remains visible in Zambian public life.[33]

---

28   Kwame Bediako, *Theology and Identity: The Impact of Culture Upon Christian Thought in the Second Century and in Modern Africa* (Oxford: Oxford Regnum, 1992), 4; Bediako, *Christianity in Africa*, 258; Kwame Bediako, *Jesus in Africa: The Christian Gospel in African History and Experience* (Yaoundé, Cameroun: Editions Clé/Akro-pong: Regnum Africa/Oxford: Regnum, 2000), 51; Kwame Bediako, *Jesus and the Gospel in Africa: History and Experience* (Maryknoll: Orbis Books, 2004), 51; Kwame Bediako, "A Half-Century of African Christian Thought: Pointers to Theology and Theological Education in the Next Half-Century," *Journal of African Christian Thought* 3, no. 1 (2000), 5–15.

29   Bediako, *Theology and Identity*, 4; Bediako, *Christianity in Africa*, 258; Bediako, *Jesus in Africa*, 51; Bediako, "African Theology," 428.

30   Ogbu Kalu, *African Pentecostalism: An Introduction* (New York: Oxford University Press, 2008).

31   Bediako, *Christianity in Africa*, ix.

32   Chammah J. Kaunda, *The Nation That Fears God Prospers: A Critique of Zambian Pentecostal Theopolitical Imaginations* (Minneapolis: Augsburg Fortress Publishers, 2018). Kaunda ruled for twenty-seven years.

33   Chammah J. Kaunda and Marja Hinfelaar, eds., *Competing for Caesar: Religion and Politics in Post-Colonial Zambia* (Minneapolis: Fortress Press, 2020).

AFRICAN PENTECOSTALISM AND THE BIBLE

Pentecostalism—described by its followers as biblical Christianity—upholds its own radical continuity with early or apostolic Christianity. The events of the Bible, both Old and New Testaments, are perceived as still happening today. Naomi Haynes observed how Zambian Pentecostals engage with the Bible by reclaiming and reconstituting the memory of the biblical events in the present through typological-participatory hermeneutics.[34] These events are not conceived to be in the past. Instead, they are regarded as ongoing Kairos moments. Similarly, Paul Gifford confirms, for African Pentecostals, the Bible "is not primarily a historical document at all."[35] It is a locus of mysterious workings and ongoing interactions of God with the community of faith; it is a spiritual gate or portal through which the believer can access the reality of the living God here and now. The promises of God in the Bible are also available and accessible through faith. For Pentecostals, to believe in the power of the Holy Spirit sometimes requires uncritically and literally interacting with the Bible as the Word of God. It is a "My Bible and Me" spirituality. The Spirit of God is the Biblical Spirit, "the Spirit of truth," who guides the believer "into all truth" (John 3:16 NIV). This kind of interaction with the Bible appears to arise from Indigenous apprehensions of reality. As Bediako reminds us, "Scripture is not just a holy book from which we extract teaching and biblical principles. Rather, it is a story in which we *participate*. When Livingstone preached in Africa in the nineteenth century, he is said to have always referred to the Bible as the 'message from the God whom you know.'"[36]

The African Pentecostal approach to the Bible is in continuum with Indigenous spiritual hermeneutics of vital participation in the totality of the community of life, which includes both the living and the dead. The

---

34 Naomi Haynes, "The Expansive Present," *Current Anthropology* 61, no. 1 (2020): 57–76.

35 Paul Gifford, "The Bible in Africa: A Novel Usage in Africa's New Churches," *Bulletin of the School of Oriental and African Studies* 71, no. 2 (2008): 203–19 (202).

36 Kwame Bediako, "Scripture as The Interpreter of Culture and Tradition," in *Africa Bible Commentary*, ed. Tokunboh Adeyemo (Grand Rapids: Zondervan, 2006), 7–8 (7).

relevance of this Pentecostal approach to the Bible stems "from the fundamental theological affirmation that in Christ, and through faith-union with Christ in the Gospel, [Pentecostals have] become 'the seed of Abraham and heirs according to the promise,' that is, the promise of Abraham and therefore 'heirs together with Israel, members together of one body.'"[37] In Christ, therefore, African Pentecostals understand themselves to have been born again to "an adoptive past,"[38] resulting in a radical ontological bondedness between the Indigenous past and the whole history of Israel. Thus, African Pentecostal hermeneutics of vital participation in the spiritual realm of Christ establish the relevance of the Bible as an adopted sacred text that has opened the way for African appropriations of the whole of Scripture and its mysteries.[39] Therefore, Pentecostals engage with the Bible as the spiritual portal through which believers participate in Christ, and thus also in the resources, powers, and the mysteries of God, which are catalyzed in the power of the Holy Spirit. African Pentecostals are rightly described as "Bible people."[40] They have an absolute love for and are at home in the Bible. Some perceive ultimate spiritual power as residing in the Bible, so they place it under their pillows at night as an act of faith in God. They "have direct and unmitigated access to the Bible, authorized, energized and qualified mainly by the Spirit."[41]

This is the same framework in which African Pentecostal notions of sexuality are interpreted and reinforced in their congregations. African Pentecostals engage culture and modernity through the hermeneutics of suspicion, in which some forms of sexuality and sexual practices from the African past that are perceived as having an affinity with biblical notions are affirmed to support their arguments, and those perceived in conflict are rejected as unbiblical.[42] To reject certain lifestyles and prefer others is what

---

37   Bediako, *Christianity in Africa*, 227. Italics added for emphasis.

38   Andrew F. Walls, *The Missionary Movement in Christian History: Studies in the Transmission of Faith* (Edinburgh: T & T Clark, 1996), 9.

39   Ibid.

40   Tinyiko S. Maluleke, "Of Africanised Bees and Africanised Churches: Ten Theses on African Christianity," *Missionalia* 38, no. 3 (2010): 369–79.

41   Ibid.

42   Chammah J. Kaunda, ed., *Genders, Sexualities, and Spiritualities in African Pentecostalism: 'Your Body is a Temple of the Holy Spirit'* (Cham: Palgrave Macmillan, 2020).

makes us human. This is reflected in the "right to freedom of thought, conscience and religion," as embedded in the Universal Declaration of Human Rights.[43] Therefore, the problem is not that Pentecostals reject certain sexuality and sexual practices but instead *how* they reject them. As demonstrated in the Zambian Pentecostal approach to homosexuality and gender below, there is a lack of spiritual empathic rejection that allows for humanization of those whose way of life is rejected and promotes what could be describe as the dialogue of life. This is embedded in the divine policy of never closing the door on any human, as reflected in the words of Isaiah 1:18, "Come now, and let us reason together." This divine policy is also conveyed in the *ubuntu* principle that I may not understand you, nor even agree with your lifestyle, but I embrace you, and respect you because we can only be human together. Spiritual empathic rejection is embedded in the theology of grace—a politics of humanization, recognition, respect, and solidarity with those whose ideas of life seem to conflict with one's own.

However, I also acknowledge that in some African Pentecostal contexts, the Bible has been going through a process of delicate decolonization. It has moved from being an imperial or colonial text to an anticolonial and liberationist text, to a postcolonial and antineocolonial text, to a text of reconstruction, human rights, gender justice, public health, ecological justice, and search for human flourishing.[44] At the same time, it has unfortunately been used to reinforce and perpetuate neocolonialism and dehumanizing rejection of homosexuality and suppression of the agency

---

43   Article 18 states, "Everyone has the *right to freedom of thought, conscience and religion*; this right includes freedom to change his *religion or belief, and freedom,* either alone or in community with others and in public or private, *to manifest his religion or belief in teaching, practice, worship and observance."* United Nations, General Assembly, *Universal Declaration of Human Rights* (Washington, DC.: Department of State Publication, 1948), 4. Italics added for emphasis.

44   Kwabena Asamoah-Gyadu, "Mediating Power and Salvation: Pentecostalism and Religious Mediation in an African Context," *Journal of World Christianity* 5, no. 1 (2012): 43–61; Joseph Quayesi-Amakye, "Pentecostalism, the Akan Religion and the Good Life," *International Journal of Pentecostal Missiology* 5 (2017): 111–28.

of women.[45] This means the Bible remains locked in between as a text of struggle for decolonial resistance and a text that legitimizes, reproduces, and perpetuates the status quo of neocolonialism. Neocolonial sovereign power manifests itself in economic exploitation, political corruption, electoral fraud and manipulation, ethnic nepotism, heteropatriarchal gender and sexual relations, abuse of religion for political gains, hierarchical power relations, and the use of various forms of violence to maintain power over the nation. In addition, many African leaders have turned a blind eye to foreign corporations' economic exploitation of local people, and enrich themselves at the expense of the wider prosperity of the nations. Many, especially Pentecostals, have appropriated the Bible in the public sphere with a biblicist framework, which subliminally sanctions neocolonial politics and legitimatizes hierarchical relational, gender, and sexual moral discourses of heteropatriarchy embedded in the so-called biblical practice of heterosexuality.

Many African Pentecostals see the Bible as the final authority in matters of morality and life. The biblically shaped heteropatriarchal structure of inequalities, injustice, and violence is therefore utilized as a public moral censure and policing constraint, within which gender and sexuality are embedded and to be experienced.[46] African Pentecostals also perceive their God-given mission as extended to public life, matters of national concern, and the claiming of nations for Christ. Pentecostal Christianity is an ardent public religion and a biblicist-informed public consciousness.[47] For instance, Adriaan van Klinken notes that Pentecostal

---

45   The Bible has a controversial history in Africa. For a detailed discussion, see Gifford, "The Bible in Africa"; Gerald West, *The Stolen Bible: From Tool of Imperialism to African Icon* (Pietermaritzburg: Cluster Publication, 2016).

46   Chammah J. Kaunda and Mutale Mulenga Kaunda, "Mobilising Religious Assets for Social Transformation: A Theology of Decolonial Reconstruction Perspective on the Ministry of National Guidance and Religious Affairs (MNGRA) in Zambia," *Religions* 9, no. 6 (2018): 176.

47   Birgit Meyer, "Pentecostalism and Globalization," in *Studying Global Pentecostalism: Theories and Methods*, ed. Allan H. Anderson, Michael Bergunder, Andre Droogers, and Cornelis van der Laan (Berkeley: University of California Press, 2010), 113–30; Asonzeh Ukah, "The Deregulation of Piety in the Context of Neoliberal Globalization: African Pentecostalisms in the

interpretations of the Bible sometimes emphasize the monolithic fixity of the Bible and tend to ignore that "from a global perspective, there are strands within Christianity that adopt different interpretations of the bible and that, even in the Zambian context, there are dissident voices."[48] It is lamentable how this non-apathetic rejectionist approach is "used normatively to define the social and political character of Zambia as a Christian nation"[49] and continuously calls for national moral purity, especially with regard to sexuality. However, some scholars also believe that Pentecostals' profound and unparalleled influence in public spheres is a capacity that, if channeled positively, has the potential to contribute to radical relational, social, economic, and political transformation in Africa.[50]

The following shows that Pentecostals utilize the Bible in the public sphere as both a tool for promoting their religious agency in legitimatizing value systems that favor their spirituality and as a symbolic power to resist certain gender identities and sexual relations.

BIBLICIZATION OF NATIONAL POLITICS AND POLITICIZATION OF THE BIBLE

Since the Declaration of Zambia as a Christian Nation (hereafter, the Declaration) by Frederick T. J. Chiluba, a Pentecostal Christian, upon inauguration as the second republican president of Zambia in 1991, the Bible has been politicized in the public sphere. This process has taken a biblicist or biblical literalist approach, which has been used by Pentecostals and some politicians who seek to biblicize the nation. Zambia is the only nation in the world that has openly declared itself a Christian Nation and enshrined it in the preamble of the

---

Twenty-First Century," in *Global Renewal Christianity: Spirit-Empowered Movements Past, Present, and Future*, vol. III: *Africa*, ed. Vinson Synan, J. Kwabena Asamoah-Gyadu, and Amos Yong (Lake Mary, FL: Charisma House Publishers, 2016), 378–79 (362–69).

48   Adriaan van Klinken, "Homosexuality, Politics and Pentecostal Nationalism in Zambia," *Studies in World Christianity* 20, no, 3 (2014): 259–81 (265).

49   Van Klinken, "Homosexuality," 265.

50   Dena Freeman, "Pentecostalism and Economic Development in sub-Saharan Africa," in *The Routledge Handbook of Religions and Global Development*, ed. Emma Tomalin (New York: Routledge, 2015), 128–40.

National Constitution (1996). The Constitution of Zambia states, "WE, THE PEOPLE OF ZAMBIA: ACKNOWLEDGE the supremacy of God Almighty; DECLARE the Republic a Christian Nation while upholding a person's right to freedom of conscience, belief or religion."[51] However, Zambia was not the first country to constitutionalize Christianity. Ireland's Constitution of 1937 explicitly stated, "In the Name of the Most Holy Trinity, from Whom is all authority and to Whom, as our final end, all actions both of men and States must be referred, We, the people of Éire, Humbly acknowledging all our obligations to our Divine Lord, Jesus Christ, Who sustained our fathers through centuries of trial . . ."[52] Whereas, Ireland's Constitution was overwhelmingly Catholic Christian informed, the Zambian Declaration was grounded in a conservative Pentecostal understanding of the Bible as the document of God's covenant with and commitment to the believer, the community of faith, and any nation that fears the Lord.[53] On October 18, 2015, the former president Edgar Lungu, demonstrating a politically driven obsession with Pentecostalism, reaffirmed the Declaration, and in 2016 he created the aforementioned MNGRA and appointed a female Pentecostal clergy, Rev. Godfridah Sumaili, as its minister. Sumaili sought to utilize the Declaration as a covenant between God and the nation in order to bring the Bible to the center of political governance. This was a way for transforming political ideals and culture, thereby giving rise to a biblico-political consciousness that could transcend human sinfulness and lead to national prosperity.[54] A Christian nation, therefore, was defined in a 2020 policy of the MNGRA as:

> A Nation that acknowledges the Divine Lordship of Jesus Christ over all its affairs. The Holy Bible guides the beliefs and values that its people espouse in family life and apply appropriately in Government and all sectors of society for enhanced welfare, peace and

---

51 Government of Zambia, Constitution of Zambia (Amendment) [No. 2 of 2016] (Lusaka: Government Printer, 2016), 9, https://tinyurl.com/2p8ar4dz.

52 Ireland, "Ireland's Constitution of 1937 with Amendments through 2015," (1937 [rev. 2015]), 3, https://tinyurl.com/mvr25z9j.

53 Kaunda, *The Nation That Fears God Prospers.*

54 Frederick T. J. Chiluba, "Zambia Christian nation declaration by President Frederick Chiluba," May 2, 2017, https://tinyurl.com/t84bj6dr.

unity. God's principles of Righteousness and Justice are the foundation for the rule of law and governance for sustained social order and morality.[55]

As indicated above, this notion of a Christian nation is embedded in Pentecostal nationalism and its religious imaginations, in which the Bible is regarded as God's seal of the covenant with critical implications for life in various dimensions. This notion also underlies victory, health, wealth, hope, and prosperity for Zambia. For many Pentecostals, "the Declaration is a covenant with God."[56] It is a biblico-political discourse that seeks to define and, in some ways, to determine the religio-political atmosphere, the public consciousness, and the political-cultural imaginations of many Zambians from the top-down and the bottom-up.[57] The MNGRA made it clear that "the Bible, the Word of God brings transformation of lives, hope and peace to people."[58] Hence, from that perspective, it appears the Bible constitutes a symbolic power and a public problem that must be engaged even before interrogating the religious characteristics of Zambian people themselves.

Although Sumaili misused the Bible in the public in several ways, in this section, I focus on her role as a Pentecostal minister in public office in the construction of a religious nationalist power structure and a discourse about sexuality that violated the rights of LGBTQI+ persons and suppressed women's agency. In what follows, I demonstrate that the Bible was not an innocent text in Sumaili's public discourse. It was a nonempathic state

---

55   MNGRA, *Ministry of National Guidance and Religious Affairs Policy* (Lusaka: MNGRA, 2020), viii.

56   Chammah J. Kaunda, "'The Ngabwe Covenant' and the Search for an African Theology of Eco-Pneumato-Relational Way of Being in Zambia," *Religions* 11, no. 6 (2020): 275, https://doi.org/10.3390/rel11060275.

57   Margaret Anderson, "Disillusionment and Fear: The Impact of Zambia's Religio-Political Climate on Sexual and Reproductive Health Organisations," *Southern African Journal of Policy and Development* 5, no. 1 (2020): Article 6, https://tinyurl.com/rh8x7j8r.

58   Speech by the Hon. Rev. Mrs. Godfridah Sumaili, MP Minister of National Guidance and Religious Affairs at the 49th Annual General Meeting Held at The Cathedral of the Holy Cross (June 24, 2017).

apparatus of symbolic power, which was used to outrightly reject, suppress dissent, exclude, and segregate those perceived as impure and sinful.[59]

"An Abomination in Zambia"

The question of LGBTQI+ rights has been disturbing for most Pentecostal Christians, to put it mildly. Most have taken a completely reactive approach. Very few think soberly or pastorally, let alone prophetically, when confronted with the question of sexual minorities. Sumaili's Ministerial approach to sexuality and LGBTQI+ persons was informed by reactive resistance rather than by empathy, dialogue, and pastoral concern. She claimed that "discussions on pervasive sexuality such as homosexuality, lesbianism, transgender are not welcome because such practices are illegal and an abomination in a Christian nation."[60] Elsewhere, we have argued that the national sexual purity discourse "is not only about resisting homosexuality; it is defined based on the Christian traditional notion of family, which allows for expression of only heteronormative romantic love as God's ideal and excludes all other sexual expressions as forms of rebellion against God."[61] Sumaili sought to reinforce the public rejection and hatred of homosexuality, which she constantly described as "a crime in Zambia." She called Zambians to "guard against foreign influences," saying, "In Zambia we do not condone gayism and this is a crime and inviting such people means we are slowly accepting this vice. We must guard against such foreign influences as they pose a risk

---

59   Adriaan Van Klinken has written on the issue of homosexuality in relation to the Declaration. See for example, their "Homosexuality, politics and Pentecostal nationalism in Zambia," *Studies in World Christianity* 20 (2014): 259–81; Adriaan Van Klinken, "Christianity and Same-Sex Relationships in Africa," in *Routledge Companion to Christianity in Africa,* ed. Elias K. Bongmba (London: Routledge, 2016), 487–501.

60   Godfridah Sumaili, "Role of Ministry of National Guidance and Religious Affairs," Paper presented at National Symposium, Equipping People of Faith to Face the Challenges of Today (Lusaka, Zambia, March 20, 2018).

61   Chammah J. Kaunda and Mutale M. Kaunda, "Mobilising Religious Assets for Social Transformation: A Theology of Decolonial Reconstruction Perspective on the Ministry of National Guidance and Religious Affairs (MNGRA) in Zambia," *Religions* 9, no. 6 (2018): 176.

of disturbing our social [fiber] as a Christian nation."[62] Like many Zambian Pentecostals, Sumaili's main concern for the nation was for the "country [to] uphold . . . Christian values as enshrined in the Bible" in order to resist "wizardry and satanism . . . secularism."[63] As indicated above, this biblicist imagination is rooted in nationality of power—how a state deploys specific technologies of subjectivation or domination to control or police its citizenry. Sumaili insisted on Zambia being a Christian nation that cannot condone or recognize the practice of homosexuality because the vice is against the law. For her, "homosexuality and lesbianism are an abomination in Zambia." The Bible is against homosexuality, and it will not be entertained in Zambia.[64]

In this way, Sumaili deployed the Bible as an apparatus of nationality of power—a tool of symbolic power through which "persuasion and consent [was] sought without necessarily parking the machine of violence."[65] The Bible was used to enact subliminal or objective violence.[66] Sumaili used "symbolic violence" embodied in biblical language in the public sphere to institutionalize specific forms of discrimination. For example, Sumaili insisted that "LGBTQI rights are NOT Human Rights." She called on the public, saying,

> Blessed people of Zambia I implore you to take a resolute and strong stand against LGBTQI. This wanton plan to distort our Christian identity and expose our people especially young people to destructive, unnatural and queer sexual orientation has no place in our culture and our Christian nation.[67]

---

62 Lusakatimes.com, "In Zambia we do not condone gayism and homosexuality, this is a crime-Sumaili," June 29, 2019, https://tinyurl.com/4ubyf692.

63 Lusakatimes.com, "HH should explain why he has scraped off Ministries of Religious Affairs and Traditional Affairs," September 19, 2021, https://tinyurl.com/ypn9e4s8.

64 National Reporter, "Gay Rights Have No Place in Zambia," April 9, 2018, https://tinyurl.com/mr2jk4ae.

65 Sabelo J. Ndlovu-Gatsheni, *Empire, Global Coloniality and African Subjectivity* (New York: Berghahn Books, 2013), 157.

66 Sabelo J. Ndlovu-Gatsheni, "Beyond the Equator There Are No Sins: Coloniality and Violence in Africa," *Journal of Developing Societies* 28, no. 4 (2012): 419–40.

67 Rev. Godfridah Sumail, "Cry My Beloved Country: Say No To LGBTQI, LGBTQI Rights Are NOT Human Rights," May 23, 2022, https://tinyurl.com/25dj76t6.

According to her, "The Word of God, the Bible is our foundation, standard and anchor from which we cannot depart as a Covenant nation." She cited Leviticus 18:22, "You shall not lie with a male as with a woman. It is *an abomination . . .* It is hypocritical to acknowledge Zambia as a Christian nation and yet *permit abominable behaviors and practices* that *are alien and contrary* to our Christian faith and values. It is also a terrible betrayal to the people of Zambia."[68] Here we see clearly the biblical language of violence that she employed in the public to describe LGBTQI+ persons.

There was also a crackdown on LGBTQI+ Zambians during Sumaili's tenure as Minister. A gay couple was sentenced to fifteen years imprisonment for what was described as "crimes against the order of nature" or "offence of sodomy or having sex against the order of nature contrary to the laws of Zambia."[69] This came after a human rights activist was detained for publicly calling for the decriminalization of same-sex relations. In addition, Somizi Mhlongo, a South African media personality, television presenter, actor, and choreographer, who openly self-identifies as gay, was refused entry into the country on account of his sexuality. Sumaili announced that people with "questionable character" such as Mhlongo were not welcome in Zambia.[70]

In post-Sumaili Zambia, Pentecostals have retained their normative form of resistance against issues of sexuality. In a recent pastoral letter, The Pentecostal Assemblies of God in Zambia (PAOGZ) recently argued that "LGBTQI ideology is in direct contradiction to these noble ideals [such as protecting and strengthening the values of African family] and for that reason stands rejected."[71] The PAOGZ called promotion of LGBTQI+ rights by international communities in Zambia as "a war against our families, present and future."[72] It claimed, "The PAOGZ believes homosexuality and lesbianism are treatable conditions which require empathy to bring affected individuals

---

68   Ibid. Italics added for emphasis.

69   Lusakatimes.com, "Jailing of Kapiri gay couple to 15 years horrifies US envoy," November 29, 2019, https://tinyurl.com/3arv8cz6.

70   Paul Shalala, "Zambia Over Homosexuality," July 3, 2019, https://tinyurl.com/496dtyu2.

71   Zambian Observer, "UPND Government must clarify if it has quietly decided to open doors to homosexuality and lesbianism, says Bishop Joshua Banda," May 25, 2022, https://tinyurl.com/87czp4fw.

72   Ibid.

to a place of liberty and healing . . . We resist this war against our consciences and our families, in the name of Jesus Christ our Lord."[73] The current President of Zambia, Hakainde Hichilema, quickly retorted that the government "will not support Gay Rights, Lesbian Rights, Zambia is a Christian Nation."[74]

Denial of Women's Agency

During her time as Minister, Sumaili's utilization of the Bible's symbolic power was not limited to LGBTQI+ rights; it was also extended to suppression of women's agency. She used the Bible as a tool of "symbolic violence" when she insisted on reversing all the progress Zambian women had made in their struggle for gender justice and equality. She used the Bible to revitalize and reinforce relational power dynamics between women and men. She introduced the "house" concept, in which the nation was defined as a home with the president as the father and citizens as children. In reducing the nation to a heteropatriarchal home, Sumaili appealed to Ephesians 6:1 which urges, "Children, obey your parents in the Lord, for this is right." At the same time, she politicized Ephesians 5:22–33: "Wives, submit to your husbands as to the Lord. For the husband is the head of the wife as Christ is the head of the church, his body, of which he is the Saviour." Zambian citizens, as children, were expected to "submit passively to the president in the same way some conservatives expect their wives and children to submit to fatherly authority in their homes. This alliance of religio-political power that projects Lungu as the father and president of the nation promotes housenization of the nation."[75] Certain forms of women's agency were also characterized as questionable in the Christian nation. For instance, Sumaili called for the banning of miniskirts for promoting immorality. In 2018 popular South African dancer and socialite, Zodwa Wabantu, was detained at the airport upon arrival in Zambia and sent back on another flight to South Africa

---

73   Ibid.

74   Hakainde Hichilema, "We will not support Gay Rights, Lesbian Rights, Zambia is a Christian Nation – HH," May 30, 2022, https://tinyurl.com/2bnx7v8x.

75   Mutale M. Kaunda and Chammah J. Kaunda, "Pentecostalism, Female Spirit-Filled Politicians, and Populism in Zambia," *International Review of Mission* 107, no. 1 (2018): 23–32. Bible verses are taken from the NIV.

because her dances were characterized as "immoral" and "unchristian." Zodwa, known for her dance moves, was described as "the highest priestess of immorality who should not be tolerated in any civilized society especially Zambia, a country that prides itself as a Christian nation."[76]

Sumaili's vision was to construct a Bible-based nation. She called on the Bible Society of Zambia to "flood this nation with the Bible. The holy Bible . . . outlines the values to guide us to fulfil the agreement with God."[77] At the same time, she restricted the sale and purchase of sex toys, even threatening jail terms for anyone caught in what she termed as "a very unnatural thing." She underlined that "God created man and woman for sexual satisfaction—but for a man or woman to use a lifeless object is immoral."[78] She also took issue with what she described as "indecent dressing and provocative dancing which she viewed as displeasing before God." She cited the Scripture (John 4:23), saying, "God is looking for worshippers who will worship in spirit and truth. We have to present ourselves in an honouring manner and should not be offensive to him and other worshipers in how we worship."[79] In many ways, Sumaili perceived herself as the arch-spiritual guardian or the arch-spiritual-mother of the nation. To legitimatize her position, she instrumentalized the Bible as an apparatus to police national morality, and control and undermine citizens' sexual and gender agency. By deploying a theology of wifely submission for the whole Zambian citizenry, Sumaili constructed what could be described as "a Sumaili State Theology." She provided a "theological justification of the status quo"[80] with its neocolonization, patriarchy, heterosexism, homophobia, sexism, corruption,

---

76 Evans Musenya Manda, "Indecent Dressing: Not Here!," March 2, 2018, https://tinyurl.com/yc5dry82.

77 Speech by the Hon. Rev. Mrs. Godfridah Sumaili, MP Minister of National Guidance and Religious Affairs at the 49th Annual General Meeting Held at The Cathedral of the Holy Cross, June 24, 2017.

78 Africanews, "Zambians engage in 'Rights vs Morals' debate over sex dolls," December 3, 2018, https://tinyurl.com/2xntjcuk.

79 Lusakatimes.com, "Twerking and provocative dressing in church irks Religious Affairs minister," November 28, 2017, https://tinyurl.com/283runs9n.

80 The Kairos Theologians, *The Kairos Document: Challenge to the Church: A Theological Comment on the Political Crisis in South Africa* (Johannesburg: Skotaville Publishers, 1986), 3.

subjugation, domination, and despotism. Sumaili misused "theological concepts and biblical texts for . . . political purposes."[81]

ANALYTICAL CONCLUSION

The foregoing discussion demonstrates how Sumaili used the Bible as tool for neutralizing popular dissent in the church and society, as a smokescreen to cover corruption and repression, and to forbid a free flow of ideas that might help realize Zambia as a democratic nation in which everyone has equal access to public resources to achieve a meaningful life. In fact, Sumaili's MNGRA policy defined the church as "A group of believers in the Lordship of Jesus Christ whose *primary source of doctrine* is the Holy Bible and *registered as such under the Zambian Law*."[82] In this definition, Sumaili tapped into the Pentecostal idea of the church. But the requirement of being registered as a group of believers is problematic and potentially persecutory. The nonempathic interpretations of the scriptures that are deployed by some Zambian Pentecostals promote a belief that theirs is not just the legitimate but also the *only* interpretation sanctioned by God, and therefore, by default, it is applicable to everyone. In extension thereof, Sumaili as a Pentecostal politician regarded her position as a divine opportunity to change the political rules of play in order for Pentecostal truth claims to become constitutive of Zambian politics.[83] This view does not promote dialogue or mutual growth, but rather it seeks to repress any view that appears contrary to a normative Pentecostal/Biblicist approach to reality. It is grounded in a process of total subjugation of Christianity and every social system of the nation by placing them under Pentecostal authority. Sumaili's Bible was a hidden tool of symbolic violence used to police sexual relations and gender norms. It was used to control "the masses, not in order to make sure that they really participate in the business

---

81 Ibid.

82 Ministry of National Guidance and Religious Affairs Policy (Lusaka: MNGRA, 2020), viii. Italics added for emphasis.

83 Carsten Bagge Laustsen, "Studying Politics and Religion: How to Distinguish Religious Politics, Civil Religion, Political Religion, and Political Theology," *Journal of Religion in Europe* 6, no. 4 (2013): 428–63 (438).

of governing the nation,"[84] but in order to remind them constantly that Zambia is a Christian nation, and citizens are expected to submissively obey the state as appointed by God to mediate intangible blessings. The Bible was deployed to defuse any idea other than the Pentecostal ideology of womanhood and sexuality. It was used to reinforce religious nationality of power and fundamentalist spiritual consciousness. It was an "ideological force behind the transfer of capital and source of legitimating discourse."[85] The Bible was leveraged to legitimize human rights abuses and undermine the inalienable dignity of many Zambians.

In this way, Sumaili's Bible functioned as an ideological apparatus of the state and legitimized the political abuse of power, corruption, exploitation, and oppression. Paul Gifford's classification of Zambia as "a corrupt and uncaring Christian nation"[86] is therefore accurate. Sumaili's Bible increasingly devalued and left the poor and marginalized behind. Its main function was to impart legitimacy to Lungu's presidency, by seeking to impose a Pentecostal monotheistic framework within which the day-to-day life and practice of Pentecostal-politics were being reproduced and perpetuated in the public sphere to influence the people at the grassroots. Hence, accusations have been made that Pentecostals support whoever becomes president in Zambia as long they promise to protect the Declaration.

However, the Bible is a multivalent sacred text. It is not easily reducible to good and bad but can be used to promote either of the two. In the case of Sumaili, it was utilized to justify symbolic violence and legitimize dominant ideologies. In the context of uncritical political alliances, the Bible can be deployed as a state apparatus to produce and reproduce relations of power in which practices of nonheterosexual and nontraditional sexualities are blamed for national underdevelopment, and considered a perpetual danger to national progress, as God was against them. Therefore,

---

84   Frantz Fanon, *The Wretched of the Earth*, trans. Richard Philcox (New York: Grove Press, 2004/1961), 181.

85   Gustavo Lins Ribeiro, "Why (Post) Colonialism and (De) Coloniality Are Not Enough: A Post-Imperialist Perspective," *Postcolonial Studies* 14, no. 3 (2011): 285–97 (293).

86   Paul Gifford, *African Christianity: Its Public Role* (London: Hurst, 1998), 205.

women's and sexual minorities' freedoms and human rights are regulated. I have argued that the deployment of the Bible in this way can be described as symbolic domination. As a politician and Pentecostal minister, Sumaili occupied a socially and pentecostally constructed position of privilege in the nation. The Bible in her hand was "symbolic power entrenched with invisible power which can be exercised only with the complicity of those who do not want to know that they are subject to it or even that they themselves exercise it."[87] Sumaili's public use of the Bible must be understood as an exercise of structured symbolic power to impose a Pentecostal socio political vision. Sumaili's Bible threatened human dignity and the democratic values of Zambia. She deployed it as a site of incontestable power, a medium of exploitation, and a construction of an elitist reality.[88] Thus, the Bible was used as a symbolic instrument for delegitimization of dissenting voices, domination of anyone perceived as resisting the social system, and robbing the voice from the citizens. Here we are dealing with the institutionalization and nationalization of the Bible as a means of controlling and undermining good governance, democracy, and democratization. Although the Bible is intended to be an instrument of liberation, emancipation, and empowerment for marginalized groups, in the end, the way it has been employed in the public by politicians and some Pentecostals has often promoted the negative mobilization of Christianity. This has seriously compromised the prophetic function and moral integrity of the church's political voice in Zambia.

---

87   Bourdieu, *Language and Symbolic Power*, 164.
88   Ibid.

CHAPTER 9

MARGINAL DESIRE AND UNSUBMISSIVE TRANSIT BETWEEN THE CENTER AND THE MARGIN OF CHRISTIANITY: TWO BRAZILIAN CASES

Ana Ester Pádua Freire

"God is desire."[1]

Desire is a category rarely used in the study of religions, especially in the Christian tradition. It has become, however, an increasingly important category of analysis to understand the various social actors who are present in the plural possibilities of Christian experience. The tense relationship between faith and sexual and gender dissidents in the history of Christianity has aroused forms of resistance through a pulsating production of Queer Theology. In Latin America, Queer Theology has intersected, at least since the 1990s, with postcolonial perspectives that move the production of knowledge to the margins of the hegemonic center. From this perspective, the margin, which for a long time was considered a destination for LGBTQI+ people, is now understood as a theologizing body-territory that celebrates sexual and gender pluri-diversity.

---

1   Marcella Althaus-Reid.

219

Using Marcella Althaus-Reid's "Indecent Theology"[2]—a queer, sexual, and postcolonial theological proposal—this chapter examines the transits that occur between the center and the margin of Christianity, which result in liberational faith experiences, such as *Evangélicxs pela Diversidade* (Evangelicals for Diversity) and the *Rede Nacional de Grupos Católicos LGBT* (National Network of Catholic LGBT Groups), both Brazilian inclusive initiatives. The choice of Althaus-Reid's Indecent Theology to guide this study is not naive. The Argentine theologian created a theological perspective that makes visible the sexual and gender dissidents who were for so long left out of the theological debate—or rather excluded from that debate.

Furthermore, the use of Althaus-Reid's theological proposal as an epistemological path for this chapter aims to:

1. Present a queer theological proposal that stems from the experiences of sexual and gender dissidents in Latin America, and

2. Narrate experiences of sexual and gender dissidence, using concepts that subvert the religious discourses of hegemonic Christianity.

The first section of this chapter presents "the marginal at the margin," and contrasts the concepts of marginal and margin. This section presents a proposal of a marginal theology and a marginal God, based on Althaus-Reid, to exemplify the importance of marginal desire as a category that cannot be denied in a theological analysis that claims to be embodied. The second section focuses on "telling marginal stories" based on two proposals of marginal Christianity in Brazil: the *Evangélicxs pela Diversidade* and the *Rede Nacional de Grupos Católicos LGBT*. The third and final section explores the "unsubmissive transit between the center and the margin of the Christian tradition," presenting an analysis of the two cases introduced in the previous section.

---

2 Marcella Althaus-Reid's Indecent Theology is mostly described in her book *Indecent Theology* (London: Routledge, 2000). Her Indecent Theology manages to escape any scheme of decency or enclosure by proposing a sexual and Queer Theology.

Finally, the conclusion considers the importance of telling sexual stories silenced by hegemonic Christianity for an analytical perspective on the theme of alterity in global Christian studies. The unsubmissive transit of these inclusive initiatives causes ruptures in the structure of Christianity and allows the recognition of the "other" to take place in an affective, desiring, and sexual way.

THE MARGINAL AT THE MARGIN

As this chapter advances an analysis of the religious phenomenon focusing on the category of desire, it is important to locate this desire. I refer not only to a geographic location but also to a social location—and therefore a political and economic one—that starts with the premise of an existing colonizing center of power that organizes and hierarchizes human relationships. The margin appears in a dialectical relationship with the center and can be understood as the place of marginalization, that is, of expulsion from the center of power.

In this chapter, desire is located on at least two sites—in Latin America and in sexual and gender dissidents. According to Fernanda Bruno, Bruno Cardoso, Marta Kanashiro, Luciana Guilhon, and Lucas Melgaço, editors of the book *Tecnopolíticas da vigilância* (Surveillance Technopolitics):

> Thinking from Latin America implies thinking from the margin—understood less as a peripheral region than as a liminal region: sometimes inside, sometimes outside the agencies that constitute the great vectors of the surveillance culture in the so-called "global North;" sometimes in consonance, sometimes in disagreement with the critical agenda and the resistance patterns in force in that same North.[3]

---

3   Fernanda Bruno, Bruno Cardoso, Marta Kanashiro, Luciana Guilhon, and Lucas Melgaço, "Apresentação," in *Tecnopolíticas da Vigilância: perspectivas da margem*, ed. Fernanda Bruno, Bruno Cardoso, Marta Kanashiro, Luciana Guilhon, and Lucas Melgaço (São Paulo: Boitempo, 2018), 9. All the quotations from Portuguese or Spanish sources were translated into English by the author.

Latin America has a vibrant theological production, which includes Liberation Theology and Indecent Theology. In indecency,[4] it is possible to think of the margin also as the territory of sexual and gender dissident bodies. After all, the center's body is mostly white, heterosexual, and cisgender. The body on the margin is the abject body, the body of *travesties*,[5] the body of indecency. It is necessary to emphasize, however, that the margin and the center are not understood here as territories separated by insurmountable borders.

On the contrary, the objective of thinking about the margin in this context is precisely to draw attention to bridges that were built, to the cracks that were opened, to the gaps that were produced on the wall of the disaffected. In this analysis, the margin offers itself as a place where desire is embodied in the dispute for fairer and more solidary relationships in relation to differences. After all, as Bruno, Cardoso, Kanashiro, Guilhon, and Melgaço explain, "to think from the margins, or from the Latin American situation, is immediately to maintain diversity"[6]—diversity of bodies, desires, and experiences of Christianity.

The desire that exists on the margin escapes the notions of homogenization of the "other." Homi Bhabha explains that "it is only by understanding the ambivalence and the antagonism of the desire of the 'other' that we can avoid the increasingly facile adoption of the notion of a homogenized 'other,' for a celebratory, oppositional politics of the margins or minorities."[7] This is one of the objectives of an analysis on the margin and from the margin—to propose ways of breaking separations by the celebration of differences.

---

4   Indecency is a category used by Marcella Althaus-Reid as the opposite to the "decency" of hegemonic theology.

5   *Travesti* (Portuguese) is a gender identity from Latin America that usually refers to a transgender woman. However, the word *travesti* refers to more than gender identity, taking into consideration other intersectionalities, such as race and class. In the past, *travesti* was used to refer to transgender women who were sex workers; today it still keeps that meaning, but it is also a political position.

6   Bruno, Cardoso, Kanashiro, Guilhon, and Melgaço, op. cit., 9.

7   Homi K. Bhabha, *The Location of Culture* (London: Routledge, 1994), 52.

Even if one were to agree with the possibilities of encounters between the margin and the center, it is essential to understand the separatist strategies of the center, as bell hooks explains:

> To be in the margin is to be part of the whole but outside the main body. . . . We focused our attention on the center as well as on the margin. We understood both. This mode of seeing reminded us of the existence of a whole universe, a main body made up for both margin and center. Our survival depended on an ongoing public awareness of the separation between margin and center and an ongoing private acknowledgment that we were a necessary, vital part of the whole.[8]

To understand sexual and gender dissidence in Christianity, more than thinking from the margin, it is necessary to *think marginally*. Such a thinking is not marginalized but it is from the minority perspective, subaltern, or diasporic.[9] The marginal avoids the assimilation from the margins to the center, and asserts itself as a powerful territory of life experience.

This important differentiation between the center, the margin, and the marginal can be better understood from the indecent theological proposal of Althaus-Reid. The theologian has repeatedly asserted that Indecent Theology is a marginal theology. Her intention was to denounce Liberation Theology and Feminist Theology, which, according to Althaus-Reid, were theologies that "visited the margins" or were "co-opted by the margins."[10] As she explains when comparing Indecent Theology to Feminist Theology:

> From Feminist Theology to Indecent Theology is not a progressive development. Rather is a transversal (queer) one in that we can

---

8   bell hooks, *Feminist Theory: From Margin to Center* (Boston: South End Press, 1984), ix.

9   Bhabha, *The Location of Culture*, 181.

10   Marcella Althaus-Reid, "Gustavo Gutiérrez Goes to Disneyland: Theme Park Theologies and the Diaspora of the Discourse of the Popular Theologian in Liberation Theology," in *From Feminist Theology to Indecent Theology*, ed. Marcella Althaus-Reid (London: SCM Press, 2004).

see how a high sexual suspicion concerning epistemology starts a process that both unsettles and discovers. In this discovery new understandings continue to interrogate the praxis of the church as action and reflection from "the margins of the margins" where a true marginal God refuses to leave and be co-opted by the center.[11]

Althaus-Reid's criticism of the Liberation Theology is concerned more with stabilities than discontinuities. According to the theologian, Liberation Theology did not break with the dogmatic and systematic approach of hegemonic Christianity, even though it elevated the poor as a preference for God's liberating proposal. Also, according to Althaus-Reid, Liberation Theology privileged a rural theology, disregarding the urban poor. It is from the urban poor, who frequent salsa bars, that Althaus-Reid proposes an Indecent Theology that destabilizes the "eternal truths" of hegemonic theology.

It is interesting to point out that Indecent Theology, despite presenting strong criticisms of Liberation Theology and Feminist Theology, asserts itself as part of the two—"but more marginal and perhaps even more messy."[12] This is because Indecent Theology is not a progression from one to the other but a radicalization of the contextuality of the bodies it represents. In this case, it is already possible to perceive a transit between the theological perspectives that points to the transit itself between the margin and the center.

However, this transit between the margin and the center should not mean the annihilation of the marginal power that inhabits the margins. An example is when the center "opens up" to divergent sex/gender experiences in a discourse of inclusion, which, for Althaus-Reid, can be dangerous because when the center captures dissident sexual and gender identities, it can actually be defined as a "theological exercise by a simple economy of inclusion."[13] This is an example of the assimilation of the margin by the center:

---

11   Althaus-Reid, "Gustavo Gutiérrez Goes to Disneyland," 9.

12   Ibid., 146.

13   Marcella Althaus-Reid, *The Queer God* (New York: Routledge, 2003), 51.

> Queer Theology takes its place not at the centre of the theological discourses conversing with power, but at the margins. It is a theology from the margins which wants to remain at the margins. To recognize sexual discrimination in the church and in the theological thinking (by selective thematic of reflection or by de-authorization of other discourses) does not mean that theology from the margins should strive for equality. Terrible is the fate of theologies from the margin when they want to be accepted by the centre! Queer Theology strives, instead, for differentiation and plurality.[14]

Indecent Theology is a queer theological perspective, produced marginally in Latin America and from marginal bodies, marginal lives. Therefore, its importance lies in transgressing the domestications of the desire and the passion by hegemonic Christianity. "Queer Theology is then," in the words of Althaus-Reid and Lisa Isherwood, "a sexual theology with a difference: a passion for the marginalized. That passion is compassion but also a commitment to social justice, because there is a wider understanding of human relationships involved."[15]

A marginal theology considers human relationships—affectionate and sexual—and does not aim to make a cultural translation of theological production to the margins but to produce theology on the margins. One of the forms of this marginal theological production is the telling of unsubmissive stories. The stories that I will share later in this chapter take place in a very specific context—Brazil. According to the *Associação Nacional de Travestis e Transexuais* (National Association of Travestis and Transexuals),[16] Brazil is the number one country in the world that kills trans people. Another important research project about LGBTQI+ in Brazil shows that "300 LGBT+ people suffered violent death in Brazil in 2021, 8% more than the previous year: 276 homicides (92%) and 24 suicides (8%).

---

14   Marcella Althaus-Reid and Lisa Isherwood, "Thinking Theology and Queer Theory," *Feminist Theology* 15, no. 3 (Los Angeles, London, New Delhi and Singapore: Sage Publications, 2007), 304.

15   Althaus-Reid and Isherwood, "Thinking Theology and Queer Theory," 308.

16   "Associação Nacional de Travestis e Transexuais," accessed May 32, 2022, https://antrabrasil.org.

Brazil continues to be the country in the world where most LGBT people are murdered: one death every 29 hours."[17]

The systemic violence against LGBTQI+ people in Brazil is the effect, among social, political, and economic realities, of a Christian moralizing discourse, which not only denies differences but also wants to exterminate them. Conservative Christian groups' insistence on blaming sexual and gender dissidents reinforces violence that is portrayed in alarming numbers. Therefore, any attempt to break with this system is an experience of unsubmission.

TELLING MARGINAL STORIES

In order to know the experiences of unsubmission in relation to Christianity, it is necessary to have attentive ears. The experiences of sexual and gender dissidents located on the fringes of tradition exist in unauthorized theological places,[18] and are silenced by the violence of the Christianity that claims to be absolute. David Jasper explains:

> Margins of many kinds are explored. People live on the margins of history and culture; they live on the margins between faith and doubt; they also live on geographical margins—or beyond them. Thus, marginalization may breed dissent, but it may also, and more powerfully, bring about a sense of exile and a sense of being an outsider who is not even in a position to articulate a dissenting voice.[19]

The dissident voices that occupy the margins have stories to tell, stories to oralize. The importance of orality is not strange to Christianity; on the contrary, it is fundamental for its construction and dissemination. The role

---

17   "Violent Deaths of LGBT+ in Brazil: 2021 Report," accessed May 31, 2022, https://tinyurl.com/5n76dxnh.

18   Althaus-Reid, "El éxodo divino de Dios," 38.

19   David Jasper, "Preface," in *Dissent and Marginality: Essays on the Boarders of Literature and Religion,* ed. Kiyoshi Tsuchiya (New York: St. Martin's Press, 1997), vii.

of orality in the Judeo-Christian tradition is well known. What is presented as a sacred text is, precisely, the transcription of oral stories. David M. Carr and Colleen M. Conway explain that "the early traditions of ancient Israel, whatever they were, evolved in their journey across the centuries of the second millennium, passing from one set of lips to another."[20]

Starting, then, from the importance of orality for the Christian tradition and, therefore, for theological production, Althaus-Reid asks about the sexual stories that are told. According to Althaus-Reid and Isherwood, Queer Theology is "a radical form of the 'love-talk of theology', that is, a theology which introduces a profound questioning into the ways of love in our lives as individuals and as society, and the things love can do in our world."[21] And they add:

> Using a perspective from Queer Theology, we may say that to reflect theologically is always an activity done with a presupposition of love. To talk theology is to talk about a loving style of relationship. Theological themes are themes of love, even if perhaps this has been obscured by centuries of using a terminology which may have lost their original transparency.[22]

But is Queer Theology the only theology speaking of love? No, because all theology is a sexual act. This means that, even though it does not claim to be sexual, hegemonic theology brings within itself a cisgender and heterosexual orthodoxy, which, as a dogma, is divinized. After all, "theology is never innocuous or sexually innocent or neutral."[23] The question that arises then is: If hegemonic Christian theology also speaks of love, what (un)love stories does it not tell?

The nonoralized sexual stories of hegemonic Christianity are those lived by sexual and gender dissidents, who are on the margins, challenging with their bodies, their affections, and their desires the unstable claims of

---

20 David M. Carr and Colleen M. Conway, *An Introduction to The Bible: Sacred Texts and Imperial Contexts* (United Kingdom: Wiley-Blackwell, 2010), 38–39.
21 Althaus-Reid and Isherwood, "Thinking Theology and Queer Theory," 303.
22 Ibid.
23 Althaus-Reid, *Indecent Theology*, 87.

hegemonic Christian morality. For Althaus-Reid, even if these stories are told, they are not heard, as she explains, "Marginality seems to be somehow the first condition of whether sexual stories are heard or not. At the top of Rubin's pyramid we can hear sexual stories told loudly and clearly, but somehow at the bottom the stories are shouted. The difference is that they are ignored."[24]

Althaus-Reid refers here to the "erotic pyramid" proposed by Gayle Rubin. In this pyramid, "marital and reproductive heterosexuals are at the top, and below are the most despised sexual castes which currently include transsexuals, transvestites, fetishists, sadomasochists, sex workers such as prostitutes and pornographic models, and below all, those whose eroticism transgresses generational boundaries."[25] For Althaus-Reid, the voices that are placed down the pyramid are not heard and, therefore, do not take part in hegemonic interactions. She explains that "once the story is heard, it becomes part of an interactive social word, and negotiates its space of meaning and signification within a network of other unheard stories, and from that actions for transformation and challenge to the status quo may take place."[26]

In this context, the indecent theological proposal rescues untold stories by making use of a transgressive orality, as explained by André Musskopf:

> Marcella Althaus-Reid recognizes a tradition of subversive sexual stories lived in Latin America that survive despite centuries of colonialism on the continent, as well as current practices of poor people in urban contexts that reveal other sexual, political and religious arrangements, made invisible, excluded or marginalized from the theological hermeneutic circle for not being harmonized within the heterosexual ideology given their conflicting, unstable and impure character. Recovering and giving visibility to these experiences through different sources, and using them in

---

24   Althaus-Reid, *Indecent Theology*, 136.

25   Gayle Rubin, "Pensando o sexo" (1984), in *Políticas do Sexo*, coleção Argonautas (São Paulo: UBU Editora, 2017), 83.

26   Althaus-Reid, *Indecent Theology*, 135.

an exercise of intertextuality, they reveal themselves as disruptive practices of a totalitarian theology and thus become redeeming practices.[27]

Orality presents itself as a fundamental instrument for disruptive practices because the stories told penetrate the social fabric, causing the transformations that are so necessary for the liberating proposal of Christianity understood from the base of the pyramid.

Althaus-Reid presents a "systematic theology from the margins of sexuality"[28] in her Indecent Theology. For her, theology is based on stories—sexual stories. The act of (re)telling these stories is "oral sex,"[29] based on recognizing private life as having important theological content because, "all theology is sexual theology."[30] As she explains, "We need to consider seriously the fact that it is oral sex we are dealing with (the retelling of sexual stories in the gathering of communities), which can build the Project of Liberation of the Kingdom better than the heterosexual reproductive stories we are used to."[31]

Starting from the concept of oral sex, in view of the insubordination that the very use of the term in a Christian context evokes, I will share the stories of two LGBTQI+ collectives in Brazil, one Protestant and one Catholic. The first one is the story of the *Evangélicxs pela Diversidade,* and the second one is the story of *the Rede Nacional de Grupos Católicos LGBT.*

Evangélicxs pela Diversidade

"We are the Evangélicxs pela Diversidade because we do not accept that any sheep of the flock of Christ are abandoned along the way because of sexual and gender diversity."[32]

---

27 André Musskopf, "Via(da)gens teológicas: itinerários para uma teologia queer no Brasil" (PhD diss., Faculdades EST, São Leopoldo, 2008), 209.

28 Althaus-Reid, *Indecent Theology,* 144.

29 Ibid., 134.

30 Ibid., i.

31 Ibid., 147.

32 "Evangélicxs pela Diversidade," accessed Feb 8, 2022, https://evangelicxs.com.

The *Evangélicxs pela Diversidade* (Evangelicals for Diversity) is the first inter-denominational LGBTQI+ evangelical[33] organization in Latin America. Founded in 2017, the collective started to work on social media in 2018. From then on, it began to organize itself in the Brazilian territory through local centers that aim to offer support and reception for LGBTQI+ and training spaces.

In 2019 *Evangélicxs* joined the Organization of American States (OAS) coalition on "Religion, Spirituality and Civil Society," focusing on the fight against religious fundamentalism and its impacts on civil society.[34]

The *Evangélicxs* aims to combat evangelical religious fundamentalism against the LGBTQI+ population by building bridges for dialogue between churches, communities, mission agencies, and other evangelical organizations that wish to think positively about the issue of gender and sexual diversity. The collective has a psychological support project called *Psis Pela Diversidade* (Psy for Diversity), and a pastoral support network.[35] The group's work is organized into four main areas of activity:

1. *Reception and pastoral care:*
    Offers support and care to LGBTQI+ people who are suffering some type of violence or oppression due to issues related to the evangelical faith, whether in their personal and family contexts, in their faith communities or in relationship networks because they understand themselves as expressing gender or sexuality differently from the cis-heteronormative pattern;

2. *Training and reflection:*
    Creates opportunities for reflection and continuous and up-to-date learning that contribute to forming and informing the Brazilian evangelical church and its organizations,

---

33 Evangelical is a synonym to Protestant. In the Brazilian context, Protestant is used more for historical denominations, such as Presbyterian and Baptist. Evangelical is an umbrella term for historical but also new Protestant denominations, such as Neo-pentecostals.

34 Ana Ester Pádua Freire et al., *Manual de Cristianismo e LGBTI+* (Curitiba: IBDSEX, 2021), 129.

35 Freire, *Manual de Cristianismo e LGBTI+*, 129.

including the production of content and didactic resources that help them become faith communities that welcome and affirm sexual and gender diversity;

3. *Articulation and public incidence:*
    Promotes and organizes the participation and engagement of evangelical people and their faith communities in actions of service to the LGBTQI+ community and in the promotion of their rights and human dignity, strengthening partnerships and articulations with organizations that also assume this vocation;

4. *Evangelization and Dialogue:*
    Promotes the vision of faith communities that welcome and affirm sexual diversity and gender identity through the expansion of spaces and channels for dialogue and exchange between LGBTQI+ people, the LGBTQI+ Movement and evangelical churches and denominations, unconditionally respecting diversities of engagement modalities.[36]

These four areas of activity are based on the *Evangélicxs's* mission to "organize a movement of evangelical LGBTQI+ people who guide sexual and gender diversity in dialogue with the evangelical faith, present nationally, with initiatives that promote its affirmation in churches, evangelical organizations and in the society."[37] And, also, they arise from the vision of "being a reference on sexual and gender diversity in an evangelical perspective, promoting emancipatory and affirmative perspectives and practices of LGBTQI+ evangelical people, in the relationship with churches, evangelical organizations and civil society."[38]

One of the important actions that *Evangélicxs* has carried out since its beginning was the "Affirmative Evangelical Leadership Training Laboratory" (FLEA.lab), which brought together young people, activists, and progressive evangelical leaders in Brazil during 2021. The training offered ninety-six hours of workshops on topics related to Christianity and sexual

---

36 "Evangélicxs pela Diversidade."
37 Ibid.
38 Ibid.

and gender diversity, such as biblical study methods, affirmative herme-neutics, HIV/AIDS, and preventing and combating abuse and violence. The project was the first with this scope in Brazil and trained twenty-seven people. The *Evangélicxs* are interested in training "affirmative leaders," that is, LGBTQI+ people and allies prepared to dispute the narratives in the religious and public debate that are, most of the time, contrary to the dignity of dissident sex-gender people.

In addition to psychological care offered through *Psis pela Diversidade* (Psis for Diversity) and training courses, another important activity of *Evangélicxs* is pastoral care. The collective is a safe space for mutual help, and through social media, it is accessed daily by people seeking help, primarily because they want guidance on how to reconcile their faith with their dissident sexuality and/or gender identity.

Rede Nacional de Grupos Católicos LGBT

> *"Collectives are spaces where we plant seeds of life that nourish and enrich us and where we leave to sow our gifts and generate good fruits, thus contributing to the construction of a world of more justice and equality, in which there is space for each one to flourish in diversity."*[39]

The *Rede Nacional de Grupos Católicos LGBT* (National Network of LGBT Catholic Groups, hereinafter called *RNGC*) presents itself as a coalition of Brazilian LGBTQI+ Catholic lay collectives. The groups were organized based on the need to create safe spaces for respectful reception, sharing experiences and living the Christian faith in the community for those people who seek to reconcile their Roman Catholic religious affiliation with their identities as LGBTQI+ people.[40]

In 2007 there emerged the first organized group of LGBTQI+ Roman Catholics in Brazil, the "Catholic Diversity," in Rio de Janeiro. After that, several other similar collectives began to emerge across the country. In 2014 the "First National Meeting of LGBT Catholics" took place, and representatives of five existing groups in the country founded *RNGC*. At the end

---

39   Freire, *Manual de Cristianismo e LGBTI+*, 115.

40   Ibid.

of 2020, the network already had twenty-one groups, and became part of the Global Network of Rainbow Catholics (GNRC) which brings together groups of "Rainbow Catholics" from around the world.[41]

The network has the following mission/ line of action/ charisma:

> Our mission is to promote and spread the Good News of Jesus Christ and the fully inclusive project of the Kingdom of God, sharing the experience of Love, Freedom, Justice and Life in abundance with all people who are excluded from the Church and/or society by virtue of their gender identity and/or sexual orientation. We believe that God created us and loves us all with Unconditional Love, that Christ embraces us and calls us friends, and that his Church is for all of us. We believe in the Spirit that breathes in our voices and our lives, and that it is our prophetic mission to contribute with our gifts and our testimonies to the construction of the Kingdom. May the peace of Christ and the loving protection of Mary, our mother, always be with each and every one of us, and with each and every one of you.[42]

The network, like the *Evangélicxs*, is committed with training its public. In 2021 for example, a course on "Plural Theologies" was offered, which covered topics such as Feminist Theology, Black Theology, and Queer Theology. In addition, the network's social media show the collective's involvement with ecumenism and interreligious dialogue.

Cris Serra, the former national coordinator of the *RNGC* (2018–2021), has done important research about this network. She explains that the intention of the first group, the "Diversidade Católica," was "to create a website providing theological resources for reconciling sexual and gender diversity with the Christian faith, especially in Roman Catholicism."[43] The website is an important tool for LGBTQI+, not only because it offers resources but also because it announces the possibilities of reconciliation

---

41   Ibid.

42   Ibid.

43   Cris Serra, "Diversity as a Gift: LGBTQI+ Roman Catholic Organizations in Twenty-First-Century Brazil," *International Journal of Latin American Religions* (November 9, 2021): 20, https://doi.org/10.1007/s41603-021-00152-4.

between Christianity and sexuality. However, the website created a demand for face-to-face meetings.

These face-to-face meetings are one of the most critical actions of the *RNGC* because the collective is organized into small groups formed in different territories in Brazil. The groups are self-generated, and provide important moments of communion for people who have historically been excluded from the communal experience of Christianity. In addition, the groups have a national meeting, where opportunities for formation and communion are offered.

It is important to highlight that "most of the groups seek the support of priests for spiritual and pastoral accompaniment and mass celebration. Many of them organize or participate in open conferences or meetings on subjects related to sexual and gender diversity, either on a theological approach or not."[44] This fact already points to an important transit between the margin and what could be considered the center of a Christian Roman Catholic tradition in an attempt to legitimize the group, as well as to cause fissures in the tradition.

THE UNSUBMISSIVE TRANSIT BETWEEN THE CENTER AND THE MARGIN OF CHRISTIANITY

The stories that have been presented in this chapter, and the countless other stories of sexual and gender dissidents in relation to Christianity, are stories of transit, stories of movement. Some observers might simply assume that these people were pushed to the margins by the center of power—and that would be the end of the journey. As Althaus-Reid explains, "The revelation that occurs in intimate acts, in the perceived chaotic history of intimate human relationships in history, has been systematically marginalized and silenced by a highly idealistic sexually hegemonic theological project, heavily dependent on a colonial model."[45] However, what is perceived is an unsubmissive transit between the center and the margin, in what could be understood as a process of continuities and ruptures.

---

44   Serra, "Diversity as a Gift," 23.

45   Althaus-Reid, *The Queer God*, 38.

The continuities occur especially in the self-affirmation of these collectives when they declare themselves Christians, despite all the violence they suffered from the Christian religious institution. One example of this self-affirmation is the preamble of the Statement of Faith of Metropolitan Community Churches, considered the world's first inclusive Christian church: "Metropolitan Community Churches is *one chapter* in the story of the Church, the Body of Christ. We are people on a journey, learning to live into our spirituality, while affirming our bodies, our genders, our sexualities."[46] They insert themselves as a chapter in the history of the church, that is, they reject the marginalization of their faith experiences.

On the other hand, the stories show significant ruptures with the tradition of Christianity through theological proposals that affirm and celebrate diversity, despite all the efforts of hegemonic theology with its "traditional androcentric methodology which tends to absorb and adapt the most radical elements which can arise from the margins."[47] The margin presents itself as a new paradigm, according to Silva Regina de Lima:

> Reality demands paradigms with a holistic conception of life, of the created world, of interhuman relationships. It demands concepts that break down barriers, build bridges, encourage dialogue, reaffirm life, and respect and value the richness of the diversity that makes up our continent. . . . To find this new paradigm it is necessary to change the place from where the world is seen, to have another point of view, another starting point. It is looking at the world from below, from the little ones. It is looking at it from the ground, with your feet planted on the ground, with a body made of earth, of fragility and firmness, a supportive body, a body part of other bodies.[48]

---

46   "Metropolitan Community Churches," accessed Feb. 8, 2022, https://tinyurl.com/mrx7k8ve.

47   Althaus-Reid, *Indecent Theology*, 6.

48   Silvia Regina de Lima, *En territorio de frontera: una lectura de Marcos 7. 24-30* (Costa Rica: DEI, 2001), 22.

This is the importance of Althaus-Reid's "oral sex"—to tell stories from the margins, creating a new paradigm of theological reflection that does not disregard the significance of the margins in the liberating project of Christianity. After all, the margin is "a non-negotiable site of Grace and freedom."[49]

From this paradigm, what can be seen is that the transit is part of these dissident and insurgent experiences. For Ihab Hassan, this journey can be understood as a "metaphor and transgression, a textuality of motion"[50] because "travel, in any case, transgresses. It oversteps time as well as space, culture as well as consciousness. Blurring boundaries, though, it recreates them; it remarginalizes areas it has smeared."[51]

The transgression of this trip may require multiple passports. "A Queer theologian has many passports because she is a theologian in diaspora, that is, a theologian who explores at the crossroads of Christianity issues of self-identity and the identity of her community, which are related to sexuality, race, culture and poverty."[52] The metaphor of passports helps to explain how this process of ruptures and continuities takes place by traveling between the center and the margins. However, this is not a compulsory journey—it is a journey of resistance that gives rise to a spirituality of resistance. "In this sense, a spirituality of resistance is urgent, which does not mean accommodation but rather persevering tenacity, capable of withstanding and facing systems of domination."[53]

Transit from the margin to the center is not "a movement from the margins into the central discourse of theology"[54] for which Althaus-Reid criticized Liberation Theology,[55] but it is a transit of resistance, which

---

49   Althaus-Reid, *The Queer God*, 107.

50   Ihab Hassan, "Travel as Metaphor," in *Dissident and Marginality: Essays on the Boarders of Literature and Religion*, ed. Kiyoshi Tsuchiya (Great Britain: Macmillan Press, 1997), 163.

51   Hassan, "Travel as Metaphor," 164.

52   Althaus-Reid, *The Queer God*, 7.

53   Lima, *En territorio de frontera*, 20.

54   Althaus-Reid, *Indecent Theology*, 25.

55   Althaus-Reid, "Gustavo Gutiérrez Goes to Disneyland."

questions the legitimacy of the tradition based on the stories of dissidence, as Serra explains from the experience of the *RNGC*:

> Having critically acknowledged the magisterium's limitations, the Brazilian LGBTQI+ Catholic groups strive for greater moral autonomy and assert their self-knowledge and their own authority to speak for themselves. . . . By doing so, they subvert the authority of the alleged holders of Sacred Truth; that, in turn, allows them to question the legitimacy of a Church capable of marginalizing, excluding, and perpetrating violence.[56]

Therefore, it is an unsubmissive transit, which does not submit to castration by hegemonic Christianity, defying orthodoxy from a praxis based on marginal lives. Althaus-Reid explains that the praxis needs to be done through sexual deviance because only that perspective can challenge the regulatory regime of the heterosexuality sacralized by Christianity. As Serra exemplifies:

> Rather than discussing sexual and gender diversity in Roman Catholicism in the third person, the Brazilian communities that avowedly organize around identities that are simultaneously "Roman Catholic" and "LGBTQI+" take the floor publicly to attest to their presence in the Church.[57]

In this process of autonomy, when talking about themselves, sexual and gender dissidents narrate/oralize their Christian experience from their own struggles, pains, contradictions, ambiguities. This is one of the main contributions of the margin as a paradigm—the possibility of knowing Christianity from incarnated experiences of marginal desire. After all, as Grada Kilomba explains, "the margin is a location that nourishes our capacity to resist oppression, to transform, and to imagine alternative new worlds and new discourses."[58]

---

56   Serra, "Diversity as a Gift," 28.

57   Ibid., 25.

58   Grada Kilomba, *Plantation Memories: Episodes of Everyday Racism* (Muster: UNRAST-Verlag, 2010), 37.

Althaus-Reid's Indecent Theology does that by moving "objects and subjects of theology around, turning points of reference and re-positioning bodies of knowledge and revelation in sometimes unsuitable ways."[59] And she explains:

> Queer theologies go into diasporas by using tactics of temporary occupation; disruptive practices which are not necessarily to be repeated, and reflections which aim to be disconcerting. At the bottom line of Queer theologies, there are biographies of sexual migrants, testimonies of real lives in rebellions made of love, pleasure, and suffering.[60]

The *Evangélicxs* and the *RNGC* perform the indecent theological proposal of Althaus-Reid by moving their dissident bodies from the margin to the center, proposing ruptures and continuities with Christianity. When the *Evangélicxs,* for example, say on their social media that "the trans body is the image of God,"[61] they are challenging the hegemonic interpretations of the book of Genesis, which claim that "man and woman were created in the image and likeness of God."

The *Evangélicxs* not only challenge biblical interpretations of exclusion but also create, from their presence on social media, a destabilization in relation to the very understanding of what the church is. Theology is no longer only done in official pulpits but is also done on social media, giving visibility to the message they claim is "good news" for sexual and gender dissidents.

These embodied experiences of Indecent Theology create "strange alleys to the quest"[62] that present a challenge:

> The point to consider now is how we can ever know theology from different centres, such as the centre of a Queer nation. This may not be called a theology from the margins any more, but a theology

---

59   Althaus-Reid, *The Queer God*, 52.

60   Ibid., 8.

61   *Evangélicxs* Instagram post from January 31, 2022 (@evangelicxs_).

62   Althaus-Reid, *The Queer God*, 33.

> from recognisable, legitimised (if not approved) and visible centres
> which have been rendered invisible. We need to reflect in the area
> of different sexual ways of knowing which could be considered
> foundational (even if always provisory, as in a process of theologi-
> cal praxis) for a new way of reflecting on God and on us.[63]

The power of the margin lies in breaking down borders by creating other
centers. Not centers that are exclusive or hegemonic but centers that
affirm diversity and that are based on relationships of solidarity, such as
the *Evangélicxs* and the *RNGC*.

CONCLUSION: MARGINAL DESIRE

The margin, as a paradigm for the recognition of alterity, is a territory
of experiences based on untold stories, stories silenced by hegemonic
Christianity. This chapter presented two experiences of Brazilian Christian collectives that organize themselves on the margins of tradition, but
not in submission to the tradition. After all, the "sexual stories from the
margins"[64] show that "theology and sexuality can be rewritten from the
margins of society, the church and systematic theologies."[65]

The *Evangélicxs pela Diversidade* and the *Rede Nacional de Grupos
Católicos LGBT* are inclusive initiatives of resistance to the historical
condemnation of dissident gender and sexuality through the creation of
solidarity networks that affirm and celebrate what, for so long, was considered a sin. These two examples are among many other experiences that
show that the presence of sexual and gender dissidents in Christianity not
only changes the history of the church but also changes the affirmations
that have for so long been held sacred.

The marginal epistemology proposed by a queer/indecent theology is
fundamental to the theories and methods for the study of Christianity and
to the theme of alterity in global Christian studies. The transit between
the margin and the center shows that the study of religions cannot be

---

63   Ibid.

64   Althaus-Reid, *Indecent Theology*, i.

65   Ibid., 4.

produced only from a cultural translation but also from a cultural experience that recognizes the belonging of dissident and insurgent inclusive initiatives that challenge Christianity.

Thus, marginal desire presents itself as a category of recognition of the experiences of sexual and gender dissidents in Latin America that aims to oralize their sexual stories. The sound of these voices creates waves of resistance that cause fissures in the borders that separate the center from the margin, and the sacred manifests itself. After all, "God is desire"[66]—marginal, in transit, and unsubmissive desire.

66   Althaus-Reid, *Indecent Theology*, 148.

CHAPTER 10

THEOLOGIZING WITH CONCUBINES:
TRUSTING IN INDECENT BODIES
IN WORLD CHRISTIANITY

Eve Parker

"The lords of Gibeah rose up against me, and surrounded the house at night. They intended to kill me, and they raped my concubine until she died."[1]

"Four upper-caste men attacked, raped and murdered the Dalit Christian woman in Hathras, Uttar Pradesh. She suffered multiple fractures, paralysis and a deep gash on her tongue."[2]

Bodily acts are theological acts that reveal secrets about God; even the most indecent bodily acts offer profound insights into society, religion, power, and our knowledge and understanding of God. Yet disembodied theologies appear to dominate in the study of Christianity, particularly in the context of Europe. This contradicts what feminist epistemologies have held to be true: that knowing is situated and varies across social locations, and that gendered power structures apparent within society impact

---

1   Judges 20:5 NRSV.

2   Bijay Kumar Minj, "Indian bishop condemns 'inhuman' rape-murder of Dalit woman," *Union of Catholic Asian News* (October 1, 2020), available online: https://tinyurl.com/5ar78d5j.

241

knowledge production.[3] The same applies when taking into consideration the dominant discourses apparent within the study of World Christianity, where there exists a lacuna for the voices of women whose narratives are situated in contexts of sexual violence, racism, casteism, and classism. This is not to deny that the study of World Christianity has journeyed into the margins to be with the poor or those who suffer from such violence but, in agreement with Marcella Althaus-Reid, "the narratives of the 'theologian from the poor', the 'Christ of the poor', and 'theology from poverty' never de-centered Christian Western theology but rather adapted it more successfully."[4] The testimonies of the women whose sexual narratives expose the gendered violence of patriarchal, capitalist, and casteist society are often invisible, and have been hermeneutically marginalized, whilst their experience and knowledge have been systematically dismissed as a consequence of epistemic injustice.[5] Even in discourses that focus on the liberation of the oppressed in World Christianity, the testimonies of the indecent poor are often missing. Let me elaborate here about what is meant by the "indecent poor." According to Althaus-Reid, the poor in Liberation Theology have been presented as "decent," their sexual narratives of both struggle and lust have been silenced in such theology, and there exists a lacuna of sexual honesty and indecent epistemology that

---

3   See Heidi E. Grasswick, *Feminist Epistemology and Philosophy of Science: Power in Knowledge* (New York: Springer, 2011), xvi.

4   Marcella Althaus-Reid, "Gustavo Gutiérrez Goes to Disneyland: Theme Park Theologies and the Diaspora of the Discourse of the Popular Theologian in Liberation Theology," in *Interpreting Beyond Borders,* ed. Fernando F. Segovia (Sheffield: Sheffield Academic Press, 2000), 39.

5   Miranda Fricker has written extensively on epistemic injustice, noting that there exists structural prejudice that leads to epistemic injustice, inclusive of testimonial injustice, where "a speaker suffers a testimonial injustice just if prejudice on the hearer's part causes him to give the speaker less credibility than he would otherwise have given." Fricker suggests there are two forms of epistemic injustice, namely "testimonial injustice, in which someone is wronged in their capacity as a giver of knowledge; and hermeneutical injustice, in which someone is wronged in their capacity as a subject of social understanding." Fricker, *Epistemic Injustice: Power and the Ethics of Knowing* (Oxford: Oxford University Press, 2007), 4.

has the potential to deconstruct moral orders of oppression. The indecent poor, therefore, refers to narratives of sexuality and sexual oppression that coincide with the intersections of poverty and struggle. Althaus-Reid notes,

> The everyday lives of people always provide us with a starting point for a process of doing a contextual theology without exclusions, in this case without the exclusion of sexuality struggling in the midst of misery.[6]

Sexual violence, patriarchy, and colonialism are interrelated realities that impact women across the globe, and intersect with religious doctrines, Christian missions, and faith practices. Such social inequalities also have epistemic consequences because the indecent testimonies of those who have experienced such sexual violence are often censored from our contemplations on God, and given less credence as worthy knowledge.

This chapter will address the silenced and indecent testimonies of Dalit women Christians in the context of South India in order to engage with multiple marginalities of caste, gender, class, religious, and economic subjugation whilst also highlighting the ways in which sexual violence against women has been silenced in dominant discourses of Christian theology and the study of World Christianity. It will argue that the theology that emerges out of violence against women brings about critical and challenging questions about God, society, and Scripture, where the bodies of women become central in helping us to contemplate God in the study of World Christianity. It will look to Indecent Theology, which in the words of Althaus-Reid, "aims to uncover, unmask and unclothe that false hermeneutics which considers itself as 'decent' and as such, proper and benefitting for women especially in sexual matters."[7] Narratives of violence against women expose the violence of heteropatriarchal colonial

---

6   Marcella Althaus-Reid, *Indecent Theology: Theological Perversions in Sex, Gender and Politics* (New York: Routledge, 2000), 4.

7   Marcella Althaus-Reid, "On Wearing Skirts Without Underwear: 'Indecent Theology Challenging the Liberation Theology of the Pueblo'. Poor Women Contesting Christ," *Feminist Theology Journal* 7, no. 20 (1999): 39–51.

Christianity, and are a source of suppressed knowledge, as the sexual narratives of the oppressed can challenge the political, economic, religious, and social matrix of power. I will therefore give voice to Dalit women's experiences in the context of South India by sharing ethnographic research paying attention to the experiences of Dalit sacred "sex workers," known as *devadāsīs*. Yet it is also important to note that I am an "outsider" looking in, and my experience as a white, British woman differs greatly from that of the women whose narratives I share. I note my own social identity as a means of being consciously epistemologically disobedient by challenging the notion that knowing can be disconnected from our own geopolitical configuration, as to act as though one's social location is irrelevant in ethnographic research is to epistemically harm the marginalized voices that I seek to highlight. The notion of "epistemic disobedience" refers to Walter Mignolo's work and gives focus to those who bare the "colonial wound" and "have been classified as underdeveloped economically and mentally."[8] I therefore cannot claim in this chapter to offer more than contemplative reflections, based upon the narratives heard and witnessed.[9]

I share testimonies in the words of Dalit women who have experienced sexual violence, in order to affirm "the racially devalued"[10] and take a decolonial turn by offering the space for such testimonies to be the starting point for contemplating God in Christian theology. This chapter applies such testimonies and experiences to Christian scripture as a means of giving greater attention to the relevance of Dalit women's experiences in the study of World Christianity. In taking this decolonial turn, I seek to prioritize the experiences of Dalit women in order to reread Judges 19, a tale of sexual oppression where a persecuted woman is silenced and

---

8   Walter Mignolo, "Epistemic Disobedience, Independent Thought and Decolonial Freedom," *Theory, Culture & Society* 26, nos. 7–8 (2009): 159–81 (161).

9   The ethnographic research took place between the years 2011 to 2014 in Tamil Nadu and Andhra Pradesh, where I researched the *devadāsī* community in the rural villages of South India. Interviews took place with informed consent, and much of the research was published in Eve Rebecca Parker, *Theologising with the Sacred 'Prostitutes' of South India: Towards an Indecent Dalit Theology* (Leiden: Brill, 2021).

10   See Mignolo, "Epistemic Disobedience," 159–81 (162).

abused throughout. Giving voice to the voiceless women of Scripture is a powerful tool of resistance used in Dalit feminist theological methodology, where, as Surekha Nelavala comments, Dalit womanist hermeneutics "engages in a parallel and comparative reading of the text and the narratives" of Dalit women.[11] I will use this method in order to engage with the testimonial injustice experienced by the "concubine" in the text, and will consider how such narratives relate to the silenced experiences of Dalit women.

DALIT WOMEN'S EPISTEMOLOGY IN CHRISTIAN THEOLOGY

Dalit women in India are described as being "thrice marginalized"—they have been persecuted as a result of their caste status, as well as their gender in a patriarchal society, and this has led to the majority of Dalit women facing significant economic deprivation. Dalit women consequently suffer religious, social, economic, and political marginalization. Reflecting on Dalit women's experiences, Prasuna Gnana Nelavala notes that they are "those who have lost their laughter, labour, and life for the sake of upper caste men and women and even their co-Dalit men."[12] Dalit women have also disproportionately experienced sexual violence and exploitation, including rape, sexual harassment, forced prostitution, and domestic violence. Female sexuality and caste are intertwined, and as "caste itself is premised on the management of female sexuality through arranged, endogamous marriage," this is also made apparent in the sexual exploitation of Dalit women where caste hegemony is entrenched through acts of abuse, rape, and harassment. Clarinda Still explains how the sexual exploitation of Dalit women has been historically rooted in acts of bonded labor, noting that "one of the most extreme manifestations of this was a practice known as *adi bapa*, that occurred in the South Indian state of Telangana, where

---

11   Surekah Nelavala, "Smart Syrophoenician Woman: A Dalit Feminist Reading of Mark 7:24–31," *The Expository Times* 118, no. 2 (2006): 64–69 (64).

12   Evangeline Anderson, "Turning Bodies Inside Out: Contours of Womanist Theology," in *Dalit Theology in the Twenty-first Century, Discordant Voices, Discerning Pathways*, ed. Sathianathan Clarke, Deenabandhu Manchala, and Philip Vinod Peacock (Oxford University Press): 211–67 (267).

a landlord had the right to take the virginity of his servant's bride on the wedding night."[13] Acts of sexual abuse and rape of Dalit women are used as a means of shaming and violently exploiting Dalits both physically and symbolically. Ajay Kumar highlights the extent of such violence, stating that in an examination of rape cases from 2009 to 2020, research found that "80% of the sexual violence cases against Dalit women and girls were committed by upper caste dominant men." Rape and gang rape have become weapons of oppression used against the bodies of Dalit women to impose caste hierarchy and patriarchal domination, and to "settle scores against Dalits mostly in rural India." There exists a culture of impunity in the face of such violence, as "about ninety percent of crimes against Dalit women are not reported to the police for the fear of social exclusion and threat to personal security and safety."[14]

Those women who experience violence are often denied justice in their capacity as a "knower," and Dalit women are faced with the reality that in classist, casteist, racist, sexist societies, their testimonies of oppression are not trusted. Miranda Fricker describes how testimonial injustice "occurs when prejudice causes a hearer to give a deflated level of credibility to a speaker's word."[15] Relying on Fricker's concept of testimonial injustice, it is apparent that Dalit women experience epistemic harm, as they are often denied of their credibility on the basis of pervasive social prejudice. Their experiences are also silenced in dominant theological discourse in the study of World Christianity that has, for the most part, not entered into spaces of Dalit women's sexual oppression. As Dalit women who have experienced the atrocities of sexual violence have not been trusted in their embodied epistemologies, consequently, the silenced, raped, and violated bodies of those who have lived experiences of such atrocities have not been heard. Yet such unheard narratives of sexual oppression have the potential to expose certain truths and failures of dominant epistemologies in Christian thought and praxis.

---

13   Clarinda Still, *Dalit Women: Honour and Patriarchy in South India* (New York: Routledge, 2017), 13–14.

14   See Ajay Kumar, "Sexual Violence against Dalit Women: An Analytical Study of Intersectionality of Gender, Caste, and Class in India," *Journal of International Women's Studies* 22, no. 2 (2021): 123–34 (125).

15   Fricker, *Epistemic Injustice*, 1.

It is for this reason that Dalit feminist hermeneutics in Christian theology has sought to give voice to such experience through rereadings of the Bible. To quote Surekha Nelavala:

> I, as a Dalit woman, approach the text looking for an interpretation that is truly liberating to Dalit women in particular and the community of the marginalised in general. I find such liberation in the model of mutual reconciliation of both the oppressed and the oppressor that involves acceptance, repentance, and a radical transformation particularly from the privileged groups of the society.[16]

Reading the Bible in the context of Dalit women's oppression enables a theologizing that is shaped by the communal experience of gendered violence against Dalit women, as, in agreement with Grasswick, "marginalised positions might have better insights, based on their social location, that could be fostered to attain knowledge."[17] It was in meeting Dalit women, who had been dedicated to the goddess Yellamma in the context of the South Indian village, and had come to be known as sacred "prostitutes," that I gained a greater understanding into the complexities of World Christianity, and the extent to which marginalized narratives of oppression offer profound insights into Christ, scripture, and doctrine. The Dalit women, known as *devadāsīs*, had been dedicated in childhood to local village goddesses as result of their caste status, due to poverty, and in response to sickness, such as smallpox, that the goddess is believed to heal. The dedicated women experience significant violence in the form of economic, religious, and sexual exploitation. Their identities are exceptionally complex, as historically, *devadāsīs* were deemed auspicious "ritual specialists," central to temple worship, and revered by their communities. Yet, as they now exist on the margins of Indian society, objectified as "harlots" and "prostitutes," they have become the templates on which

---

16　Surekha Nelavala, "Jesus Asks the Samaritan Woman for a Drink: A Dalit Feminist Reading of John 4," *lectio difficilior* no. 1 (2007): 2–3.

17　See Grasswick, *Feminist Epistemology*, xvi.

the empires of the past and the ideologies of caste and patriarchy in the present have sought to impose their rule and order.

Many of the women whom I encountered had "converted" to Christianity in response to church reform initiatives that sought to "save" the women from what the church maintained was "sinful" behavior. The epistemology of the *devadāsīs* offered radical insights into a lived practical Christian theology, noting that, "for the converted *devadāsī*, Jesus responds when he is called upon, whether that be for food, comforting, disease, or rain . . . he becomes real for the *devadāsī* when he participates in her struggles and suffering."[18] The dedicated *devadāsī* Dalit women whom I met narrated a profound understanding of Jesus, as well as the goddess, that was relevant to their struggles, and to their hybrid religious belonging, where they confessed faith in both the goddess and Jesus. As one *devadāsī* commented: "Jesus is like a mother to me, one that did not give me away, has never left my side, she is always there for me, when I ask, she responds."[19]

In observing the Dalit Christian theology of the *devadāsīs*, I therefore found a Christian religiosity that was fluid in the manner in which it negotiated multiple religious realities—a fluidity shaped by the day-to-day needs of the women. This included their prayers to the goddess for healing from rape, menstrual pains, and the wrath of the landlord, alongside worship of Jesus, who became a local village deity, as one woman described:

> He is with me now, next to me, just as he was when I would do bad things, he is with me when I have sex with people for the goddess, he is with me when I get called bad names and when I pray to him, he always answers.[20]

It was through ethnographic research in the South India village with the dedicated women that I attained knowledge about Christ that was

---

18   Parker, *Theologising with the Sacred 'Prostitutes' of South India*, 163.

19   Ibid., 166.

20   Mathamma Kanagarathinam, interview, Nagalapuram, Andhra Pradesh, December 12, 2014. Quoted in Parker, *Theologising with the Sacred 'Prostitutes' of South India*, 158.

otherwise silenced. Such lived Christianity challenges imposed colonial norms—where Indigenous religiosities were deemed to be heathen practices and epistemologically silenced in the process. The lived Christianity of the dedicated women was also indecent, as it exposed the limitation of rigid notions of morality and decency that have dictated the boundaries of belonging in Christianity. Therefore, entering into spaces of indecency allows us to be "drawn into a space where theological limit and theological transgression are seen as mutually dependent."[21] In doing so, we can witness how the colonial matrix of power continues to impact the lives of the subaltern, as capitalism, racism, and patriarchy intersect in order to silence the knowledge that the colonized produce.

In agreement with Mignolo, I find that it is not possible to be a "neutral seeker of truth and objectivity,"[22] nor should we be neutral in the face of oppression. Dalit women's epistemology is therefore vital in contemplating World Christianity, which has predominantly neglected the lived Christianity of the "indecent poor,"[23] and as Nelavala remarks, "it is equally important not only to raise the issues of oppression and liberation but also to explore the interconnections between the Dalit woman's world

---

21   Jeremy Carrette, "Radical Heterodoxy and the Indecent Proposal of Erotic Theology: Critical Groundwork for Sexual Theologies," *Literature and Theology: Queering Religion* 15, no. 3, (2001): 286–98 (289).

22   Mignolo, "Epistemic Disobedience," 159–81 (162).

23   Studies of World Christianity vary greatly. This is apparent in Raimundo C. Barreto Jr. et al., eds., *World Christianity as Public Religion* (Minneapolis: Fortress Press, 2017), where scholars engage with World Christianity as a form of public religion looking to ethics, politics, gender, and intercultural perspectives. Issues of identity in the study of World Christianity have also been explored with profound reflections on issues of belonging, multiple religious belonging, and the impact of cultural and social locations on lived Christianity. See Corey L. Williams and Afe Adogame, "Christianity and Multiple Identities," *Studies in World Christianity* 25 (2019): 1–4. Scholars have also debated the methodological considerations to be made in the study of World Christianity, noting the importance of multidisciplinary approaches. See Dorottya Nagy and Martha Theodora Frederiks, eds., *World Christianity: Methodological Considerations* (Leiden: Brill, 2020). However, there exists a lacuna for the sexual narratives of the oppressed Christians whose identities and lived Christianity offer profound insights into Christ.

and the biblical world with the intention of transforming Dalit women."[24] When we privilege the testimonies of Dalit women in Christian theology, we are able to gain a greater understanding of the Christian faith and its scriptures by recognizing both how the Bible and doctrine have been used as weapons of oppression and how the Bible can become a tool of resistance. The Bible requires a non-neutral lens in light of violence against women, particularly when we take into consideration what Phyllis Trible referred to as "texts of terror" in the Bible,[25] such as Judges 19, a narrative of horrific violence, rape, and the murder of a silenced and tortured woman.

Whilst for many readers, such a text tells the tale of an unthinkable atrocity, such a narrative speaks directly to the violence and fear of violence experienced daily by Dalit women in India where the mutilation and dismemberment of Dalit women continue to be enacted as a means of instilling caste hierarchy and gendered subjugation. This has come to light recently in the brutal rape and murder of a nameless Dalit Christian woman in Uttar Pradesh in 2021. She was nineteen years old and was gang raped and murdered when "four upper-caste men attacked the Dalit woman in Hathras. She suffered multiple fractures, paralysis and a deep gash on her tongue."[26] The woman was never given the chance to tell her story. Her tongue, her weapon of voice, was taken from her, her body used, abused, and violated in the most horrific way. We owe deference to the silenced epistemology of this woman in our theology because patriarchy, caste, colonialism, and capitalism have all denied her of the trust her testimony and narrative deserves.

The Testimonial Injustice of the Concubines in Christian Theology

In Christian scripture, we see similar shocking narratives of violence against women. In Judges 19, we read of a Levite residing in a remote part

---

24   Prasuna Gnana Nelavala, "Caste Branding, Bleeding Body, Building Dalit Womanhood," in *Dalit Theology in the Twenty-first Century, Discordant Voices, Discerning Pathways,* ed. Sathianathan Clarke, Deenabandhu Manchala, and Philip Vinod Peacock (Oxford: Oxford University Press, 2010), 265–76 (271).

25   Phyllis Trible, *Texts of Terror* (Philadelphia: Fortress Press, 1984).

26   Minj, "Indian Bishop condemns inhuman rape-murder of Dalit woman."

of Ephraim who "took to himself a concubine from Bethlehem in Judah" (19:1). The story that unravels is one of grave gender-based violence, rape, and murder. The concubine, who remains without a name in the text, attempts to escape from the Levite man and goes to her father's house. However, the Levite persuades her to come back to him (19:3); we are to assume she accepts, but since her father so willingly welcomes the man into his home, the woman's choice in the matter seems of little consequence. The father of the concubine makes the Levite man feel welcome despite whatever difficulties the man and his daughter had been going through, and together the men go on to eat and drink over a number of days (19:4–9). Eventually the man leaves with the woman, his servant, and donkeys, and they seek shelter on their travels in Gibeah (19:15). As no one will take them in, they rely on the hospitality of a "foreign" man from Ephraim, who was residing in Gibeah (19:21). The stranger welcomes them and feeds them, but "while they were enjoying themselves, the men of the city, a perverse lot, surrounded the house, and started pounding on the door" (19:22). The men threaten to rape the Levite, but the owner of the house refuses to allow this to happen and says, "Here are my virgin daughter and his concubine; let me bring them out now. Ravish them and do whatever you want to them; but against this man do not do such a vile thing" (19:24). The men grabbed the concubine, gang-raped her, abused her body all through the night until the morning (19:25).[27] As far as we can assume, the woman's body could not take any more pain and suffering, and she died on the doorstep of the house that her master had been welcomed into—she was murdered in the most violent of ways. The Levite man threw the corpse of her body onto the back of his donkey, and when he reached his home, he took a knife and dismembered her, chopping up her tortured corpse into "twelve pieces, limb by limb and sent her throughout all the territory of Israel" (19:29).

Judges 19 is a story about power, rape, testimonial injustice, and epistemic injustice. The gendered and violated body of a woman, known as a concubine, is central to the text, and yet she is voiceless and nameless throughout, much like the Dalit woman who faced such violence.

---

27   See Eve Parker, *Trust in Theological Education: Dismantling Trustworthiness for a Pedagogy of Liberation* (London: SCM Press, 2022), 39–40.

Systemic patriarchy, apparent in both the world of the murdered concubine and that of today, determines that women, as social agents, have less power. They are often not granted the basic levels of epistemic authority, as their voices and experiences are too often not trusted. A rereading of Judges 19 in the context of the epistemic and testimonial injustice of the nameless concubine enables us to give voice to similar experiences today, and to call for radical change in both our theology and praxis. For Trible, it is a tale of contrast between male "power, brutality, and triumphalism" and female "helplessness, abuse, and annihilation."[28] In the text, we read of how the woman attempts to escape her predicament, and yet her own father forces her back into the arms of the man who will eventually cause her brutal death. Many Dalit women are forced into arranged marriages, where they are often abused, and in the case of the Dalit *devadāsī* women, marriage is central to the control of the dedicated women. In the process of dedication, *devadāsī* women are married off to the goddess in childhood, also leading to their sexual abuse, social vilification, and control. As one *devadāsī* named Mathamma commented, "If I want to get married to one person it is believed that, that man will die and so we never get married."[29] Yet twentieth-century Christian reformists used marriage as a means of making the women "decent" and "moral." This often came at the expense of the women's agency, as marriage became "a necessary means of rehabilitation for those sacred sex workers who accept Christ."[30] Both the Christian reformists and the high-caste Hindus deem Dalit women's sexuality as needing to be controlled. Nitya Rao makes this point, noting that "marriage and sexuality is hence politicized, with numerous strategies, individual and collective, used to weaken women's agency and bargaining power."[31] We know the concubine in the text resists her oppression as she flees to her father. However, we are not told what she is running from— her testimony is omitted from the narrative. Likewise, violence against Dalit women is often met with a culture of impuntity by both society and

---

28   Trible, *Texts of Terror*, 65.

29   Parker, *Theologising with the Sacred 'Prostitutes' of South India*, 21.

30   Ibid., 112.

31   Nitya Rao, "Marriage, Violence, and Choice: Understanding Dalit Women's Agency in Rural Tamil Nadu," *Gender & Society* 29, no. 3 (2015): 410–33 (413).

normative Christian thought. Further, when Dalit women protest against caste and gender discrimination, those with power use sexual violence as a weapon to silence the women.

In Judges 19, the father takes the side of his own daughter's oppressor. Male epistemology is prioritized throughout the story, and in the words of Jessie Bernard, "Since virtually all human knowledge is a male creation, such knowledge deals only with a world seen through male eyes."[32] The world of the concubine is depicted only through the eyes of the men who seek to control and oppress her, and this text has also predominantly been interpreted by men who continue to silence her. Similarly, despite the numerous accounts of rape and violence against Dalit women, there is minimum recognition of their suffering in the study of World Christianity, and their lived experience is deemed irrelevant to dominant ways of knowing and seeing the world. Yet sexual violence and gendered oppression are what, in part, make the world of women different from that of men. Such sexual narratives of oppression provide unique and vital realities of life that are excluded from dominant ways of knowing, as the male world that also dominates our theological discourses has been observed, researched, interpreted, and contemplated through the male gaze. Althaus-Reid makes this point, stating, "Sexual stories are not components of abstract worlds but they are rooted in political communities and obey concrete conditions of production, limited by race, class, age, degrees of accepted sexual normative discourse or resistance."[33] This has had a significant impact on the way in which we have come to understand the Christian faith. Due to the "male bias in human learning, it is almost impossible even to conceive of a female world as an entity in and of itself, with its own character, its own validity, its own legitimacy. It is invisible."[34] Thus for most Christian interpreters who have been influenced by this male bias, the world of the concubine is rendered invisible in the text—it is only in rape and death that she becomes visible, as an object to be manipulated and abused by the powerful. Her death represents a grave testimonial injustice where

---

32   Jessie Bernard, *The Female World* (New York: The Free Press, 1981), 12.

33   Althaus-Reid, *Indecent Theology*, 134.

34   Bernard, *The Female World*, 12.

she is unable to voice her struggles and truth, she is not deemed credible, and she is dehumanized in the process. Such testimonial injustice is also apparent in dominant discourses of World Christianity and Christian theologizing where structural biases against certain groups exist to the extent that they are not considered to be credible in their epistemology.

Exposing Murdered Knowledge in World Christianity

In Judges 19, we witness the impact of such structures in the Levite man's response, as he remains concerned about his own ill-treatment and the inhospitality he received, as opposed to the violent rape and murder of the woman. He even continues to violate the voiceless body of the corpse of the dead woman by dismembering her (19:28–29). For Hamley, "The dismembering becomes an attempt to erase her and the memory of a crime that was first directed against him."[35] However, the very fact that this story exists as a sacred text makes it relevant to the sexual narratives of the oppressed. From narratives such as that of the Dalit *devadāsīs,* for example, who worship Christ alongside the local village goddess as a means of responding to their situated individual needs, we learn things about God and local village religiosity that are otherwise invisible to us. The sacred becomes relevant to the lives of the oppressed. Yet, the world of the Dalit *devadāsīs* has been invisible in dominant discourses of World Christianity that often remain inattentive to sexual injustices and violence against women.[36] The exclusion of such narratives is of significant importance to the future of the study of World Christianity. Denying such realites disembodies and dismembers the lived reality of global Christianity, where the indecent poor are marginalized from sacred spaces, as one *devadāsī* stated: "The Church will not let me and my children be baptised, I am not welcome to come to church services, I am not welcome because I am a prostitute,

---

35 Isabelle M. Hamley, *Unspeakable Things Unspoken: An Irigarayan Reading of Otherness and Victimization in Judges 19–21* (Eugene, Oregon: Pickwick Publications, 2019), 223.

36 Dalit theologians have also been critiqued for silencing the experiences of Dalit women. See Clarke, Manchala, and Peacock, *Dalit Theology in the Twenty-first Century.*

what hope is there for me?"[37] When we center the epistemology of those who have been raped and violated instead of silencing such truths in Christian theology, we come to learn and unlearn the truth of the dangers and violence of patriarchy within the Christian faith tradition that would otherwise go unchallenged.

Apparent within both the biblical narrative and the narratives of Dalit women are the binaries of worthy/unworthy, man/woman, pure/impure, ruling class/working class, decent/indecent, virgin/whore. The woman is consciously depicted as indecent and in need of controlling from the beginning, so her body is ranked as worthless in comparison to the "decent" woman and the men. The Dalit theologian Evangeline Anderson-Rajkumar notes that "violence against women, especially those targeted on the wombs and bodies of women, should be seen as ways of driving women and men back into respective boundaries of patriarchal power."[38] There exists a need in patriarchal societies and theologies to deny women of power and autonomy, even if this to leads to violence. The body of the concubine can be compared to the colonial "other," where the colonizers' power is realized in their assumed superiority to those they encounter in their conquests. Because the bodies of Dalit women were considered to be colonial conquests under British imperial rule, their religious and social identities were silenced, and they were depicted as "indecent" and in need of controlling. To do theology in resistance to such power dynamics is to ackowledge the way colonial difference operates and instead allow for "indigenous practices, values, and ideas that were targeted for eradication by colonizers, exploring ways of writing/thinking/practicing theology that would begin deconstructing embedded power imbalances, and establishing decolonial metholodologies."[39] This also highlights the extent to which the oppressive frameworks must be exposed, and how the narratives

---

37   Parker, *Theologising with the Sacred 'Prostitutes' of South India*, 114.

38   Evangeline Anderson-Rajkumar, "Turning Bodies Inside Out: Contours of Womanist Theology," in *Dalit Theology in the Twenty-first Century, Discordant voices, Discerning Pathways*, ed. Clarke, Manchala, and Peacock (Oxford: Oxford University Press, 2010), 199–214 (211).

39   Oscar García-Johnson, *Spirit Outside the Gate: Decolonial Pneumatologies of the American Global South* (Illinois: InterVarsity Press, 2019), 3.

of the marginalized must be given the space to disrupt and dismantle, as the study of World Christianity offers a space to center the voices of the most marginalized Christian communities in order to address the intersections of systemic violence.

The concubine's brutal murder also forces us to consider the ways in which her knowledge was murdered with her. In life she could not speak her truth, and in death she is dismembered by her oppressor, and her body, through the dismemberment and sending to the territories of Israel (19:29), is used to tell her oppressors' version of events. The truth is that even if the woman had survived the horrors of the violence inflicted against her, her word, her truth, her embodied suffering, would likely not be trusted by those with power. It would likely, as is the case for many Dalit women today, be met with indifference. Her knowledge about the evils of societal violence and gendered persecution would not be given a platform to be heard, as often occurs "in places and circumstances where the putative 'knower' can, for a range of personal and situational reasons, be discounted because of who he or she is."[40] The author of the text attempts to dismiss her worth from the outset by presenting her as an adulteress who runs away from her forgiving master. This same technique continues to be used today to dismiss the experiences of rape and trauma survivors, where their characters are assassinated, presented as "indecent," "whores," "troublesome," or "liars" in order to discount their worth before the courts and God. The impact of such indifference to the suffering of women was expressed by one dedicated *devadāsī*, who questioned, "How can I believe in a god that is a man, when it is men who force me to suffer. This god man will not know my pain—so how can he be a god to me?"[41]

Rereading Judges 19 through Dalit feminist hermeneutics enables the concubine's epistemology to be brought to life in her silenced oppression. As the abused body of the concubine is prophetic, in that it speaks of sex as an act of dominion and control, it forces us to behold the indecent sexual

---

40   Lorraine Code, "Feminist Epistemology and the Politics of Knowledge: Questions of Marginality," in *The Sage Handbook of Feminist Theory*, ed. Mary Evans, Clare Hemmings, Marsha Henry, Hazel Johnstone, Sumi Madhok, Ania Pomien, and Sadie Wearing (Los Angeles: Sage, 2014), 9–25 (18).

41   Parker, *Theologising with the Sacred 'Prostitutes' of South India*, 165.

narratives of the oppressed in our Holy Scriptures, and ask: Why is this text of terror sacred? Who is this nameless woman, and how can the violence inflicted against her and her story be heard and inform our contemplations on God? This rereading therefore challenges dogmatic norms that have silenced the sexual narratives of oppressed bodies and sustained patriarchal norms because "at the core of any discussion on sexuality lies the threat of destabilizing dogmas and ecclesiologies which have made God a resource of heterosexual authority."[42] Rereading the silenced testimony of the tortured concubine through a Dalit feminist lens enables us to reflect on women's suffering in World Christianity as a means of valuing the knowledge and lived experiences of those who have been silenced and othered by patriarchy, caste, and colonialism, whilst also highlighting the way in which marginalized Christian communities use Scripture as resistance.

CONCLUSION: TRUST IN THE TESTIMONIES OF THE INDECENT OPPRESSED

Rereading Judges 19 in the context of Dalit women's struggles puts trust in the bodies of women who have been silenced, not only as a means of remembering the women of Scripture who were rendered voiceless but also to act in solidarity with the women who experience such horrors today and demand the church and society take notice. For Trible, "Reading these texts of terror involves a wrestling with demons and an absent deity who does not intervene."[43] However, the notion of an absent deity in the text can itself be challenged in light of the faith expressed and lived by the Dalit Christian *devadāsīs*. For example, the testimony of the *devadāsī* who narrated her struggles described how "Jesus is with me when I have sex for money, when my landlord beats me, when I am raped, just as the goddess is with me,"[44] and thereby she presented a deity who is far from absent in her suffering.

---

42   Marcella Althaus-Reid, *From Feminist Theology to Indecent Theology* (London: SCM, 2004), 102.

43   Phyllis Trible, *Texts of Terror: Literary-Feminist Readings of Biblical Narratives*, 40th Anniversary Edition (Minneapolis: Fortress Press, 2022), xi.

44   Mathamma Kanagarathinam, interview by author, Nagalapuram, Andhra Pradesh, December 12, 2014.

Because the personal and indecent lived religiosity takes God into indecent spaces, we are forced to consider the notion that God was with the concubine when she was raped and dismembered, and to raise the question: Was God therefore raped and dismembered with her in the process, just as the deity for the dedicated Dalit women knows their pain and suffering? In Judges 19, we are not given the concubine's testimony, so she is therefore not allowed the chance to voice her theology. This is an act of testimonial injustice. Such injustice forces us to consider our own complicity in silencing such testimonies, as we must ask: What role do we play in this narrative, who do we put our trust in, and how have we silenced the theological truth claims of the indecent oppressed? How do we understand and contemplate God when such narratives are happening in the here and now, and yet are silenced in the dominant discourses of World Christianity? Hanning remarks on how "many Global South women live in an in-between world, a world of uncertainties, ambiguities and contradictions; a space between indigenous worldviews and contemporary social and cultural life constructed by modernity/coloniality."[45] Such complexities are often overlooked in dominant discourses of theology and the study of World Christianity that focus instead on the narratives that are removed from the "indecent" and violated bodies.

The absence of such epistemology indicates a failure to trust in the knowledge of the oppressed, and, consequently, our understanding of World Christianity is made "decent" in the process, and therefore void of the sexual narratives that expose the realities of a God who is arguably dismembered with the sexually violated. This void is an act of hermeneutical injustice, and a result of systematic prejudice, for "it is not an accident that members of socially and politically marginalized groups lack the tools to understand and communicate their own experiences . . . they are denied the epistemic authority to contribute toward and influence the body of accepted and acceptable interpretive resources."[46] Such hermeneutical

---

45   Jennifer Manning, "Decolonial Feminist Theory: Embracing the Gendered Colonial Difference in Management and Organisation Studies," *Gender Work Organisation* 28 (2021): 1203–19 (1204).

46   Debra L. Jackson, "Date Rape: The Intractability of Hermeneutical Injustice," in *Analyzing Violence Against Women,* ed. Wanda Teays (Switzerland: Springer Nature, 2019), 39–51 (40).

injustice has theological consequences, as we learn to "know" God not through the eyes or testimonies of the oppressed but only through that of their oppressor.

If the study of World Christianity remains a patriarchal world where intersectional injustices, tyrannies, and evils of patriarchy are able to go unchallenged, unrecognized, and unacknowledged, then it denies the testimonies of the most marginalized. Putting trust in the indecent narratives of the oppressed challenges such a world and encourages us to contemplate God in ways that may enable a praxis of resistance and liberation for the sexually violated and most marginalized. Trust is central to such theologizing, as we must learn to distrust the dominant ways of knowing and enter into indecent spaces of oppression to put trust in the unknown, complex, disturbing, violent, and "impure" narratives of oppression. It was a result of the concubine being distrusted in her capacity as a knower that she was ultimately murdered. Trust in the testimonies of the oppressed is therefore required as a means of epistemic justice for the oppressed. Such justice in the study of World Christianity calls for epistemic resistance, where the knowledge of the marginalized is prioritized and undermines and challenges the oppressive normative ways of knowing that have sustained the structures of oppression.

Narratives of rape and violence against women are bodily acts that must not be silenced in our contemplations on God. If the study of World Christianity is to be epistemologically just, it must therefore overcome the fear of entering into indecent spaces of oppression, and instead witness the structural sins of our dominant ways of knowing that have silenced the testimonies of women. The intersectional struggles and profound religiosity of Dalit women encourage us to be epistemologically disobedient to our dominant ways of knowing and understanding the world and the Christian faith. In doing so, those learning and hearing such realities may become critically aware of their own social identity and positionality. When we become conscious of such oppression, we can actively work to redistribute the knowledge of the oppressed, so that we may gain a deeper and more profound understanding of the Christian faith that better helps us to reflect critically on how we can work collectively to end such violence against women.

CHAPTER 11

ASCETICISM, CORPOREALITY, AND VIOLENCE: THE WOMAN IN THE BOOK OF REVELATION

Kenner R. C. Terra[1]

For a long time, the Book of Revelation was read as a description of reality, as a text with ciphered language having direct connections with the Roman Empire, as if the text could reflect facts using apocalyptic symbols. In recent years, especially due to advances in biblical language studies, we have witnessed a change in the hermeneutical key, causing this enigmatic work to be understood as using a rhetorical-discursive[2] strategy and narrativization of memories. Consequently, Revelation is now seen as an example of the narrative strategy used in Christian literature of the first century. The images that appear in this work by the prophet John reveal a framework of order that reflects the mythical structuring of the world. In the visionary's work, places are remade, and grotesque bodies reformulate religious and social practices, while they denounce and/or strengthen oppression discursively. In other words, in Revelation's symbolic construction of reality, social places are resignified, and inversions are established.

The apocalyptic language is permeated by symbols of violence and hope. At the limit of metaphors, the book's discursive images are

---

1   Translated by Monika Ottermann.

2   Elisabeth Schüssler Fiorenza, *The Book of Revelation: Justice and Judgment*, 2nd ed. (Minneapolis: Fortress Press), 1998; Elisabeth Schüssler Fiorenza, "The Followers of the Lamb: Visionary Rhetoric and Social-political Situation," *Semeia* 36 (1986): 123–47.

instruments of identity construction and world organization. Following the Second Temple tradition, the visionary prophet John invites the interlocutors of the seven churches of Asia to interpret the Roman Empire as the abode of chaos, which would demand strict asceticism from the faith communities of the Asian region of the first century. As a counterdiscourse, Revelation contradicts the imperial propaganda of order and *pax* by describing reality as the dwelling place of the dragon (Rev 12–13; 17), a situation that would require total cultural separation.

John's strategy, as defended by current research in the light of discursive analysis, establishes strict boundaries that strengthen the symbolic limits between the followers of the Lamb and the Beast. In this scenario of identity construction, female corporeality is treated as part of the evil system. In light of this, following the methodological guidelines that understand the text as a result of enunciation strategies based on discourse theories, this chapter will show how images linked imagetically to the feminine serve as symbolic material in John's ascetic discourse. The hypothesis of this essay is that the language of Revelation, despite presenting a harsh criticism of the Empire, reinforces ideas of gender violence in contemporary readers, and can potentially legitimize misogyny. This situation obliges us to read the text with critical care and symbolic inversion. I will examine this hypothesis taking into consideration the reading of Revelation, and its potential relation with violence against women in the Brazilian context.

According to data from the last census (2010) by the IBGE (*Instituto Brasileiro de Geografia e Estatística*/Brazilian Institute of Geography and Statistics), 86.8 percent of the Brazilian population declare themselves to be Christian (Catholics: 64.6 percent; Evangelicals: 22.2 percent), while at the same time, as shown in the Map of Violence Against Women,[3] every 17 minutes, a woman is physically assaulted in Brazil. Research shows that every half hour, a woman suffers psychological or moral violence; every 3 hours, there is a case of home captivity; and 75 percent of the victims experience some sort of violence on a weekly basis. As if such data were not

---

3   Câmara dos Deputados, *Mapa da Violência Contra a Mulher*, 2018. Câmara Legislativa do Brasil, https://tinyurl.com/38m7hasj.

enough, the Atlas of Violence[4] shows that, although the general indicators of violence in Brazil have improved over the last decade, violent deaths of women increased by 4.2 percent between 2008 and 2018. Additionally, Black women, who are the majority in Brazilian evangelical Christianity, were the main targets, as the homicide rate among them increased by 12.4 percent in the same period, while among non-Black women, this rate dropped.[5] Considering that in Brazil, violence against women has a deep relationship with religious language[6]—and feminist biblical hermeneutics demonstrate how much the Judeo-Christian text uses symbolic material to uphold the idea of the dangerousness of the female body[7]—it is important to look accurately at the images of women in the book of Revelation in order to resignify social locations and denounce expressions of oppression.

In the symbolic archive of Revelation,[8] female bodies have an important place. If, on the one hand, the mythical woman dressed in the sun is threatened by the Dragon (Rev 12), on the other, Jezebel is seductive, and her body leads the disciples/men to prostitution (Rev 2:20). At the same time that Revelation gives new meaning to Roman masculinity, it simultaneously describes demonic beings with feminine traits, such as the locusts of Revelation 9. This imagery can be described as the cultural establishment of places of power. In response to that, interpretations that

---

4   Daniel Cirqueira and Samira Bueno, eds., *Atlas da Violência 2020* (IPEA –Instituto de Pesquisa Econômica Aplicada, 2020), https://tinyurl.com/49965av5.

5   Marília de Camargo César, *O Grito de Eva: A Violência Doméstica em Lares Cristãos* (São Paulo: Thomas Nelson Brasil, 2021), 25, 26.

6   Lemos Fernanda, "Discurso Religioso e Violência de Gênero – Uma Análise da Linguagem Episcopal no periódico Conexão," *Mandrágora* 7/8, São Bernardo do Campo (2001/2002): n.p.; Gustavo Vilella Silva, "A violência de gênero no Brasil e o gemido das mulheres evangélicas," *Discernindo* 1 (2013): 131–42.

7   Kenner Terra, "Misoginia Cósmica na Literatura Judaico-cristã," *Revista Jesus Histórico* 15 (2015): 103–9.

8   I apply the term "archive" as a set of cultural memories in the light of the perspectives of Jan Assmann. See Jan Assmann, "Communicative and Cultural Memory," in *Cultural Memory Studies: An International and Interdisciplinary Handbook*, ed. Astrid Erll and Ansgar Nünning (Berlin: Walter De Gruyter, 2008), 109–18.

denounce expressions of symbolic violence and point to a narrative-literary resignification are necessary, since they oppose symbolic strategies that encourage violence, and announce new relationships based on the Christian traditions in Brazilian territory.

The following three sections will first interpret the apocalyptic genre in opposition to violence, then consider the significance of feminine imagery in the Book of Revelation, and finally propose a liberatory reading of John's Revelation, as an urgent task for the church in Brazil.

Jewish Apocalyptic and Female Corporeality
Reading in Opposition to Violence

The Book of Revelation is embedded in Jewish cultural textuality whose literary imagination and memories are composed of shared themes and discursive strategies. As Richard Bauckham explained well, the Hebrew Bible and the Jewish hermeneutical strategies applied to sacred texts permeate Revelation.[9] It is precisely in the visionary's appropriations that the establishment of social loci and the construction of worlds and networks of symbolic power take place.

It is possible to understand the apocalyptic as a literary expression, a symbolic set and social representation.[10] Paul Hanson classifies Jewish apocalyptic into three areas: *apocalypse* (literary genre), *apocalyptic eschatology* (worldview present in literatures related to apocalypticism), and *apocalypticism* (socioreligious movement and social-historical group). In this literature, the female body and its potential are treated as dangerous and destabilizing. Despite considering the historical distances (so as not to fall into anachronisms), we can find in these texts expressions of misogyny, perceived in expressions of hatred against women or everything related to the feminine. In more specific terms, misogyny is

---

9   Richard Baukham, *The Climax of Prophecy* (London: T & T Clark, 1993), xi.

10 Paul D. Hanson, "Apocalypse, Genre"; "Apocalypticism" in *The Interpreter's Dictionary of the Bible: Supplementary Volume*, ed. Keith R. Crim (Nashville: Abingdon Press, 1976); Martinus de Boer, "A influência da apocalíptica judaica sobre as origens cristãs: gênero, cosmovisão e movimento social," *Estudos de Religião* 19 (2000): 11–24.

an ideology or system of beliefs that accompanied (and still accompanies) patriarchal cultures, and thus subordinated women, limiting their power and autonomy.[11] Hatred against the feminine is closely related to the tradition of fear that surrounds the image of women and their corporeality. This psychocultural experience permeated Antiquity, was very present in the Middle Ages, and until today permeates the imagination of many different cultures. In light of contemporary research, the main problem for patriarchal societies is the female body, seen as terrifying, as it carries an indomitable danger. In apocalyptic literature, one of the many reasons to fear women is the relationship between feminine beauty and the destabilization of the cosmic order. We find this imagery in several texts in which the woman appears as an agent of destruction of celestial orders and established cosmologies.

A tradition considered to have originated in the apocalyptic genre and important to this discussion is the myth of the Watchers,[12] as preserved in the book of the Watchers,[13] which comprises chapters 1–36 in the first book of Enoch. In this work, the Watchers (angels) do not resist female beauty and they cohabit with the daughters of men, transgressing the boundaries established by God, a situation that produces immeasurable and irremediable catastrophes (1 Enoch 6:1–5). In contact with humans, the Watchers taught them the art of metallurgy and weapon making. To the women, they taught the art of embellishing themselves (such as adornment with makeup), along with the art of divination, magic, incantations, astrology, and cultivation of roots (1 Enoch 8:1–3). The importance of this narrative can be seen in the presence of the Watcher's myth in much of the Jewish and, later on, Christian tradition.[14] Following those tracks, some texts can

---

11   Michael Flood, ed., *International Encyclopedia of Men and Masculinities* (New York: Routledge, 2007).

12   Annette Yoshiko Reed, *Fallen Angels and the History of Judaism and Christianity: The Reception of Enochic Literature* (New York: Cambridge University Press, 2005), 3.

13   The first book of Enoch (an apocryphal text) is formed by five separate writings.

14   J. Vanderkam, *Enoch and the Growth of an Apocalyptic Tradition.* CBQMS 16 (Washington, DC: CBA, 1984); J. Vanderkam, "The Interpretation of Genesis

help us understand how the images of this myth instilled fear and hatred against women in this literary genre, leading to the demonization of the feminine one finds in the Book of Revelation.

A Jewish text similar to the Book of the Watchers is Jubilees (second century BC). Jubilees claims that the wickedness of the world and the origin of demons are linked to the female body, whose beauty produced all disorder. Therefore, this Jewish work claims that wickedness increased on earth, and God sent the deluge. After the catastrophe, Noah prays against the polluted demons who were leading astray, blinding, and killing his grandchildren. Thus, God orders the angels to bind the demons, and Mastema, their leader, asks God to leave a tenth of the demons with him. Once again, female sexuality is the cause of evil, and the origin of demonic beings on earth.

At Qumran the myth is read once more, and appears in the *Damascus Document*, 4Q180, 1Q23, and others. The same symbolic order is preserved in these Dead Sea texts when speaking of the fall of angels and their relationship with sexually dangerous women. In the *Damascus Document*, for example, the lustful gaze and obstinacy against God are criticized. Another Jewish text that is influenced by the Watchers myth is the Testament of Reuben,[15] which calls the community to flee from the women because they had bewitched the Watchers: "Forbid your wives and your daughters to adorn their heads and faces! For every woman who resorts to these wiles brings eternal punishment upon herself. It was like this that they also bewitched the Guardians before the flood" (T. Reu. 5:4–5). In the Testament of Reuben, again, the female body and beauty are seen as dangers and causes of the seduction of angels, needing to be tamed. Therefore, women should not beautify themselves. Thus, if sexuality is seen as an instrument of power and used cunningly by women, patriarchal domination is legitimized to maintain social and cosmic order.

---

in 1 Enoch," in *The Bible at Qumran. Text: Shape and Interpretation*, ed. Peter W. Flint (Grand Rapids: CBA, 2000).

15   This is one of the books comprising *The Testaments of the Twelve Patriarchs*. See R. H. Charles, *The Testaments of the Twelve Patriarchs* (Sheffield, England: Sheffield Academic Press, 2001).

Some parts of the New Testament also resemble images from the myth of the Watchers (Jude 6; 1 Peter 3:18–21; 2 Peter 2:4).[16] The First Letter to the Corinthians presents a very obscure passage, but it becomes clear when we know this Enoch myth. The text says: "For this reason a woman should wear a sign of dependence on her head, because of the angels" (1 Cor 11:10). Letting one's hair down was extremely lewd in Jewish and Roman tradition.[17] Therefore, Paul asks women to hide this erotic feature because it could seduce the angels, as happened in primordial times, according to the myth of the Watchers. That is, once again the woman and her beauty threaten the order established in heaven. The same idea appears in the Pastoral Letters. 1 Timothy 3:11 teaches that the woman should not be a curser, which in Greek shares the same root as the word "devil." In 1 Timothy 2:12–15, as the narrative of Adam and Eve is recalled, the text still presupposes the dangerous figure of the woman, so she must remain silent and limit herself to motherhood for her salvation. In 1 Peter 3:3–4, like the Testament of Reuben and 1 Timothy 2:9–11, the ornaments and adornments are placed in the background so that modesty and submission are priorities. In these examples, we see the control of the woman's body represented in the discourse around clothing and ornamentation, the result of the fear of women's sexual potential.

The imagery of ancient apocalyptic literature not only demonizes the feminine but also blames it for the evil in the world and the origin of demons. In the New Testament, these beings, contrary to the kingdom and promoters of chaos, are indispensable characters for the necessary establishment of the new era, the Kingdom of Heaven, because the victory over them would be synonymous with the victory of God in the cosmos. Therefore, female sexuality and corporeality would always be under suspicion, as women are seen as the direct cause of this evil reality. Such imagery has devastating force and directly affected the language of the Book of Revelation. We must therefore understand the text's literary strategies in order to resignify the feminine imagery and announce other models of

---

16   Robert A. Kugler, ed., *The Book of Enoch or 1 Enoch* (Oxford: Clarendon, 1912). See the chapter titled "The Influence of *1 Enoch* on the New Testament," 182.

17   J. L. Sebesta, "Women's Costume and Feminine Civic Morality in Augustan Rome," *Gender e History* 9, no. 3 (1997): 529–41.

relationships. Thus, we move to discuss some hermeneutical paths that consider new rhetorical strategies, which expose such symbolic acts of violence.

ENGAGING REVELATION FROM LATIN AMERICA: INTERPRETATION AND VIOLENCE

For a long time, especially in Latin American exegesis, the Book of Revelation was read as a text that reflected realities of oppression and even martyrdom caused by the structural violence the Roman Empire perpetrated in the time of Domitian. In this perspective, Revelation was written to help Jesus's followers keep faith during tragic times, with the promise that the great tribulation and the end of the world were immanent. Eusebius's statement that "the victims of Domitian's cruelties were many" (Hist. Eccl. 3.17) is accepted as historically accurate in the research on Revelation.[18] However, other scholars accept Irenaeus's text (*Adversus haereses* 5.30.3) and identify Revelation's images of violence and death as mirrors of Nero's reign.[19] In other words, the text is seen as a gateway to the bloody reality marked by persecutions. An example of this interpretation exists in the classic Brazilian commentary by Carlos Mesters and Francisco Orofino,[20] in which we find the expectation that Revelation reflects at some level the reality of persecution experienced in the Roman Empire.

Another Latin American text that follows this perspective, with only a few modifications, is the work of Pablo Richard.[21] In the wake of Paul Hanson's assertions that apocalyptic literature always appears in spaces of

---

18   Leonard L. Thompson, "Ordinary Lives: John and His First Readers," in *Reading the Book of Revelation: A Resource for Students*, ed. David L. Barr (Atlanta: Society of Biblical Literature, 2003), 30.

19   Christopher A. Frilingos, *Spectacles of Empire: Monsters, Martyrs, and the Book of Revelation* (Philadelphia: University of Pennsylvania Press, 2004), 2–3.

20   C. Mesters and F. Orofino, *O Apocalipse de São João: A teimosia da fé dos pequenos* (Petrópolis: Vozes, 2002).

21   Pablo Richard, *Apocalipse: Reconstrução da Esperança* (Petrópolis: Vozes, 1996).

deprivation,[22] Richard treats Revelation as the work of marginalized, poor, and humiliated sectors of society that produce an alternative historical or theological vision. Thus, he defines three types of situations in which the oppressed can live and from which apocalyptic texts can be born: disintegration, persecution, and oppression. For Richard, a reality of oppression and exclusion exists behind the lines of the text, which materialized in the economic, cultural, religious, political, quotidian, and family spheres.[23]

Richard's historical reconstruction is one more example of the way in which the Book of Revelation was read on Latin American soil. In such a reading, the presence of suffering and persecution serves as the hermeneutical background. Despite the important contribution of these works, recently we have witnessed new interpretive orientations in Latin America, following the paradigmatic changes after the linguistic turn and the emergence of text theories. Researchers since the twentieth century have relativized the image of a world full of violence and conflicts perceived in the description of the Book of Revelation. In these new horizons, Revelation is appreciated as a narrative strategy that accesses the larger *apocalyptic discourse*—a constellation of topics[24]—for rhetorical persuasion.

Thompson, for instance, after analyzing Eusebius's claims and arguments in the light of Roman texts and Jewish and Christian traditions, came to the following conclusion: "For the reasons given under each of the points above, Eusebius's view is untenable. Domitian was not a mad tyrant. There is little evidence that he persecuted Christians. And the notion that he banished John to the island of Patmos has no credibility."[25] In the Sibylline Oracles (in Book 12), for example, the reign of Domitian is characterized as a "great kingdom whom all mortals will love."[26] This shows, according to Thompson, that Domitian was not hated, even in a text as anti-Roman as the Sibylline Oracles.

---

22   Paul Hanson, *The Dawn of Apocalyptic: The Historical and Sociological Roots of Jewish Apocalyptic Eschatology* (Philadelphia: Fortress Press, 1983).

23   Ibid., 48–49.

24   Greg Carey and Gregory Bloomquist, eds., *Vision and Persuasion: Rhetorical Dimensions of Apocalyptic Discourse* (St. Louis: Chalice, 1999).

25   Thompson, "Ordinary Lives: John and His First Readers," 34.

26   Ibid., 30.

Even the references to the death of Antipas (Rev 2:13) and the multitude that comes out of the great tribulation (Rev 6–7) are not proof of institutional persecution. Furthermore, the verbs are in eschatological language, as an *expectation*, typical of the apocalyptic imagination, and do not reveal a situation lived in structural terms. They are "merely symbolic," as is common in religious language.[27] If there was a generalized persecution, we would have to explain how in Asia Minor during that period, we find a favorable attitude toward the state and society. For this reason, it does not make sense to talk about institutional persecution before the period of Pliny's epistle to Trajan (112 CE). This finding is important, as it forces us to read Revelation based on its discursive strategies. Therefore, by the late twentieth century, research on the last book of the canon by scholars like Elisabeth Schüssler Fiorenza followed other paths that understand the context as a semiosphere,[28] and the text as a discursive reality.

Fiorenza's research is of fundamental importance, as it shows the symbols and images of Revelation as rhetorical strategies.[29] Fiorenza argues that Revelation uses images discursively for persuasion. The author, in turn, argues that the poetic and the rhetorical are different. Poetic oeuvres refer to works that organize or create imaginary experiences, while rhetorical oeuvres "persuade" or "push" toward certain actions.[30] Without making innocent dualities, Fiorenza states that some texts are rhetorically poetic, that is, poetic and rhetorical elements can be interlaced in one and the same work. In this sense, Revelation is a poetic-rhetorical text.[31] The rhetorical strategy as a lens for reading the images of Revelation responds to the question she raises of whether the persecutions are current or foreseen

---

27 Nogueira, *Imagens de Violência no Apocalipse de João*, 223.
28 Semiosphere is a term coined by cultural semiotics that serves to understand the relations of meaning in culture. By analogy with the concept of biosphere, semiosphere is the functioning of meaning systems of various types and levels of organization. A semiosphere is formed by texts of a culture that are in continuous interaction and without which they would not exist. See Juri M. Lotmann, *La Semiosfera I: Semiótica de la Cultura e del Texto* (Madrid: Ediciones Cátedra, 1996).
29 Fiorenza, *The Book of Revelation*; Fiorenza, "The Followers of the Lamb."
30 Fiorenza, "The Followers of the Lamb," 129.
31 Ibid., 130.

(a proximate risk). Fiorenza questions whether John actually wants to destabilize the complacency of some who prospered during Domitian's reign.[32]

Fiorenza says the book was written as a prophetic word to be read in the assembly. Moving away from Adela Collins's interpretation, Fiorenza argues that Revelation created a new framework of plausibility and a "symbolic universe" as an alternative world in the face of persecution or possible execution. In this sense, there is no governmental persecution but rather social ostracism, which the symbolic universe of Revelation enables readers to transcend. Fiorenza's work allows the book to be read as an instrument of rhetorical persuasion that uses images capable of creating worlds and interpreting reality. However, it is not necessary to follow the hypothesis that there is some foreseen or experienced persecution. And it is in this network of symbolic use that the female body, based on the memories of apocalyptic language, is demonized and oppressed. To understand this further, we must move on to another author who deepens the discussion, Leonard Thompson.[33]

Thompson explains that the prophet's discourse is not simply a description "in universal code" observable in the social reality of Jews, Christians, or the Roman Empire, but it creates a symbolic universe that transforms and represents social reality in terms of John's own interpretation.[34] Therefore, the "reality" of John's literary world is found in the interconnection of his language and not in any external correspondence to the Roman world.[35] Based on this claim, Thompson analyzes the expressions of tribulation in Revelation, which in his opinion, are prevalent in 4:1–22:5. He concludes that the symbolic universe of the narrative has its own spatial-temporal framework, which does not indicate any relationship with the historical or social "time" of the churches in Asia Minor.[36] In this sense, when analyzing the tribulation narratives,

---

32 Fiorenza, *The Book of Revelation*, 20.

33 Leonard Thompson. "A Sociological Analysis of Tribulation in the Apocalypse of John," *Semeia* 36 (1986): 147–74; Leonard Thompson. *The Book of Revelation: Apocalypse and Empire* (New York: Oxford University Press, 1990).

34 Thompson, "A Sociological Analysis of Tribulation," 147.

35 Ibid., 147.

36 Ibid., 148.

such as chapter 7, he does not locate the tribulation in either the past, present, or future. These important images in the book need to be read within their own literary framework. According to the author, tribulation and suffering do not refer to a specific moment in history but refer to an expression of those who are faithful—a testimony of those who follow the slain lamb.[37]

Thus, based on the narrative evidence of tribulation, Thompson shows how the text's rhetorical construction of reality does not directly reflect the reality of the world that surrounds the visionary. This is the "true" condition of Revelation's audience in the light of the world perceived by the visionary prophet. The conflict is not due to persecution or any deprivation but results from the division of the two discursively created worlds: that of the prophet, and that of the Roman world.[38]

The Roman Empire offered its citizens the rhetorical expression, materialized in the emperor and in the *Pax Romana*, of order and coherence that united the most fundamental social spheres of common life. For the prophet John, this order was false, and should be seen from another angle to understand in a visionary fashion the chaotic side represented by the system. To give authority to his discourse and interpretation of the world, John begins his text by demonstrating what kind of force his narrative has: the revelation of Jesus Christ (1:1).[39]

For Thompson, Christians at the end of the first century lived peaceful lives, not unlike other provincials. The economy, as usual, had its ups and downs, and the government kept the peace and demanded taxes.[40] Therefore, the sources from Domitian's reign do not show a tyrannical and cruel, megalomaniac emperor. Even the imposition of the cult of the emperor, although being an unquestionable reality and having an important social function in the time of Augustus, was not Domitian's obsession—he did not demand, for example, the use of the title *dominus et deus noster* (Lord and our God). There are no clear indications that

---

37   Ibid., 147.
38   Ibid., 169.
39   J. J. Collins, "Pseudonymity, Historical Reviews and the Genre of the Revelation of John," *Catholic Biblical Quarterly* 39, no. 3 (1977): 329–43.
40   Ibid., 95.

Domitian demanded honors greater than those accorded to his predecessors or successors.[41]

Thompson believes that the problem lies in the rhetoric of the Empire and the visionary's interpretation. In John's view, the peace and prosperity of the discourse of Roman society cannot be celebrated by faithful Christians: the seven heads of the Beast are the seven hills of Rome (Rev 17:9); they also represent seven Roman emperors (Rev 17:10). Rome is Babylon, the harlot who rides the scarlet beast, and has become a prison (Rev 18:2; 20:7). In Revelation, the political order of Rome is totally corrupt, it belongs to the satanic kingdom. Thus, Thompson argues that the conflict exists only in John's imagination, and not in the actual society. The crisis is an orientation proper to the apocalyptic genre, and not necessarily related to the social reality. As Thompson says, the crisis situation is a "*topos*" in the apocalypse genre.[42] The discursive force that destabilizes the rhetoric of the *pax romana* ends up exposing the dehumanizing place of women because if, on the one hand, the Empire is criticized, on the other, it is the female metaphors that end up composing its counterargument. And as Robert Royalty argues, in addition to the crisis against Rome, there is a dispute over authority in Christian circles.[43] Thus, a sectarian rivalry is also behind the images of Revelation, and female leadership is heavily criticized in the visionary's work. Evidence of this hypothesis appears in the opening of Revelation, which presents seven churches in Asia Minor, where there were Christians like Jezebel.[44] According to Royalty, who shares the view of Paul Duff,[45] the churches that received Revelation were urban and socially diverse. In other words, external crises were secondary; their biggest concern was with internal opponents, among which were female leaders.[46] Thus, through using rhetorical analysis, it is possible to identify how the language of the Apocalypse produces symbolic violence against women.

---

41   Ibid., 107.

42   Ibid., 175.

43   R. Royalty, *The Streets of Heaven: The Ideology of Wealth in the Apocalypse of John* (Macon, GA: Mercer University Press, 1998).

44   Frilingos, *Spectacles of Empire*, 4–5.

45   Paul B. Duff, *Who Rides the Beast? Prophetic Rivalry and the Rhetoric of Crisis in the Churches of the Apocalypse* (New York: Oxford University Press, 2001).

46   Frilingos, *Spectacles of Empire*, 5.

THE GROTESQUE AND THE FEMALE BODY: REREADING THE REVELATION OF JOHN FOR LIBERATION

As we have seen, the symbolic webs of Revelation impose values on the culture that are received by the readers of the Bible, a situation that requires sensitivity and resignification in order to avoid reproducing acts of violence. Christopher A. Frilingos, when reading Revelation in the context of the imagination of Roman spectacles, states that in the visions of monsters and martyrs present in the book, we find the same desire or "spirit of the age" that stirred the spectacles in the Roman arenas.[47] Because of its language, the Book of Revelation causes its listeners to interpret the "other" as threatening.[48] This "other" was portrayed as a distant barbarian within the structure of the Empire, or as a stranger incarnated in the coward gladiator. Applying concepts from critiques of Orientalism, Frilingos shows that the Roman public exhibition enabled the "other" to be known and dominated.

Revelation is an expression of the culture of spectacle typical of the Roman Empire. From this perspective, due to the very methodology of reading and interpretation of the literary genre, the book's images must be connected to the Roman imaginary, and this requires observing the performance of the shows whose objective was to define enemies, friends, and the "self."[49] The male and female readers of Revelation, like the spectators of the arenas, were involved in the network of images in a performative frame. Monsters and martyrs are common in the images of the Apocalypse, and they cover a wide range of content with grotesque features, including the arsenal of images related to the symbols of Christianity. It is precisely these monsters that interest Frilingos, for in them, he perceives Revelation's approach to the Roman world.

In the Roman arena, for example, exotic animals from the outskirts of the Empire were displayed and hunted. Paradoxographies, literary collections of "wonders," and accounts of fabulous creatures who lived on the fringes of civilization were common in the culture in which the

---

47   Ibid.

48   Ibid., 12–13.

49   Ibid., 11.

visionary prophet John and the Asian churches lived. Therefore, the language of Revelation is loaded with the expressions that contribute to the structuring of social locations. As Carlin Barton has observed, "The ambiguous, the paradoxical, the enigmatic, the obscure and the uncategorized—in short, the monster—was the great and greatest temptation for the ancient Romans."[50] Thus, to understand the meaning of the monstrous for Romans is to perceive the meaning of the bestial/monstrous in Revelation.

In the monsterization of the body or in the use of the grotesque to define identities, the female image in Revelation is disfigured and takes on a connotation of a terror that must be fought. Therefore, internal and external enemies carry traces of femininity. Among the images in the composition of Revelation that define the groups to be unconfigured and symbolically resisted are Babylon and Jezebel (Rev 2:18–25). The latter would represent the internal and sectarian danger, the former the external. However, the two share the language of the "feminine" and its risks, especially in relation to sexuality.

Tina Pippin explains that Babylon is described in Revelation as an interconnection between desire and death in a way that the resentment against the female figure is blatant, which forces Pippin to believe that the misogyny in the subaltern structures of this text is extreme.[51] Despite identifying the cathartic value of the work of the visionary prophet John, she explains that, in relation to the gender discussion, female characters are victimized in the text.[52]

The demonization of Babylon/Rome (Rev 12; 17) finds strength in its feminization. If we add the identification of the mythical woman adorned and dressed in purple (Rev 17:3-7), her description as a whore and the interconnection between Rome and the Beast of Revelation 13, we will realize how much the feminine symbols, which refer to previous apocalyptic literature, are potent in producing ideas that treat the feminine as something monstrous. In John's language, this would be a proof of their

---

50   Ibid., 8–9.

51   Ibid., 103.

52   T. Pippin, "Eros and the End: Reading for Gender in the Apocalypse of John," *Semeia* 59 (1992): 191.

malignity. Likewise, the description of the purity and sanctity of the army of the followers of the Lamb, the 144,000 men, indicates the danger of the female body and encourages asceticism: "These are they who were not defiled (μολύνω) with women; they are virgins and these are the ones who follow the Lamb wherever he goes" (Rev 14:4). In texts such as this, sexuality and the very body of the woman signify impurity, which recalls the hybrid relationship between heavenly and human beings in apocalyptic literature. The text's force of contamination revolves around cosmic instability because, since the time of the Watchers in 1 Enoch, the world has been at risk of being disorganized and weakened due to the disruptive force of the feminine. Therefore, the character Jezebel, a figure known in the Hebrew Bible for seducing her husband and popularizing idolatry, is evoked by the visionary, and her ecstatic-prophetic experience is deauthorized with John's accusation: "You tolerate the woman[53] Jezebel, who calls herself a prophetess" (Rev 2:20). She seduces, deceives, and leads her male peers into prostitution (Rev 2:20–21).

Viewed in a panoramic way, the 144,000 are Johannine prototypes of those who were not deceived by women, which have Ahab's wife as their prototype. Pippin, delving deeper into the imaginary strategies of female corporeality and its forms in Revelation, indicates that the book deals especially with gender issues:

> The New Jerusalem is a woman, but women are not included in the utopian city. God's future world excludes women but not before marginalizing them first. Of the four females in the text, Jezebel and the Whore are destroyed, the Woman Clothed with the Sun is left in exile, and the Bride is submissive and controlled.[54]

Therefore, any reading of Revelation needs to consider these literary strategies, and its male and female readers must not ignore this political imagination of the masculine and feminine. It is precisely in this space of interpretive disputes that issues such as desire, death, and violence gain

---

53　The expression τὴν γυναῖκα has a depreciative rhetorical connotation, as if its "non-masculine" condition would already disqualify it.

54　Pippin, *Eros and the End*, 196.

contours and practical application. In the world of God exposed in John's visions, the metaphors linked to the female body are a source of demonization that, on the one hand, serves as hope before the colonizer (Rome), but at the same time, reveals misogynistic expressions in the depth of the text, opening the door to the possibility of eliminating the grotescalized "other stranger," namely, the woman. In the case of Revelation, the world is described as the place of the Dragon and of evil through metaphors linked to the feminine world. Insofar as religious language establishes ways of understanding the world, such literary-rhetorical expressions cannot be underestimated. On the contrary, it is necessary to reread them and deconstruct their powers.

In Latin America, and specifically in Brazil, these images are fundamental, as Christian colonization ingrained these biblical forms in the culture. Revelation, in turn, especially among dispensationalist Pentecostal communities, for whom this book holds an important place, has always been a source of faith inspiration and imagination. Therefore, reimagining its symbols and redefining its interpretations, aided by decolonial and womanist hermeneutic perspectives, could significantly affect the reality of life for women in Brazil. A good example was the work of Danielle Ventura Bandeira de Lima who applied the theory of conflict in dialogue with feminist hermeneutics and realized that the woman in Revelation 12 should be seen as an image endorsed with strength and power, whose body represented Christian communities. This reverses the symbolic power of death into a force for female liberation and empowerment.[55]

CONCLUSION

The body receives the marks of history. It is an expression of identity and freedom, without which it would not be possible to experience our existence. In the images found in Judeo-Christian traditions generally or in apocalyptic literature specifically, the woman's body gains connotations of the grotesque, is disputed among celestial beings, seduces, destabilizes the

---

55   Danielle Ventura Bandeira de Lima, "Apocalipse Doze: Uma Análise da Leitura Conflitual e da Hermenêutica Feminista," *Fragmentos de Cultura* 21 (2011): 37–49.

cosmos, and finally, needs to be denied, excluded, or even cloistered. The praise of the 144,000 males uncontaminated by women serves as a good example of how much this literature retaliates against the female body, described as dangerous and frightening. And if we consider the reception history of these texts, we will perceive the image of women linked to cosmic catastrophes. Therefore, to understand the apocalyptic imagination is to unveil a world of polysemic images whose powers of meaning can demonize gender relations or even legitimize violence since interpretation will always be a meeting between worlds—a meeting between text and male/female readers.

Depending on interpretive procedures, we will continue to witness the language of Christianity helping to promote symbolic violence in Brazil. Thus, in Revelation, the images impregnated with violence and misogyny are either like pearls to be polished or targets of our criticism. In Latin America, feminist hermeneutics has demonstrated that such a task is urgent and possible.[56] And this need is confirmed by the alarming fact that 40 percent of victims of domestic violence in Brazil are female evangelicals.[57] In other words, research has shown the intimate relationship between gender violence and fundamentalist Christian discourse on Brazilian soil,[58] which finds its source and breath in biblical readings. Revelation in particular challenges us to perceive the symbolic memories developed in culture over a long period of time, and how the appropriation of those memories served as an instrument of criticism of the Empire while at the same time demonizing female bodies. And as texts continue to act in faith communities, and in culture today, it is up to us to develop hermeneutics more sensitive to the cloistered reality of female bodies. For the church in Brazil, this task is urgent.

---

56   Elza Tamez, *Hermenêutica Feminista Latino-americana: una restropectiva. Entre la Indignacion y la esperanza* (Colômbia: [s.d.], 1988).

57   Valéria Vilhena, *Uma Igreja Sem Voz: Análise de Gênero da Violência Doméstica entre Mulheres Evangélicas* (São Paulo: Fonte Editorial, 2019).

58   Alexandre de Jesus dos Prazeres, "Fundamentalismo, Bíblia e Relações de Gênero," *Revista Eletrônica Correlatio* 20 (2021): 63–85.

PART 4

POLITICS OF MARGINALITY IN LATIN AMERICAN CHRISTIANITY

CHAPTER 12

EVANGELICALS ON THE LEFT IN CONTEMPORARY BRAZIL: A STUDY BASED ON THE 2020 ELECTIONS

Christina Vital da Cunha[1]

INTRODUCTION

In 2018 Brazil's presidential election was won by Jair Messias Bolsonaro. During his previous twenty-seven years in national politics as a city council member, state deputy, and later congress representative, he was perceived as an extremist character who defended the military dictatorship. His victory at the polls in 2018 caused euphoria among his supporters, though surprising political scientists and other scholars, as well as ordinary citizens who did not vote for him. As president, Bolsonaro continued to affirm his anti-human rights agenda, whether on social media or by revoking public policies that supported and protected Black communities, women, Indigenous peoples, LGBTQI+ persons, homeless populations, and other marginalized groups. In the first year of his term, in 2019, he lost the support of many voters and his allied base in the National Congress. In the face of this change, many different social segments in Brazil feared one of two possible outcomes to the 2020 municipal elections: either the authoritarian right established in the federal government would continue to ascend, making democratic life in the country a chimera, or the left would organize, re-emerge at the

---

1   Translated by Monika Ottermann.

281

polls, and inhibit the growth of antagonistic political forces with a view to reversing the game in the 2022 presidential elections. As a result of the municipal elections of 2020, most of the center and center-right parties were strengthened. Growth among left and center-left parties was also observed.[2]

Since 2018 and, notably in the 2020 elections, left-wing evangelicals have been mobilizing to participate in partisan political dispute. In this chapter, I examine two groups in particular, *Bancada Evangélica Popular* (Popular Evangelical Caucus) and *Cristãos Contra o Fascismo* (Christians Against Fascism), reflecting on the strategies, controversies, performances, and disputes that occurred in the 2020 election, especially those involving leftist or progressive evangelical identity. Other cases are also useful for my analysis: city council candidacies of evangelical men and women in left and center-left parties in Rio de Janeiro, São Paulo, Belo Horizonte, Recife, Salvador, Goiânia, Porto Alegre, and Belém do Pará.[3] In a recent article, I analyzed the various issues addressed by those left-wing evangelical candidates during the campaign, including matters of gender and race.[4] In this chapter, however, I highlight the performances, disputes, and controversies surrounding leftist evangelical identity, and the relations between the Christian left and the secular left.

My intention is not to exhaust the possibilities of analysis on these issues but to offer some interpretive keys that contribute to the understanding of the contemporary interface of religion in the Brazilian public

---

2   Christina Vital da Cunha, "Irmãos contra o império: evangélicos de esquerda nas eleições 2020 no Brasil," *Debates do NER*, Porto Alegre 21, no. 39 (January/July 2021): 13–80. Brazil holds elections every two years. In each of the elections, majority (also called Executive) and proportional (also called Legislative) positions are voted on. In 2020 mayoral and city council elections were held. In the 2022 elections, voters chose the President of the Republic, governors, congress representatives, senators, and state deputies. For more information about evangelicals in Brazil's 2020 election, see also Christina Vital da Cunha, "Identidades, partidos, cristianismo global na análise sobre evangélicos," *Debates do NER* 21, no. 39 (January/July 2021): 157–71.

3   Data collected through a partnership between ISER, *Núcleo de Estudos da Religião* (Religious Studies Group, NER-UFRGS) and GeAfro – UFRGS, represented by Érico Carvalho and Ari Pedro Oro.

4   Vital da Cunha, "Irmãos contra o império," 13–80.

sphere, in the wake of other undoubtedly significant works.[5] The data that supports the analysis results from the survey *Esquerda evangélica nas eleições 2020* (Evangelical Left in the 2020 Elections), carried out by *Instituto de Estudos da Religião* (Institute of Religious Studies) in partnership with *Heinrich-Böll-Stiftung* (Heinrich Böll Foundation).[6] In addition to monitoring candidacies through social networks and traditional

---

5   Emerson Giumbelli, *O Fim da Religião: Dilemas da liberdade religiosa no Brasil e na França* (São Paulo: Attar Editorial, 2002); Eduardo Dullo, "Política secular e intolerância religiosa na disputa eleitoral," in *Religiões e Controvérsias Públicas: experiências, práticas sociais e discursos*, ed. Paula Montero (São Paulo/Campinas: Terceiro Nome/Unicamp, 2015), 27–47; Paula Montero, "Religious Pluralism and Its Impacts on the Configuration of Secularism in Brazil," *Secular Studies* 2 (2020): 14–2; Paula Montero, "Controvérsias religiosas e Esfera Pública: repensando as religiões como discurso," *Religião & Sociedade* 32 (2012): 15–30; Paul Freston, "Protestantismo e Democracia no Brasil," *Lusotopie* (1999): 329–40; Ari Pedro Oro, "No Brasil as tendências religiosas continuam: declínio católico e crescimento evangélico," *Debates do NER* 20, no. 37 (2020): 69–92; Roberto Dutra and Karine Pessoa, "Guerras culturais e a relação entre religião e política no Brasil contemporâneo," *Revista brasileira de história das religiões* 13 (2021): 233–56; Ronaldo Almeida, "Evangélicos à direita," *Horizontes Antropológicos* 26 (2020): 419–36.

6   The data collection for the *Esquerda evangélica nas eleições 2020 survey* took place from July through December 2020. I was the project proponent and coordinator of the survey, and João Luiz Moura was my direct assistant. LePar members (Gabrielle Herculano, Rafaela Marques, and Wallace Cabral) assisted us during the interviews and transcriptions. Gabrielle Abreu and Matheus Pestana worked directly in monitoring the campaigns of right-wing and left-wing evangelical candidates on social media, under the coordination of Magali Cunha. Pestana also prepared several databases, some already available on ISER's Religion and Power (*Religião e Poder*) platform. My survey team met weekly with members of another survey team researching right-wing evangelical candidatures, carried out by ISER with support from the Ford Foundation, under the coordination of Lívia Reis. In these opportunities, all of us, in an integrated way, shared research findings, reflections, and readings. At each meeting, Regina Novaes, Ana Carolina Evangelista, and Clemir Fernandes provided us with important comments on the topics discussed. I thank all these dear interlocutors for the insights I seek to develop here. I share the successes with them and take responsibility for any analytical incompleteness that may be found in this chapter.

communication vehicles, I conducted interviews with candidates, activists, theologians, and pastors.[7]

Theoretical-methodological references on the production of discourses and social situations are important to this study insofar as the actors' narratives are treated in a way that values their production and priorities.[8] Another important aspect of the analysis that follows concerns the treatment of the political behavior of different actors as performances, based on Jeffrey Alexander's contributions. According to him, in the realm of cultural sociology, access to moral, cultural, political, and social meanings involves the observation of performances by social actors in direct interaction with other actors and/or discourses. For the author, "modern social life is a series of continuous performances by various actors."[9] His elaboration is inspired, in part, by Erving Goffman's use of theater theory to observe and reflect on social and political dynamics. Another point of inspiration in Alexander's work comes from the understanding of performance as a mechanism aimed at manipulating impressions.

In Brazil, Alexander is well known for his article "The Centrality of the Classics," published in a collection organized by Anthony Giddens.[10]

---

7   Christina Vital da Cunha and João Luiz Moura, "Evangélicos à esquerda no Brasil: entrevistas com lideranças e coletivos nas eleições 2020," *Comunicações do ISER* 40, no. 73 (2021): https://tinyurl.com/5znzfpkr. Interviews were conducted with the articulators of *Frente de Evangélicos pelo Estado de Direito* (Evangelicals for the State under the Rule of Law), Pastor Ariovaldo Ramos, Nilza Valéria, and the following candidates: Thiago Santos (CCF coordinator), Fellipe Gibran, Jonatas Arêdes, Djenane Vera, Kenia Vertello, and Samuel Oliveira (BEP coordinator).

8   Max Gluckman, "Análise de uma situação social na Zululândia moderna," in *Antropologia das Sociedades Contemporâneas*, ed. Bela Feldman Bianco (São Paulo: Global, 1987), 227–67; Moacir Palmeira et al., *Relatório de pesquisas do Projeto Emprego e mudança socioeconômica no Nordeste* (Rio de Janeiro, Museu Nacional/UFRJ, vol. 4, 1977); Pierre Bourdieu, "A ilusão biográfica," in *Usos e abusos da história oral* (Rio de Janeiro: Editora Fundação Getúlio Vargas, 1996).

9   Jeffrey Alexander, "Entrevista com Jeffrey Alexander," *Revista Estudos Políticos* 5, no. 2 (2014): 362.

10   Anthony Giddens, Jonathan Turner, eds., *Social Theory Today* (Cambridge: Polity Press, 1987), 11–57.

In an article published in Brazil, Australian sociologist Raewyn Connell makes a critical reference to Alexander as one of the contemporary authors responsible for reinforcing a kind of colonial fantasy about the foundation of sociology.[11] Despite this, Alexander's contribution to updating Goffman's work[12] and his readings on the production of political and social performances are of great interest to my proposed analysis. My aim is to reflect on strategies that involve manipulation of impressions, stigmas, and exercises in moral cleansing. This last point is especially important when political actors aim to impress the perception of the truth upon themselves and impute the stain of untruth, of lies, on their opponents.

In this chapter, I present the two movements, *Bancada Evangélica Popular* (Popular Evangelical Front) and *Cristãos Contra o Fascismo* (Christians Against Fascism), exploring the profile of candidates, their main agendas and engagements, and some quantitative data on leftist evangelical candidacies in these elections, in order to offer a general picture of this segment in the elections. Then, I reflect on the accusations and identifications against progressive, popular, and/or leftist identity among leftist evangelicals. Finally, I present some considerations about identity performances, exploring them in the light of the intersectionality that animates them.[13]

The *Bancada Evangélica Popular* (BEP) in the 2020 Elections

On July 5, 2020, in a live session on Facebook, the *Bancada Evangélica Popular* (BEP) was officially launched at the initiative of eight evangelical leaders: Ariovaldo Ramos (pastor, founder, and then Coordinator of Evangelicals for the Rule of Law); Daniel Santos (pastor at the Christian

---

11   Raewyn Connell, "O Império e a Criação de Uma Ciência Social," *Contemporânea – Revista de Sociologia da UFSCar* 2, no. 2 (July–December 2012): 309–36.

12   Alexander, "Entrevista com Jeffrey Alexander," 362; Jeffrey Alexander, "Lutando a Respeito do Modo de Incorporação: Reação Violenta contra o Multiculturalismo na Europa," *Revista Estudos Políticos* 5, no. 2 (2014): 399–426.

13   A longer version of this analysis was presented in an article published in Portuguese in Vital da Cunha and Moura, "Evangélicos à esquerda no Brasil."

Community in the East Zone/SP); Eliad Dias (pastor at the Methodist Church of Luz/SP); João Paulo Berlofa (pastor at *Igreja da Garagem* [Church of the Garage], coordinator of *Coletivo Inadequados* [Inadequates Collective]); Ricardo Assunção (leader of the *Frente de Luta por Moradia* [Front of Struggle for Housing], pastor at Church of the Metropolitan Community of São Paulo); Samuel Oliveira (activist, member of Evangelicals for the Rule of Law, member of the Christian Community in the East Zone/SP); Valéria Vilhena (pastor and coordinator of Evangelicals for Gender Equality, Methodist Church of Luz), and William Carvalho (presbyter in the Christian Community in the East Zone/SP).

Regarding the origins of the BEP, Pastor Ramos, then coordinator of Evangelicals for the Rule of Law (FEED)[14] and one of the founders of the *Bancada*, says: "When we started the Front, back in 2016, one thing became clear: we had not only taken a stand against the coup d'état, but also against the attempt at hegemony of the *Bancada Evangélica* [Evangelical Caucus] [in the National Congress], mainly the attempt to draw a unique profile for evangelicals." Ariovaldo goes on to present the importance of the dispute for evangelical identity and the "struggle against empire" through institutional politics: "We need to do this confrontation at the ballot box. If we don't do this confrontation at the ballot boxes, all our speech dies on the beach [is in vain]."[15]

The objectives of the Popular Evangelical Front were to combat the political hegemony of the Evangelical Parliamentary Caucus in the National Congress (whose profile is mostly right-wing) and the social identification of evangelicals exclusively with right-wing political parties, with moral conservatism, and with the promotion of capitalism. The Front would endorse evangelical candidates who supported the defense of the secular state, the fight to overcome poverty, the protection of individual

---

14   FEED stands for Frente de Evangélicos pelo Estado de Direito. For a detailed study of the Evangelicals for the Rule of Law, see Gabrielle Silva Herculano, "Nosso Luto Vem do Verbo Lutar: Uma análise do ativismo progressista evangélico através da Frente de Evangélicos pelo Estado de Direito" (Master's thesis, Universidade Federal Fluminense, Rio de Janeiro, 2021).

15   Ariovaldo Ramos, interview by the author and Wallace Cabral Ribeiro, João Luiz Moura, and Gabrielle Herculano by Google Meet on September 23, 2020.

freedoms, and the struggle against social, racial, and gender inequality, through an egalitarian Christian perspective. Thus, the Front advanced a common biblical interpretation for the campaign, articulating political affinities with a sense of transforming mission inspired by the figure of Christ. Messages and quotations centered on love and inclusion of those on the margins of society gained prominence in campaign material, and on the social networks of candidates supported by BEP.

Samuel Oliveira, a college philosophy student, a PCdoB (*Partido Comunista do Brasil*, Communist Party of Brazil) candidate for the São Paulo city council, and one of the founders of the BEP, said that the choice of the term "popular" in the movement's name was aimed at expanding the dialogue "with the people." According to Samuel:

> We chose this term because we believed that it places us in dialogue with the people. . . . the term "popular" makes it clear, I think, that [the Front] is part of this process of this progressive identity, this identification with the people, the poorest ones, but, at the same time, it doesn't convey the idea you get when you address a person who is already super closed to dialogue, who grew up in a conservative logic and who learned that progressive is a PT [*Partido dos Trabalhadores*, Workers' Party] thing, that it's this and that, and who will avoid the conversation because they already identified it with something that they reject. So, since our intention is to expand dialogue and not to close doors, without losing our identity, we understood that the term "popular" could better serve this intention.[16]

A pendular articulation of people/people of God is a strategy Catholics and evangelicals in past decades used in a messianic sense when the emphasis on social justice for the poorest emerged as a unifying agenda of these religious groups.[17]

---

16   Ibid.

17   Ronaldo Laurentino de Sales Jr. and Jorissa Danila Aguiar, "A fé do povo latino-americano: entre o cristianismo da libertação e as lutas populares," *Religião e Sociedade* 40, no. 2 (2020): 99–121.

Those seeking the BEP endorsement in the past election cycle were encouraged to take political formation courses offered by FEED,[18] and also by Rudá Ricci,[19] given that most of them were in their first electoral contest or had previously run for office but had never won. The formation courses offered by the Front seek to develop in its members a "progressive spirituality" characterized by socialist values, an emphasis on eco-socialism, and an egalitarian perspective based on the New Testament. From FEED's perspective, this was "naturally" a Christian spirituality.

BEP ambitions are of a national scope, although it has endorsed candidacies primarily in São Paulo, with lower incidence in other states in the South and Southeast regions. The multiparty character intended by the movement was asserted with candidacies from parties such as REDE (Rede Sustentabilidade [Sustainability Network]), PT (*Partido dos Trabalhadores* [Workers' Party]), PSOL (*Partido Socialismo e Liberdade* [Socialism and Liberty Party]), and PCdoB. BEP was able to formally endorse five candidacies. This process was quite bureaucratic, at that time making it difficult for a larger number of candidates to participate.[20]

Cristãos Contra o Fascismo (CCF) in the 2020 Elections

The Christians Against Fascism collective (*Cristãos Contra o Fascismo*, CCF) was created in 2018, and is made up of evangelicals and Catholics who self-identify as progressives. There are more Catholics in the collective than evangelicals, and among the former are several priests and nuns. There are also evangelical pastors involved. CCF originated from social networks. It emerged from the grassroots activism of Tiago Santos, a theologian and candidate for Porto Alegre (RS) city councillor in 2020, who said in an interview:

---

18   FEED has local chapters in several States of the Federation, which have autonomy to organize local initiatives. Thus, the courses are not the same in each chapter, but some emphases are common: race, gender, class egalitarianism, valuing democracy, secular state, human rights.

19   Ricci is a political scientist and the general director of *Instituto Cultiva*. See: https://institutocultiva.com.br.

20   See Vital da Cunha, "Irmãos contra o império."

> On Facebook, I launched an event called Christians Against Fascism calling for the *Ele Não* [Not Him] event [a demonstration against then presidential candidate Jair Bolsonaro] here in Porto Alegre. So, I launched it, created quickly a little design on the computer and put it there. It happened to get a very strong adhesion, an adhesion that we did not imagine, did not expect. The idea is surprising because there is a common sense that every evangelical is conservative. That every Christian somehow supported Bolsonaro's discourse, you know? [Then people realize] that this is not the case, that this discourse is not hegemonic, that Christians are not a monolithic bloc, that there are these differences in discourse, in interpretation.[21]

The event Santos created was reproduced in other cities, gaining space in both alternative and conventional media.

In the 2020 elections, CCF supported forty-two candidates, out of a total of sixty names (many were so-called "collective candidacies"). CCF's support involved the dissemination of candidatures on the movement's networks, the recording of endorsement videos by evangelical personalities, media guidance, and legal guidance through the *Advogados contra o Fascismo* collective (Lawyers against Fascism). Among the supported candidates, two were elected (including Duda Salabert, the most voted councillor in the city of Belo Horizonte in 2020). Another thirteen came in second place in their parties (four of them collectives).

Progressive, Popular, Leftist: Controversies over Evangelical Political-Religious Identity

For the members of Evangelicals for the Rule of Law, the Popular Evangelical Front, and Christians Against Fascism, it is important to affirm and value their identities as both progressives or leftists and evangelicals. The

---

21 Tiago Santos, interview by the author and João Luiz Moura, Rafaela Marques, Wallace Cabral Ribeiro, and Gabrielle Herculano by Google Meet on October 29, 2020.

accompaniment of these present-day groups brings to mind others that were very active in the past, such as the *Movimento Evangélico Progressista* (Evangelical Progressive Movement, MEP) itself. What relationships can we imagine between the members of these groups and their action strategies, both in the past and in contemporary Brazil?

MEP was created in 1990, and its statute was presented during the III CONMEP—*Congresso Nacional do Movimento Evangélico Progressista* (National Congress of the Evangelical Progressive Movement)—on July 6, 1997.[22] With the publication of *Cristianismo e Política: Teoria Bíblica e Prática Histórica* (Christianity and Politics: Biblical Theory and Historical Practice) in 1985,[23] Robinson Cavalcanti became one of the main references for what would come to be known as left-wing evangelicals.[24] The intellectual and activist work carried out by Cavalcanti, as well as by Paul Freston, another prominent evangelical intellectual, was inspired by the *Teologia da Missão Integral* (Theology of Integral Mission).[25] In light of his perception of the political opportunism of right-wing evangelical leaders during the Constituent Assembly in Brazil, Cavalcanti understood the need for a type of political thinking that could guide both center and left-wing evangelicals.

Thus, in addition to the political and theological dimensions of this reflection, the affirmation of a distinct identity in contrast with that of politicians associated with the emerging Evangelical Caucus in the National Congress was part of the task this and other progressive groups undertook. If before the 1964 military coup in Brazil the maxim "(Evangelical)

---

22   MEP continues to exist under the coordination of Canon Daniel Barbosa, of the Anglican Orthodox Church of Brazil.

23   Robinson Cavalcanti, *Cristianismo e Política: Teoria Bíblica e Prática Histórica* (Viçosa, Brazil: Editora Ultimato, 1985).

24   Zózimo Trabuco, *À direita de Deus, à esquerda do povo: Protestantismos, esquerdas e minorias (1974–1994)* (Salvador: Sagga, 2016).

25   The Theology of Integral Mission is based on a view of evangelism that preaches the Word while also offering social, psychological, and spiritual assistance to everyone, with special attention to the most socioeconomically needy. Churches inspired by this model emphasize the importance of practicing God's love unreservedly, as Jesus Christ did. See C. René Padilla, *O que é a Missão Integral?* (Viçosa, Brazil: Ultimato, 2009).

believers don't get involved in politics"[26] prevailed, with the beginning of redemocratization process in the 1980s, the motto "brother votes for brother"[27] would increasingly become the organizational principle of the evangelical segment, especially those who developed an "entrepreneurial mindset."[28] The instrumentalization of politics by large denominations produced outrage: "Commenting on an instigating text by Monteiro on Churches, sects and agencies, [Rubem] Alves asked: Are we before a 'religious phenomenon' or a 'spiritualization of the economy'?"[29]

A progressive evangelical profile emerged then in response to that indignation. According to Cavalcanti, "more and more young lay people and pastors are adhering to a holistic, incarnated theological vision, committed to an Integral Mission of the Church, aiming to awaken our values and talents for a service perspective. These competent brothers [sic], instead of comfortably bemoaning the present situation, can change it by changing themselves. Converted individuals, acting as a community, will be able to convert culture, society and the State."[30]

According to the *Tribunal Superior Eleitoral* (Superior Electoral Court, TSE), in 2020 around 8,000 candidates in right-wing parties ran for city council offices across the country using religious titles such as a pastor, brother, sister, or missionary. By contrast, 1,804 did so representing center-left and left parties. Among the candidates linked to BEP, CCF, and other left-wing evangelical activism collectives that we followed in the *Esquerda evangélica nas eleições 2020 survey*, the majority were under thirty-five years of age and were Black females. Their campaigns highlighted the problem of land ownership in rural and urban areas, the defense of the environment,

---

26   Antonio Flávio Pierucci, "Representantes de Deus em Brasília: a bancada evangélica na Constituinte," *Ciências Sociais Hoje* 11 (1989): 123. After a coup by the armed forces in 1964, Brazil was under a military regime until 1985.

27   Josué Sylvestre, *Irmão vota em Irmão: Os evangélicos, a constituinte e a Bíblia* (Lisboa: Editora Pergaminho, 1986).

28   Rubem Alves, *Protestantismo e Repressão* (São Paulo: Ática, 1979).

29   Leonildo Campos, "O discurso acadêmico de Rubem Alves sobre 'protestantismo' e 'repressão': Algumas observações 30 anos depois," *Religião e Sociedade* 28, no. 2 (2008): 102–37.

30   Robinson Cavalcanti, *A utopia possível: Em busca do cristianismo integral* (Belo Horizonte: Editora Ultimato, 1993), 149.

and the fight against racism, gender and sexual discrimination, and social inequality. Several candidates shared the trauma of having to disconnect from their churches and subsequently engaging in small evangelical communities, many maintained in a very fluid and informal way. One of the candidates interviewed said, "One starts discovering oneself as an activist from the moment one disagrees with the church. The church showed me a series of things that I didn't like, that I didn't agree with, that I didn't think were right. And the church environment got hostile as hell to me. That's when I discovered that there was a universe beyond the church, and then was catapulted into militancy."[31]

In the midst of this subjective splitting process, the support activists receive from groups that share their same religious and social perspective emerges as fundamental for their reintegration into public life in order to overcome that conflict. One of the interviewed candidates whose family had congregated since his childhood in the Assemblies of God said:

> Every evangelical who comes from a fundamentalist background and who awakens to a more progressive faith goes through a moment of indignation, revolt with the churches, and all the rest. I think it's almost a general rule in these cases. The Front [of Evangelicals for the of Rule of Law] was a very important space for me to realize the possibility of being evangelical and being different, inclusive, to help me understand the importance for us to embrace our identity as evangelicals and in a short time to value in reality this evangelical activism, this progressive evangelical activism. The Front helped me in this process. I never lost my Christian identity, but, for a while, I stopped identifying myself as an evangelical in an attempt to dissociate myself from this majority field.

The "political struggle," according to the interviewees, is not disconnected from their lives, weaving "daily struggles" against misogyny, racism, poverty, and homophobia. During this research, I noticed the efforts to define progressive or leftist identity. Ariovaldo Ramos, for example,

---

31   All interviews cited in this chapter come from the *Esquerda evangélica nas eleições 2020 survey.*

considered questions such as: "Are you against the destruction of the Rule of Law? Are you against neo-liberalism? Are you against this slaving movement behind the coup d'état that took place?"[32] If the answers to all the questions were yes, the individual would be a progressive evangelical. For other interviewees, it was redundant to say that they were progressive evangelicals. In this reading, which inverts the majority perception of evangelicals in Brazil, it is "the fundamentalists" who should explain themselves, who should formulate biblical, political, and social justifications for their positions. Progressivism was the modus operandi of Jesus Christ, who fought the status quo, who opposed the tradition of his time. An expression of this argument emerges in the interview with Tiago Santos, coordinator of the CCF:

> When we say we are followers of Jesus, and we need to say we are progressive, this seems redundant. But, at the same time, it is necessary because the message of Jesus Christ is progressive in the sense of being a counterpoint to the conservative, to tradition, of being able to outline a possibility of rethinking society, of rethinking established structures. So, for me, being progressive is . . . being in constant updating, in constant reform. It may seem redundant to say I am a Christian, and I am a feminist, to be a Christian and in favor of human rights, but today it is necessary because there are those who claim to be Christian and do not defend any of this. So this is an important narrative matter.

Along the same lines, Jonatas Arêdes, candidate for city councillor in the *Plural* collective candidacy in Belo Horizonte (Minas Gerais State), argues, "I'm leftist, I'm progressive, and I'm Christian. I think that we live in a context in which, as redundant as it may seem, in my view, to say that I am evangelical and progressive, I think it is important for us to delimit it, to name our identities, because the history of Brazil is based on three main elements: machismo, racism and latifundium."

---

32 Editors' note: the coup d'État mentioned here refers to the impeachment President Dilma's opponents orchestrated against her in 2016 without a plausible cause.

On the other hand, interviewees questioned the notion of progressivism. In the words of one interviewee:

> I have not seen a theological construction either. I have seen a lot of repetition of this progressive discourse. Then, we arrange it as if we were cool evangelicals, always emphasizing, "Look, there are cool evangelicals, I am one of them; look, cool evangelicals exist, and we are these cool evangelicals." "We are here, we are evangelicals, too." It's just that, without any theological construction. . . . So, I've actually seen this takeover of identity, everyone taking over the identity, as if that was the main point. And I think that building this theology, in this way, would help us if we had someone to talk to, right? I have been very suspicious of our ability to talk to our brothers. I think this has been my fatigue, right, my fatigue from the struggle comes precisely from that. I say: "Guys, be careful not to be determined by social media."[33]

In this perspective, the so-called progressive identity would be mobilized either as a way of speaking out politically in the face of an effervescent agenda on social networks or as an exercise in moral cleansing because, with this public stamp, the evangelical would be seen as "cool."

The criticism contained in this interpretation identifies a theological void within the progressive evangelical identity, preventing efficient communication within and outside their religious communities. According to another criticism, progressive evangelicals disregard Christ's soteriological character and accentuate the social dimension, emptying the mystical and salvationist dimension. One of the interviewees, reflecting on the testimony of a Rio de Janeiro professional in the beauty industry, stated:

> Then, he has an encounter with this Christ that transforms his reality. So, today, he is a successful professional, and this figure of

---

33   The entire interview with Nilza Valéria is available in Vital da Cunha and Moura, "Evangélicos à esquerda no Brasil." Valéria is one of the founders of "Frente de Evangélicos Pelo Estado de Direito," an important group formed in 2016 and composed of progressive and liberal evangelicals.

Christ is fundamental for him. And I'm not belittling the figure of Christ, because religion is personal experience . . . I can look at his reality and see something else, but what he sees is a boy who once was saved. He saw his friends being killed by drug dealers. He lived there in Antares, in Santa Cruz. His mother gave him a little electric razor. He began to charge each friend 20 *centavos* to cut their hair, and the business went through the roof. So, my criticism of this image of Jesus that Christians Against Fascism use . . . is that it lacks this element, this Jesus, this transforming faith.

For another interviewee, in evangelical "common sense," the term "progressive" means to be on the side of a sexual minority: "So, I realize that this progressive banner has been translated into the following, 'a believer who is in favor of gays.' This is the most popular error."

Another layer of interpretation advances a distinction between leftist activism and progressivism, emphasizing some dimensions already highlighted in other interviews, and even in the specialized literature. One of the candidates of the Plural Collective says:

> I also work with the distinction of the terms leftist and progressive. Left for me is related to the economic aspect, an expansionist policy, income distribution, social justice, and I defend that. The progressive person is exactly the opposite of conservatism. So, we want gender equality, dignity for black people, dignity for LGBTs, historic reparation for our native peoples, for Indigenous and Quilombolas peoples . . . I think it's very important to bring these identities to the fore, and our party, the UP [União Popular, Popular Union], is a left-wing party in a revolutionary perspective.[34]

In the same vein, another interviewee predicts:

> For me, what is really problematic in this notion of progressive is . . . I have preferred to use the term leftist rather than progressive. It seems that being progressive is buying a complete package,

---

34 Vital da Cunha, "Irmãos contra o Império."

including agendas, and I'm not against identity political agendas. But it's as if, at this moment, being progressive means just looking from those identity agendas. I don't know if that makes sense, but this has been a big problem for us who have been fighting within this segment for a long time. This is making a real mess. So, the progressive terminology has bothered me a lot. It seems that everything was thrown in there, and if we don't buy the whole package, they start saying that we are no longer in this field.[35]

In this way, BEP's use of the term "Popular" proved to be strategic, as we saw in the statement by Oliveira above, but it did not exempt the organization from accusations during the campaign.

Accusations against Leftist Evangelicals in the 2020 Elections

On July 31, 2020, *Folha Universal*, the most widely circulated print newspaper in Brazil, published an article titled "What is behind the Popular Evangelical Front: Leftist group wants to create a socialist front focused on Christians."[36] The opening of the article highlighted the (supposedly) deceptive nature of BEP, claiming, "For a superficial reading, the group's message seems to evoke coherent values. However, first, it is necessary to understand the context in which this faction is inserted." The next issue announces, "The 'Left' in Practice," continuing the lie vs. truth tone of the previous issue. The article argues that the left's ideal is libertarian, but in practice, it restricts individual freedoms and persecutes Christians. The next paragraph informs readers about the evangelical front's socialist and

---

35   Interview with Nilza Valéria in Vital da Cunha and Moura, "Evangélicos à esquerda no Brasil," 31.

36   Folha Universal, "O que está por trás da Bancada Evangélica Popular," *Folha Universal*, July 31, 2020, accessed July 31, 2020, https://tinyurl.com/mwmy9n79. Created in 1992 as a vehicle for evangelization by the largest neo-Pentecostal denomination in Brazil, the Universal Church of the Kingdom of God, *Folha Universal* is distributed weekly to its faithful, and also to people on the streets of the city.

communist ideas based on Karl Marx and Friedrich Engels, stressing that the former was strongly opposed to the religions, having said that they were "the opium of the people."[37]

Another article titled "Leftist Evangelical Front?" begins by stating, "This is a group of pre-candidates for city councilor. Understand why this wave will not last."[38] The article then affirms the inconsistency between evangelical and left-wing identities, saying, "Left-wing Christian? This is a kind of movement that comes up to try to misrepresent the Word of God. There are two reasons to justify the fact that a Christian is a leftist: either he doesn't understand what it means to be leftist, or he doesn't know what it means to be a Christian." The article goes on to claim that BEP aims to generate disunity among evangelicals and distorts the Bible. It quotes passages from the books of Matthew and Corinthians to support the importance of unity and peace among people. The article concludes by urging evangelicals not to be deceived: "It is necessary to pay attention to movements that have 'beautiful' and populist 'discourses', in addition to knowing their origin and the faith they profess. That way, you'll be able to identify the deceit that is coming up."[39]

Marina Lacerda points out that in 2014, "accusations of communism" began to gain strength among conservative evangelicals in Brazil in relation to their antagonists. Analyzing the votes of these evangelical parliamentarians, the author explains that, since 2013, of the thirteen evangelical congress representatives most active in defense of the patriarchal family, twelve argued against some expression of twenty-first century socialism, whether against Bolivarianism or against the examples seen in Cuba, Bolivia, and Venezuela. The arguments are varied: sometimes they are made in the name of Christianity, sometimes for economic reasons, sometimes because Bolivarianism (as well as Petism) would be an evil in itself.[40]

---

37   Ibid.

38   Folha Universal, "Bancada evangélica de esquerda?" *Folha Universal*, September 27, 2020, accessed September 27, 2020, https://tinyurl.com/tvtmvuv4.

39   Ibid.

40   Marina Basso Lacerda, *O novo conservadorismo brasileiro: de Reagan a Bolsonaron* (Porto Alegre: Zouk, 2019). Supporters of PT, *Partido dos Trabalhadores*

During the 1989 presidential elections, evangelical leaders exploited similar fears to gain votes for candidate Fernando Collor de Mello (PRN), in opposition to Luiz Ignacio Lula da Silva (PT). The evangelical fears were related to the persecution of religions by communists. On the other hand, they saw in the PT candidate a Catholic–communist alliance that should be defeated.[41] These and other political evangelical positions generated the perception that "Evangelicals are naturally anti-Petists," as Alexandre Brasil Fonseca recalled in a recent report. His critical perspective argues:

> There is no natural Evangelical anti-Petism. What exists instead is a strong and significant investment of sectors in this group, for several years, aiming to undermine this segment in relation to any position on the left. This is not a new reality and is an important part of North American history, for example. . . . There is certainly an Evangelical segment in Brazil that is anti-PT, as there are in other sectors. In the Evangelical case, these are middle class segments, with medium and higher education, white and with income between 2 and 5 minimum wages. In this segment, more Baptist and Presbyterian, the non-voting for PT has always happened. The resistance of this segment of the population is very visible and is the same found in sectors with the same profile among Spiritists and Catholics.[42]

The Universal Church of the Kingdom of God, in the case of the 2020 elections, certainly joined other evangelical denominations in the production of disinformation, accentuating anti-communist, anti-PT sentiments and fears about the flourishing of left-wing evangelical groups in politics. Along the same lines, the first *Folha Online* article mentioned above, published on July 31, 2020, reads, "It is worth noting that the idea here is

---

(Worker's Party), are often called *petistas* (Petists); their ideas, then, are descried as *petismo* (Petism).

41   Ricardo Mariano and Antônio Flávio Pierucci, "O Envolvimento dos pentecostais na eleição de Collor," *Novos Estudos CEBRAP* 34 (1992): 92–106.

42   Alexandre Brasil Fonseca, "O PT e o voto evangélico," *Instituto Humanitas Unisinos,* October 19, 2020, accessed October 22, 2020, https://tinyurl.com/3at99hzx.

not to defend the 'political right,' although this is more coherent with the need of the people."[43]

In response to the article published in *Folha Universal*, BEP released a disapproval note via Facebook, on October 4, 2020, affirming its commitment to social justice, the defense of quality public health and education, and the fight against poverty, contrary to what the Evangelical Parliamentary Caucus would be doing. Two days later, it held a live broadcast on BEP's Facebook page.

The accusations and misinformation about left-wing evangelicals in the 2020 elections were not limited to these articles published in *Folha Universal*. In a video released on Twitter on October 16, 2020, under the title "VERY IMPORTANT ALERT! Attention, evangelicals and Christians in general. Watch and share!," the founder of the Assemblies of God Victory in Christ (*Vitória em Cristo*), Silas Malafaia, named all the parties that would be deceiving Brazilian Christians, saying, "For 4 years the left-wing parties PT, PDT, PSB, PCdoB, PSOL have been against our values, and during elections they come with a '*sambarilove*,'[44] a miserable lip service, trying to deceive us."

In addition to promoting their political and party interests, several of these conservative evangelical leaders seek to assert their view of evangelical identity as a strategy for consolidating their hegemony.[45] One of the interviewees explains:

> They appear on the radio with these discourses. So, I understand that the impression society generally has is that whoever is not a Christian in that way is less Christian or not a real Christian. . . . So, we understand that we need to occupy these spaces and present to society that there is another discourse, that these people are not speaking alone.[46]

---

43 Folha Universal, "O que está por trás da Bancada Evangélica Popular," op. cit.

44 "Sambarilove," said to be a spoofed version of "somebody love," became famous as a cry of triumph by the comedy figure Armando Volta, nicknamed Sambarilove, when achieving an undeserved advantage.

45 Joanildo Burity and Emerson Giumbelli, "Minorias Religiosas: identidade e política em movimento: editorial," *Religião e Sociedade* 40, no.1 (2020): 9–18 (12).

46 *Esquerda evangélica nas eleições 2020 survey.* See Vital da Cunha, "Irmãos contra o Império."

In this same way, Fábio Diniz, one of the members of the collective candidacy *Nós Por Nós* (We for Ourselves, PSOL) in Belo Horizonte, stated, "The great challenge [in this dialogue] is to break down prejudice and understand that a progressive is not someone who denies faith, denies the precepts of the Bible, the Christian faith. Jesus was a progressive. He showed [us] a new gospel, a new way of looking at things, a new way of doing, seeing, loving, practicing."[47]

The social perception of this conservative evangelical identity as hegemonic, added to modern Western notions regarding the private place of religion, provided mounting difficulties for the presentation of left-wing evangelical candidacies among the secular left. An emblematic case was the Instagram post by left-wing network Mídia Ninja, on October 18, 2020.[48] The headline read: "Progressive Evangelical candidates to know and vote." The publication caused numerous reactions, including the following:

> "One doesn't mix politics and religion. Isn't the chaos we're experiencing enough already????? F**K"

> "One doesn't mix politics with religion, but if it's progressive one can! Greetings from coherence."

> "Progressive Evangelical, I never laughed so much."

> "And the Secular State!?"

> "The one who uses religion to support himself is Bolsonaro, folks."

> "If a person wants to be Evangelical, Muslim, or Candomblecist, among others, feel free to be it at home, in their place of religious practice, in socializing with their friends, not in politics. The problem starts with choosing candidates based on their religion."

---

47 Brasil de Fato, *Conheça as pré-candidancies evangélicas que desafiam o conservadorismo cristão em MG*, accessed September 20, 2020, https://tinyurl.com/2s47y6tx.

48 Mídia Ninja (@midianinja), "Candidatos Evangélicos progressistas para conhecer e votar" ("Progressive Evangelical candidates to know and vote.") *Instagram*, October 18, 2020, https://tinyurl.com/yc9uaebs.

"They can be progressive trillions of times, but also Evangelical? It doesn't work, right? Let's separate these things properly."

"The politician who uses the name of God to be elected does not get my vote."

"I didn't understand the post. One doesn't mix religion and politics! I didn't expect this from this webpage."

"You are kidding! It's not possible."

"Sorry to say this . . . But there is no such a thing as a progressive Evangelical."

These comments convey a call for reflection on what seemed to be opportunism from Mídia Ninja, opportunism of the candidates themselves, or an inconsistency of the secular left when announcing candidacies of religious people who mobilize support around their religious identities in the dispute. In either case, the affirmation of the secular state and an identification of the evils present in Brazilian institutional politics with the growth of the evangelical presence seem recurrent. Along the same lines, the comments exhibit a disbelief, a distrust in relation to the progressive evangelical identity— as if it were incompatible, a cunning attempt to hide wolves under sheepskins. On the other hand, fewer comments were made on this Instagram page in defense of progressive evangelical candidacies, arguing that the historic participation of religious people in politics ensured the achievement of many rights, whether in the context of a country's independence from colonialism or in the advancement of minorities in their own countries:

> Guys, I understand you. I also don't want any more Christians in politics if they are like the well-known ones who are already there. But don't stigmatize all evangelicals. If Pastor Martin Luther King hadn't left his pulpits for political militancy, I don't know what would have become of the struggle for civil rights. I could cite Gandhi, Wilberforce, Desmond Tutu, Jaime Wright and so many other religious [leaders] who made a difference in politics . . . It's time for honest and decent people to speak up on behalf of the church in parliament.

To think that Evangelicals are all like Silas Malafaia, Damares and the like of them is a strategic mistake that has cost us leftists very much. Evangelicals are also the working people, the exploited ones. They are also LGBT, feminist, anti-racist and anti-fascist. The picture is much more complex than this simplistic polarization—and for a long time, the far right has understood that!

It is very disappointing to see the comments on this post. Is this how we differ from bolsonarists? Discriminating against those who think differently?? It is very clear that the purpose of these candidacies is to show that not all Evangelicals are right-wing. So, what do some leftists do? They berate left-wing Evangelicals! This is unbelievable . . . And then they don't understand how Bolsonaro came to power.

I understand the majority's point in saying 'one doesn't mix politics with religion,' but what do you expect, voting for atheist candidates?? Being Evangelical is just part of who they are, not a power project (I believe).

Two points in these comments deserve to be highlighted: first, they signal the historical contribution of religious activists to the consolidation of democracy, and second, they distinguish between a religious candidate and a candidacy with a religious project, the latter being, in all the cases, the target of criticism for violating the secular state. For example, Samuel Oliveira, articulator of the BEP, asserts that his commitment is to a popular mandate and that religion should not be the reason for voting for him:

Evangelicals cannot have as their only political alternative these candidates who have been occupying political offices for years to sustain a neoliberal power structure in its enterprise of privileges for the ruling class. The Evangelical people, as well as the whole society, need to have alternatives that represent a popular project and that can also share the faith identity. We, as a counterpoint to the (traditional) Evangelical caucus or the Bible caucus currently installed in all political instances, do not want to be elected because we are Evangelicals. This is just an identity that we maintain, as well as several others do in other segments and around other issues, which brings candidates closer to their voters.[49]

William Siri, a successful PSOL candidate for councillor in the city of Rio de Janeiro, used the controversy to express himself and capture attention for his campaign. He began with an understanding tone in relation to the distrust about the evangelical names announced there, and affirmed the secular nature of the state, inviting internet users to a conversation:

> I understand all the criticisms and concerns raised here. It's not without reason. When we hear about Evangelical politicians, we immediately remember the religious leaders who enrich themselves at the expense of people's faith or of the Bible caucus. But those people don't represent me! . . . There are many people out there who live the Gospel based on love and the defense of human rights. Being a Christian moves us to fight against all forms of oppression. Almost 90% of all Brazilians are Christians! . . . You can't put all these hardworking and honest people in the same bag with a few charlatans. You can't talk about social, popular, real change without considering these people of faith.[50]

These various reports reveal the difficulties of evangelicals on the left in making their religious identity public not only in front of conservative evangelicals but also among activists on the secular left. This difficulty results, first, from the social perception of evangelicals in Brazil as conservatives and extremists. Second, it concerns a diffuse belief in the Brazilian left and center left that the consolidation of a secular state would be able to retract the strength that religion has in national public life, and also in politics today. Despite internal difficulties, left-wing parties in 2020 began to expand their spaces for dialogue with evangelicals with a view to vying for the votes of this segment. This movement within left-wing parties can contribute to reducing the resistance of the secular left, and of other religious groups in relation to evangelicals in Brazil.

---

49   See Vital da Cunha, "Irmãos contra o Império."
50   Ibid.

FINAL CONSIDERATIONS

In Brazil, as in other Latin American countries, and even in the US, the dominant social perception of evangelicals is that they are conservative and to the right on the political spectrum. In fact, Christian institutionality, whether Catholic or evangelical, is hegemonically conservative, and tends to present itself based on values identified with the right. The political language of most right-wing politicians in Brazil today is Christian, and above all, Pentecostal. Jair Bolsonaro, then President of the Republic,[51] himself is a major example of that. Since his presidential campaign in 2018, his pronouncements have been filled with references to the Bible (especially to Christian eschatology), to the Mosaic laws (especially referring to images of force and order calling for the recovery of a mythical Israel present in some Pentecostal eschatologies),[52] while reinforcing the view that to be a Christian, especially an evangelical, is to side with the political right. This strategy of transforming religious language into political language, among other tactics, ensured Bolsonaro's victory at the polls, supported by 70 percent of the evangelical voters. Besides presenting himself as a Christian sliding between a Catholic and an evangelical identity, he mobilized a rhetoric based on loss, thus communicating with feelings dispersed in the population, especially the poorest voters, whose losses were experienced in the previous decade in regard to authority, morals, security, customs, and family.

Part of the conservative religious activism that underpinned Bolsonaro's 2018 campaign began to demobilize in his first year in office. In 2019 several conservative groups left his support base, including *Movimento*

---

51   On October 30, 2022, Brazilian President Jair Bolsonaro lost his reelection bid to the Workers' Party's candidate Luiz Inácio Lula da Silva, whose inauguration took place on January 1, 2023.

52   For an important reflection on this construction of a mythical Israel in Brazilian Pentecostalism and Neo-Pentecostalism, see Edlaine Gomes, *A Era das Catedrais: a autenticidade em exibição* (Rio de Janeiro: Garamond, 2011). For a more recent discussion of Israel's place among the new right in Brazil, see Mônica Grin, Michel Gherman, and L. Caracinki, "Beyond Jordan River's Waters: Evangelicals, Jews, and the Political Context in Contemporary Brazil," *International Journal of Latin American Religions* 4 (2019): 1–21.

Brasil Livre[53] and *Escola Sem Partido*,[54] among others. In 2020, during the worst health crisis the country experienced in many decades, the crisis' inefficient management by the Bolsonaro administration, along with corruption scandals, and the repeated replacement of health ministers for their refusal to ignore the warnings from the scientific community, caused a new series of criticisms, resulting in the retrieval of government support on the part of some religious groups.[55] This was the case of the National Association of Evangelical Jurists [56] However, the political crisis led the government to identify in evangelical media leaders fundamental supporters of its crisis management. In this context, the dispute over the evangelical identity in the country became even more virulent. These media leaders asserted that to be evangelical was to be right-wing, conservative, and defenders of the family, of a binary gender pattern, and of economic liberalism, in line with the public identity of Catholics and evangelicals in other national contexts. These events intensified the association of the public identity of evangelicals with the political right, making the existence of evangelicals critical of these political and moral positions increasingly invisible.

However, over the last three decades, evangelical movements avowedly on the left have been organizing themselves in society, seeking space in the churches themselves as a way of living the Christian faith in line with their values. In Brazil, in the 1990s, left-wing evangelicals formed different groups under the aegis of the Integral Mission. The dominant

---

53   The Free Brazil Movement (MBL) is a morally conservative and politically liberal movement active since 2014.

54   Non-Partisan Education. This movement was created in 2014 under the leadership of a jurist with the aim of preventing left-wing ideologies from being present in schools and universities in Brazil. Under the aegis of a defense of freedom, they proposed punishment for teachers who spoke out on issues such as sex education, gender, social inequality, critical rights, etc.

55   Two health ministers were replaced for not agreeing with the president's direction regarding the use of chloroquine as an alleged preventive treatment for COVID-19. See Christina Vital da Cunha, *Mandonismo e Sadismo durante a pandemia no Brasil: Analisando a gestão de Bolsonaro à luz da obra de Gilberto Freyre* v.6 (São Paulo: Editora Recriar, 2020): 30.

56   *Associação Nacional de Juristas* Evangélicos (ANAJURE).

profile of the leaders of that movement at the time was male, white, and linked mainly to historically Protestant denominations. The quest to improve the lives of the poorest, the fight against corruption, and the resulting "social justice" work united those religious activists. As mentioned earlier, one of the groups that gained prominence in this period was the Progressive Evangelical Movement (MEP). Youth groups also began to take a leading role in defending a Gospel that was geared toward meeting the needs of the weakest in society. This was the case of the FALE (Speak Up) Movement. The 2000s and 2010s saw the emergence of hundreds of other groups organized around themes that were not as prominent in MEP and other groups formed in the 1990s or earlier. Thus, the work of the Black Evangelical Movement, the Evangelical Front for the Rule of Law, Evangelixs (gathering the evangelical LGBTQI+ population), the Black Evangelical Women Network, and the Evangelical Front for the Legalization of Abortion, among others, has gained public repercussion in the past decade.

By examining two left-wing Christian collectives in the 2020 elections, namely Christians Against Fascism and Popular Evangelical Front, this chapter sought to give visibility to the growing political organization of these particular actors in Brazil. This political mobilization with an aim to occupy elective positions is relatively new, and also produces a difference in relation to the evangelical social movements previously formed in the 1990s. A series of political performances were triggered by these candidacies of evangelicals on the left in order to circumvent the distrust of evangelicals in the social base who were assuming an anti-PT stance (the Workers Party [PT] is the largest left-wing party in Brazil and became very identified in the media with the corruption scandals that allegedly involved members of the governments of former presidents Luiz Ignacio Lula da Silva and Dilma Rousseff). Thus, we observed that the political challenges these candidates faced around their religious identities assumed an inward (either in relation to their religious social base, or in front of media leaders linked to large denominations) and an outward face (in this case, with the secular left and liberal elites).

In some of the analyzed cases, the difficulty in overcoming a misconstrued distrust regarding the candidates' evangelical identity made it impossible for electoral success. In this way, the use of strong performances, in the terms described by Alexander (as seen in the introductory paragraphs of this chapter), was mobilized with a view to circumventing challenges such as the budgetary limitation of these candidacies and internal disputes within the religious group (such as that related to their evangelical identity), among others. Evidently, multiple causes directly and indirectly influenced the electoral success of the candidacies we followed. However, these internal disputes in the evangelical field overflow the supposed borders of the religious, producing social situations, narratives, and performances that inform other fields of life, such as the political, economic, and electoral, as we saw in the cases discussed in this chapter.

CHAPTER 13

PATRIARCH KIRILL, POPE FRANCIS, AND CUBA: THE ORTHODOX "OTHER" IN LATIN AMERICA

Graham McGeoch

INTRODUCTION

This chapter addresses an often-overlooked aspect of religion in the Latin American region: the Orthodox "other." First, the chapter provides an overview of Orthodox Christianity in Latin America, giving preference to the Russian diaspora. It contextualizes the discussion of the Orthodox diaspora in light of the recent decisions of the Holy and Great Council of the Orthodox Church, held in Crete in 2016. Second, the chapter presents the Joint Declaration of Patriarch Kirill[1] of Moscow and All Russia and Pope Francis from Havana, Cuba, in 2016. It discusses aspects of the Joint Declaration related to ecclesial and geopolitics. Specifically, it addresses inter-Orthodox relations, the relations of the Orthodox Church with other Christian traditions, and the witness of the Orthodox Church today (themes under discussion for over one hundred years within Orthodoxy in preparation for the Great and Holy Council). Third, the chapter discusses the political ambitions of the Russian Orthodox Church in Latin America, in light of the Joint Declaration and the Holy

---

1   In this article, I follow the Russian Orthodox Church publications regarding the transliteration of Patriarch Kirill into English. In other publications, the name sometimes appears as Patriarch Kyrill.

and Great Council. Particular attention is given to ongoing inter-Orthodox tensions, as well as Orthodox relations with other churches and the contemporary world.

Despite its historical presence in Latin America, the Orthodox "other" in Latin America rarely features in publications about either Orthodoxy or Latin American Christianity. On the one hand, publications that address the Orthodox diaspora tend to focus on Western Europe and North America. On the other hand, the monumental church history project of *Comision de Estudios de Historia de la Iglesia en America Latina* (CEHILA) does not devote any attention to Orthodox Christianity in Latin America. It approaches Orthodox Christianity as part of the "proto-history of the Latin American church."[2] It offers a description of Oriental Christianity and Slavonic Christianity (covered in just seven pages of a 723-page introductory volume) up to the Middle Ages. In reconstructing the history of the church in Latin America, its focus is on Roman Catholicism and Protestantism. Other standard church histories of Latin America essentially follow the CEHILA model.

Equally, Latin America rarely features in considerations of the Orthodox diaspora. Furthermore, its intellectuals and theologians overlook Latin America's Orthodox diaspora. The Americas are represented by the USA, particularly the theologians from St. Vladimir's Theological Seminary, Holy Cross Orthodox School of Theology, and Fordham University. In Europe, France has been integral to the Orthodox intellectual and theological diaspora, particularly L'Institute de Theologie Orthodoxe St. Serge in Paris. The diaspora in Western Europe and North America has drawn the most attention, and been the focus of the vast majority of research projects.

Despite this, according to the Pew Research Center, Orthodox Christianity has grown in Latin America over the last one hundred years. In 1910 Mexico had an estimated 1,000 Orthodox Christians. This number has risen to over 110,000.[3] Equally, in Brazil, in 1910, there were an

---

2   Enrique Dussel, ed., *Historia General de la Iglesia em America Latina* (Salamanca: Ediciones Sigeme, 1983), 175–82.

3   Neha Sahgal and Alan Cooperman et al., *Orthodox Christianity in the 21st Century* (Washington: Pew Research Center, 2017), 24.

estimated 3,000 Orthodox Christians. The number is now over 130,000.[4] Of course, while the numbers throughout Latin America demonstrate a growing Orthodox presence, this community is still very much at the margins of global Orthodox Christianity, and at the margins of Christian presence in Latin America. Orthodox Christians in Latin America make up less than 1 percent of global Orthodoxy.[5] This is significantly different from the composition of global Roman Catholicism or even Protestantism, as Latin Americans constitute 40 percent and 13 percent of these populations, respectively.[6] As the Pew Research Center notes, one hundred years ago, all three major branches of Christianity were highly concentrated in Europe. Roman Catholicism and Protestantism have globalized.[7] The Orthodox diaspora has grown—particularly in Africa—but it has not globalized to the same extent as Roman Catholicism and Protestantism. In the Americas, the largest Orthodox diasporas are located in the USA (1.8 million), Canada (470,000), Brazil (130,000), and Mexico (110,000).[8]

The Orthodox "Other" in Latin America: History

Orthodox Christianity has been present in Latin America for over one hundred years. The first Russian Orthodox Church was consecrated in Buenos Aires in 1901. Orthodox dioceses have flourished across Latin America, particularly in Argentina, Brazil, Colombia, Costa Rica, Cuba, Dominican Republic, Guatemala, Haiti, Mexico, Panama, and Venezuela, amongst other countries. Despite this, Sonia Maria de Freitas, in her work on Russian migration to Brazil, has noted that there is an "academic silence" about Orthodox communities in Latin America.[9] She attributes this partly

---

4   Ibid.

5   Ibid., 8.

6   Ibid.

7   Ibid., 6.

8   Ibid., 24.

9   Sonia Maria De Freitas, "Identity, Religion and Resistance of Russian people in Brazil," in *Migration and Public Disource in World Christianity*, ed. Afe Adogame, Raimundo Barreto, and Wanderley Pereira Rosa (Minneapolis:

to ideological reasons related to Russia's communism in the twentieth century and the avowedly anti-communist dictatorships installed in many Latin American countries in the same period.

The waves of Russian migration to Latin America in the twentieth century were shaped by three motivating factors: first, the events prior to the 1917 Revolution, second, the consequences of the 1917 Revolution, and third, the effects of World War II. Accordingly, different social groups dominate the three different waves of Russian migration to Latin America and reflect their interests accordingly. The overwhelming majority of migrants pre-1917 were peasants drawn to agricultural work in Latin America.[10] The second wave was composed of urban and intellectual elites fleeing the consequences of the 1917 Revolution. The third wave was mostly made up of impoverished urban workers fleeing the devastation of World War II and those who were seeking an exit from what would later be called the Iron Curtain.

These Russian Orthodox migrants to Latin America are part of the Orthodox diaspora. Ivana Noble recalls that in speaking about diaspora, one has to clarify two aspects of the term's use within Orthodoxy. First, it is used to primarily refer to movements of Orthodox Christians to Western Europe from the eighteenth century onward. In Western Europe, Orthodox Christians deemed it natural to form church communities linked to their ethnicity, with language, culture, and identity helping to form a church home in a foreign land.[11] In Latin America, the Orthodox diaspora

---

Fortress Press, 2019), 99. Sonia Maria de Freitas is a historian. Her work is perhaps symbolic of some of the work now just beginning in Latin America in relation to Orthodox Christianity. There are some ethnographical and historical studies of "foreign national" communities—Russian, Greek, etc.—which may or may not make explicit study of religion within these communities. I have done some preliminary work on the Greek and Russian communities in Espirito Santo, Brazil: Graham McGeoch, "Of Greeks and Russians: Orthodox Christianity in the State of Espirito Santo, Brazil," *Salt: Crossroads of Religion and Culture* 1 (2022): 242–50.

10   The Brazilian government had a policy of distributing land and offering financial incentives to European immigrants. The coffee industry benefited from this subsidized migration policy.

11   Ivana Noble, "L'avenir de la «diaspora» orthodoxe," *Contacts* 65, no. 243 (July–September 2013): 477.

followed a similar pattern to that in Western Europe. In this sense, the consecration of the Russian Orthodox church in Buenos Aires in 1901, and subsequent churches throughout the region, was the establishment of an ethnic church—a Russian church for the Russian peoples in the diaspora in Latin America. The ethnic churches are designed to attend the needs of Russians (or Greeks, or any other Orthodox ethnicities). They are not missionary endeavors—in the Western sense of the term—looking to make new converts amongst Latin Americans.

This phenomenon from the eighteenth century onward brought with it an idea of diaspora and ethnicity significantly different from the idea of Orthodox diaspora established by Canon 28 of Chalcedon, which stated that:

> The bishops of the aforesaid dioceses who are amongst the Barbarians, shall be ordained by the above-mentioned most holy throne of the most holy Church of Constantinople.[12]

Chalcedon defined the diaspora as those living "among the barbarians" (i.e., outside the empire, and therefore outside Christendom). It gave jurisdiction of this diaspora to the Patriarch of Constantinople. According to Chalcedon, the concept of Orthodox diaspora is linked to those Orthodox living outside Christendom. The eighteenth-century concept of Orthodox diaspora, discussed by Ivana Noble, points to a broadening use of the term to include Orthodox Christians living outside Orthodox lands. In the case of Western Europe and Latin America, additionally, the Orthodox diaspora lives in a broadly Christian, albeit Western, space.

The Orthodox diaspora from the eighteenth century onward was not established in a territory easily identifiable as outside the bounds of Christendom, whereby the Patriarch of Constantinople would naturally have jurisdiction. The Orthodox diaspora settled in countries with a long Christian tradition, even if it was a tradition derived from the Latin Church. This post-eighteenth-century Orthodox

---

12   J. Stevenson, *Creeds, Councils and Controversies: Documents Illustrating the History of the Church, AD 337–461* (London: SPCK, 1989), 362.

diaspora therefore ushered in multiple jurisdictions. In other words, each Orthodox ethnicity established a church in the spheres of Latin Christianity (Western Europe and Latin America, Protestant and Roman Catholic), but not subject to the jurisdiction of the Latin Church. Equally, each Orthodox church has not necessarily been under the jurisdiction of the Ecumenical Patriarchate. This situation is viewed historically by Orthodoxy as noncanonical, due to Canon 28 of Chalcedon. However, the noncanonical situation is complicated by the fact that neither Western Europe nor Latin America is "among the barbarians," at least in the original terms envisaged by Chalcedon. Nor is it reflective more widely of Orthodox ecclesiology. After the Russian Revolution in 1917, the Orthodox diaspora boomed with political exiles or deportees fleeing the Revolution and its consequences. This new diaspora has contributed to ongoing difficulties with the question of ethnic churches and jurisdiction in Latin America.

According to Noble, it is worth noting a second aspect of Orthodox movement, understood as "Orthodox diaspora," that has helped to change perceptions of the diaspora. In recent years, diaspora figures like the Russian religious philosophers led by Nicholas Berdyaev and Sergius Bulgakov, and theologians including Georges Florovsky and Vladimir Lossky, have played a significant role in the development of Orthodox theology.[13] This group also had an influence on liberation theologies in Latin America.[14] In other

---

13   Paul L. Gavrilyuk has reflected on diaspora theologians and their influence on Russian, and more widely Orthodox, theology. He divides them into "Fathers" and "Children" to reflect Tugenev's novels. He also notes the difference between what he calls the "pre-exilic period" (1890s–1910) inside Russia and the "exilic period" (1920s–1940s) with the expulsion of theologians. The Russian diaspora was affected in different ways by its exiling, and this is sometimes reflected in their work. Paul L. Gavrilyuk, *Georges Florovsky and the Russian Religious Renaissance* (Oxford: Oxford University Press, 2014), 42–59.

14   There is a gap in research on this topic. However, Juan Luis Segundo wrote his doctoral dissertation in France on Nicholas Berdyaev (an influential Russian religious philosopher). The title of the dissertation was *Berdiaef: une reflexion chretienne sur la personne.* Segundo's early books can be interpreted as a theological and pastoral application of Berdyaev's philosophical ideas

words, the Orthodox diaspora has contributed richly to contemporary Orthodox theology.

It is theologians in the wider diaspora of the Americas who have rethought the concept of diaspora in terms of the "local church." Florovsky, Alexander Schmemann, and John Meyendorff have all contributed to helping the Orthodox diaspora in North America understand itself as a local church rather than a diaspora. In particular, Meyendorff has reflected that pluralism—from the use of language and aesthetic practices to national churches—is one of the contemporary marks of the catholicity of local churches.[15] Meyendorff admits that the dangers of divisiveness and division from overidentifying a local church exclusively with a particular ethnicity are an ongoing challenge for Orthodoxy. However, Meyendorff (and others in North America) can point to the emergence of the Orthodox Church in America as a "local church," which is not an ethnic church, and which has taken its place in the catholicity of local churches in Orthodoxy.

Latin America has not replicated this North American movement. None of the Latin American countries have developed anything close to the Orthodox Church of America, for example. This means that the tensions that Ivana Noble highlights in her text between a "local church" and an "ethnic church" are very present in Latin America. Many of the Orthodox churches in Latin America are still configured by ethnic considerations. This means that the dangers of divisiveness and division, to which Meyendorff alludes in his consideration of the pluralism within Orthodoxy, are particularly present in Latin America.

---

in Latin America. Segundo himself exerts influence on what came to be known as "theology of liberation." José Comblin also turned to Berydaev in his reflections on freedom and liberation. Paul Evdokimov (a Russian theologian who taught at L'Institute de Theologie Orthodoxe St. Serge in Paris) is also viewed as an influence on emerging Trinitarian liberation theologies. See Olivier Clément, "Orthodox Reflections on 'Liberation Theology'," *St. Vladimir's Theological Quarterly* 29 (1985): 62–72. Evdokimov also has a particular influence on Leonardo Boff's work.

15   John Meyendorff, *Catholicity and the Church* (New York: St. Vladimir's Seminary Press, 1983), 139.

THE ORTHODOX DIASPORA AND THE HOLY AND GREAT COUNCIL

Resolving the complexity of issues related to the Orthodox Diaspora was one of the priorities of the Holy and Great Council of the Orthodox Church convened in Crete, Greece, in 2016. The Holy and Great Council is an inter-Orthodox meeting of church leaders to discuss and collaborate on different challenges facing Orthodoxy. While the Holy and Great Council had a broad agenda, of particular interest for this chapter is the way in which the Orthodox diaspora is reorganized by the Council. Preparations for the Holy and Great Council began in 1902, and an inter-Orthodox preparatory committee first met in 1930. Among the seventeen topics under consideration for a Great and Holy Council were autocephaly, relations with other churches and Christian confessions, and the political fallout from World War I. Understanding this long history, setting the agenda for the Holy and Great Council is important in order to understand the broader ecclesial and geopolitical implications of the meeting between Patriarch Kirill and Pope Francis in Cuba in 2016.

Shortly after World War II, Patriarch Athenagoras injected some urgency to the inter-Orthodox process, and the first panorthodox preparatory meeting was convened at Rhodes in 1961. Relations between the Orthodox Churches, relations of the Orthodox Churches with the rest of the Christian world, and the witness of the Orthodox Church in the world were among the topics for discussion. The first meeting of the preconciliar panorthodox conference in Chambesy in 1976 decided to focus on the same three topics.

By the fourth meeting of the preconciliar panorthodox conference in Chambesy in 2009, a final text was adopted on the Orthodox diaspora, dividing the world and its jurisdictions into twelve areas: (1) North and Central America, (2) South America, (3) Australia—New Zealand—Oceania, (4) Great Britain—Ireland, (5) France, (6) Belgium—Netherlands—Luxembourg, (7) Austria, (8) Italy and Malta, (9) Switzerland, (10) Germany, (11) Scandinavia, (12) Spain and Portugal. Significantly, the signatories to the document on the Orthodox diaspora included both the Ecumenical Patriarchate of Constantinople and the

Russian Orthodox Church.[16] The document reflected the globalizing of Orthodox Christianity, and sought to bring some jurisdictional order to the Orthodox diaspora.

The adopted document begins:

> It is affirmed that is the common will of all of the most holy Orthodox Churches that the problem of the Orthodox Diaspora be resolved as quickly as possible, and that it be organized in accordance with Orthodox ecclesiology, and the canonical tradition and practice of the Orthodox Church.[17]

The Orthodox diaspora has been a persistent problem for Orthodoxy because diaspora practices have deviated from the Canons of the Council of Chalcedon, and diaspora practices have sometimes deeply challenged Orthodox ecclesial self-understanding, bringing significant tensions into relations between Orthodox churches.

In light of this history, the Chambesy document goes on to suggest a transition period whereby Episcopal Assemblies[18] of all canonically recognized bishops be formed. These Episcopal Assemblies ought, in the first instance, "to be chaired by the first among the prelates of the Church of Constantinople [Ecumenical Patriarchate] and, in the absence of thereof, in accordance with the order of the Diptychs."[19] The formation of twelve

---

16   In all, fifteen Orthodox hierarchs signed the Chambesy document. John of Pergamon (Chairman), Sergios of Good Hope, John in Western and Central Europe, Hesychios of Capitolia, Hilarion of Volokolamsk, Irenaeus of Batschka, Irenaeus of Oltenia, Neophytos of Roussis, Gerasimos of Zoukdidi and Tsaisi, George of Paphos, Chrysostom of Peristerion, George of Siemiatise, John of Korytsa, Tikhon of Komarno, and Jeremias of Switzerland (Secretary).

17   "The Orthodox Diaspora, Decision," Report on the 4th Pre-Conciliar Pan-Orthodox Conference Chambesy (Ecumenical Patriarchate: Constantinople, 2009), https://tinyurl.com/y3fzprnv.

18   In Orthodox literature, sometimes the "Episcopal Assembly" is referred to as a "Synaxis."

19   "The Orthodox Diaspora, Decision." The order of the diptychs (a recognized order of the leaders of the autocephalous, or autonomous, Orthodox

Episcopal Assemblies in the Orthodox diaspora aims to manifest the unity of the Orthodox, promote pan-Orthodox action in the contemporary world, and identify a pan-Orthodox representative vis-a-vis other faiths and society. However, the formation of Episcopal Assemblies in no way deprives member bishops of administrative competencies or canonical character in the Orthodox diaspora. In other words, in the Orthodox diaspora, canonical jurisdiction continues with the church of origin and not the newly formed Episcopal Assemblies. While striving for a common mind amongst Orthodox Christians, the document recognizes that each bishop remains responsible to his own church, and continues to express the views of that church with regard to "the outside world," meaning the diaspora, external relations, etc.

The text and agreement of the preconciliar panorthodox conference in Chambesy in 2009 is important because the text was presented to the Holy and Great Council in 2016. At the Holy and Great Council, it was adopted with some changes. The American diaspora was reorganized. The Chambesy text had agreed to divide the Americas into two Episcopal Assemblies: (1) North and Central America and (2) South America. The Holy and Great Council decided on three regions in the Americas: (1) Canada, (2) the United States of America, and (3) Latin America. Recalling the information drawn from the Pew Research Center on Orthodoxy in the Americas, the new division brings a greater numerical balance to the Episcopal Assemblies. The document at the Holy and Great Council was signed by the delegations from ten Orthodox churches.[20]

At almost the same time as the meeting of the Holy and Great Council, the Russian Orthodox Church (which would not be present) was pursuing another political strategy in terms of relations with the Orthodox diaspora and relations with the rest of the Christian world. Patriarch

---

churches, implying some form of communion between the churches) is (1) Constantinople, (2) Alexandria, (3) Antioch, (4) Jerusalem, (5) Russia, (6) Serbia, (7) Romania, (8) Bulgaria, (9) Georgia, (10) Cyprus, (11) Greece, (12) Poland, (13) Albania, (14) Czech Lands and Slovakia.

20   The Churches of Antioch, Russia, Bulgaria and Georgia did not participate, even though two of these four churches—Antioch and Russia—had signed the preconciliar documents.

Kirill met with Pope Francis in Latin America in February 2016, just four months before the convening of the Holy and Great Council in Crete in June of that year. While the Roman Catholic Church and the Ecumenical Patriarchate of Constantinople have enjoyed "brotherly and sisterly" relations, given special impetus by the Common Declaration of Pope Paul VI and Patriarch Athenagoras on the occasion of the Vatican II, the relationship between the Ecumenical Patriarchate and the Russian Orthodox Church has become increasingly fraught in recent years. This is some of the context for the meeting of Patriarch Kirill and Pope Francis in Latin America and the absence of the Russian Orthodox Church from the Holy and Great Council. The Russian Orthodox Church prepared and signed the Chambesy text, and it would also have been fully aware of the changes in the proposed text about the Orthodox diaspora forthcoming at the Holy and Great Council (2016), although it chose not to send a delegation. Patriarch Kirill's meeting with Pope Francis in Havana needs to be set within this wider Orthodox perspective.

This historic meeting drew on over one hundred years of Orthodox presence in Latin America, and over one hundred years of preparation for the Holy and Great Council. It was also an important meeting in its own right in the history of World Christianity, being the first meeting between the leaders of the Churches of Rome and Moscow. In his informative book, *The Orthodox Church*, Kallistos Ware notes that from the fifteenth century onward, Moscow began to think of itself as "the third Rome."

> The first Rome (so they argued) had fallen to the barbarians and then lapsed into heresy; the second Rome, Constantinople, had in turn fallen into heresy at the Council of Florence, and as a punishment had been taken by the Turks. Moscow therefore had succeeded Constantinople as the third and last Rome, the centre of Orthodox Christendom.[21]

The loss of Constantinople in 1453, the rejection of the Council of Florence (1431), and the election of a Metropolitan by the Russian bishops without reference to Constantinople (1448) are important historic marks in the

---

21   Kallistos Ware, *The Orthodox Church* (London: Penguin, 1997), 103.

self-understanding of the "third Rome." Communications from both the Vatican and the Department of External Church Relations of the Russian Orthodox Church regarding the meeting between Patriarch Kirill and Pope Francis were keen to stress this historic aspect of the meeting.

The meeting also can be seen as an attempt by Patriarch Kirill to exert the jurisdictional influence of the Russian Orthodox Church on both the Russian diaspora in Latin America and the leadership of the wider Latin American Orthodox diaspora beyond the Russian Orthodox Church. Normally, the Ecumenical Patriarchate has jurisdiction over the Orthodox diaspora, in line with Canon 28 from Chalcedon. And, in terms of the proposals for the diaspora from Chambesy and the Great and Holy Council, the Episcopal Assemblies chaired by the first prelate of the Patriarchate of Constantinople (thereafter following the diptychs), the exertion of Russian influence may raise some eyebrows. In the meeting between Patriarch Kirill and Pope Francis, Eastern and Western Christianity met in the Orthodox diaspora. Patriarch Kirill was able to position his church in the Orthodox geopolitics of the Orthodox diaspora and also in the internal politics of Orthodoxy in the struggle (now a standoff, following the autocephaly of the Ukrainian Orthodox Church) for ascendency between Constantinople and Moscow (the second and third Rome).[22]

The Joint Declaration of Pope Francis and Patriarch Kirill from Havana

In 2016 Havana and the Cuban government hosted a remarkable encounter between the leaders of the two largest churches in the world: the Roman Catholic Church and the Russian Orthodox Church. The meeting between the two leaders was remarkable for two reasons. First, it was the first time that the bishops of Rome and "third Rome" met, providing a significant

---

22   The terms "first," "second," and "third," which are used to describe the geopolitical relations between Rome, Constantinople, and Moscow in this article, are not used canonically by each of these churches in their self-understanding. However, Kallistos Ware, in his classic introduction to Orthodoxy, presents the history of the Orthodox Church using these terms. See Ware, *The Orthodox Church*.

moment in Christian unity and the search for the expression of the catholicity of the church.

Second, and perhaps more remarkably, the meeting was hosted by a communist government—and one that has been inspirational for revolutionary movements across the Latin American continent since the 1960s[23]—which had previously tried to suppress Christianity. Indeed, in the wider global context, it is worth recalling that Christianity in Russia was brutally persecuted during the twentieth century by a communist government, just as it was in Cuba.

It should be noted that Cuba's communist government has hosted other church leaders, including the Ecumenical Patriarch Bartholomew when he consecrated the Orthodox Church of St. Nicholas in Havana in 2004. Pope John Paul II also visited in 1998. Fidel Castro's increasing openness to certain kinds of religion in Cuba was documented in his groundbreaking interview with the Brazilian journalist and theologian, Frei Betto.[24] The visits and hosting of church leaders in post-Soviet era Cuba has been one significant change in a wider foreign policy approach to building new alliances with the aim of pressuring the US blockade. In contrast to the visits of Pope John Paul II and Patriarch Bartholomew, however, in the meeting between Pope Francis and Patriarch Kirill, the Cuban government hosted a meeting between two church leaders on church business not necessarily related to Cuban political questions.

I would now like to consider the Joint Declaration from the meeting, and the context of the meeting, with relation to the changing geopolitics and ecclesial politics of Orthodoxy in the twenty-first century. As mentioned in the previous section, Orthodoxy is frequently overlooked or not accounted for in the religious history of Latin America. Yet the meeting in Havana in 2016 between Patriarch Kirill and Pope Francis is important

---

23   For a fuller understanding of Cuba's political contribution to Latin American politics, see Boaventura de Sousa Santos, *A Difícil Democracia: reinventar as esquerdas* (Sao Paulo: Boitempo, 2016).

24   Frei Betto conducted his interview with Fidel Castro in 1985. It has been published in many languages. Frei Betto, *Fidel and Religion: Castro Talks on Revolution and Religion with Frei Betto* (New York: Simon & Schuster, 1987).

to both Roman Catholic and Orthodox religious history in Latin America, even if the scholarship is still to emerge.

The Joint Declaration of Pope Francis and Patriarch Kirill of Moscow and All Russia is carried on the internet sites of the Roman Catholic Church and the Moscow Patriarchate in multiple languages, reflecting the global nature of the two churches and the global reach of the historic encounter.[25] The Joint Declaration has also led to annual encounters between the Roman Catholic Church and the Russian Orthodox Church on matters raised in the text from the meeting. Cardinal Koch of the Pontifical Council for Promoting Christian Unity and Metropolitan Hilarion Chair of the Department for External Church Relations have led these conferences.

The Joint Declaration notes the shared tradition of the first millennium, placing particular emphasis on the martyrs:

> We thank God for the gifts received from the coming into the world of His only Son. We share the same spiritual Tradition of the first millennium of Christianity. The witnesses of this Tradition are the Most Holy Mother of God, the Virgin Mary, and the saints we venerate. Among them are innumerable martyrs who have given witness to their faithfulness to Christ and have become the "seed of Christians."[26]

The declaration gives expression to the joy of speaking face to face as brothers, quoting from the Second Letter of John:

> We have met like brothers in the Christian faith who encounter one another "to speak face to face" (2 Jn 12), from heart to heart,

---

25   Joint Declaration of Pope Francis and Patriarch Kirill of Moscow and All Russia, February 12–18, 2016, available via The Russian Orthodox Church Department of External Church Relations, https://tinyurl.com/2txt6xyt. There is extensive Russian media coverage carried on the website of the Department related to the Joint Declaration. The Vatican also lists the Joint Declaration in its digital archive of documents: https://tinyurl.com/47mkjcks.

26   Joint Declaration of Pope Francis and Patriarch Kirill of Moscow and All Russia.

to discuss the mutual relations between the Churches, the crucial problems of our faithful, and the outlook for the progress of human civilization.[27]

The meeting in Havana was the first face-to-face meeting in the history of Christianity of the leaders of its two largest churches. The Joint Declaration describes the significance of meeting in Havana, a "crossroads" for both the "new world" and for the dramatic events of the twentieth century. Colonization and communism, though, are absent in word, if not in spirit, from the document.

While the declaration describes a fraternal meeting that gives expression to a shared spiritual tradition, it is forthright in noting that there is no Eucharistic communion between Orthodox and Roman Catholic, and that divisions have been inherited through old and new conflicts, and through differences in doctrinal expressions of the Trinity.

> Notwithstanding this shared Tradition of the first ten centuries, for nearly one thousand years Catholics and Orthodox have been deprived of communion in the Eucharist. We have been divided by wounds caused by old and recent conflicts, by differences inherited from our ancestors, in the understanding and expression of our faith in God, one in three Persons—Father, Son and Holy Spirit.[28]

These are by no means simple matters to resolve. However, the document goes on to cite implicitly the modern ecumenical movement, stating:

> We are pained by the loss of unity, the outcome of human weakness and of sin, which has occurred despite the priestly prayer of Christ the Saviour: "So that they may all be one, as you, Father, are in me and I in you . . . so that they may be one, as we are one" (Jn17:21).[29]

---

27   Ibid.

28   Ibid.

29   Ibid.

It draws, too, on the language of the Vatican II document *Unitatis Redinte-gratio,* with a call for Christians to pray together: "May our meeting inspire Christians throughout the world to pray to the Lord with renewed fervor for the full unity of all His disciples. In a world which yearns not only for our words but also for tangible gestures, may this meeting be a sign of hope for all people of goodwill!"[30]

However, the majority of the Joint Declaration (at least twenty-one of the thirty paragraphs of the text) addresses the pastoral role of the church and Christian witness in the contemporary world. The document speaks sympathetically of the suffering church in Africa and the Middle East. It issues a call for interreligious dialogue, recalling that "interreligious dialogue is indispensable in our disturbing times. Differences in the understanding of religious truths must not impede people of different faiths to live in peace and harmony."[31] And it celebrates the revival of faith in Russia as an expression of religious freedom:

> In affirming the foremost value of religious freedom, we give thanks to God for the current unprecedented renewal of the Christian faith in Russia, as well as in many other countries of Eastern Europe, formerly dominated for decades by atheist regimes. Today, the chains of militant atheism have been broken and in many places Christians can now freely confess their faith. Thousands of new churches have been built over the last quarter of a century, as well as hundreds of monasteries and theological institutions. Christian communities undertake notable works in the fields of charitable aid and social development, providing diversified forms of assistance to the needy. Orthodox and Catholics often work side by side. Giving witness to the values of the Gospel they attest to the existence of the shared spiritual foundations of human co-existence.[32]

It also celebrates the growth of Christian faith in Latin America:

---

30 Ibid.

31 Ibid.

32 Ibid.

> It is a source of joy that the Christian faith is growing here in a
> dynamic way. The powerful religious potential of Latin America,
> its centuries-old Christian tradition, grounded in the personal
> experience of millions of people, are the pledge of a great future
> for this region.[33]

Normally, scholars of religious studies draw attention to Pentecostal contributions to Christianity's growth in Latin America. However, the Roman Catholic Church remains the largest church in the region, and the Orthodox diaspora, including the Russian Orthodox Church, has contributed to a growth of the presence of the Orthodox church in the region. It is also possible that the "growth" referred to in the document is not only numerical but growth in terms of "maturity."

The Joint Declaration speaks about justice and peace, as well as morality. Only a few short lines are dedicated to the family, marriage, and abortion. However, the short lines reinforce the political and religious pact on "tradition" that both churches seek to forge with partners in light of the shifting debates on these topics, particularly when countries' constitutions are being revised or changed to reflect the changing concepts of family, marriage, and abortion.

To some extent, the Joint Declaration follows the structure set for the Holy and Great Council since 1902, with regard to addressing autocephaly, relations with other Christians, and Christian witness in the contemporary world. The issue of autocephaly (pertaining to Ukraine) is documented in paragraphs 26 and 27. The Joint Declaration, however, should be read in light of the preparations for the Holy and Great Council at Crete. It is part of an ongoing conversation about autocephaly, rather than documentation of the more open conflict between Moscow and Constantinople after the Holy and Great Council at Crete:

> We deplore the hostility in Ukraine that has already caused many
> victims, inflicted innumerable wounds on peaceful inhabitants and
> thrown society into a deep economic and humanitarian crisis. We

---

33   Ibid.

invite all the parts involved in the conflict to prudence, to social solidarity and to action aimed at constructing peace. We invite our Churches in Ukraine to work towards social harmony, to refrain from taking part in the confrontation, and to not support any further development of the conflict.

It is our hope that the schism between the Orthodox faithful in Ukraine may be overcome through existing canonical norms, that all the Orthodox Christians of Ukraine may live in peace and harmony, and that the Catholic communities in the country may contribute to this, in such a way that our Christian brotherhood may become increasingly evident.[34]

It is worth noting that subsequent events in Ukraine, particularly the 2022 invasion, have demonstrated that this issue is more pressing than ever in intra-Orthodox relations, with some foreseeing potential for the fourth great schism in Christianity.[35]

Obviously, relations with other churches and Christian confessions appear in the document too, as does the contemporary political context. The Joint Declaration concludes by calling Roman Catholic and Orthodox "to work together fraternally in proclaiming the Good News of salvation," declaring:

In the contemporary world, which is both multiform yet united by a shared destiny, Catholics and Orthodox are called to work together fraternally in proclaiming the Good News of salvation, to testify together to the moral dignity and authentic freedom of the person, "so that the world may believe" (Jn 17:21).[36]

---

34 Ibid.

35 Kallistos Ware's keynote address at the inaugural International Orthodox Theological Association (IOTA) in Romania in 2019 touched on the problem. See Kallistos Ware, "Synodality and Primacy in the Orthodox Church," IOTA, accessed July 19, 2022, https://tinyurl.com/35kd55bh.

36 Joint Declaration of Pope Francis and Patriarch Kirill of Moscow and All Russia.

THE RUSSIAN ORTHODOX CHURCH'S FOREIGN POLICY

It is generally acknowledged that the Russian Revolution in 1917 deci-mated the Russian Orthodox Church. The brutal murder of Metropolitan Vladimir of Kiev in 1918 is often taken as a symbol of the horror suffered by the church.[37] The Russian Orthodox Church of today is a result of this destruction and rebirth. According the Irina Papkova, the literature is still "underdeveloped"[38] on the relationship between the Russian Orthodox Church and the Russian state, with much "analysis" feeding off two misplaced assumptions about Orthodox political theology. The widely held misconceptions about "caesaropapism" and "symphonia," partic-ularly as threatening to democracy and vulnerable to identity politics, often overemphasize the influence and presence of the Russian Orthodox Church in state policy and politics.[39] Caesaropapism is a particular model of church–state relations that denotes the harmonious role of emperor and bishop in governance. Symphonia—a model derived from Byzantine Christianity—emphasizes the symbiosis and harmony between church and state (there being no "secular space," at least in the Western under-standing of "secular"). Nikolas Gvosdev's work was among the first that looked at the Russian Orthodox Church as the most significant actor in post-Soviet civil society, noting it refused the status of "state church."[40] This more nuanced understanding of the relationship between church and state has gained traction in recent scholarship, as Papkova's study demonstrates.

At the same time, it is important to note with Lucian Turcescu that the Soviet regime (1917–1991) "was characterized by radical antireligious policies that did away with many of the pre-Soviet features of religious life in Russia. Many Orthodox Church leaders were imprisoned, killed, and eventually replaced with leaders who were subservient to the regime;

---

37   Ware, *The Orthodox Church*, 125.

38   Irina Papkova, *The Orthodox Church and Russian Politics* (New York: Oxford University Press, 2011), 5.

39   Ibid., 6.

40   Nikolas Gvosdev, *Emperors and Elections: Reconciling the Orthodox Tradition with Modern Politics* (New York: Troista Books, 2000), 23.

monasteries and churches were closed, monks and nuns imprisoned . . . while other churches [Protestants] were completely obliterated."[41]

Within the Soviet period, persecution of Christians and religious communities ebbed and flowed. Krushchev launched an aggressive antireligious state campaign, after which followed a détente, and by the 1970s, the state tacitly (not publicly) acknowledged the existence of the Orthodox Church. Krushchev's antireligious policies and their aftermath are important with regard to Latin America as they coincide with the Cuban Revolution and the rise of Liberation Theology. The roots of the Cuban Revolution are more related to the internal political questions on the island and changes more broadly sweeping Latin America. Likewise, Liberation Theology is a response to the failure of developmentalism in Latin America and thrives in struggles for redemocratization across the region. However, the Soviets heavily supported and later sponsored the sustaining of the Cuban Revolution, introducing antireligious policies and perspectives to Fidel Castro's regime. Cuban churches thus suffered under communism, even if Castro did famously reconsider the role of Christianity in the Cuban Revolution in his seminal interview with Frei Betto.[42]

However, of direct interest to the practice of the Russian Orthodox Church's foreign policy is the post-Soviet period (1991–present). An early contributor to this debate is Nikolai Mitrokhin, who characterizes the Russian Orthodox Church as a political party that is antiliberal, anti-Western, xenophobic, authoritarian, statist, and antimarket. While there is a greater plurality within the church than this, Mitrokhin's description has found resonance with Orthodox and Western scholars alike when assessing the Russian Orthodox Church. This resonance can also perhaps partly be interpreted as a consequence of the long debate about "the Russia idea"—pointing to the distinctiveness of Russia from the West—shaped by

---

41   Lucian Turcescu, "Eastern Orthodox Constructions of 'the West' in the Post-Communist Discourse: The cases of the Romanian and Russian Orthodox Churches," in *Orthodox Constructions of the West,* ed. George Demacopoulos and Aristotle Papanikolaou (New York: Fordham University Press, 2013), 219.

42   Frei Betto, *Fidel e a Religiao* (Sao Paulo: Brasiliense, 1985), 212.

the Slavophiles and Westernizers with Russian church and society from the nineteenth century onward.[43]

Likewise, while the Russian state is often criticized for similar positions as the church, it is, in fact, more plural and nuanced in its dealings with the Russian Orthodox Church, and indeed religion more widely. For example, Lucian Turcescu notes that the post-Soviet period can be characterized by three phases that influenced Russia's view of the West or wider world.[44] From the early to mid-1990s, the state was characterized by an attitude of neutrality to all religions. Russia became a "mission field" for Western churches, and there was intense foreign missionary activity provoking problems around proselytism. The second period (from the late 1990s to the mid-2000s) saw a strengthening of the Russian Orthodox Church, an increased correlation between religion and ethnicity, and clashes with the Roman Catholic Church over proselytism. In the Russian parliament, religious freedom laws were framed in terms of the historical and cultural context. The third period (from the mid-2000s to present) has seen the Russian Orthodox Church attempt to increase its influence on state and society and to turn its attention to the wider role of the Russian Church and state in the world. Papkova questions if, in fact, this supposed influence correlates to reality within Russia. Her study of church–state relations in Russia concludes with a much more ambivalent perspective about the influence of the church due to the internal divisions on political questions within the Moscow Patriarchate, coupled with disinterest on the part of the Russian population toward the political priorities of the Russian Orthodox Church.

The 2016 Havana meeting between Patriarch Kirill and Pope Francis took place within this third phase. But it also happened within the wider narrative of Russian Christianity's oppression and resurrection in its recent history (communist and post-communist). Cuba's government was close to the Soviet regime that almost destroyed the Russian Orthodox Church. However, this third phase has seen a geopolitical shift with relation to Russia and Latin America. Perhaps symbolic of this shift—and, for

---

43   Susanna Rabow-Edling, *Slavophile Thought and the Politics of Cultural Nationalism* (Albany: State University of New York Press 2006), 136.

44   Turcescu, "Eastern Orthodox Constructions of 'the West,'" 220.

some, a demonstration of the strengthened position of the church within the *Russky Mir* (the Russian world) project—was the consecration of the Russian Orthodox Cathedral in Havana (Our Lady of Kazan) in 2008 by then Metropolitan Kirill (as head of the Department of External Relations). Fidel Castro was present at the consecration.[45] Then Metropolitan Kirill called it "a monument to Russian–Cuban friendship and all the efforts that have preserved our relations during the most difficult moments of the Cold War."[46] Patriarch Kirill returned to Cuba to meet Pope Francis in 2016. Communist President Raul Castro hosted the two religious leaders. Patriarch Kirill was focused on reclaiming the Russian diaspora and its history in Latin America. The location is symbolic for two reasons: the political context (Communism-Church) and the historical context (Cuba is the neighboring island to Hispaniola, the meeting point of the "Old" and "New" Worlds).

According to political analyst Vladimir Rouvinski:

> Now Russia promotes, in conjunction with the Orthodox Church, its strong support for "universal traditional values" on a global scale, a message that resonates well in many conservative sectors of Latin American societies. From this perspective, the meeting in Havana served as yet more evidence that Russia is returning to the region with an agenda that is not limited to sporadic arms sales and contacts with anti-American governments. Today, Russia seeks to establish a longer-term, multifaceted presence in the Western Hemisphere.[47]

Rouvinski highlights the "return of the Russians" to the region through strategic alliances with those troubled by the "northern neighbour" (the

---

45   The consecration of the Russian Orthodox Cathedral in Havana (Our Lady of Kazan) in 2008 echoes the consecration of the Orthodox Church of St. Nicholas in Havana in 2004 by Patriarch Bartholomew, also with Fidel Castro present.

46   "Cuba opens first Russian Church," *BBC News*, last modified October 20, 2008, https://tinyurl.com/yc6npsb7.

47   Vladimir Rouvinski, *Understanding Russian Priorities in Latin America* (Washington: Woodrow Wilson Center, 2017), 2.

USA). Russia's foreign policy has sought to draw in Latin American leaders swept to power during the "pink tide" of the late 1990s through the 2000s. It has tried to close trade deals "primarily from the energy sector and military–industrial complex."[48] It has also been keen to remind the region that it was once part of the "near abroad" of the Soviet Union, and therefore that Russian interests must continue to be taken into account in the region. The Russian Orthodox Church has provided helpful assistance to restoring this "near abroad" in geopolitical terms through its developing attention to the Orthodox diaspora in Latin America.

Conclusion

This chapter is part of preliminary research about the Orthodox "other" in Latin America. It draws attention to a gap in the research and the literature in both World Christianity and Orthodox Studies. World Christianity often overlooks the presence and contribution of the Orthodox "other" in Latin America, while Orthodox Studies often overlooks Latin America in its reflections on the Orthodox diaspora. The overwhelming attention by scholars is on Roman Catholicism and, more recently, Protestantism (including Pentecostalism) in Latin America.

Yet the Orthodox "other" has been present and practicing there for over one hundred years, and is present today in a variety of countries from Argentina to Mexico, with larger and active communities in Brazil. As this chapter discusses, Latin America, specifically Cuba, hosted the historic meeting between Pope Francis and Patriarch Kirill. The meeting and the Joint Declaration these leaders produced are significant for Eastern and Western Christianity, for Christianities of the Global North and the Global South.

The Joint Declaration of 2016, and the fact that the meeting of Patriarch Kirill and Pope Francis took place in Cuba, is significant for the Russian Orthodox Church for three broad reasons. First, it demonstrates that the church is an integral actor in Russian foreign policy (one might say a "soft power" in advancing Russian strategic interests). This forms part of the Russian Orthodox Church's strategy (post-2000 if following

---

48   Rouvinski, *Understanding Russian Priorities in Latin America*, 2.

Lucian Turcescu's periodization) to exert influence on Russian state and society and to banish the effects of communism. While this might be the Russian Orthodox Church's perspective, political analysis of the relationship between the church and state in Russia is more ambivalent among scholars, with many like Gvosdev and Papkova keen to demonstrate that the position and influence of the church should not be overstated.

Second, the Joint Declaration positions the Russian Orthodox Church as a leading Orthodox Church in the Latin American region. It is not the only Orthodox Church in the region as the work of the Holy and Great Council testifies. Indeed, the desire to overcome the problem of the Orthodox diaspora by organizing Episcopal Assemblies, including a Latin America Assembly created by the Holy and Great Council, demonstrates the attempts to resolve questions of jurisdiction of the Orthodox "other" in Latin America. However, the Holy and Great Council can only fully resolve the question of jurisdiction in the Orthodox diaspora in Latin America if all the Orthodox churches participate, including the Russian Orthodox Church. While the newly formed Episcopal Assemblies are to be chaired by the bishop from the Ecumenical Patriarchate, Patriarch Kirill's meeting with Pope Francis in Latin America can be seen as an attempt by the Russian Orthodox Church to show Orthodox leadership in the newly created diaspora region.[49] The meeting also demonstrates the ongoing tensions in the relationship between the Ecumenical Patriarchate of Constantinople and the Russian Orthodox Church, and indicates how these tensions are experienced by the Orthodox "other" in Latin America. The Ecumenical Patriarchate was, curiously, absent from the Havana meeting (even though sending a "regional representative.")

Third, in the ongoing "dispute" between Constantinople and Moscow for leadership of Orthodoxy—particularly pressing with the Ukrainian question—the Joint Declaration gives visibility to the Russian Orthodox Church, speaking on behalf of Orthodoxy to the contemporary world, and not only in the Latin American diaspora. Although it is beyond the scope of this chapter, it is worth noting the Russian Orthodox Church's

---

49   The Episcopal Assembly was formally approved only later in 2016 at the Holy and Great Council, but it was already enacted "in principle" from 2009 onward.

support for "universal traditional values." This support has consequences for others, not only the Orthodox "other," in Latin America. A pro-family political agenda is also often an anti-LGBTQI+ global agenda. The synergies between right-wing politics—and their transnational alliances—and the issues that the Russian Orthodox Church chooses to address in the contemporary world do not go unnoticed by scholars and observers alike.

Achille, Mbembe. "Necropolitics." *Public Culture* 15, no. 1 (2003): 11–40.

Adogame, Afe, Raimundo C. Barreto, and Wanderley Pereira de Rosa, eds. *Migration and Public Discourse in World Christianity*. Minneapolis: Fortress Press, 2019.

Aguilar, Mario I. "Public Theology from the Periphery: Victims and Theologians." *International Journal of Public Theology* 1 (2007): 21–337.

Almeida, Ronaldo. "Evangélicos à Direita." *Horizontes Antropológicos* 26 (2020): 419–36.

Alsultany, Evelyn, and Ella Shohat, eds. *Between the Middle East and the Americas: The Cultural Politics of Diaspora*. Ann Arbor: University of Michigan Press, 2013.

Althaus-Reid, Marcella. "On Wearing Skirts Without Underwear: 'Indecent Theology Challenging the Liberation Theology of the Pueblo.' Poor Women Contesting Christ." *Feminist Theology Journal* 7, no. 20 (1999): 39–51.

______. "Gustavo Gutiérrez Goes to Disneyland: Theme Park Theologies and the Diaspora of the Discourse of the Popular Theologian in Liberation Theology." In *Interpreting Beyond Borders* edited by Fernando F. Segovia, 36–58. Sheffield: Sheffield Academic Press, 2000.

______. *Indecent Theology: Theological Perversions in Sex, Gender and Politics*. New York: Routledge, 2000.

______. *The Queer God*. New York: Routledge, 2003.

______. *From Feminist Theology to Indecent Theology*. London: SCM, 2004.

______. "Thinking Theology and Queer Theory." *Feminist Theology* 15, no. 3 (2007), 302–14.

Alves, Rubem. *Protestantismo e Repressão*. São Paulo: Ática, 1979.

Ammerman, Nancy, ed. *Everyday Religion: Observing Modern Religious Lives*. New York: Oxford University Press, 2007.

Ana, Julio de Santa. "The Ecumenical Movement at the Crossroads." *Student World* 1 (2003): 11–23.

Anderson, Allan H. "Stretching Out Hands to God: Origins and Development of Pentecostalism in Africa." In *Pentecostalism in Africa: Presence and Impact of*

Pneumatic Christianity in Postcolonial Societies, edited by Martin Lindhardt, 54–74. Leiden: Brill Academic, 2015.

Anderson-Rajkumar, Evangeline. "Turning Bodies Inside Out: Contours of Womanist Theology." In *Dalit Theology in the Twenty-first Century, Discordant voices, Discerning Pathways*, edited by Sathianathan Clarke, Deenabandhu Manchala, and Philip Vinod Peacock, 199–214. Oxford: Oxford University Press, 2010.

Andraos, Michel, ed. *The Church and the Indigenous Peoples in the Americas: In Between Reconciliation and Decolonization*. Eugene, OR: Cascade Books, 2019.

Andrews, William L., Frances Smith Foster, and Harris Trudier, eds. *The Oxford Companion to African American Literature*. New York: Oxford University Press, 1997.

Ari, Pedro Oro. "A política da Igreja Universal e seus reflexos nos campos religioso e político brasileiros." *Revista Brasileira de Ciências Sociais* 18, no. 53 (2003): 53–69.

______. "No Brasil as tendências religiosas continuam: declínio católico e crescimento evangélico." *Debates do NER* 20, no. 37 (2020): 69–92.

Asamoah-Gyadu, Kwabena. "Mediating Power and Salvation: Pentecostalism and Religious Mediation in an African Context." *Journal of World Christianity* 5, no. 1 (2012): 43–61.

______. *Contemporary Pentecostal Christianity: Interpretations from an African Context*. Oxford: Regnum Books, 2013.

______. *Sighs and Signs of the Spirit: Ghanaian Perspectives on Pentecostalism and Renewal in Africa*. Eugene, OR: Wipf & Stock Publishers, 2015.

______. *Pentecostalism in Africa: Experiences from Ghana's Charismatic Ministries*. Oxford: Regnum, 2021.

Austin, John. *How to Do Things with Words*. Cambridge: Harvard University Press, 1962.

Ballestrin, Luciana. "America Latina e o Giro Decolonial." *Revista Brasileira de Ciência Política* 11 (2013): 89–117.

Barbosa, José Carlos. *Slavery and Protestant Missions in Imperial Brazil: "The Black Does Not Enter the Church, He Peeks in from Outside."* Lanham, MA: University Press of America, 2008.

Barnes, Andrew E. *Global Christianity and the Black Atlantic: Tuskegee, Colonialism, and the Shaping of African Industrial Education*. Waco: Baylor University Press, 2017.

Barr, David L., ed. *Reading the Book of Revelation: A Resource for Students*. Atlanta: Society of Biblical Literature, 2003.

Barreto, Raimundo C. "The Epistemological Turn in World Christianity: Engaging Decoloniality in Latin American and Caribbean Christian Discourses." *Journal of World Christianity* 9, no. 1 (2019): 48–60.

_____. "Vatican II, Medellin, and Ecumenism: A Brazilian Protestant Perspective." *Journal of World Christianity* 9, no. 2 (2019): 187–202.

_____. "World Christianity and Global Justice: Ecumenical Demands and Possibilities." *The Ecumenical Review* 74, no. 1 (2022): 16–3.

_____. "The Challenge for Christian Unity and Reconciliation Today from a Decolonial Perspective." *International Review of Mission* 111, no. 1 (2022): 70–87.

Barreto, Raimundo C., and Chaves, João. "Christian Nationalism Is Thriving in Brazil: Bolsonaro's Faith-Based Enablers." *The Christian Century* 138, no. 24 (2021): 22–25.

Barreto, Raimundo C., and Roberto Sirvent, eds. *Decolonial Christianities: Latinx and Latin American Perspectives*. New York: Palgrave Macmillan, 2019.

Barreto, Raimundo C., Ronaldo Cavalcante, and Wanderley Pereira da Rosa, eds. *World Christianity as Public Religion*. Minneapolis: Fortress Press, 2017.

Baukham, Richard. *The Climax of Prophecy*. London: T & T Clark, 1993.

Bawardi, Hani. *The Making of Arab Americans: From Syrian Nationalism to U.S. Citizenship*. Austin: University of Texas Press, 2014.

Bayoumi, Moustafa. *This Muslim American Life: Dispatches from the War on Terror*. New York: New York University Press, 2015.

Beaver, R. Pierce. *American Protestant Women in World Mission: History of the First Feminist Movement in North America*. Grand Rapids, MI: Eerdmans, 1980.

Beavers, Herman. "The Autobiography of an Ex-Colored Man." In *The Oxford Companion to African American Literature*, edited by William L. Andrews et al., 39–40. New York: Oxford University Press, 1997.

Bediako, Kwame. *Theology and Identity: The Impact of Culture Upon Christian Thought in the Second Century and in Modern Africa*. Oxford: Oxford Regnum, 1992.

_____. "African Theology." In *The Modern Theologians: An Introduction to Christian Theology in the Twentieth Century*, edited by J. Ford, 428–43. Cambridge: Blackwell, 1997.

_____. "A Half-Century of African Christian Thought: Pointers to Theology and Theological Education in the Next Half-Century." *Journal of African Christian Thought* 3, no. 1 (2000), 5–15.

_____. *Jesus in Africa: The Christian Gospel in African History and Experience*. Yaoundé, Cameroun: Regnum Africa, 2000.

_____. *Jesus and the Gospel in Africa: History and Experience*. Maryknoll, NY: Orbis Books, 2004.

_____. "Scripture as the Interpreter of Culture and Tradition." In *Africa Bible Commentary*, edited by Tokunboh Adeyemo, 7–8. Grand Rapids, MI: Zondervan, 2006.

bell hooks. *Feminist Theory: from Margin to Center*. Boston: South End Press, 1984.

Bernard, Jessie. *The Female World*. New York: The Free Press, 1981.

Betto, Frei. *Fidel and Religion: Castro Talks on Revolution and Religion with Frei Betto.* New York: Simon & Schuster, 1987.

Bhabha, Homi K. *The Location of Culture.* London and New York: Routledge, 1994.

Biney, Moses O. *From Africa to America: Religion and Adaptation among Ghanaian Immigrants in New York.* New York: New York University Press, 2011.

Biney, Moses O., Kenneth Ngwa, and Raimundo C. Barreto Jr., eds. *World Christianity, Urbanization and Identity.* Minneapolis: Fortress Press, 2021.

Birman, Patrícia. *Religião e Espaço Público.* São Paulo: Attar Editorial/CNPq/PRONEX, 2003.

Blassingame, John W. *Slave Community: Plantation Life in the Antebellum South.* Rev. ed. 1972, repr., New York: Oxford University Press, 1979.

Boer, Martinus de. "A influência da apocalíptica judaica sobre as origens cristãs: gênero, cosmovisão e movimento social." *Estudos de Religião* 19 (2000): 11–24.

Boodoo, Gerald, ed. *Religion, Human Dignity and Liberation.* São Leopoldo, Brazil: Oikos Editora, 2016.

Boskin, Joseph. *Sambo: The Rise and Demise of an American Jester.* New York: Oxford University Press, 1986.

Burity, Joanildo, Lara Grigoletto Bonini, and Thaís Serafim. "Religião e Espaço Público: Entrevista com Joanildo Burity." *Debates do NER* 16, no. 28 (2015): 127–47.

Burity, Joanildo and Emerson Giumbelli. "Minorias Religiosas: identidade e política em movimento: editorial." *Religião e Sociedade* 40, no.1 (2020): 9–18.

Burrows, William R., Mark R. Gornic, and Janice A. McLean. *Understanding World Christianity: The Vision and Works of Andrew F. Walls.* Maryknoll, NY: Orbis Books, 2011.

Campos, Leonildo. "O discurso acadêmico de Rubem Alves sobre 'protestantismo' e 'repressão': Algumas observações 30 anos depois." *Religião e Sociedade* 28, no. 2 (2008): 102–37.

Carey, Greg, and Gregory Bloomquist, eds. *Vision and Persuasion: Rhetorical Dimensions of Apocalyptic Discourse.* St. Louis: Chalice, 1999.

Carrette, Jeremy. "Radical Heterodoxy and the Indecent Proposal of Erotic Theology: Critical Groundwork for Sexual Theologies." *Literature and Theology: Queering Religion* 15, No. 3, (2001): 286–98.

Casselberry, Judith, and Elizabeth A. Prichard, eds. *Spirit on the Move: Black Women and Pentecostalism in African and the Diaspora.* Durham: Duke University Press, 2019.

Cavalcanti, Robinson. *Cristianismo e Política: Teoria Bíblica e Prática Histórica.* Viçosa, Brazil: Editora Ultimato, 1985.

_____. *A utopia possível: Em busca do cristianismo integral.* Belo Horizonte: Editora Ultimato, 1993.

César, Marília de Camargo. *O Grito de Eva: A Violência Doméstica em Lares Cristãos*. São Paulo: Thomas Nelson Brasil, 2021.

Chaves, João B. *The Global Mission of the Jim Crow South: Southern Baptist Missionaries and the Shaping of Latin American Evangelicalism*. Macon, GA: Mercer University Press, 2022.

Chisale, Sinenhlanhla Sithulisiwe. "Politics of the Body, Fear and Ubuntu: Proposing an African Women's Theology of Disability." *HTS Teologiese Studies/Theological Studies* 76, no. 3 (August 2020): 1–10.

Cho, Min-Ah. "Stirring up Deep Waters: Korean Feminist Theologies Today." *Theology Today* 71, no. 2 (2014): 233–45.

Choi, Man-Ja. "Feminist Theological Interpretation of Korean Shamanism." *Korean Journal of Christian Studies* 7, no. 1 (1990): 244–45.

______. "Feminine Images of God in Korean Traditional Religion." In *Frontiers in Asian Christian Theology: Emerging Trends*, edited by R.S. Sugirtharajah, 80–89. Maryknoll, NY: Orbis Books, 1994.

______. "The Acceptance, Development, and Influence of Feminist Theology in The Korean Church and Society in the 1980s." *Christianity and History in Korea* 18 (2003): 86–87.

Chuba, Bwalya S. *A History of Early Christian Missions and Church Unity in Zambia*. Ndola: Mission Press, 2013.

Chung, Hyun Kyung. *Struggle to Be the Sun Again: Introducing Asian Women's Theology*. Maryknoll, NY: Orbis Books, 1990.

______. "Opium or the Seed for Revolution? Women-Centered Religiosity in Korea." In *The Power of Naming: A Concilium Reader in Feminist Liberation Theology*, edited by Elisabeth Schüssler Fiorenza, 275–83. Maryknoll, NY: Orbis Books, SCM Press, 1996.

Chung, Jae-Yeon. "Religion and Korean Women: Rethinking Korean Shamanism from the women's theological perspectives." *Han'gugyŏsŏngsinhak* 6 (1991): 38–41.

Chung, Meehyun. *Another Story of Women's Theology*. Seoul: South Korea: Handŭlch'ulp'ansa, 2007.

Clément, Olivier. "Orthodox Reflections on 'Liberation Theology'." *St. Vladimir's Theological Quarterly* 29 (1985): 62–72.

Close-Barry, Kirstie. *A Mission Divided: Race and Culture & Colonialism in Fiji's Methodist Mission*. Acton, Australia: ANU Press, 2015.

Crenshaw, Kimberlé. "Demarginalizing the Intersection of Race and Sex: A Black Feminist Critique of Antidiscrimination Doctrine, Feminist Theory and Antiracist Politics." *University of Chicago Legal Forum* 1, no. 8 (1989): 141–56.

Dasilio, Derval. *Jaime Wright: O Pastor dos Torturados*. Rio de Janeiro: Metanoia Editora, 2012.

Davis, Edwin Adams, ed. *Plantation Life in the Florida Parishes of Louisiana, 1836–1846, as reflected in the Diary of Bennet H. Barrow.* New York: AMS Press, 1943.

Dah, Ini Dorcas. *Women Do More Work Than Men: Birifor Women as Change Agents in the Mission and Expansion of the Church in West Africa (Burkina Faso, Côte d'Ivoire and Ghana).* Eugene, OR: Wipf & Stock, 2018.

Delany, M. R., and Robert Campbell. *Search for a Place: Black Separatism and Africa, 1960.* Ann Arbor: University of Michigan Press, 1969.

Dolamo, Ramathate. "Botho/Ubuntu: The Heart of African Ethics." *Scriptura* 112 (2013): 1–10.

Demacopoulos, George, and Aristotle Papanikolaou, eds. *Orthodox Constructions of the West.* New York: Fordham University Press, 2013.

Domenici, Eloisa. "Samba de Roda and the Threat of Epistemicide on the North Coast of Bahia." *MUSICultures* 48 (2021): 142–67.

Dorrien, Garry. *Social Ethics in the Making: Interpreting an American Tradition.* West Sussex: U.K. John Wiley & Sons, 2011.

Douglass, Frederick. *My Bondage and My Freedom*, edited by John David Smith. 1855. repr., New York: Penguin Books, 2003.

Du Bois, W. E. B. *The World and Africa: An Inquiry into the Part which Africa Played in World History.* New York: International Publishers, 1965.

______. *The Souls of Black Folk.* 1903. repr., New York: Barnes & Noble Classics, 2003.

Dube, Musa W. "Searching for the Lost Needle: Double Colonization & Postcolonial African Feminisms." *Studies in World Christianity* 5, no. 2 (January 1, 1999): 213–28.

Duff, Paul B. *Who Rides the Beast? Prophetic Rivalry and the Rhetoric of Crisis in the Churches of the Apocalypse.* New York: Oxford University Press, 2001.

Dullo, Eduardo. "Política secular e intolerância religiosa na disputa eleitoral." In *Religiões e Controvérsias Públicas: experiências, práticas sociais e discursos*, edited by Paula Montero, 27-47. São Paulo/Campinas: Terceiro Nome/Unicamp, 2015.

Dusen, Henry P. Van. *World Christianity: Yesterday, Today, Tomorrow.* New York: Abingdon-Cokesbury Press, 1947.

Dussel, Enrique, ed. *Historia General de la Iglesia em America Latina.* Salamanca: Ediciones Sigeme, 1983.

______. "Agenda for a South-South Philosophical Dialogue." *Human Architecture*, 11, no. 1 (2013): 3–18.

Dutra, Roberto, and Karine Pessoa. "Guerras culturais e a relação entre religião e política no Brasil contemporâneo." *Revista brasileira de história das religiões* 13 (2021): 233–56.

Ebenezer, Obadare. *Pentecostal Republic: Religion and The Struggle for State Power in Nigeria.* London: Zed Books Ltd., 2018.

Elkins, Stanley. *Slavery: A Problem in Institutional and Intellectual Life*, 2nd ed. Chicago: University of Chicago Press, 1968.

Ellis, Stephen, and Gerrie ter Haar. *Worlds of Power: Religious Thought and Political Practice in Africa*. London: C. Hurst & Co., 2004.

Espin, Orlando O. *Idol and Grace: Traditioning and Subversive Hope*. Maryknoll, NY: Orbis Books, 2014.

Esquivel, Juan Cruz, and Toniol, Rodrigo. "The Presence of Religion in the Latin American Public Space: Notes for a Debate." *Social Compass* 65 (2018): 1–18.

Fiorenza, Elisabeth Schüssler.*The Book of Revelation: Justice and Judgment*, 2nd ed. Minneapolis: Fortress Press, 1998.

______. *Changing Horizons: Explorations in Feminist Interpretation*. Minneapolis: Fortress Press, 2013.

______. "The Followers of the Lamb: Visionary Rhetoric and Social-political Situation." *Semeia* 36 (1986): 123–47.

Flood, Michael, ed. *International Encyclopedia of Men and Masculinities*. New York: Routledge, 2007.

Foner, Philip S., ed. *Frederick Douglass: Selected Speeches and Writings*. Chicago: Lawrence Hill Books, 1999.

Fonseca, Alexandre Brasil. "O PT e o voto evangélico." *Instituto Humanitas Unisinos* (October 19, 2020). Accessed October 22, 2020, https://tinyurl.com/3at99hzx.

Frederiks, Martha, and Dorottya Nagy, eds. *World Christianity: Methodological Considerations*. Boston: Brill, 2021.

Freeman, Dena. "Pentecostalism and Economic Development in Sub-Saharan Africa." In *The Routledge Handbook of Religions and Global Development*, edited by Emma Tomalin, 128–140. New York: *Routledge*, 2015.

Freire, Ana Ester Pádua et al. *Manual de Cristianismo e LGBTI+*. Curitiba: IBDSEX, 2021.

Freston, Paul. "Protestantismo e Democracia no Brasil." *Lusotopie* (1999): 329–40.

Fricker, Miranda. *Epistemic Injustice: Power and the Ethics of Knowing*. Oxford: Oxford University Press, 2007.

Frilingos, Christopher A. *Spectacles of Empire: Monsters, Martyrs, and the Book of Revelation*. Philadelphia: University of Pennsylvania Press, 2004.

Gandolfo, Elizabeth O'Donnell, and Laurel Marshall Potter. *Re-Membering the Reign of God: The Decolonial Witness of El Salvador's Church of the Poor*. New York: Lexington Books, 2022.

García-Johnson, Oscar. *Spirit Outside the Gate: Decolonial Pneumatologies of the American Global South*. Westmont, IL: InterVarsity Press, 2019.

Gavrilyuk, Paul L. *Georges Florovsky and the Russian Religious Renaissance*. Oxford: Oxford University Press, 2014.

Gebara, Ivone. *Out of the Depths: Women's Experiences of Evil and Salvation*. Minneapolis, MN: Fortress Press, 2002.

Gherman, Michel, and Klein, Misha. "Aquela Noite: o lugar da Israel imaginária na nova direita brasileira." *Revista Anthropológicas* 32, no. 2 (2021): 111–40.

Gifford, Paul. *African Christianity: Its Public Role*, London: Hurst, 1998.

_____. "The Bible in Africa: A Novel Usage in Africa's New Churches." *Bulletin of the School of Oriental and African Studies* 71, no. 2 (2008): 203–19.

_____. *Ghana's New Christianity: Pentecostalism in a Globalizing African Economy.* Bloomington: Indiana University Press, 2004.

Giumbelli, Emerson. *O Fim da Religião: Dilemas da liberdade religiosa no Brasil e na França.* São Paulo: Attar Editorial, 2002.

_____. "Public Spaces and Religion: An Idea to Debate, a Monument to Analyze." *Horizontes Antropológicos* 24 (2018): 279–309.

Gnanadason, Aruna. "Jesus and the Asian Woman: A Post-Colonial Look at the Syro-Phoenician Woman/Canaanite Woman from an Indian Perspective." *Studies in World Christianity* 7, no. 2 (2001): 162–77.

Gnanadason, Joy. *A Forgotten History: A Story of the Missionary Movement and the Liberation of People in South Travancore.* Columbia, MO: South Asia Books, 1996.

Gomes, Edlaine. *A Era das Catedrais: a autenticidade em exibição.* Rio de Janeiro: Garamond, 2011.

Gonzalez, Michelle A. *Sor Juana: Beauty and Justice in the Americas.* Maryknoll, NY: Orbis, 2003.

Gordon, David M. *Invisible Agents: Spirits in a Central African History.* Athens: Ohio University Press, 2012.

Granberg-Michaelson, Wesley. *From Times Square to Timbuktu: The Post-Christian West Meets the Non-Western Church.* Grand Rapids, MI: Eerdmans, 2013.

Grasswick, Heidi E. *Feminist Epistemology and Philosophy of Science: Power in Knowledge.* New York: Springer, 2011.

Green, Todd H. *Presumed Guilty: Why We Shouldn't Ask Muslims to Condemn Terrorism.* Minneapolis: Fortress Press, 2018.

Grin, Mônica, Michel Gherman, and L. Caracinki. "Beyond Jordan River's Waters: Evangelicals, Jews, and the Political Context in Contemporary Brazil." *International Journal of Latin American Religions* 4 (2019): 1–21.

Gualtieri, Sarah M. A. *Between Arab and White: Race and Ethnicity in the Early Syrian American Diaspora.* Berkeley: University of California Press, 2009.

Gvosdev, Nikolas. *Emperors and Elections: Reconciling the Orthodox Tradition with Modern Politics.* New York: Troista Books, 2000.

Hamley, Isabelle. *Embracing Justice.* London: SPCK, 2021.

Hamley, Isabelle M. *Unspeakable Things Unspoken: An Irigarayan Reading of Otherness and Victimization in Judges 19–21.* Eugene, OR: Pickwick Publications, 2019.

Hanciles, Jehu J., ed. *World Christianity: History, Methodologies, Horizons.* Maryknoll, NY: Orbis, 2021.

Hanson, Paul. *The Dawn of Apocalyptic: The Historical and Sociological Roots of Jewish Apocalyptic Eschatology*. Philadelphia: Fortress Press, 1983.

Harper, Charles R. O. *Acompanhamento: Ecumenical Action for Human Rights in Latin America, 1970–1990*. Geneva: WCC Publications, 2006.

Hassan, Ihab. "Travel as Metaphor." In *Dissident and Marginality: Essays on the Boarders of Literature and Religion*, edited by Kiyoshi Tsuchiya, 163–78. New York: Macmillan Press, 1997.

Hassan, Waïl S. "The Rise of Arab-American Literature: Orientalism and Cultural Translation in the Work of Ameen Rihani." *American Literary History* 20, no. 1–2 (2008): 245–75.

Haynes, Naomi. "The Expansive Present." *Current Anthropology* 61, no. 1 (2020): 57–76.

Hegel, G. W. F. *The Philosophy of History*. Mineola: Dover Press, 1956.

Herculano, Gabrielle Silva. "Nosso Luto Vem do Verbo Lutar: Uma análise do ativismo progressista evangélico através da Frente de Evangélicos pelo Estado de Direito." Master's thesis, Universidade Federal Fluminense, Rio de Janeiro, 2021.

Hinfelaar, Marja. "Legitimizing Powers: The Political Role of the Roman Catholic Church, 1972–1991." In *One Zambia, Many Histories: Towards a History of Post-colonial Zambia*, edited by Jan-Bart Gewald, Marja Hinfelaar, and Giacomo Macola, 129–43. Lusaka: Lembani Trust, 2009.

Hooper, S. M., and Culshaw W. J. *Bible Translations in India, Pakistan and Ceylon*. Bombay: Oxford University Press, 1963.

Irvin, Dale. "World Christianity: An Introduction." *Journal of World Christianity* 1, no. 1 (2008): 1–26.

———. "Specters of a New Ecumenism: In Search of a Church 'Out of Joint.'" In *Religion, Authority, and the State: From Constantine to the Contemporary World*, edited by Leo D. Lefebure, 3–32. New York: Palgrave Macmillan, 2016.

———. "World Christianity: A Genealogy." *Journal of World Christianity* 9, no. 1 (2019): 5–22.

Isasi-Díaz, Ada María. *Mujerista Theology: A Theology for the Twenty-First Century*. Maryknoll, NY: Orbis, 1995.

Jackson, Debra L. "Date Rape: The Intractability of Hermeneutical Injustice." In *Analyzing Violence Against Women*, edited by Wanda Teays, 39–51. Switzerland: Springer Nature, 2019.

Jacobs, Linda. "Playing East: Arabs Perform in Nineteenth-Century America." *Mashriq & Mahjar* 2, no. 2 (2014): 85–118.

Johnson, James Weldon. "*The Autobiography of an Ex-Colored Man*." In *James Weldon Johnson: Writings*, edited by William L. Andrews. New York: Literary Classics of the United States, 2004.

Johnson, Todd M., and Gina A. Zurlo, eds. *World Christian Database*. Leiden/Boston: Brill, 2016.

Joint Declaration of Pope Francis and Patriarch Kirill of Moscow and All Russia, February 12–18, 2016, available via The Russian Orthodox Church Department of External Church Relations, https://tinyurl.com/2txt6xyt.

Jones, Arun W. *Missionary Christianity and Local Religion: American Evangelicalism in North India, 1836–1870.* Waco, TX: Baylor University Press, 2017.

Jones, Arun W., ed. *Christian Interculture: Texts and Voices from Colonial and Postcolonial Worlds.* University Park: Pennsylvania State University Press, 2021.

Joseph, M. P. *Theologies of the Non-person: The Formative Years of EATWOT.* London: Palgrave Macmillan, 2015.

Kallistos, Ware. *The Orthodox Church.* London: Penguin, 1997.

Kalu, Ogbu U. *African Pentecostalism: An Introduction.* Oxford University Press, 2008.

———. *The Collected Essays of Ogbu Uke Kalu, vol. 1: African Pentecostalism: Global Discourses, Migrations, Exchanges, and Connections,* edited by Wilhelmina J. Kalu, Nimi Wariboko, and Toyin Falola. Africa World Press, 2010.

Kang, Namsoon. "Reclaiming Theological Significance of Women's *Religious Choice-in-Differential*: Korean Women's Choice of Christianity Revisited." *Journal of World Christianity* 3, no. 1 (2010): 18–46.

Kaunda, Chammah J., and Marja Hinfelaar, eds. *Competing for Caesar: Religion and Politics in Post-Colonial Zambia.* Minneapolis: Fortress Press, 2020.

Kaunda, Chammah J., and Mutale Mulenga Kaunda. "Mobilising religious assets for social transformation: A theology of decolonial reconstruction perspective on the Ministry of National Guidance and Religious Affairs (MNGRA) in Zambia." *Religions* 9, no. 6 (2018).

Kaunda, Chammah J., ed. *Genders, Sexualities, and Spiritualities in African Pentecostalism: 'Your Body is a Temple of the Holy Spirit.'* Cham: Palgrave Macmillan, 2020.

———. *The Nation That Fears God Prospers: A Critique of Zambian Pentecostal Theopolitical Imaginations.* Minneapolis: Augsburg Fortress Publishers, 2018.

———. "'The Ngabwe Covenant' and the Search for an African Theology of Eco-Pneumato-Relational Way of Being in Zambia." *Religions* 11, no. 6 (2020), https://doi.org/10.3390/rel11060275.

Kendall, Laurel. *Shamans, Nostalgias, and the IMF: South Korean Popular Religion in Motion.* Honolulu: University of Hawaii Press, 2009.

Kent, Eliza F. *Converting Women: Gender and Protestant Christianity in Colonial South India.* New York: Oxford University Press, 2004.

Kidd, Thomas S. *American Christians and Islam: Evangelical Culture and Muslims from the Colonial Period to the Age of Terrorism.* Princeton, NJ: Princeton University Press, 2018.

Kilomba, Grada. *Plantation Memories: Episodes of Everyday Racism.* Muster: UNRAST-Verlag, 2010.

Kim, Grace Ji-Sun, and Hilda P. Koster. eds. *Planetary Solidarity: Global Women's Voices on Christian Doctrine and Climate Justice*. Minneapolis: Fortress Press, 2017.

Kim, Helen Jin. *Race for Revival: How Cold War South Korea Shaped the American Evangelical Empire*. Oxford: Oxford University Press, 2022.

Kim, Jin. "Musoksinanggwa hanŭi sinhak (Shamanistic Faith and the Theology of Han)." *Theological Thought* (Sinsang) 67 (1989): 992–94.

Kim, Tae-gon. "What Is Korean Shamanism?" In *Korean Shamanism: Revivals, Survivals, and Change*, edited by Keith Howard, 15–31. Seoul: The Royal Asiatic Society, Korea Branch, 1998.

Kim, Ŭnhŭi. *Life Stories of Women Shamans*. Seoul: Muneyŏn'gusa, 2004.

Kinnamon, Michael, ed. *Signs of the Spirit: Official Report of the Seventh Assembly of the World Council of Churches*. Geneva; Grand Rapids, MI: WCC Publications/World Council of Church Internet Archives, 1991.

______. *Can a Renewal Movement be Renewed? Questions for the Future of Ecumenism*. Grand Rapids, MI: Eerdmans, 2014.

Kippenberg, Hans G. "In Praise of Syncretism: The Beginning of Christianity Conceived in the Light of a Diagnosis of Modern Culture." In *Syncretism in Religion: A Reader*, edited by A. M. Leopold and J. S. Jensen, 29–38. London: Equinox, 2004.

Klinken, Adriaan van. "Homosexuality, Politics and Pentecostal Nationalism in Zambia." *Studies in World Christianity* 20, no, 3 (2014): 259–81.

______. "Christianity and Same-Sex Relationships in Africa." In *Routledge Companion to Christianity in Africa*, edited by Elias K. Bongmba, 487–501. New York and London: Routledge, 2016.

Kumar, Ajay. "Sexual Violence against Dalit Women: An Analytical Study of Intersectionality of Gender, Caste, and Class in India." *Journal of International Women's Studies* Vol. 22, Issue 2 (2021): 123–34.

Kumar, Kanithi Ranjit. "The Element of Bhakti in the Lyrics of Acharya A.B. Masilamani: Its Implications for Mission and Its Relevance to the Convention of Baptist Churches in the Northern Circars." Master's thesis, Serampore University, 2005.

Küster, Volker. *A Protestant Theology of Passion: Korean Minjung Theology Revisited*. Studies in Systematic Theology, vol. 4. Leiden; Boston: Brill, 2010.

Kwok, Pui-lan. "Christianity and Women in Contemporary China." *Journal of World Christianity* 3, no. 1 (2010): 1–17.

______. "Interfaith Dialogue from the Perspective of Feminist Theology in the Multireligious and Multicultural Context of Asia." In *Women and Christianity*, edited by Pui-lan Kwok, 229–39, vol. 3. London: Routledge, 2010.

______. *Introducing Asian Feminist Theology*. Sheffield: Sheffield Academic Press, 2000.

Kwok, Pui-lan, ed. *Asian and Asian American Women in Theology and Religion: Embodying Knowledge.* Cham: Palgrave Macmillan, 2020.

Lacerda, Marina Basso. *O novo conservadorismo brasileiro: de Reagan a Bolsonaro*n. Porto Alegre: Zouk, 2019.

Lange, Ernst. *And Yet It Moves.* Geneva: WCC Publications, 1979.

Lee, Jonghyun. "Shamanism and Its Emancipatory Power for Korean Women." *Journal of Women and Social Work* 24, no. 2 (May 2009): 186–98.

Leistle, Bernhard, ed. *Anthropology and Alterity.* New York: Routledge, 2017.

Lester, Julius. *Black Folktales.* New York: Grove Press, 1991.

Lima, Danielle Ventura Bandeira de. "Apocalipse Doze: Uma Análise da Leitura Conflitual e da Hermenêutica Feminista." *Fragmentos de Cultura* 21 (2011): 37–49.

Lima, Silvia Regina de. *En territorio de frontera: una lectura de Marcos 7. 24–30.* Costa Rica: DEI, 2001.

Lior, Mika Lillit. "Circling With/In the Saint: Bahian Candomblé's Feminist Poiesis and Dark Horse Kinetics." PhD diss., University of California, 2021.

Machingura, Francis. "'A Woman Should Learn in Quietness and Full Submission' (1 Timothy 2:11): Empowering Women in the Fight Against Masculine Readings of Biblical Texts and a Chauvinistic African Culture in the face of HIV and AIDS." *Studies in World Christianity* 19, no. 3 (2013): 233–51.

Mackay, John. *Ecumenics: The Science of the Church Universal.* Englewood Cliffs, NJ: Prentice-Hall, 1964.

Mackenzie, John M. "David Livingstone – Prophet or Patron Saint of Imperialism in Africa: Myths and Misconceptions." *Scottish Geographical Journal* 129, no. 3–04 (2013): 277–91.

Macqueen, Ian. "Ecumenism and the Global Anti-Apartheid Struggle: The World Council of Churches' Special Fund in South Africa and Botswana, 1970–75." *Historia* 62, no. 2 (2017): 87–111.

Maldonado-Torres, Nelson. "Enrique Dussel's Liberation Thought in the Decolonial Turn." *Transmodernity* 1, no. 1 (2011): 1–30.

______. *Against War: Views from the Underside of Modernity.* Durham, NC: Duke University Press, 2008.

Maluleke, Tinyiko S. "Of Africanised Bees and Africanised Churches: Ten Theses on African Christianity." *Missionalia* 38, no. 3 (2010): 369–79.

Manning, Jennifer. "Decolonial Feminist Theory: Embracing the Gendered Colonial Difference in Management and Organisation Studies." *Gender Work Organisation* 28 (2021): 1203–19.

Mariano, Ricardo, and Pierucci, Antônio Flávio. "O Envolvimento dos pentecostais na eleição de Collor." *Novos Estudos CEBRAP* 34 (1992): 92–106.

Marteijn, Elizabeth. "Between Ruins and Remnants: Religious Reinvention and Renewal among Christians in West Bank Palestine." PhD diss., University of Edinburgh, 2022.

Masuzawa, Tomoko. *The Invention of World Religions. Or, How European Universalism Was Preserved in the Language of Pluralism*. Chicago: University of Chicago Press, 2005.

Matt, Susan J. *Homesickness: An American History*. New York: Oxford University Press, 2011.

McGeoch, Graham. "Of Greeks and Russians: Orthodox Christianity in the State of Espirito Santo, Brazil." *Salt: Crossroads of Religion and Culture* 1 (2022): 242–50.

Mesters C., and Orofino, F. *O Apocalipse de São João: A teimosia da fé dos pequenos*. Petrópolis: Vozes, 2002.

Meyendorff, John. *Catholicity and the Church*. New York: St. Vladimir's Seminary Press, 1983.

Meyer, Birgit. "Pentecostalism and Globalization." In *Studying Global Pentecostalism: Theories and Methods*, edited by Allan H. Anderson, Michael Bergunder, Andre Droogers, and Cornelis van der Laan, 113–30. Berkeley: University of California Press, 2010.

Mignolo, Walter. *The Darker Side of Western Modernity: Global Futures, Decolonial Options*. Durham/London: Duke University Press, 2011.

_____. "Epistemic Disobedience, Independent Thought and Decolonial Freedom." *Theory, Culture & Society* 26, no. 7–8 (2009): 159–81.

Mignolo, Walter D., and Catherine E. Walsh. *Decoloniality: Concepts, Analytics, Praxis*. Durham, NC: Duke University Press, 2018.

Montero, Paula. "Religião, pluralismo e esfera pública." *Novos Estudos CEBRAP* 74 (March 2006): 47–66.

_____. "Controvérsias religiosas e Esfera Pública: repensando as religiões como discurso." *Religião & Sociedade* 32 (2012): 15–30.

_____. "Religious Pluralism and Its Impacts on the Configuration of Secularism in Brazil." *Secular Studies* 2 (2020): 14–29.

Moon, Hellena. "Genealogy of the Modern Theological Understanding of Han." *Pastoral psychology* 63, no. 4 (August 2014): 419–35.

Morrison, Toni. *The Source of Self-Regard: Selected Essays, Speeches, and Meditations*. New York: Alfred A. Knopf, 2019.

Moses, Wilson Jeremiah. *Black Messiahs and Uncle Toms: Social and Literary Manipulations of a Religious Myth*. University Park: The Pennsylvania State University Press, 1993.

Moyo, Fulata Lusungu. "A Quest for Women's Sexual Empowerment through Education in an HIV and AIDS Context: The Case of Kukhonzekera Chinkhoswe caChikhristu (KCC) among Amang'anja and Ayao Christians of T/A Mwambo in rural Zomba, Malawi." PhD diss., University of KwaZulu-Natal, South Africa, 2009.

_____. "Called to Lament Injustice and Prophesy Equality, Justice, Peace and Healing for All – Honoring Rev Dr Nyambura Njproge." In *That All May Live: Essays in*

Honour of Nyambura J. Njoroge, edited by Ezra Chitando, Esther Mombo, and Masiiwa Ragies Gunda, 47–57. Bamberg: University of Bamberg Press, 2021.

Mudimbe, V. Y. *The Invention of Africa: Gnosis, Philosophy, and the Order of Knowledge*. Bloomington: Indiana University Press, 1988.

———. *The Idea of Africa*. Bloomington: Indiana University Press, 1994.

Musskopf, André. "Via(da)gens teológicas: itinerários para uma teologia queer no Brasil." PhD diss., Faculdades EST, São Leopoldo, 2008.

Mwewa, Charles. *Zambia, Struggles of My People & Western Contribution to Corruption and Underdevelopment in Africa*. Lusaka: Maiden Publishing House, 2011.

Myers, Kathleen Ann. *Neither Saints nor Sinners: Writing the Lives of Women in Spanish America*. Oxford: Oxford University Press, 2003.

Nair, Janaki. "The Troubled Relationship of Feminism and History." *Economic and Political Weekly* 43, no. 43 (October 25–31, 2008): 57–65.

Ndlovu-Gatsheni, Sabelo J. "Beyond the Equator There Are No Sins: Coloniality and Violence in Africa." *Journal of Developing Societies* 28, no. 4 (2012): 419–40.

Nelavala, Prasuna Gnana. "Caste Branding, Bleeding Body, Building Dalit Womanhood." In *Dalit Theology in the Twenty-first Century, Discordant voices, Discerning Pathways*, edited by Sathianathan Clarke, Deenabandhu Manchala, and Philip Vinod Peacock, 265–276. Oxford: Oxford University Press, 2010.

Nelavala, Surekha. "Jesus Asks the Samaritan Woman for a Drink: A Dalit Feminist Reading of John 4." *lectio difficilior* 1 (2007): 1–12.

Nelson, Sarah Milledge. *Shamanism and the Origin of States: Spirit, Power, and Gender in East Asia*. Walnut Creek, CA: Left Coast Press, 2008.

Ninh, Thien-Huong T. *Race, Gender, and Religion in the Vietnamese Diaspora: The New Chosen People*. New York: Palgrave, 2017.

Noble, Ivana. "L'avenir de la «diaspora» orthodoxe." *Contacts* 65, no. 243 (July–September, 2013): 477–97.

Oduyoye, Mercy A. *African Women's Theologies, Spirituality, and Healing: Theological Perspectives from the Circle of Concerned African Women Theologians*. New York: Paulist Press, 2019.

———. *Daughters of Anowa: African Patriarchy*. Maryknoll, NY: Orbis, 1995.

Oduyoye, Mercy A., and Musimbi R. A. Kanyoro, eds. *The Will to Rise: Women, Tradition, and the Church in Africa*. Eugene, OR: Wipf & Stock, 1992.

Oladdemo, Oyeronke. "New Dimensions in Nigerian Women's Pentecostal Experience: The Case of DODIM, Nigeria." *Journal of World Christianity* 5, no. 1 (2012): 62–74.

Oliveira, Andréa Carvalho. "Direito à memória das comunidades tradicionais: organização de acervo nos terreiros de candomblé de Salvador, Bahia." *Ciência da Informação* 39, no. 2 (2010): 84–91.

de Oliveira, Rafael Soares et al., eds. *Ecumenismo, Direitos Humanos e Paz: A Experiência do Fórum Ecumênico Brasil*. Rio de Janeiro, Brazil: Fe Brasil, 2006.

Olsen, Ted. "*One African Nation under God.*" *Christianity Today* 46, no. 2 (2002): 36–43.

Omenyo, Cephas. *Pentecost Outside Pentecostalism: A Study of the Development of Charismatic Renewal in Mainline Churches in Ghana.* Boekencentrum Publishing House, 2006.

Padilla, C. René. *O que é a Missão Integral?* Viçosa, Brazil: Ultimato, 2009.

Papkova, Irina. *The Orthodox Church and Russian Politics.* New York: Oxford University Press, 2011.

Park, Shalon. "The Politics of Impeaching Shamanism: Regulating Religions in the Korean Public Sphere." *Journal of Church and State* 60, no. 4 (2018): 636–60.

Parker, Eve. *Trust in Theological Education: Dismantling Trustworthiness for a Pedagogy of Liberation.* London: SCM Press, 2022.

Parker, Eve Rebecca. *Theologising with the Sacred 'Prostitutes' of South India: Towards an Indecent Dalit Theology.* Leiden: Brill, 2021.

Pauw, Christoff Martin. *Mission and Church in Malawi. The History of the Nkhoma Synod of the Church of Central Africa, Presbyterian 1889–1962.* Wellington, South Africa: Christian Literature Fund Publishers, 2016.

Phiri, Isaac. "Why African Churches Preach Politics: The Case of Zambia." *Journal of Church and State* 41, no. 2 (1999): 323–47.

_____. *Proclaiming Political Pluralism: Churches and Political Transitions in Africa.* Westport, CT: Praeger, 2001.

Pierce, Yolanda. "'Leaving Husband, Home, and Baby and All' African American Women and Nineteenth-Century Global Missions." *Journal of World Christianity* 6, no. 2 (2016): 277–90.

Pierucci, Antonio Flávio. "Representantes de Deus em Brasília: a bancada evangélica na Constituinte." *Ciências Sociais Hoje* 11 (1989): 104–34.

Pineda-Madrid, Nancy. *Salvation and Suffering in Ciudad Juárez.* Philadelphia: Fortress Press, 2011.

Pippin, T. "Eros and the End: Reading for Gender in the Apocalypse of John." *Semeia* 59 (1992): 193–210.

dos Prazeres, Alexandre de Jesus. "Fundamentalismo, Bíblia e Relações de Gênero." *Revista Eletrônica Correlatio* 20 (2021): 63–85.

Premawardhana, Devaka. *Faith in Flux: Pentecostalism and Mobility in Rural Mozambique.* Philadelphia: University of Pennsylvania Press, 2018.

Quayesi-Amakye, Joseph. "Pentecostalism, the Akan Religion and the Good Life." *International Journal of Pentecostal Missiology* 5 (2017): 111–28.

Quinn, Anne-Lise. "Holding on to Mission Christianity: Case Studies from A Presbyterian Church in Malawi." *Journal of Religion in Africa* XXV, no. 4 (Nov. 1995): 387–411.

Raj, Pulidindi Solomon. "Christian Prabhandha Literature." In *Striving for Excellence: Educational Ministry in the Church,* edited by Siga Arles and Brian Wintle, 393–409. Bangalore: Center for Contemporary Christianity, 2007.

Rao, Nitya. "Marriage, Violence, and Choice: Understanding Dalit Women's Agency in Rural Tamil Nadu." *Gender & Society* 29, no. 3 (2015): 410–33.

Rao, Rayi R. Sundara. *Telugulo Chraistava Sahityam.* Chennai: Rayi Foundation, 2016.

Reade, W. Winwood. "Efforts of Missionaries among Slaves." *Journal of the Anthropological Study of London* (1865): 163–83.

Reed, Annette Yoshiko. *Fallen Angels and the History of Judaism and Christianity: The Reception of Enochic Literature.* New York: Cambridge University Press, 2005.

Rhie, Deok-Joo. *A Study on the Formation of the Indigenous Church in Korea, 1903–1907.* Seoul: The Institute of the History of Christianity in Korea, 2000.

Ribeiro, Gustavo Lins. "Why (Post) Colonialism and (De) Coloniality Are Not Enough: A Post-Imperialist Perspective." *Postcolonial Studies* 14, no. 3 (2011): 285–97.

Richard, Pablo. *Apocalipse: Reconstrução da Esperança.* Petrópolis: Vozes, 1996.

Robert, Dana L. *American Women in Missions: A Social History of their Thought and Practice.* Macon, GA: Mercer University Press, 1996.

______. "Gender Roles and Recruitment in Southern African Churches, 1996–2001." In *Communities of Faith in Africa and the African Diaspora,* edited by Casely B. Essamuah and David K. Ngaruiya, 116–34. Eugene, OR: Pickwick Publications, 2013.

______. "Shifting Southward: Global Christianity since 1945." *International Bulletin of Missionary Research* 24, no. 2 (April 1, 2000): 50–58.

______. "World Christianity as a Women's Movement." *International Bulletin of Missionary Research* 30, no. 4 (2006): 180–88.

Rotberg, Robert I. *Christian Missionaries and the Creation of Northern Rhodesia 1880–1924.* Princeton, NJ: Princeton University Press, 1965.

Rouvinski, Vladimir. *Understanding Russian Priorities in Latin America.* Washington: Woodrow Wilson Center, 2017.

Royalty, R. *The Streets of Heaven: The Ideology of Wealth in the Apocalypse of John.* Macon, GA: Mercer University Press, 1998.

Rubin, Gayle. "Pensando o sexo" (1984). In *Políticas do Sexo,* coleção Argonautas, translated by Jamille Pinheiro Dias. São Paulo: UBU Editora, 2017.

Ryu, Tongshik. *Korean Religions and Christianity.* South Korea: Taehan'gidokkyo-sŏhoe, 1993.

______. *The History and Structure of Korean Shamanism,* translated by Jeong-il Moon. Seoul: Yonsei University Press, 2012.

Sahgal, Neha, and Alan Cooperman et al. *Orthodox Christianity in the 21st Century.* Washington: Pew Research Center, 2017.

de Sales, Ronaldo Laurentino Jr., and Jorissa Danila Aguiar. "A fé do povo latino-americano: entre o cristianismo da libertação e as lutas populares." *Religião e Sociedade* 40 no. 2 (2020): 99–121.

Samuel, Sudha Ratnanjali. *Purshothama Chowdari Jeevitha Charitra.* Chennai: Christian Literature Services, 1997.

Sanneh, Lamin. *Translating the Message: The Missionary Impact on Culture.* Maryknoll, NY: Orbis, 1989.

______. *Whose Religion Is Christianity? The Gospel Beyond the West.* Grand Rapids, MI: Eerdmans, 2003.

Sanneh, Lamin, and Michael McClymond, eds. *The Wiley Blackwell Companion to World Christianity.* Hoboken, NJ: Wiley-Blackwell, 2016.

Santos, Boaventura de Souza. *If God Were a Human Rights Activist.* Stanford, CA: Stanford University Press, 2015.

______. *A Difícil Democracia: reinventar as esquerdas.* Sao Paulo: Boitempo, 2016.

Schouten, Lucy Jane. "'Everyone Has a Story': Jordanian Churches Reimagine Middle Eastern Christianity in Response to Refugees." PhD diss., University of Edinburgh, 2022.

Sebesta, J. L. "Women's Costume and Feminine Civic Morality in Augustan Rome." *Gender e History 9,* no. 3 (1997): 529–41.

Serra, Cris. "Diversity as a Gift: LGBTQI+ Roman Catholic Organizations in Twenty-First-Century Brazil." *International Journal of Latin American Religions* (November 9, 2021). https://doi.org/10.1007/s41603-021-00152-4.

Shenk, Wilbert R., ed. *Enlarging the Story: Perspectives on Writing Christian World History.* Maryknoll, NY: Orbis Books, 2002.

Shor, Ira, and Freire, Paulo. "What Is the 'Dialogical Method' of Teaching?" *The Journal of Education* 169, no. 3 (1987): 11–31.

Silva, Gustavo Vilella. "A violência de gênero no Brasil e o gemido das mulheres evangélicas." *Discernindo* 1 (2013): 131–42.

Snow, Jennifer. "The Civilization of White Men: The Race of the Hindu in *United States v. Bhagat Sindh Thind.*" In *Race, Nation, and Religion in the Americas,* edited by Henry Goldschmidt and Elizabeth McAlister, 259–80. Oxford: Oxford University Press, 2004.

So, Youn-Jung. "A Critical Study on Pluralistic Theism by Jung, Hyun Kyung: A Perspective in Holy Spirit." *Pogŭmgwa sŏn'gyo* 9, no.1, (2008): 215–51.

Stevenson, J. *Creeds. Councils and Controversies: Documents Illustrating the History of the Church, AD 337–461.* London: SPCK, 1989.

Still, Clarinda. *Dalit Women: Honour and Patriarchy in South India.* New York: Routledge, 2017.

Suh, David Kwang-sun. *Theology, Ideology and Culture.* Hong Kong: World Student Christian Federation, Asis/Pacific Region, 1983.

Suh, Nam Dong. "Towards a Theology of Han." In *Minjung Theology: People as the Subjects of History,* edited by Yong Bock Kim and Christian Conference of Asia, 51–65. Singapore: Commission on Theological Concerns, 1981.

Sylvestre, Josué. *Irmão vota em Irmão: Os evangélicos, a constituinte e a Bíblia*. Lisboa: Editora Pergaminho, 1986.

Synan, Vinson J., Kwabena Asamoah-Gyadu, and Amos Yong, eds. *Global Renewal Christianity: Spirit-Empowered Movements Past, Present, and Future*, vol. III: Africa. Lake Mary, FL.: Charisma House Publishers, 2016.

Tamez, Elza. *Hermenêutica Feminista Latino–americana: una restropectiva. Entre la Indignacion y la Esperanza*. Colômbia: [s.d.], 1988.

_____. *Teólogos da Libertação Falam sobre a Mulher: Entrevistas*. São Paulo: Loyola, 1989.

_____. ed. *Through Her Eyes: Women's Theology from Latin America*. Eugene, OR: Wipf & Stock, 2006.

Tan, Jonathan Y., and Anh Q. Tran S. J., eds. *World Christianity: Perspectives and Insights*. Maryknoll, NY: Orbis Books, 2016.

Taneti, James Elisha. *Caste, Gender, and Christianity in Colonial India: Telugu Women in Mission*. New York: Palgrave, 2013.

Taylor, Charles. "The Politics of Recognition." In *Multiculturalism*, edited by Amy Gutmann, 25–73. Princeton, NJ: Princeton University Press, 1994.

Terra, Kenner. "Misoginia Cósmica na Literatura Judaico-cristã." *Revista Jesus Histórico* 15 (2015): 103–9.

Thomas, Sonja. "'Studying Up' in World Christianity: A Feminist Analysis of Caste and Settler Colonialism." *Journal of World Christianity* 11, no. 2 (2021): 195–209.

Thompson, Leonard. *The Book of Revelation: Apocalypse and Empire*. New York: Oxford University Press, 1990.

Thompson, T. Jack. *Christianity in Northern Malawi. Donald Fraser's Missionary Methods and Ngoni Culture*. Leiden: E. J. Brill, Studies in Christian Mission, 1995.

Tjorhom, Ola. "An 'Ecumenical Winter'? Challenges in Contemporary Catholic Ecumenism." *The Heythrop Journal* 48 (2008): 841–59.

Trabuco, Zózimo. *À direita de Deus, à esquerda do povo: Protestantismos, esquerdas e minorias (1974–1994)*. Salvador: Sagga, 2016.

Trible, Phyllis. *Texts of Terror: Literary-Feminist Readings of Biblical Narratives*, 40th Anniversary Edition. Minneapolis: Fortress Press, 2022.

Tsosie, Rebecca. "Anthropology, and the Legacy of Epistemic Injustice." In *The Routledge Handbook of Epistemic Injustice*, edited by Ian James Kidd, Jose Medina, and Gaile Pohlhaus, Jr., 356–68. New York: Routledge, 2019.

Turner, Richard Brent. *Islam in the African-American Experience*. Bloomington: Indiana University Press, 2003.

Vanderkam, J. *Enoch and the Growth of an Apocalyptic Tradition*. Washington, DC: CBA, 1984.

Vilhena, Valéria. *Uma Igreja Sem Voz: Análise de Gênero da Violência Doméstica entre Mulheres Evangélicas*. São Paulo: Fonte Editorial, 2019.

Vital, Christina. *Mandonismo e Sadismo durante a pandemia no Brasil: Analisando a gestão de Bolsonaro à luz da obra de Gilberto Freyre v.6*. São Paulo: Editora Recriar, 2020.

______. "Identidades, partidos, cristianismo global na análise sobre evangélicos." *Debates do NER* 21, no. 39 (January/July 2021): 157–71.

______. "Irmãos contra o império: evangélicos de esquerda nas eleições 2020 no Brasil." *Debates do NER*, Porto Alegre 21, no. 39 (January/July 2021): 13–80.

Vital, Christina, and João Luiz Moura, "Evangélicos à esquerda no Brasil: entrevistas com lideranças e coletivos nas eleições 2020." *Comunicações do ISER* 40, no. 73 (2021): https://tinyurl.com/5znzfpkr.

Vogelstein, Rachel. *Ending Child Marriage: How Elevating the status of Girls Advances U.S. Foreign Policy*. New York/Washington: The Council on Foreign Relations, 2013.

Walker, Alice. *In Search of Our Mothers' Gardens: Womanist Prose*. New York: Harcourt Brace Jovanovic, 1983.

Walls, Andrew F. *The Missionary Movement in Christian History: Studies in the Transmission of Faith*. Edinburgh: T & T Clark, 1996.

______. *The Cross-Cultural Process in Christian History: Studies in the Transmission and Appropriation of Faith*. Maryknoll, NY: Orbis Books, 2001.

Ware, Kallistos. "Synodality and Primacy in the Orthodox Church." IOTA. Accessed July 19, 2022. https://tinyurl.com/35kd55bh.

Wariboko, Nimi. *Nigerian Pentecostalism*. Rochester Studies in African History and the Diaspora. Rochester, NY: University of Rochester Press, 2014.

______. *The Pentecostal Hypothesis: Christ Talks, They Decide*. Eugene OR: Cascade Books, 2020.

Wariboko, Nimi, and Ebenezer Obadare, eds. *African Pentecostalism and World Christianity: Essays in Honor of J. Kwabena Asamoah-Gyadu*. Eugene, OR: Pickwick Publications, 2020.

West, Gerald. *The Stolen Bible: From Tool of Imperialism to African Icon*. Pietermaritzburg: Cluster Publication, 2016.

White, Owen, and J. P. Daughton, eds. *In God's Empire: French Missionaries and the Modern World*. Oxford: Oxford University Press, 2012.

Wilkinson, Doris Y., and Ukah Asonzeh, eds. *The Black Male in America: Perspectives on His Status in Contemporary Society*. Chicago: Nelson-Hall, 1977.

Willis, Alan Scott. *All According to God's Plan: Southern Baptist Missions and Race, 1945–1970*. Lexington: University Press of Kentucky, 2005.

Womack, Deanna Ferree. "Middle Eastern Christianity in the Context of World Christianity." In *The Rowman & Littlefield Handbook of Christianity in the Middle East*, edited by Mitri Raheb, Meredith Riedel, and Mark A. Lamport, 548–58. Lanham, MD: Rowman & Littlefield, 2020.

_____. *Protestants, Gender and the Arab Renaissance in Late Ottoman Syria.* Edinburgh: Edinburgh University Press, 2019.

Yi, Buyŏng. *The Korean Shamanism and Analytical Psychology with Special Reference to the Symbols of Suffering and Healing.* Seoul: Han'gilsa, 2013.

Young, Richard Fox, ed. *World Christianity and Interfaith Relations.* Minneapolis: Fortress Press, 2022.

Zwetsch, Roberto E. "Apresentação." In *Conviver Ensaios para uma Teologia Intercultural Latino-Americana*, edited by Roberto E. Zwetsch, 17–23. São Leopoldo, Brazil: Editora Sinodal/EST, 2015.

INDEX

B

C

Church Missionary Society (CMS) 33, 35, 80
Church of Central Africa Presbyterian (CCAP) 21, 121, 123, 128, 129, 131, 132, 133n21, 136, 137, 139
Church of Pentecost (CoP) 102
Churches Witnessing with Migrants (CWWM) 59, 60, 62, 66
Circle of Women Theologians in Sub-Saharan Africa, the 8
Colombia 18, 60, 278n56, 311
colonial
colonialist-missionary mentality 10
coloniality of being 9nn10 and 11
coloniality of knowing 9n10
coloniality of power 9
Comision para el Estudio de Historia de la Iglesia en America Latina (CEHILA; Commission for Historical Studies of the Church in Latin America) 310
Comissão Ecumênica dos Direitos da Terra (CEDITER; Ecumenical Commission on the Rights of the Land) 63
communal relations 21, 130
concubine 22, 241–59
Confucianism 154, 158
Convention of Baptist Churches (Northern Circars) 85, 86n17
Converts ix, 10, 31, 78, 81, 177, 313
Convivência 75
Coordenação Ecumênica de Serviço (CESE; Ecumenical Service Coordination) 63, 64
Corporeality 261–77
Cristãos Contra o Fascismo (Christians Against Fascism) 23, 282, 285, 288, 289, 295, 306
critical Race theory xi, 5
Cuba
Cuba 23, 61, 297, 309–33
Cuban Revolution 328

D

da Silva, Luiz Ignacio Lula 298, 304, 306
Dalit
Dalit Christians 79, 82, 86, 92
Dalit Feminist Hermeneutics 247, 256
de Santa Ana, Julio 54
decolonial
decolonial lens 19
decolonized 3
Delaney, Martin R. 177, 187, 188
deliverance 104, 105, 108
demonic 108, 263, 266
devadāsīs 22, 244, 247, 248, 254, 257
Domitian 268, 269, 271, 272, 273
Douglass, Frederick 182, 183
Druze 43
Du Bois, W. E. B. 173, 174, 176
Dussel, Enrique 11, 12, 24n37, 58, 98n3, 310

E

Ecclesiology 314, 317
ecological crisis 19
ecumenical
Ecumenical Association of Third World Theologians (EATWOT) 59, 66, 157
Ecumenical Center of Documentation 65
Ecumenical Committee of the Presbyterian Church of Korea 146, 149
Ecumenical Forum Act Brazil (FEACT) 65, 66, 67
Ecumenical Patriarchate of Constantinople 316, 319, 332
Ecumenical Studies 49
Ecumenics xi, xii, 49, 50, 52, 114
Ecumenismo 19, 49–76, 115, 233
El Salvador 17n29, 60
Elkins, Stanley 180, 181

Ellacuria, Ignacio 18
Enoch 265, 266n14, 267, 276
Episcopal Assemblies 317, 318, 320, 332
Epistemic
    epistemic justice 8, 49, 52, 53, 66, 73,
        259
    epistemicide 71n59, 72
    epistemologies 5, 24, 57, 98, 241, 246
Espin, Orlando 74, 75
Ethics 4, 11n17, 18, 20, 21, 115, 116, 118,
    121, 129, 130, 136, 148, 242n5, 249n23
Euro-American 6, 30, 33, 98, 112, 171
Eurocentric ix, 3, 5, 6, 7, 9, 24, 25, 32, 46,
    52, 53, 57
European xi, 5, 10, 11, 13, 31, 32–34, 36, 53,
    54, 58, 62, 68n54, 78, 113, 175, 176, 197,
    200, 312n10
Eusebius 52, 268, 269
evangelical
    Evangelical Front for the Rule of
        Law 306
    Evangelicalism 16n28, 20, 77–95,
        145n9
    Evangélicxs pela Diversidade
        (Evangelicals for Diversity) 220,
        229, 230, 231n36, 239
Everyday Religion 116, 117, 118
Exorcism 105, 108, 162
Exteriority 11, 99n5, 111n33
Fawcett, John 85

F
feminism
    feminista 277n55, 278n56
    feminist ethics of care 21, 129n15,
        130
    feminist ethics of *ubuntu* (FEU) 121,
        129, 130, 136, 138
    feminist epistemologies 241
Ferree Womack, Deanna 3, 7n7, 10n13,
    17n31, 19, 27, 36, 44, 143
Folktale 168, 169, 173, 189n83

Fourth Global Baptist Peace Conference
    60
Francis, Pope 23, 309–33
Freire, Paulo 63n38, 64
Fricker, Miranda 242n5, 246
Frilingos, Christopher A. 268n19,
    273nn44 and 46, 274

G
Gaze 11, 138, 253, 266
Gendered 153, 159, 241, 242, 247, 250,
    251, 253, 256, 258n45
Genders 15n25, 204n42, 235
German 17n32, 32, 55, 80, 83, 84, 189, 316
German Pietistic Missionaries 80, 84
Ghana 7n7, 100n7, 101n8, 102, 105–109
Gibran, Khalil 36, 45
global
    Global Ministries 60
    global missions 7, 14n24
    Global Network of Rainbow
        Catholics (GNRC) 233
    Global North xi, xii, xiii, 4, 9, 16, 20,
        25, 221, 331
    Global South ix, xii, xiii, 3–25, 47, 48,
        51–59, 100, 255n39, 258, 331
Glorious Word and Power Ministry 107
Gnanaratnamma, Philip 79, 95
Granberg-Michaelson, Wesley 51, 52n9
Greek Orthodox 36nn21–22, 42
Gualtieri, Sarah 37, 43n42
Guatemala 60, 311

H
Hamites 33
han (unresolved sadness/suffering) 21,
    144, 153, 155
han-pu-ri (ritual to resolve *han*) 143–65
healing 8n9, 41n41, 104, 106, 108, 109,
    115, 125n11, 130, 136, 138, 139, 141, 162,
    171, 213, 248
Hegel, G. W. F. 99, 174, 175, 176, 186